W9-AFO-878

1992
.8
S35
E87
2008

THE ESSENTIAL SCIENCE FICTION TELEVISION READER

ESSENTIAL READERS IN
CONTEMPORARY MEDIA AND CULTURE

This series is designed to collect and publish the best scholarly writing on various aspects of television, film, the Internet, and other media of today. Along with providing original insights and explorations of critical themes, the series is intended to provide readers with the best available resources for an in-depth understanding of the fundamental issues in contemporary media and cultural studies. Topics in the series may include, but are not limited to, critical-cultural examinations of creators, content, institutions, and audiences associated with the media industry. Written in a clear and accessible style, books in the series include both single-author works and edited collections.

SERIES EDITOR
Gary R. Edgerton, Old Dominion University

THE ESSENTIAL
SCIENCE
FICTION
TELEVISION
READER

Edited by
J. P. Telotte

THE UNIVERSITY PRESS OF KENTUCKY

Scholarly publisher for the Commonwealth,
serving Bellarmine University, Berea College, Centre College of Kentucky,
Eastern Kentucky University, The Filson Historical Society, Georgetown
College, Kentucky Historical Society, Kentucky State University, Morehead
State University, Murray State University, Northern Kentucky University,
Transylvania University, University of Kentucky, University of Louisville,
and Western Kentucky University.
All rights reserved.

Editorial and Sales Offices: The University Press of Kentucky
663 South Limestone Street, Lexington, Kentucky 40508-4008
www.kentuckypress.com

12 11 10 09 08   5 4 3 2 1

Unless otherwise indicated, all images are from the volume editor's collection.

Library of Congress Cataloging-in-Publication Data

The essential science fiction television reader / edited by J. P. Telotte.
    p. cm. — (Essential readers in contemporary media and culture)
Includes bibliographical references and index.
ISBN 978-0-8131-2492-6 (hardcover : alk. paper)
1. Science fiction television programs—History and criticism.
I. Telotte, J. P., 1949-
PN1992.8.S35E87 2008
791.45'615—dc22   2007048493

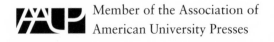 Member of the Association of
American University Presses

CONTENTS

ACKNOWLEDGMENTS

A great many people contributed to the creation of this book and deserve special mention. Foremost among them are the various colleagues who took it on faith that this project would see the light of day and readily agreed to contribute their time and creative efforts. Gary Edgerton, the series editor, encouraged the project and provided very valuable commentary on the finished volume. My chair, Ken Knoespel, was his usual supportive self and provided me the leave time needed to move this volume to completion. And my students at Georgia Tech, especially those who have worked in my classes on science fiction and film and television, proved an invaluable resource, as always. In this group there are many who deserve to be acknowledged, but let me give special thanks to Betsy Gooch, Rory Gordon, Torey Haas, Kevin Hicks, John Swisshelm, and Brad Tucker.

I also want to express my appreciation to those at the University Press of Kentucky who contributed at each stage to the creation and production of this text. Leila Salisbury was encouraging and attentive throughout the process. David Cobb oversaw the editing and production process and managed to keep the project moving at a refreshingly swift pace. Anna Laura Bennett was easily the most conscientious copyeditor with whom I have worked, and she contributed immeasurably to the volume. Will McKay attended to details that I overlooked. This group worked together to make the creation of this volume one of my most pleasant publishing experiences.

INTRODUCTION

The Trajectory of
Science Fiction Television

J. P. Telotte

Todd Gitlin has suggested that too often today we "take a media-soaked environment for granted . . . and can no longer see how remarkable it is" (17). Certainly, that observation has much validity for any discussion of television, a media form that twenty years ago Mark Crispin Miller had already described as constituting "the very air we breathe" (8). But the point takes on an added weight when we consider science fiction television (SFTV). For although the genre has been a part of broadcast television practically from the medium's inception, science fiction was early on often perceived as children's programming or niche fare, and it has seldom enjoyed a dominant place in regular broadcast schedules. In part, it has suffered the same prejudice that, for many years, attached to science fiction literature, which was seldom seen as an equivalent to "serious" fiction and, in fact, as Edward James has observed, was more often dismissed "as escapism" (3). Yet clearly something has changed. Today, in the major television market area where I live, I could watch on a weekly basis as many as twenty-two science fiction series.[1] Since television itself is so pervasive, it may well be difficult for many people to "see how remarkable" this relatively recent profusion of "escapist" fare really is or to register that development as anything more than another lamentable sign of cultural debasement. Certainly, it is still hard for many to recognize that the science fiction series might represent an important voice for an increasingly technologized and science-haunted world. But one symptom of that new presence is the very existence of this book, a volume called into being because of this inescapable shift. And a chief aim of this volume is to help us see this phenomenon, place it in context, and better understand it—in short, to remark on a significant cultural development.

The remarking that follows focuses largely on the dominant form that science fiction has taken on television, the extended series offered on network or cable broadcast. Working from this focus, my collaborators and I provide an introduction to the study of SFTV for general readers, for devoted fans of the various series (many of which, like *Star Trek*, *Doctor Who*, and *The X-Files*, have attracted large cult followings), and for more advanced students of the genre. One guiding principle for this book is to emphasize the development of an independent identity for the televisual form of the genre, which has moved from weak imitations of cinematic science fiction, particularly that model found in the movie serials, to its own mature productions, which have, in turn, now begun to reenvision—and energize—the genre itself, making it so remarkable today. That maturation is evidenced by the development of a network specifically devoted to the genre (the Sci-Fi Channel), the increasing migration of television series titles to the big screen (in addition to vice versa), the creation of various spin-off series, and the development of a complex industry devoted to producing novel, comic book, and online continuations of the more successful series—a development that recalls the dominant role played by the television western in the 1950s. Indeed, given that mature identity and its attendant influence across various media forms, one might well argue that SFTV is now well positioned to become the most influential mode of a genre that has largely managed to cast off the escapist label and has established itself as one of the key mirrors of the contemporary cultural climate.

In order to better describe this development, the essays that follow look both *outside* the central form, examining some of the key influences on the development of SFTV, and *into* some of the genre's more noteworthy accomplishments, particularly into some of the series that have practically become landmarks in television history. While the volume hardly pretends to offer a comprehensive account of the genre's role in television and television history or even of its place in the international market—discussion focuses largely on Anglo-American series—it does try to provide readers with a broad historical context, a sense of the key issues involved in thinking about science fiction on television, models for considering specific series, speculation on the form's future trajectory, and tools for learning more about the place of SFTV in the larger generic and cultural contexts. In short, it aims to provide "essential" background for anyone interested in studying this increasingly influential form of science fiction narrative.

I want to begin our exploration of the form by starting at the end, that is, by considering the current condition of SFTV, the kind of crossroads situation in which it finds itself. For that situation nicely frames both its current state and what I have already termed its mature identity. In *American Science Fiction TV*, a study devoted to the genre's growth in the post–*Star Trek* years, Jan Johnson-Smith observes how, even though science fiction has now attained a new level of popularity and even acceptance in the television mainstream, it also finds itself in a difficult position, for "many of its staple themes are now science, not fiction" (2). The computer, rockets, space travel, robotics—these formerly innovative concerns that provided some of the form's basic iconic trappings have "become an accepted part of life" (2) and thus pose increasing challenges for science fiction narrative, particularly in terms of its ability to move beyond this new everyday world and to visualize an even more speculative—and perhaps far more spectacular—vision of what the future might hold and what we might yet achieve. In his survey of this same material, M. Keith Booker strikes a similar note as he describes "the growing maturity (or perhaps exhaustion) of the genre of science fiction television" (192). That problematic status between maturity and exhaustion results, as he says, from the advent of a new century and an increasingly sophisticated science fiction audience that has witnessed "what had once been the science fiction future" giving way to "a present that had not, in general, lived up to the expectations of the science fiction novels, films, and television series of earlier decades" (192). The result is an ongoing challenge to meet or surpass those expectations.

On one level, both of these assessments point to the basic strength—and perhaps the greatest attraction—of the form: its speculative power, its ability to speak to the wonder and curiosity that are ultimately bound up in our scientific and technological developments, and that have always energized the literature of science fiction. On another, these observations also suggest the difficulties that impinge on that power and that might well limit the genre's articulations in the coming years—difficulties that are both cultural and technological, as I explore below. In any case, that the two assessments converge on a note of formulaic exhaustion even as they similarly point out the need for new lines of development suggests that SFTV has indeed reached a level of maturity and warrants more detailed study.

As I have noted, one problem underlying these commentaries is cultural, and it partly follows from science fiction's status today. Whether as literature, film, or television, it has simply become a text of choice for a postmodern world. Because of its generic emphasis on the constructed nature of all things, including human nature, and an increasing willingness to explore new narrative shapes, or as Brian McHale more allusively puts it, because it is a "self-consciously 'world-building' fiction, laying bare the process of fictional world-making" at every level (12), science fiction invariably evokes postmodernism's reflexive and rather ahistorical sensibility. The result is that the genre's narratives often seem less a continuation of our own historical circumstances than, to evoke one of the more popular series, a quantum leap to another history. And series science fiction, typically characterized by story arcs that function as self-conscious efforts at "filling in" an absent context, invariably projects the sense of a world in which both history and reality itself are simply being constructed as needed—a notion that resonates powerfully with contemporary audiences not because it is a permit for escapism but because it corresponds so closely with the conditions in which they live.

Another side of that cultural problem can be glimpsed in an aesthetic shift described by Jean-François Lyotard. In his effort at "reporting" on the postmodern condition, he describes a change in how our narratives typically work, as emphasis increasingly turns "from the ends of action to its means" (37). We can see that shift playing out in the way that many series have begun to deemphasize some of the genre's traditional speculative thrust in favor of drawing out the implications of its usual actions and events—those that readily reflect and comment upon the contemporary world. We might think, for example, of the way in which the revived version of *Battlestar Galactica* uses its context of a conflict between humans and their robotic creations, the Cylons, to frame in ever more complex terms its own examination of the role of women in society—pointedly reflecting our own urgent efforts at negotiating between traditional gender roles and expectations and the shifting sense of gender identity in contemporary culture. Although science fiction has, to some extent, always provided a stage for acting out our cultural anxieties—as the cinema's tales of atomic holocaust and alien invasion at the height of the cold war attest—television's increased emphasis in this direction should be seen less as a problem or symptom of "exhaustion" than as evidence of its growing importance as a tool of cultural deliberation and ideological exploration.

The technological issue I have noted has a similarly double character that, in various ways, has always been linked to the genre's identity. For rightly or not, audiences have consistently gauged science fiction in terms of its ability to give life to its visions—an ability that assumes a special prominence in the genre's film and televisual forms, where it too easily translates into the power of special effects. In fact, Michele Pierson, in her study of the special effects tradition, suggests that this link is a natural one, the response to "a cultural demand for the aesthetic experience of wonder" (168), a notion frequently evoked in histories of literary science fiction as well.[2] The cinema, of course, has vast resources for addressing such challenges, including larger budgets, longer and more flexible production schedules, and more elaborate special effects resources (including the top personnel in the field), whereas television typically has had to contend with restrictions built into its very media identity: limited budgets, tight schedules, scaled-down effects, and even a different visual style (one emphasizing the close-up and medium shot rather than the more spectacular long shots and panoramas, for example). So in its efforts to satisfy the demand Pierson identifies—and produce the sort of pleasure it implies—SFTV has traditionally had to work at a disadvantage. The space operas of the late 1940s and early 1950s are nearly legendary in this respect, with a highly successful show like *Captain Video and His Video Rangers* achieving its rather limited effects on a twenty-five-dollar-per-episode budget (Fulton 91). And even a landmark series like *Star Trek* often had to make capital from its technical and budgetary constraints. As Johnson-Smith reminds us, the series' well-known transporter effect was invented "to avoid the costs of filming a shuttlecraft landing on a weekly basis" (106).

Although such constraints have never kept the broadcast form of the genre from successfully evoking its own sort of wonder, audiences of science fiction cinema have always expected something more, and that something more has become part of its rather different identity. In fact, Albert La Valley has described the whole history of the film genre as "a kind of Oedipal cold war" of effects, one in which the latest science fiction films "aim to demonstrate the current state of the art" in special effects technology by employing "greater and greater budgets to overpower their predecessors" (149). Primed by that cinema experience, and with the television experience itself becoming ever more technologically sophisticated, audiences have begun to anticipate similar advances in effects from SFTV. Fortunately, the advent of computer-generated special effects (more generally termed CGI), the quickly dropping costs of those effects, and relatively easy access to the technology for achieving them have placed SFTV in a more competitive situation. While still constrained by tighter schedules, it is now generally capable of playing much the same "what if" game as the movies, as it finds itself able (within financial reason) to visualize practically anything its creators imagine. Having attained a kind of technological maturity, many of the series are now commonly marked by the sort of amazing imagery that previously could be found only in big-budget, big-screen spectacles of the *Star Wars* variety.

If this advent has provided more potential for achieving that aesthetic experience of wonder, it has also brought a problem that similarly plagues much of our cinematic science fiction. For the advent of new digital technologies has not only transformed the way that films are produced, distributed, and exhibited; it has also increasingly made them, especially our science fiction efforts, seem almost effects driven. And this is a problem with which a mature SFTV must likewise contend. The very effects that have allowed our television series to compete more successfully with films could also easily dominate them. *Stargate SG-1*'s wormhole effects, *Battlestar Galactica*'s deep-space combat between human and Cylon starships, and *Eureka*'s weekly visions of technologies drawn from our wildest imaginings threaten not only to dominate but also to completely formularize their narratives, turning them essentially into showcases of wonder and, in the process, rendering the instances of wonder all too predictable. Yet to their credit, the best of our most recent series have managed to strike an effective balance between narrative and effects, suggesting more the sort of "maturity" to which Booker points than the "exhaustion" of which he warns.

What I suggest is that the diagnosis offered by both Booker and

Johnson-Smith ultimately points more to the healthy dynamism characterizing the form today than to a real problem. Human culture, after all, is neither going to run out of technological challenges nor, one would hope, simply become jaundiced in the face of them. As Paul Virilio, a historian of technology, notes, art "never just sleeps in front of new technologies, but deforms them and transforms them" (159) to fit our cultural needs, particularly the needs of the imagination. And SFTV, despite a hesitation by some to admit to its status as art, has proven well placed to participate in that vital deformation and transformation. In the course of negotiating a balance between the speculative and the ahistorical and between the demands of narrative and its special effects impulses, science fiction has increasingly been able both to fit within the constraints of the television medium and to help stretch those boundaries, enriching the medium and offering it a path of growth. More particularly, I suggest that the form has helped television itself better address prevailing cultural concerns. Certainly, even the earliest television space operas, as Wheeler Winston Dixon's essay in this volume nicely chronicles, offered rather slant reflections of their era's anxieties. But because of the different historical attitude we have noted and a progressively more technological cultural climate, science fiction has come to provide one of the most effective stages for addressing our own period's key concerns—as society itself becomes ever more technologized—as well as for demonstrating series television's ability to participate in our ongoing cultural negotiations on such topics.

To better situate this sense of SFTV's maturing and dynamic character, we also need to go back to the start, to look back over the history of a form that is now nearly sixty years old—almost as old as broadcast television itself. Indeed, its early history looks back even further, to that competing medium of film and a narrative model that flourished there beginning in the 1910s: the serial. Marked by its action orientation, low budgets, and cliff-hanger endings, the serial provided ready and exciting material for television programming in the late 1940s and early 1950s, particularly since its one- and two-reel formats could easily fit—along with commercials—into the typical half-hour programming block. In fact, as early as 1948, both ABC and the DuMont television network were devoting blocks of prime-time programming to various film shorts, including serials, and many local stations used available serials (a number of which, such as *The Phantom Empire* [1935] and *The Lost City* [1935], were in the public domain) to create their own programming, as in the case of New York's *Serial Theater*.[3] Moreover, since many of those serials were essentially science fiction efforts, they early on helped to establish a place for the genre in network programming.

Perhaps more important, these early crossover programs, such as the *Flash Gordon* serials (1936, 1938, 1940), *Buck Rogers* (1939), *King of the Rocket Men* (1949), and *Flying Disc Man from Mars* (1951), helped to provide a generic model for a developing SFTV. The space opera form, marked by its interplanetary settings, heroic figures, outsized actions, and melodramatic situations[4] and heavily influenced by the comics and the space adventure novels of E. E. "Doc" Smith, Jack Williamson, and Edmond Hamilton, would be toned down somewhat to provide the template for a first generation of SFTV, but that pattern would continue to influence the genre's development. From 1949 through 1955, shows like *Captain Video* (1949–1955), *Space Patrol* (1950–1955), *Tom Corbett, Space Cadet* (1950–1955), *Rod Brown of the Rocket Rangers* (1953–1954), and *Rocky Jones, Space Ranger* (1954) addressed in a generally formulaic manner an audience presumed to be largely composed of children. As Patrick Lucanio and Gary Coville describe them, these shows "were all woven from a common fabric: adventurous themes played out before a milieu of scientific gadgetry that was often described in the most prolix manner" (116). As this description suggests, although these programs easily deployed a common formula, it was one that did not lend them a solid identity, for even though they spoke to and of the rising fascination with science and technology in the post–World War II era, this element had little substance and was always precariously balanced against their serial-like nature. In fact, they remained so much in the vogue of the cinematic serial that one program would eventually be adapted as a serial (*Captain Video*), another would use a serial protagonist and shoot its episodes on the same sets employed for its film original (*Commando Cody: Sky Marshal of the Universe*), others would regularly rely on the narrative cliff-hanger popularized by the serials (*Rocky Jones, Space Ranger*), and all would effectively disappear at almost the same time that the last film serial left theaters in 1956.

Tom Corbett, Space Cadet: Dr. Joan Dale (Margaret Garland) welcomes Tom (Frankie Thomas) back to his rocket ship.

Trying to stake out a rather different direction for development while addressing much the same audience, Walt Disney's *Disneyland* series (1954–1983) introduced its Tomorrowland-themed shows with a group of episodes collectively titled "Man in Space."[5] While these shows were animation heavy, provided a humorous view of earlier beliefs about space, space travel, and alien life, and even satirized the typical space opera of the period (see especially the "Mars and Beyond" episode), they balanced these elements with serious discussions by some of the key experts of the time, many of whom would become involved in the U.S. space program, most notably Heinz Haber, Ernst Stuhlinger, and Wernher von Braun. Although these shows were critically praised and attracted international attention, their mix of science fiction and the hard science of the space race would produce few imitators, and by 1961 the Tomorrowland segment of Disney's anthology show would disappear.

A more adult-directed form of science fiction did appear in the early years of broadcast television, although it too was in a form that owed much to other media. Anthology shows like *Lights Out* (1949–1952), *Out There* (1951–1952), *Tales of Tomorrow* (1951–1953), and *Science Fiction Theatre* (1955–1957) drew heavily on the traditions of both live and radio drama. In fact, *Lights Out* began on the radio in 1934, and by 1950 weekly radio shows like *Dimension X* and *2000 Plus* were providing futuristic tales drawn from the work of some of the top young science fiction writers of the day. Building upon this pattern, the anthology television programs offered live drama, adapted from the works of both classic science fiction writers like H. G. Wells and that new breed of authors, including Ray Bradbury, Arch Oboler, and Rod Serling, seeking to make their stories accessible in various media. Although clearly emphasizing the fantastic, these shows also benefited from the fact that they fit into a readily recognized television format. In fact, the live anthology drama was one of the new medium's most successful types of programming throughout its first decade, as typified by such long-running and critically acclaimed series as *General Electric Theater*, *Goodyear TV Playhouse*, and *Playhouse 90*. Although none of the fantasy anthologies managed the longevity, popularity, or acclaim of these more traditional live-action drama shows, the science fiction programs were notable for their use of big-name stars, their ability to attract top writing talent, and, in the case of the semidocumentary *Science Fiction Theatre*, a much greater concern with real science than any of the era's space operas ever exhibited. Perhaps more important, they helped to demonstrate the potential flexibility of the science fiction narrative, as they ranged across a wide variety of story types while treating a number of serious and timely themes.

These early anthology shows are also significant because they opened the door for two of the most important series in the early history of SFTV. *The Twilight Zone* (1959–1964) and *The Outer Limits* (1963–1965) built upon the legacy of the earlier anthology efforts, mixing science fiction tales with narratives of horror and the supernatural, drawing in top acting talent, and attracting major writers. Although *The Twilight Zone* was produced, hosted, and largely scripted by Rod Serling, who would win two Emmy Awards for episodes he wrote, it also included in its initial run sixteen scripts by Richard Matheson and twenty-two by Charles Beaumont. It quickly established a reputation for the psychological dimension of its programs, often flavored with an ironic twist. Although *The Outer Limits* would become noted for emphasizing monsters rather than ironic or surreal twists, it generally

The Outer Limits: Trent (Robert Culp) speaks to his hand in "The Demon with a Glass Hand."

stayed closer to the science fiction tradition and established a similar record of attracting top writers. During its two-season run, it included stories by young science fiction writer Harlan Ellison, who would win a Writers Guild of America award for his "Demon with a Glass Hand" episode; Joseph Stefano, who scripted Alfred Hitchcock's *Psycho* (1960); and Jerry Sohl, who also contributed numerous scripts to *The Twilight Zone* and would become a key writer for one of the most important of all science fiction series, *Star Trek*.

Beyond the quality of their scripts, both series proved noteworthy for their use of fantastic landscapes to comment upon contemporary American culture. In fact, Johnson-Smith describes the pair as among "the more daring shows" of the era—in any genre—specifically because they "grasped the potential for social commentary" (58) in television. Ranging across a variety of themes, including alien encounters, space exploration, time travel, futuristic societies, and even genetic alterations, *The Twilight Zone* especially established that those typical science fiction themes could offer an important perspective on our culture. Appearing at the very height of the cold war, it managed to address not only the expected fears and anxieties of that era but also a broad array of social issues—and rather courageously, given the political sensitivities of the time. Among them we might particularly include American culture's generally conformist values, repressed racism and xenophobia, creeping governmental control, and problematic gender relations. Based on its treatment of such themes, its consistently adult level of address, and its overall quality, *The Twilight Zone* clearly deserves Booker's recognition as "the series that marked the maturation of science fiction television as a genre" (6).

An additional legacy of these anthology series is the variety of science fiction shows that followed them in the 1960s. For in ranging over a wide spectrum of subjects and employing diverse narrative modes, *The Twilight Zone* and *The Outer Limits* demonstrated that science fiction was hardly a monolithic story type, certainly not just the space opera, and that, far from being a niche form, it could effectively address a broad spectrum of the television audience. Consequently, the 1960s saw the development of a varied array of science fiction series: shows about extraordinary explorations of various types (*Lost in Space* [1965–1968], *Time Tunnel* [1966–1967]), extraordinary technology (*Voyage to the Bottom of the Sea* [1964–1968]), extraordinary encounters (*The Invaders* [1967–1968], *Land of the Giants* [1968–1970]), comic science fiction (*My Favorite Martian* [1963–1966]), and even animated assays on the genre (*The Jetsons* [1962–1963], *The Adventures of Jonny Quest* [1964–1965]). One of the guiding lights of this variety and arguably the most influential figure in the SFTV of this period was Irwin Allen, an Academy Award–winning director, writer, and producer who created four of those series. He adapted *Voyage to the Bottom of the Sea* from his own successful film of the same title and then, in quick succession, mined its scientific adventure formula to produce *Lost in Space, Time Tunnel,* and *Land of the Giants.* In these series Allen, later to be known as the "master of disaster" thanks to his productions of such key disaster films as *The Poseidon Adventure* (1972), *The Towering Inferno* (1974), and *The Swarm* (1978), seldom took on the sorts of cultural issues that were so often the concern of *The Twilight Zone*; instead, his works had a more basic human focus, as they consistently explored the various ways people respond when faced with unusual circumstances. Yet more important, thanks to his shows' slightly larger budgets, large

Sparks fly as Robot protects the Robinson family in *Lost in Space.*

13

Doug (Robert Colbert) and Tony (James Darren) prepare for another adventure in Irwin Allen's *Time Tunnel*.

casts, and use of filmlike special effects, he brought a big-screen look to SFTV, along with larger expectations for the genre.

Allen's death in 1991 followed by only a few days that of the other key figure of SFTV in this period, one who has arguably wielded the greatest influence over the form's development, Gene Roddenberry. A television writer, most often of westerns, Roddenberry created the concept for *Star Trek* (1966–1969) by pitching it as "*Wagon Train* to the stars," alluding to one of the top western series of the era. The resulting adventures of the starship *Enterprise* in the twenty-third century would prove only moderately successful in the show's initial run—it ranked fifty-second among all series in its peak season (Brooks and Marsh 1119)—but would go on to attract a new and highly loyal audience in syndication, inspire a series of feature films, spawn an animated series (1973–1975), and provide the seed for a host of even more ambitious spin-offs extending into the following century. Roddenberry would claim that the primary reason for the impact of *Star Trek*, and indeed for the success of the entire franchise that he founded with it, was its level of social commentary, for he found that, by focusing on "a new world with new rules, I could make statements about sex, religion, Vietnam, unions, politics and intercontinental missiles" (quoted in Fulton 429). But just as crucial to its reception was its optimistic vision, or as Booker terms it, a "compelling (and heartening) future image" (51), suggesting that humanity's problems could be worked out, that technology would prove a truly useful servant, and that humanity is not alone in the universe.

Yet *Star Trek*'s importance to the development of SFTV rests in more than the affirmative and liberal vision that it—and Roddenberry—managed to articulate. With his original notion of *Wagon Train* in space, Roddenberry set out a formula that has dominated the genre to the present day. The key injunction offered in its well-known epigraph—"to boldly go where no man has gone before"—not only readily evoked a new kind of frontier but also easily differentiated the show from Allen's *Lost in Space*, as it pointed to the starship's purposefully directed travels through space, with its racially and even species-diverse crew tasked with exploring and mapping part of the universe as representatives of the United Federation of Planets. The adventurous exploring, interactions of a wide variety of characters (a variation on the old "ship of fools" motif), and strong sense of purpose or promise would prove to be a significant evolution of the space opera formula and a legacy to the medium.[6]

The pattern also characterized to some extent a much longer-running series that has had a similar influence outside the United States. The BBC-produced series *Doctor Who* aired between 1963 and 1989, becoming the longest continuously running science fiction series in television history. Some measure of its impact can be seen in the several *Doctor Who* films, television specials, and spin-off series it has inspired and in its resurrection in 2005 as a new series, coproduced by BBC Wales and the Canadian Broadcasting Company and airing in the United States (beginning in 2006) on the Sci-Fi Channel. A further measure of that impact is the large cult following the series has generated, one that closely resembles the "Trekkie" subculture that the *Star Trek* franchise has produced. In fact, the most ambitious study of SFTV fandom, John Tulloch and Henry Jenkins's *Science Fiction Audiences*, focuses precisely on the parallel development of the devoted fan bases for these two series in an effort not only to better understand "the different ways that producers, journalists, critics, and audience members have conceptualized" the typical science fiction viewer (5) but also to counter a general attitude of "condescension" by many mainstream writers and critics who tend to see such devotion as evidence of SFTV's more "infantile" lure (16). The very investment that so many viewers around the world have made in these two series, Tulloch and Jenkins suggest, strongly argues for their consequence, and particularly for their ability to speak meaningfully to and for a large audience.

In contrast to *Doctor Who*, with its long run and dedicated audience base, many American science fiction series of the 1970s would prove ephemeral, drawing a comparatively modest viewership and hinting that the genre might appeal largely to a niche audience. Once more turning to film for inspiration, American television would offer the adaptations *Planet of the Apes* (1974) and *Logan's Run* (1977–1978), neither of which would last more than a season. The main, yet still moderate, successes of this period were two linked series, both focusing on a new area for science fiction, that of biotechnology. *The Six Million Dollar Man* (1974–1978) and its spin-off *The Bionic Woman* (1976–1978) both told the stories of government employees who were seriously injured, then reconstructed by government scientists and, in the process, transformed into more realistic versions of comic book superheroes. Although other superhero series (e.g., *The Man from Atlantis* [1977–1978]) would try to capitalize on this trend, a key to the success of these two shows probably rested in their real-world context, marked by the corresponding headlines scientists were then beginning to make by producing such real prostheses as the first artificial heart.

That real-world influence would, however, prove rather short lived,

Logan (Gregory Harrison) and Jessica (Heather Menzies) on the run in the short-lived television adaptation of *Logan's Run*.

as film once again exerted its powerful influence on SFTV, in this instance through the appearance of one of the most significant movies in the genre's history, *Star Wars* (1977). George Lucas's phenomenally successful film revisited a number of elements that we have noted in earlier SFTV: it recalled the serials, as its scroll title and in medias res narrative suggest; its general formula was that of the space opera writ large and dashed with humor; it offered a motley assortment of charac-ter—and species—types; and it clearly drew on ingredients of other popular formulas, especially the western. In updating these elements and coupling them to state-of-the-art special effects, it posed a new challenge to SFTV, but one that the medium was quick to take up and that would help mark a development that Johnson-Smith has character-ized as a shift "from a predominantly verbal medium into a predomi-nantly visual medium" (61).

Among the host of *Star Wars* imitators that illustrate SFTV's response to George Lucas's popular culture phenomenon, we might give special attention to three series. The most ambitious of these was *Battlestar Galactica* (1978–1980), which detailed the wanderings of a fleet of spaceships bearing humanity's ancestors after their home planets are destroyed by the robotic race of the Cylons. The epic scope of the series was matched by its budget—reportedly the highest ever for a prime-time series at a million dollars per one-hour episode (Brooks and Marsh 93)—and it employed that budget to generate elaborate special effects that, thanks to the efforts of producer and effects coordinator John Dykstra, who had also worked on *Star Wars*, established a new stan-dard for SFTV. Similarly well-budgeted and effects-oriented, *Buck Rog-ers in the 25th Century* (1979–1981) updated the original Universal serial of 1939 as well as an older, short-lived television series (1950–1951). Far more in the tradition of the earlier space operas, it pointedly cast its story of a twentieth-century astronaut revived in the future as a comic space adventure, patterning Buck after *Star Wars*' Han Solo and providing him with a robot assistant, Twiki, that inevitably recalled R2D2 and C3PO of Lucas's film. While sharply contrasting in tone, the BBC's modestly budgeted *Blake's 7* (1978–1981)—described by Booker as "one of the darkest science fiction series ever to appear on television" (83)—found its focus in the same story of struggle and resistance that was at the heart of *Star Wars*. Detailing the efforts of a ragtag group of rebels using a captured alien spaceship to subvert the dominant Federation, *Blake's 7* gave less attention to special effects than to character and situations, suggesting its additional indebtedness to such series as *Star Trek* and *Doctor Who*. While all three of these series point up the extent to which television still closely tracked and readily responded to popular cinematic science fiction, they also demonstrate the range of that response and thus the developing flexibility in the medium.

During the 1980s, SFTV would generally follow two noteworthy lines of development, one tracing current cinematic fashion and the other staking out the form's own territory. The first of these developments was the return of a motif practically identified with American films of the 1950s, that of alien invasion, and revisited in the 1980s in a variety of modes with such works as *E.T., the Extra-terrestrial* (1982), *The Thing* (1982), *Aliens* (1986), *The Hidden* (1987), *Predator* (1987), and *Alien Nation* (1988). Reflecting this development, the alien figure, both predatory and benevolent, would become the focus for series like

Commander Adama (Lorne Greene) on the bridge of his ship in the original *Battlestar Galactica* series.

A Cylon Centurian attacks in the original *Battlestar Galactica* series.

V (1984–1985), *Alien Nation* (1989–1991), and *War of the Worlds* (1988–1990). Based on two miniseries, *V* (for "visitors") details the gradual revelation of a plan by seemingly benevolent alien visitors to take over the Earth and the resistance to their scheme, led by a television newsman. *Alien Nation*, adapted from the film of that title, uses its

Buck (Gil Gerard) and Wilma (Erin Gray) in *Buck Rogers in the 25th Century.*

story of the accidental crash of an alien slave transport to explore contemporary race relations, as the suddenly freed "newcomers," as they are termed, struggle to overcome human prejudice and assimilate into Earth culture. Although it evokes a heritage in Orson Welles's 1938 radio broadcast and the 1953 film of the same title, suggesting that its events are simply a continuation of those earlier narratives, *War of the Worlds* bears little true relationship to these forerunners. Its plot of dormant aliens awakened by a toxic spill and, in the second season, joined by humanoid invaders from another planet simply allows for a vision of civilization on the brink of destruction and reflects a growing cultural paranoia, one that would eventually find a more coherent focus and a more flexible narrative vehicle for its expression in the long-running *The X-Files* (1993–2002).

A more noteworthy development in this same period was Gene Roddenberry's return, as he reformulated his *Star Trek* series with a new cast in *Star Trek: The Next Generation* (1987–1994). Set in the twenty-fourth century—approximately eighty years after the events of the original series—the new program offered an even more diverse crew,

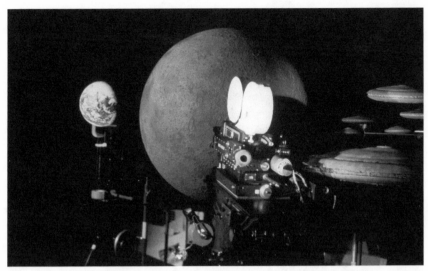

Shooting a special effects model scene of the invasion of Earth for *V.*

placed them in an updated starship, *Enterprise*-D, and sported first-rate special effects (thanks in part to its much higher budget). Yet as Johnson-Smith notes, the *Star Trek* formula had been "carefully forged" over the years and set in the imaginations of its loyal fans. Thus Roddenberry was careful not to alter it too substantially and risk upsetting "the established audience dynamic" (108). As a result, the key element of the original series, its use of future settings and situations to explore contemporary social and cultural issues, remained paramount. However, thanks to its much longer run, *The Next Generation* would eventually be able to explore the lives of its characters in far greater depth than the original *Star Trek*—a factor that would help pave the way for a new series of spin-off films and additional series that would further follow those lives in which audiences had become emotionally and intellectually invested.

Produced expressly for syndication to better target its desired audience, *The Next Generation* proved highly successful and inspired a host of other shows. In fact, even before *The Next Generation* had finished its original run, another syndicated effort was launched, *Star Trek: Deep Space Nine* (1993–1999), and there eventually followed two additional series, *Star Trek: Voyager* (1995–2001) and the prequel narrative *Enterprise* (a.k.a. *Star Trek: Enterprise*, 2001–2005). Together, these series would provide an elaborate expansion—in both space and time—of the established *Star Trek* mythology: by referring to characters and situations of the other series, by having characters from one series appear in another, by tracing out a history of the United Federation of Planets and the work of its Starfleet, and by elaborating on a number of the most popular motifs and plot threads, such as the menace of the Borgs and the conflict between the Cardassians and the Bajorans. If the overlap and continuity of these series helped to produce what Booker has described as "an unprecedented period of richness and innovation" (108) in the genre, they also underscored the new ability of SFTV to generate, independently of the film industry, a powerful and compelling narrative world—one that would, in fact, flourish in the new distribution environment provided by the explosion of cable and satellite outlets in the 1990s and the appearance of the dedicated Sci-Fi Channel, launched September 24, 1992.[7]

One of the most successful efforts in this same period, *The X-Files* (1993–2002), was launched by one of those new outlets, the Fox network (which debuted in 1986), and it little resembled anything then available on the large screen. Although it ranged across a variety of fantasy, including horror, supernatural phenomena, and urban legends, *The X-Files'* primary narrative focused on the investigation of a government cover-up of alien activity, including a planned invasion of Earth. The series' two central figures, FBI agents Fox Mulder and Dana Scully, represent two sides in the public debate about UFOs and other unexplained phenomena, with Mulder a firm believer in such things and Scully, a trained forensic scientist, always the skeptic, even after she is abducted and becomes an X file herself. The show's epigraph, "The truth is out there," neatly sums up its guiding narrative trajectory, as explanations prove ever more convoluted, appearances consistently deceive, and final truths remain elusive—within the show's precincts, even the seemingly dead sometimes come back to life. While *The X-Files'* contemporary setting provided little in the way of conventional science fiction trappings, its "postmodernist mode of epistemological skepticism" (Booker 142) and unfolding narrative approach proved highly attractive, leading to a feature film version (1998), generating a short-lived spin-off series, *The Lone Gunmen* (2001), and helping build a cult following nearly rivaling that of *Star Trek*.

Science fiction done in a noir key: *The X-Files'* Scully (Gillian Anderson) and Mulder (David Duchovny).

Although *The X-Files'* skeptic/paranoiac vision has found few imitators in recent years (the quasi–science fiction effort *Lost* [2004–present] is perhaps its closest kin), a number of other important and long-lived series that draw heavily on the narrative model developed in the various *Star Trek* series have flourished in the new viewing environment of cable and satellite television, with their ability to target specific audiences. Of particular note are shows like the syndicated *Babylon 5* (1994–1998), *Stargate SG-1* (1997–2007), *Farscape* (1999–2003), and the new *Battlestar Galactica* (2004–present). All are in the updated space opera mode of the *Star Trek* franchise (what Gary Westfahl terms the "postmodern space opera" [207]), all depend heavily on digital special effects, and, with the exception of *Stargate SG-1*, which was inspired by the 1994 film *Stargate*, all seem more indebted to the world of SFTV than to the cinema. In effect, they attest to the narrative maturity and contemporary popularity of the form.

In assessing the state of recent SFTV, Johnson-Smith suggests that all of these series must still deal with a common problem: "As broadcast technology has advanced and increased, so have our expectations, and we demand so much more" (252). The contemporary shows cited above both corroborate and qualify that assessment. For both *Babylon 5* and *Battlestar Galactica* have set a new standard for SFTV, as they are truly epic in proportion and elaborately supported by special effects. The first follows a preset, five-year narrative arc aboard a space station that is designed to serve as a kind of interstellar United Nations but eventually becomes a political entity in itself and is involved in a series of complex political intrigues and conflicts that ultimately determine the fate of the galaxy. The latter essentially reimagines human history, taking its fifty thousand survivors of a Cylon attack on an *Odyssey*-like journey through the universe in search of the lost human colony of Earth. In visual style, narrative execution, and ideas, these two series outdistance much narrative television today, even as both excel at doing what has always worked best in the medium—introducing and developing complex characters, in this case, many of them aliens. Although *Stargate SG-1* and *Farscape* are to some extent less ambitious series, both also find ways of taking audiences where they have not gone before. Through its plot device of a Stargate, a technology that allows wormhole travel from one planet to another, *Stargate SG-1*'s human explorers encounter a wide variety of civilizations, both primitive and technologically far advanced—situations that also challenge them to respond appropriately, humanly, even as they employ the genre's emphasis on wonder to reflect on our cultural attitudes toward the other. Its success can be gauged by the fact that it became the longest-running American SFTV series and, like *Star Trek*, produced a popular spin-off, *Stargate Atlantis* (2004–present). *Farscape* draws upon a similar wormhole conceit: Its protagonist, the astronaut John Crichton, is sucked through one and eventually finds himself pursued by the alien Scorpius, who wants to obtain knowledge of wormholes to advance his own evil plans. Suddenly set down in an unknown corner of the universe, one inhabited by both humanoids and strange-looking creatures (crafted by Jim Henson's Creature Shop), Crichton tries to survive in this amazing new environment while constantly struggling, much like Odysseus, "to get back home," as he notes at the start of each episode. Although Crichton's situation is unusual in

The visually "other" world of *Farscape*: Zhaan (Virginia Hey), D'Argo (Anthony Simcoe), and Crichton (Ben Browder) attend to Aeryn (Claudia Black).

that he is the real alien here, that circumstance repeatedly motivates a fundamental examination of just what it means to be human.

In fact, while all of these contemporary series effectively visualize other worlds and other, highly complex, even similarly self-conscious species, they also manage to use those fantastic visions, in one of the abiding traditions of science fiction, to interrogate our own nature and our own condition, particularly as we confront an age in which history seems to have lost much of its relevance, the future is mysterious, and our humanity is often perceived as just a construct of various forces beyond our full understanding and control. Obviously, these are all large issues, the stuff of mainstream fiction and film, and SFTV's ability to address them helps explain its increasingly important place in contemporary media culture. As a further sign of the genre's health and significance, other, similarly ambitious shows, like *Eureka* (2006–present) and *Heroes* (2006–present), have begun to attract attention and to suggest further narrative possibilities for the form. Their brief notice here reminds us that every history, but especially the sort of simple overview of SFTV I have tried to offer, must omit much—including much of promise and importance.

This short survey of SFTV has focused on series television and thus excluded a number of important miniseries, science fiction episodes of other series, and made-for-television movies. That decision follows from the belief that SFTV has in the series form achieved its greatest success and, indeed, established much of its identity. The series is also arguably the most complex incarnation of the genre on television. These notions inform the rest of this volume, in which we have chosen to focus attention largely on series science fiction. Even so, no set of articles could fully describe the scope and richness of the increasingly complex, important, and international body of work that is SFTV. The works collected here cannot treat in any depth more than a handful of the more than 150 series that have aired in the United States and the United Kingdom during broadcast television's history, a number of which—for example, *Star Trek*, *The Twilight Zone*, *Babylon 5*, *Doctor Who*, and *The X-Files*—have themselves already been the subjects of book-length studies, and in some cases multiple studies. Both this short history and the following essays have to gloss over a number of shows, including some that are simply anomalous types (such as *The Man and the Challenge* [1959–1960]), others that rework earlier programs (like the remake of *The Outer Limits* [1995–2002]), and still others that, despite their quality, had only brief runs (including the truly compelling series created by Joss Whedon, *Firefly* [2002]). The videography at the end of this volume should help to flesh out that history, although a proper view of the territory demands a full-length study of a sort that has yet to be written. But the very daunting nature of that task is also both inviting and encouraging, since it underscores the truly remarkable wealth of material that merits study and allows the various contributors to help stake out some of the territory of SFTV that remains to be explored, and thereby to become, it is hoped, essential guides to this field.

A general sense of the genre's history, as sketched above, is certainly one essential for contextualizing the broad trajectory SFTV has followed from the late 1940s to the present. Yet in emphasizing titles, dates, and key figures, as such brief histories typically do, we risk making context seem little more than such details, perhaps inviting readers to forget how much the television genre owes to work that has occurred outside it, helping to lay the foundation for SFTV's emergence and development. And here I would point especially at the development of television itself, the diverse body of science fiction and fantasy literature, science fiction film, the comics, and the general cultural fascination with science and technology. Consequently, the first section of the present volume, "Background," starts to sketch out this deeper context by addressing some of that lineage of SFTV. The essays there speak to the early science fictional conceptualization of television itself, to some of the literary influences on SFTV, and to a few of the ways in which film, perhaps the most obvious predecessor, has been adapted to or has inspired the genre's televisual forms. While these context pieces by no means function as comprehensive surveys, they should begin to trace the cultural imaginary from which SFTV has drawn for its identity.

The next section, "The Shape of the Ship," focuses on some of the narrative practices and forms that have also influenced the development of the genre on television and helped give it such a rich and flexible character. One of these narrative models is the anthology form that we find in such early efforts as *Ray Bradbury Theater*, *The Outer Limits*, and *The Twilight Zone*. This model allowed for great diversity in form while opening the door to some key writers—Bradbury, Ellison, Serling—who have fundamentally influenced the nature of SFTV. A second narrative investigation focuses on the early space opera, the picaresque stories of space voyaging exemplified by some of the first science fiction series, such as *Captain Video* and *Space Patrol*, which also, as we have noted, helped shape many later efforts like *Star Trek*, *Farscape*, and the recent and critically praised *Firefly*. A third considers the influence of animation, a form that has periodically surfaced in U.S. SFTV, from Walt Disney's early Tomorrowland forays on his *Disneyland* show to the recent *Futurama* (1999–2003), but has established its most significant presence in Japan in the form of anime, a form that, as Dennis Redmond here observes, has also played an important role in the emergence of a new "cultural logic" in Asia.[8]

Although they are not specifically addressed here, several other significant narrative explorations of the genre deserve mention. One is the "special event" approach to SFTV, in the form of the made-for-TV movie or the limited series. An example that has gone unnoted in other accounts is the PBS-sponsored adaptation of Ursula K. Le Guin's *The*

Three of the characters—Zoe (Gina Torres), Mal (Nathan Fillion), and Jayne (Adam Baldwin)—central to *Firefly*'s complex revisioning of the space opera.

Lathe of Heaven (1980), a landmark for SFTV not only for the close cooperation of Le Guin but also for the cultural validation that PBS's involvement in the production brought. In fact, Susan Marchand of PBS's marketing and distribution reported that this show has been "the most requested program in the history of the public television archives" (quoted in Garcia). Another narrative development worth noting is the melding of science fiction with the situation comedy, illustrated by works like *My Favorite Martian*, *Mork and Mindy* (1978–1982), and *3rd Rock from the Sun* (1996–2001). Surprisingly the most consistently successful science fiction shows in terms of ratings (the three cited were all among the top thirty Nielsen-rated shows during their initial runs), these hybrids have opened the genre to a broader audience while further attesting to its narrative flexibility. All of these narrative developments have helped to grow the syntax of a constantly evolving SFTV.

The following section, "What Fuels These Flights," emphasizes some of the genre's recurrent semantic components, offering detailed analyses of several of the important concerns of science fiction as it has developed on television—concerns that, for a variety of reasons, have not always been the same as those that dominate film versions of the genre.

One of those key elements is the role that women typically play in the science fiction narrative. This issue is particularly significant since it addresses a charge that has been lodged against science fiction literature and used to argue against the production of science fiction series: that it is a predominantly masculine genre and thus one with a limited appeal, aimed at only a small segment of the viewing audience. With an increasing cultural emphasis on the constructed nature of gender, particularly in the wake of Donna Haraway's influential work in this area, that assumption no longer seems tenable.[9] And several recent series, most notably the remake of *Battlestar Galactica*, have clearly offered their own challenges to this notion by foregrounding gender issues. In addition to giving attention to the construction of gender, "What Fuels These Flights" addresses several other constructions that are crucial to the genre. One is a simple yet fundamentally iconic element of the form—the spaceship, which has undergone great transformations from *Rocky Jones*'s bullet-shaped *Orbit Jet* to *Star Trek*'s iconic *Enterprise* and *Farscape*'s organic *Moya*. The evolving nature of this most fundamental conveyance of science fiction speaks across a broad register of narratives about our changing attitudes toward the technological and, as Samantha Holloway argues, our very human trajectory. Rather more sweeping in its implications is the science fiction fascination with constructing alternate realities or worlds—long a mainstay of the genre's literary form. Our ability to envision other realities in these series not only reflects on available effects technology but also opens onto the genre's ability—and its postmodern proclivity—to interrogate all of our certainties, but especially our sense of what constitutes the real. The selected discussions in this section are intended to point up some of the recurring and more important interior concerns of the genre while suggesting different approaches that might be used to think about other primary motifs that regularly surface in SFTV.

The largest segment of this volume, "The Best Sights 'Out There,'" provides analyses of a number of the most influential series with a special emphasis on those that typify the form today. As one principle of limitation, this section focuses primarily on American series, although British scholar Mark Bould demonstrates the genre's cross-cultural implications as he surveys the key offerings from the United Kingdom with special emphasis on *Doctor Who*. To provide an additional sense of historical impact—on both television in general and on the science fiction genre more particularly—this segment includes a treatment of another major landmark of the genre, *Star Trek*. Because of their recent impact on the genre's development, several of the most successful contemporary series are also addressed in this section—*Babylon 5*, *Stargate SG-1*, and *The X-Files*. Finally, to bring the issue of generic identification back into focus, an essay by David Lavery examines the hit series *Lost* (as of this writing, the only SFTV series consistently in the Nielsen top twenty ratings) in the context of shifting notions of what constitutes science fiction. While *Lost* often foregrounds many conventions associated with science fiction, it also, like a number of other recent shows, just as often slips away from any easy classification, and it thus provides an intriguing opportunity for meditating on the nature and appeal of the form today. And as this last contribution should also underscore, these essays are not intended simply as surveys or historical accounts; rather, they are aimed at demonstrating specific ways of thinking about these series and thus at suggesting fertile strategies for approaching the larger body of series SFTV.

The conclusion to this volume, "The Landing Zone," briefly discusses the growing range of SFTV's influence as its popularity and impact extend into other media while further exploiting another element of the *Star Trek* legacy, the form's devoted fan following. Certainly, one noteworthy development is the extent to which television has become not simply an arena for adapting other media but itself a fertile ground for adaptation—as the cinematic offspring of *Star Trek*, *The X-Files*, and *Firefly* readily attest—and an inspiration for other series. Yet just as significant for the genre is the extent to which science fiction series have prompted the production of a variety of related fan texts that now readily reach across all media boundaries. The conclusion, consequently, looks at blogs, Webisodes, video podcasts, and other phenomena to focus primarily on the proliferation of science fiction fan cultures but also on the new media's role in providing viewers with an expanded relation to television and especially its science fiction texts. Negotiating among different analyses of fan cultures, this section situates the ways in which SFTV's fans actively engage with their favorite shows and with entertainment culture in general. It thereby offers a most fitting conclusion for this collection by—in the spirit of all good science fiction—

pointing beyond, to some of the ways in which this television genre opens onto a new world of media experience and even promises a new sense of agency in the formation of popular culture.

I hope that the trajectory followed by these essays will lead students and fans of SFTV in some new directions while filling an important gap in science fiction and media scholarship. For while the science fiction film genre has generated a library of histories and critical studies, the television form has only lately drawn serious attention. The bibliography provided here lists much of that emerging body of criticism, along with works that, I believe, afford important cross-over perspectives and so should prove key starting points for additional research. Similarly, the videography of more than 150 major prime-time science fiction series that have appeared on network and cable television in the United States and the United Kingdom should prove a crucial tool for those who want to do more extensive examinations or undertake more nuanced historical accounts of SFTV. The proliferation of important and ambitious new series, the flourishing of the genre-specific Sci-Fi Channel, the ready availability of full seasons of series through DVD release (which is itself prompting new ways of viewing and thinking about these series that also should provoke study), and the fan-generated creation of texts online all remind us that we now face a suddenly crowded universe of science fiction texts that challenge us to address them and—what has always been one of the chief appeals of science fiction—their ideas. In addition to mapping some of the territory for this activity, *The Essential Science Fiction Television Reader* should provide a useful, perhaps even an essential, launching point.

Notes

1. In a single, randomly chosen week at the time of writing this introduction, my local cable provider was offering the following science fiction series (some in first run, others in syndication): *Star Trek, Star Trek: The Next Generation, Star Trek: Voyager, Enterprise, Eureka, Heroes, Battlestar Galactica, Doctor Who, Stargate SG-1, Stargate Atlantis, The Twilight Zone, Andromeda, Futurama, The Outer Limits, The X-Files, Dark Angel, Lost, Phil of the Future, Smallville, Jake 2.0, Red Dwarf,* and *Farscape.*

2. As examples of that emphasis on the experience of wonder, we might note David Hartwell's history of science fiction, *Age of Wonders,* and Neil Barron's bible of science fiction scholarship, *Anatomy of Wonder.*

3. For information on the serial and early television programming, I am indebted to Alan Barbour's *Cliffhanger* (234) and Brooks and Marsh's *The Complete Directory to Prime Time Network and Cable TV Shows.*

4. Whereas some have rather dismissively described the space opera as a "western in space," Edward James in his history of science fiction more nearly captures the spirit of the space opera as he emphasizes its exaggerated actions and situations, along with the element of awe it can inspire, even though he ultimately terms it a "type of preposterous galaxy-spanning adventure" (47). For a more detailed overview of the form with an emphasis on its recent development, see Gary Westfahl's "Space Opera."

5. For more detailed background on the Disney *Man in Space* shows and the larger Disney flirtation with science and science fiction, see my article "Disney in Science Fiction Land."

6. In describing the history of the space opera as a literary type, Westfahl underscores its narrative flexibility. As he notes, the form "must continually reinvent itself" so that "as one form of space opera falls out of favour . . . another, improved form of space opera emerges for discriminating readers" (198).

7. The Sci-Fi Channel is owned by General Electric as part of its NBC Universal branch.

8. Although it is essentially a genre to itself, Japanese anime represents a major presence in world SFTV, one that has increasingly come to influence live-action programs. *Cowboy Bebop* (1998–1999 in Japan, 2001 in the United States), for example, clearly fed into the complex heritage of Joss Whedon's *Firefly.* For a brief commentary on some of the key themes of anime, see my *Science Fiction Film,* 112–16. For an extended analysis of the form, see Susan J. Napier's *Anime from* Akira *to* Howl's Moving Castle: *Experiencing Contemporary Japanese Animation.*

9. See Haraway's pioneering work, *Simians, Cyborgs, and Women: The Reinvention of Nature,* as well as Claudia Springer's application of these gender concerns to science fiction film in *Electronic Eros: Bodies and Desire in the Postindustrial Age.*

Works Cited

Barbour, Alan G. *Cliffhanger: A Pictorial History of the Motion Picture Serial.* New York: A and W.

Barron, Neil. *Anatomy of Wonder: A Critical Guide to Science Fiction.* 5th ed. Westport, CT: Libraries Unlimited, 2004.

Booker, M. Keith. *Science Fiction Television: A History.* Westport, CT: Praeger, 2004.

Brooks, Tim, and Earle Marsh. *The Complete Directory to Prime Time Network and Cable TV Shows, 1946–Present.* 8th ed. New York: Ballantine, 2003.

Fulton, Roger. *The Encyclopedia of TV Science Fiction.* 3rd ed. London: Boxtree, 1997.

Garcia, Frank. "The Return of *The Lathe of Heaven*: Making Dreams Come True." *Mania TV*. April 17, 2000. http://www.mania.com/20579.html.

Gitlin, Todd. *Media Unlimited: How the Torrent of Images and Sounds Overwhelms Our Lives*. New York: Holt, 2002.

Haraway, Donna. *Simians, Cyborgs, and Women: The Reinvention of Nature*. London: Routledge, 1991.

Hartwell, David. *Age of Wonders: Exploring the World of Science Fiction*. New York: McGraw-Hill, 1984.

James, Edward. *Science Fiction in the 20th Century*. New York: Oxford University Press, 1994.

Johnson-Smith, Jan. *American Science Fiction TV: Star Trek, Stargate and Beyond*. Middletown, CT: Wesleyan University Press, 2005.

La Valley, Albert J. "Traditions of Trickery: The Role of Special Effects in the Science Fiction Film." In *Shadows of the Magic Lamp: Fantasy and Science Fiction in Film*, edited by George E. Slusser and Eric S. Rabkin, 141–58. Carbondale: Southern Illinois University Press, 1985.

Lucanio, Patrick, and Gary Coville. *Smokin' Rockets: The Romance of Technology in American Film, Radio, and Television, 1945–1962*. Jefferson, NC: McFarland, 2002.

Lyotard, Jean-François. *The Postmodern Condition: A Report on Knowledge*. Translated by Geoff Bennington and Brian Massumi. Minneapolis: University of Minnesota Press, 1984,

McHale, Brian. *Constructing Postmodernism*. London: Routledge, 1992.

Miller, Mark Crispin. *Boxed In: The Culture of TV*. Evanston, IL: Northwestern University Press, 1988.

Napier, Susan J. *Anime from* Akira *to* Howl's Moving Castle: *Experiencing Contemporary Japanese Animation*. Rev. ed. London: Palgrave, 2005.

Pierson, Michele. *Special Effects: Still in Search of Wonder*. New York: Columbia University Press, 2002.

Springer, Claudia. *Electronic Eros: Bodies and Desire in the Postindustrial Age*. Austin: University of Texas Press, 1996.

Telotte, J. P. "Disney in Science Fiction Land." *Journal of Popular Film and Television* 33, no. 1 (2005): 12–21.

———. *The Science Fiction Film*. Cambridge: Cambridge University Press, 2001.

Tulloch, John, and Henry Jenkins. *Science Fiction Audiences: Watching* Doctor Who *and* Star Trek. London: Routledge, 1995.

Virilio, Paul. *Virilio Live: Selected Interviews*. Edited by John Armitage. London: Sage, 2001.

Westfahl, Gary. "Space Opera." In *The Cambridge Companion to Science Fiction*, edited by Edward James and Farah Mendlesohn, 197–208. Cambridge: Cambridge University Press, 2003.

PART I

BACKGROUND

Lifting Off from
the Cultural Pad

LOST IN SPACE

Television as Science Fiction Icon

J. P. Telotte

Before science fiction television (SFTV) could come into being, the medium itself had to be created (both physically and imaginatively), find an audience, and establish its own identity. This historical emergence corresponds most obviously to a series of key developments that made television both a technical possibility and a potential component of the domestic environment. However, it also involves a cultural context that enabled those developments, inflected television's early reception, and produced an incubation space for SFTV. For at its inception, television was seen not simply as one more new technology among the many others that were ushered in by the machine age, that period from the turn of the century to the beginning of World War II; it was, for many, something that seemed to have sprung forth from the pages of that newly popular genre—science fiction. Before becoming a fixture in American homes and a purveyor of its own brand of science fiction, television was itself, quite simply, an icon of science fiction, and that character inevitably conditioned both its reception and that of the texts it offered audiences.

Paul Virilio notes that, during World War II, what he terms the "vision machine" rapidly emerged as a significant, perhaps even the most important, weapon for all combatants, opening the way for the ongoing "cinematization" of the contemporary world. Yet the "new industrialization of vision" (*Vision* 59) that has often been linked to the emergence of television was already well under way prior to the war, with early developments during the machine age. In fact, the popular perception of television was taking shape even while the technology itself was still largely a futuristic fantasy, a science fiction. For in this period we find the popular imagination already conceptualizing television in various roles—optimistically, as a kind of ultimate communication device, but also more darkly, as a means of surveillance, a tool of deception, even a potentially deadly force. I want to examine that early conceptualization as it took shape in another component of the larger "vision machine," our popular science fiction films. By looking at how television functions iconically in such movies—works like *Metropolis* (1927), *The Tunnel* (a.k.a. *Transatlantic Tunnel*, 1935), *Murder by Television* (1935), *The Phantom Empire* (1935), *The Invisible Ray* (1936), and *S.O.S.—Tidal Wave* (1939)—we can better understand both these varied perceptions and the context that was being created for the later introduction of regular broadcast television. In isolating this point at which one type of fantasy glimpses another's arrival, we see reflected not only what Cecelia Tichi, in her study of technology in the era, describes as "the alternating attitudes" and mixed responses "of people whose culture is in rapid transition" (*Shifting* 29) but also signs of a deep-seated cultural resistance to the work of that emerging vision machine, and particularly to its impact on our sense of public and private space.

This particular element of the larger vision machine was certainly very much in the headlines throughout the machine age, although television was hardly ready to take its eventual place as a competitor to the cinema, much less as a generator of its own influential science fiction texts. In the late nineteenth century, conditions were in place for the fusion of two constituent technologies, photography and the telephone, and by the turn of the century the term "television" had already been coined by the Russian scientist Constantin Perskyi. The mid-1920s saw the appearance of two primary television technologies: Vladimir Zworykin and Philo Farnsworth demonstrated systems based on the cathode ray tube, and John Logie Baird exhibited his Televisor, a mechanical system based on rotating metal disks. Both systems made headlines in the late 1920s and early 1930s with a series of well-publicized firsts, mostly centered on the transmission of images over ever greater distances: broadcasting from one city to another, from one country to another, from one continent to another, and, in Baird's case, even from England to an ocean liner in the mid-Atlantic (Moseley and Chapple 17). The BBC had begun regular broadcasts early in the decade using the Baird equipment, and German, French, and American transmissions soon followed, although few sets were available in any of these countries to receive the broadcasts. By the time of that signal machine age event, "Building the

World of Tomorrow," the 1939 New York World's Fair, television had clearly entered the popular consciousness if not popular use. As David Gelernter notes, "TV was all over the fair" (37), featured in the Westing-house, General Electric, Ford, RCA, and Crosley Appliance exhibits, in various demonstration kiosks that allowed fairgoers to see their own tele-vised images, and in President Roosevelt's opening speech, beamed by NBC from atop another machine age icon, the Empire State Building. Yet despite this showcasing of the new technology as an essential part of "the world of tomorrow," a survey of fairgoers found fewer than one in seven "expressed an interest in buying a set in the near future" (Corn and Hor-rigan 27). Even after World War II, *Fortune* speculated that "television could conceivably turn into the biggest and costliest flop in US industrial history" (Miner 107). Apparently, many people remained reluctant to embrace this new technology, in part because of what William Boddy terms the "larger cultural ambivalence regarding [all] new communica-tions technologies" (1).

Despite its being ballyhooed in repeated newspaper reports, show-cased in national magazines like *Life*, and explained in specialized jour-nals like *Modern Mechanics*, *Television Today*, and *Radio and Television*,[1] television remained more a cultural idea than a practical appliance. Or rather, we might describe it as a series of ideas, for as Joseph Corn and Brian Horrigan suggest, in the 1920s and 1930s, "the idea of television in our future heated the popular imagination as few technologies ever have," producing a wide spectrum of predictions that were also a bit "outlandish," even for this highly speculative era (24). In keeping with the headlines noted above, those who tried to shape the idea of television focused mainly on its ability to revise our sense of distance and thus on one of the technology's key characteristics: as Boddy puts it, "the technical indifference of broadcast signals to national boundaries" (4). Speaking to this spatial dimension, RCA's David Sarnoff envisioned a future with obvious science fiction over-tones, as he noted how "physical limitation" would be "swept away" by television, leaving as humanity's only "boundaries . . . the limits of the earth itself," thereby helping to foster a new era of global under-standing (16).

On a more practical level, television's boosters suggested that doc-tors would abandon home visits in favor of diagnosing patients from their offices, that the military would adopt it to watch our skies and borders to detect far-off invaders, that spouses would use it to keep track of each other, and that parents would employ it like an electronic nanny to monitor their children's activities.[2] Like most new technologies, television was the subject of great speculation, albeit speculation that typically saw it in a science fictional context, like other popular speculations of the era: rocket ships, death rays, life-prolonging machines. Only over much time would it, like many other, older icons of science fiction, become "annexed by the everyday" (173), as Gwyneth Jones nicely describes the process, and eventually settle into the role that Tichi, responding to its later pervasiveness, terms the new "electronic hearth"—a metaphor reflecting not just television's domestication but also the shift from its early association with the conquest of distance to a new sense of intimacy.

Of course, today, many of these promises no longer seem quite as outlandish as they did then. Television has not only become ubiquitous but has come to exert an influence on our sense of space, particularly its very real potential for intrusiveness and surveillance, that has made it the subject of public debate and legislation, as well as the latest fashion in military acquisition as surveillance becomes the key component of deterrence. For better or worse, with its annexation by the everyday, television has surrendered its iconic science fictional status to become part of the common cultural landscape—and arguably the most popular purveyor of science fiction. Yet Mark Crispin Miller has suggested that this commonness disguises a lingering fantastic dimension of the technology, that in modern times television has "itself *become* the environment," an electronic atmosphere from which we seem to draw life. As he offers, television's aim is "to be *everywhere:* not just to clutter our surroundings, but to become them," in fact, to become the electronic "air we breathe" (8). This notion is akin to Virilio's description of the various technologies that have helped shape the contemporary visual regime as having delivered us to a *Matrix*-like world, "a realm of fictitious topology in which all the surfaces of the globe are directly present to one another." Replacing the older sense of distance—and our amazement, even unease, at how easily we traverse it—is "the imposture of immediacy" (*War* 46), a situation in which our sense of real space dissolves into a new experience of mediated space, into a "cinematized" or video world that holds itself out as intimately available to us. Film and now television have not just become our primary access to the world but insinuated themselves as the very world in which we live.

We can trace out some of the steps in this gradual shift—a shift by which contemporary existence has come to seem the stuff of science fiction and the genre's icons have been normalized—in these early efforts to envision television, that is, as one component in that cinematizing process contemplates another. Certainly, even within the science fiction context, television was not always depicted as extraordinary. In fact, it was, with some prescience, often viewed as a common appliance and thus just a part of the futuristic trappings for many of these narratives. *Just Imagine* (1930), for example, shows it used to monitor apartment doors, enabling those inside to quite literally screen visitors. In *Just Imagine*, *The Tunnel*, and *Things to Come* (1936), among other films, the television is also mated to the telephone as a device for personal communication. Additionally, *Things to Come* shows the video screen, linked to a database of historical images, as a tool for instructing children. And, perhaps most nearly anticipating contemporary use, all of the films cited above, as well as *Men Must Fight* (1932) and *S.O.S.—Tidal Wave*, depict television as a primary purveyor of news. But such films typically present these rather commonplace applications as parts of a world still in the offing, a world that is finally not like our own, so even under domestic disguise, television remains an icon of distance,[3] another semantic element of science fiction narrative.

The Tunnel, a film about technological efforts to conquer physical space, fittingly offers one of the more striking analyses of the effects built into this new medium that advertised itself as dissolving distance. The film's protagonist, the engineer Mack McAllan, who is spearheading the construction of a transatlantic tunnel, is repeatedly shown flying back and forth across the Atlantic to resolve political problems, secure additional funding, and maintain enthusiasm for his project. And throughout these flights we see him resort to the videophone to connect to family and friends, explaining why he has, once again, missed his son's birthday or had to cancel an engagement with his wife, or asking a friend to stand in for him with his family. The device thus becomes an ironic measure of the great personal distances and strained relationships that his work is producing. In fact, television chronicles the gradual

In *The Tunnel* (1935), the television measures out personal and emotional distance.

disintegration of his marriage for us, as his wife, in London, finds she can keep track of her husband's activities only through the news accounts of his appearances in New York society, where he is accompanied by the beautiful daughter of one of the tunnel's key backers. Repeatedly, his wife sees these images that suggest romantic connections and assumes that the TV reports accurately measure changes in his emotional life. While both television and videophone serve as electronic versions of the narrative's larger concern with the transatlantic tunnel as a device for linking people over vast distances, they also inject a heavy irony into those technological efforts, suggesting how much of human relationships, of our most private connections, might become lost in space despite television's promises of telepresence and electronic intimacy.

Another and perhaps more immediately unsettling version of that effect shows up in the more frequent depiction of television as a component in a panopticon culture. Joh Frederson, the master of *Metropolis*'s dystopian city, can readily summon the workers' foreman or watch as he hurries about his tasks by dialing him in on the monitor in his office overlooking the city. However, that monitor simply underscores the point made by Frederson's lofty positioning and the quickness with which he fires his assistant Josephat for not properly surveilling the workers' activities: that both his control and the workers' subjection are tied to his technological ability to see everywhere and everything. And his own failure to empathize with the workers, his own intellectual and emotional distance from them, is again ironically measured by his very intrusive surveillance. The point is, of course, also made comically in Chaplin's *Modern Times* (1936), wherein we see the modern factory monitored at all key points by the factory president, who can suddenly appear on a television screen even in the restroom, admonishing the Little Tramp to "get back to work." In this case the television is simply presented as a logical extension of the modern factory system, serving to ensure the efficient operation of the assembly line by governing it— and the workers, who become components of the line—from a distance. But the possibility of television's intruding a distant eye into our most

The master of Metropolis sends orders to his foreman via television in *Metropolis* (1927).

intimate spaces, of turning its voyeuristic potential back on the viewer, was certainly one of the most common concerns that clustered around this icon.

This surveillance mode is a particularly common element of the period's serials, as we see in works like *The Phantom Empire*, *Undersea Kingdom* (1936), *Buck Rogers* (1939), and *The Phantom Creeps* (1939). *The Phantom Empire* is perhaps the most telling example, since every episode involves the use of a "master television" by Queen Tika, ruler of the futuristic underground empire of Murania. With this device she maintains control over her realm and constantly wards off threats— from within and without—as its large circular screen, a "master eye," allows her to see anywhere on Earth, even without the aid of a camera. When her chancellor Lord Argo is mysteriously absent and not even her secret police can locate him, she angrily questions one of her ministers, "Didn't you try the television screen? Nitwit!" Her expression of irritation not only underscores how easily television might be turned into a

Gene Autry commandeers the master television controls of Murania in *The Phantom Empire* (1935).

monitoring device but also suggests how commonplace that panopticon possibility might become, assumed as a fact of daily life in a futuristic, highly technological society like Murania, where there simply is no more intimate or private space, where the television eye is everywhere, empowering dictatorial rule and control.

Although it is more murder mystery than science fiction film, the ominously titled *Murder by Television* amplifies the anxiety bound up in the introduction of this intrusive new technology. Set against a backdrop of the development and demonstration of the possibilities of international television broadcasting—which was, as we have noted, very much in the headlines during this period—the film quickly frames its key icon within a science fictional context, as it opens with a portentous epigraph, asserting that "television is the greatest step forward we have yet made in the preservation of humanity. It will make of this earth a paradise we have always envisioned but never seen." Pairing that need for preservation with the utopian promise of a future paradise not only speaks to the conflicted atmosphere of the Depression era but also establishes the supposed stakes for the action here, the importance of this new icon. Underscoring this utopian hope, James Houghland, the inventor of the new television device, explains that he believes "television should be something more than just another form of amusement"—a form it takes in such non–science fiction films of the era as *Elstree Calling* (1930) and *International House* (1933), which use it as a device to introduce vaudeville-type acts. In support of that contention, Houghland proposes a series of demonstration broadcasts to showcase how television, following Sarnoff's assertion, might foster international relations. In the first of these he shows images from Paris, China, and "dear old London," as he terms it. Yet that international emphasis betrays a dark side, and thus the equally divisive potential of the new technology, when the various intrigues to acquire Houghland's invention surface and he is mysteriously killed in the middle of another transmission. The suspects prove to be an international group of characters, including Houghland's Chinese houseboy, who confesses to being one of several spies his country has sent throughout the world to gather information on television development. In fact, all of the suspects are in various ways linked to efforts at obtaining the new invention for rival governments or concerns. Emphasizing this sense of conspiracy, as well as television's panoptic implications, the federal agent Arthur Perry notes, when he exposes the real murderer, that he has been under government surveillance for some time and that his "contacts with foreign governments interested in television are known."

Yet the more significant development lies in the very way in which Houghland is killed—literally by television. In the middle of his second demonstration of long-distance broadcasting, he suddenly collapses in pain and is, as one spectator notes, "killed by his own invention." With his death spectacularly broadcast on that invention and witnessed by many, the film insinuates a dangerous, even deadly potential within the new technology that resonated with another frequent icon or motif of science fiction. As Perry explains, the killer planted a device in the television studio that, when triggered by a telephone call, radiated waves that altered Houghland's television transmission: "They created an interstellar frequency, which is *the death ray*!" Early discussions of television, such as that of Moseley and Chapple, shed some light on this sort of sensationalistic suggestion, for even as they attempt to provide technical accounts of the workings of the new technology, they also lend a note of mystification as they vaguely explain how the televised image is produced by "rays" and describe Baird's experimental efforts at transmitting nighttime television signals "by flooding the 'sending' room by *infra* red rays" (6). As Boddy chronicles, this sort of mystification was quite common, for throughout this period, electronic communication, including television, retained "a long association with the magical and uncanny" (5), here evoked in television's easy transformation into a death ray, enabling it to kill at a distance.

In fact, a similar conflation occurs in another film released in 1935, *The Invisible Ray*. It opens with a planetarium-like show of our galaxy many thousands of years ago and of an asteroid striking Earth, bringing with it a special form of radium. The images are the work of the scientist Janos Rukh, who has captured a beam of light from Andromeda—which he describes as a natural broadcasting agent—and fed it into a radium-driven television transmitter that breaks down the beam into a visual record of the past and projects it onto the ceiling of his laboratory. After discovering a more powerful form of radium, the Radium X revealed by the light from Andromeda, Rukh harnesses it not to capture images or even to cure blindness, as his rival Dr. Benet does, but rather to emit rays that destroy from a distance, much like the death ray described in *Murder by Television*. Although it is hardly a film about television—in fact, Rukh never names his various devices—*The Invisible Ray* clearly cobbled together its central technological attraction from the various conceptions that were constellating around television in this era, most notably its ability to send images across great distances (here, interstellar distances), the popular sense that this new technology depended upon rather mysterious rays, and the suspicion that, like so many other new technologies, a great danger attached to it.

Although it brackets off television's mysterious dimension, *S.O.S.—Tidal Wave* further develops its dangerous potential and frames that effect within a similar sense of distance. In this instance, television has, in an unspecified near future, become part of the fabric of everyday life, supplanting radio as a primary conduit for national and international news. An early montage, for example, shows pedestrians gathered in front of a store window, café patrons dining, and a family at home all watching the latest news. The narrative plays out this new function against the backdrop of a local election, as television's role in influencing public opinion—and thus deciding the political future—becomes the film's central focus. Its protagonist, Jeff Shannon, is a former newspaper reporter who has become a star of the new medium. As one of his admirers offers, "There's not another man like him. . . . He photographs his own stuff, projects it, and describes it." Anticipating the future star status of the national news anchor, Jeff is also described as a potential molder of public opinion, even though he has pointedly avoided political issues and concentrated his efforts on sensationalistic broadcasts—as one viewer casually notes, "We seem to have plenty of fires in the television newsreels today." Given the larger political issues in the world at the time and America's official isolationist attitude, this stance seems to offer a clear comment on that public policy, while it also argues for the inevitable political consequences of a technology that knows no "national boundaries."

Mirroring that contemporary international situation and its impact on America, the narrative shows how Jeff is gradually dragged into the middle of an election to combat a corrupt candidate supported by gangsters as well as a rival television station. In fact, most of the narrative dramatizes Jeff's difficult decision, as his wife Laura puts it, to do "his duty as a private citizen"—a decision that involves exposing Laura, their son, and another television celebrity, Uncle Dan, to the threats of the opposition, potentially getting into "trouble with sponsors," and abandoning his comfortable apolitical stance. After Jeff decides to become involved, we see him in a montage suggesting what we today term investigative journalism, as he energetically films scenes for his television show documenting the illegal activities of the corrupt politician Clifford Farrow, with the avowed purpose, as Jeff says, of putting him "out of the race." But following threats to his family and a bombing at the television station, Jeff wavers in his resolve, withdraws his investigative programming, and substitutes innocuous reports on a local ladies' club, a ship launching, and a bicycle race. Only the death of Uncle Dan, who was preparing his own television report on Farrow's background, and injuries to his wife and son draw Jeff back to his civic duty and enable him to demonstrate the political power of the new medium with an election-day exposé.[4]

Yet troubling that progressive effort is another assertion of the medium's darker potential, as Jeff's broadcast indicting Farrow is followed by what seems to be another breaking news story, one that suggests how distant images might impact the local world. As a voice announces that a tidal wave is approaching the Atlantic coast, we see broadcast scenes of a storm, of panic in the streets of New York and other cities, and of massive destruction—including the collapse of the Empire State Building. In keeping with these apocalyptic images, the anonymous newscaster warns, "All states within one hundred miles of the Atlantic coastline, evacuate," and prods listeners into near hysteria with comments like "Run for your lives!" and "Men and women of America—this is the end!" The montage of panicked citizens we then see in the streets of Jeff's town, one that replays the images glimpsed on television, dramatizes the reach and the power of television, as well as an unexpected consequence of a promise—or warning—articulated by Sarnoff in the same year, that "television will finally bring to people . . . instantaneous participation in the sights and sounds of the entire world" (42).

In this instance, that promise is twisted for political ends, as the film demonstrates how easily the "instantaneous participation" Sarnoff describes might be manipulated. For Jeff discovers that Farrow's campaign has arranged for the rival television station to broadcast scenes of a disaster film, accompanied by the voice of a live announcer, to disrupt the election. The station manager's subsequent excuse, that "we forgot to announce it was a film transcription,"[5] and Farrow's apology in which he notes that "it was intended as a harmless amusement. We didn't anticipate anybody would take it seriously," stir echoes of the most famous media hoax of the era, Orson Welles's *War of the Worlds* broadcast in the previous year. And as Farrow's subsequent defeat suggests, those disingenuous explanations do no better than Welles's public apology to placate a deceived public. Moreover, they hardly mask a string of dangers revealed here: of political forces eager to control the new medium of television, of a medium already aware of the reach and power of its voice, of the ease with which television might manipulate and even panic the citizenry, and of our own quick transformation into the fully cinematized culture Virilio would later describe.

Of course, like many other B films of the era, *S.O.S.—Tidal Wave* sounds these warnings in an exaggerated manner that invariably paints television in like colors. But coming as it does at the close of the machine age and linking the looming force of television to the sort of media manipulation recently experienced in the Welles broadcast, it helps us better see some of the cultural perceptions of this new technology, as well as its potential subject matter, that were already coming into focus. Like all of the other films considered here, it pointedly identifies television's real province not as entertainment but as news and public service presentations—areas that the film industry might well have been willing to cede to this potential competition. And with its parallel editing of "televised" scenes of panic in New York and other seaboard cities with the similar "live" images in Jeff's city, it underscores not only the perceived power of this new medium but also its ability to collapse space, that is, the way its distant dealing with subjects can become locally intrusive, reaching even into the individual human psyche. In fact, this latter effect finds an added comic punctuation in the film's conclusion when Jeff's assistant Peaches tells his girlfriend Mable, "Now that we're alone, how about a little kiss?" only to find that their kiss is inadvertently broadcast over television. Although that translation of private space into the public arena is presented as an accidental practical joke, it further underscores how television might itself become a cultural practical joker, potentially everywhere, as Miller suggests, always ready—unsettlingly—to share with the world our most intimate moments, as it becomes the very "air we breathe."

As Gwyneth Jones reminds us, the icons of science fiction—including television in the films discussed here—are ultimately more than contextual components; they "warn . . . that this is a different world; and at the same time constitute that difference" (163). In these machine age films, television clearly helps to constitute a rather different sort of world, a science fictional realm marked not so much by futuristic cities or rocket travel but by a new sense of space and by technologies that foreground that sense of space. On a note of optimism, these films suggest the optical expansion of our personal world that television would usher in, and indeed one that was soon visualized in the spate of space operas that populated American television in the late 1940s and 1950s. More of our world and its people could be seen—whether they wished it or not—instantaneously. Yet these films locate a darker possibility as well, finding in that seeing an uncomfortable collapse of space. For even if the prying eye of television could not quite reach everywhere, as *The Phantom Empire, Undersea Kingdom, The Invisible Ray,* and other works that play fast and loose with the technological facts would suggest, it was certainly seen as compromising our most intimate spaces, as Peaches and Mabel in *S.O.S.—Tidal Wave* find out. It is an icon, then, that may help us not only to better gauge the levels of uncertainty and anxiety surrounding such technological developments but also to more accurately measure the extent to which the machine age, in its early fascination with televisual technologies, was already invested in that cinematized world that Virilio describes and that we now obviously inhabit.

Of course, it might well be argued that the film industry was simply casting into a negative light a potential competitor and that television as we have long known it—along with its suspicious brother the cinema—is already a bit out of date, on the verge of being absorbed into the digital world of multimedia and virtual reality. Indeed, recent developments have rendered many of the early cinematic visions of television irrelevant, making those video dreams no longer so outlandish, no longer science fictional, simply ordinary—at least with one key exception. For that strange relation to space that we find in these early visions of television and the impact of that relation on our sense of self still evoke something of the authentic atmosphere of science fiction, an atmosphere that inheres in much early SFTV. Virilio has described the modern malady of "technological vertigo or purely cinematic derealization, which affects our sense of spatial dimension" (*War* 85). Perhaps in these early visions of television we are seeing some symptoms of this malady, as space is beginning to slip from our control, to become not something we have technologically mastered but something that might master us. That fantastic ability to see across oceans and continents, into outer space or through time, in fact, to position the prying eye anywhere our desires might wish,[6] finally leaves the figures of these machine age films, not unlike audiences today, strangely unanchored, lost in space (as we would see in one of the more popular SFTV series, *Lost in Space* [1965–1968]), and even threatened because of its correlative implications for our most intimate spaces. But for this reason these films still merit our attention as what Jones terms warnings, as they forecast our own science fictional fate as inhabitants of that fictitious topology Virilio describes, and as they point toward a fully realized SFTV that might be seen as another step in the relentless process of cinematization.

Notes

An earlier version of this essay appeared in *Journal of Popular Film and Television* 33, no. 4 (2006): 178–86.

1. It is worth noting that Hugo Gernsback, one of the key figures of early science fiction, edited a variety of journals that took the new medium of television as their primary focus, including *Radio and Television*, *Television*, and *Television News*. Gernsback was also one of those most responsible for bringing the very term "television" into popular usage. In one of his earlier magazines, *Modern Electrics*, he published articles on early television as well as stories in which this new technology played a central role, including his own serialized science fiction novel *Ralph 124C41+*. Often described as a gadget story, the novel depicts the distant future of 2660, an era largely transformed by the triumphs of science and technology, especially television.

2. For a litany of these popular conceptions of television's role, see Corn and Horrigan's account (24–27) as well as Sarnoff's predictions (48–50).

3. My study *A Distant Technology* provides an extended discussion of the metaphor of distance across a wide range of machine age science fiction films. It is a trope that runs through the films of many nations in this era and speaks to that cultural reconfiguration of private and public space implicated in the new broadcast technologies.

4. Caught in the quandary between doing his duty and exposing his family

and friends to harm, Jeff winds up trying to avoid his problems by drinking them away in the aptly named Looneyville Bar. The implication that trying to retreat from the political realities of the day is simply "looney" seems one of the film's more intriguing commentaries, particularly in light of the film industry's own general tendency in this era to avoid much direct commentary on the world situation—on its own Jeff-like attitude.

5. This comment gains resonance from the fact that *S.O.S.—Tidal Wave* is working its own variation on this television strategy, for it has lifted this fairly convincing disaster footage from a combination of newsreels and other feature films. Most notably, the New York scenes are taken from another machine age science fiction film, RKO's *Deluge* (1933).

6. The notion that the eye of television can see anywhere, without the aid of a camera, is rather common in films of this era. As *The Invisible Ray* exaggeratedly suggests, some believed that television was essentially a device for focusing rays of light from remote locations. The conclusion of the serial *The Phantom Empire* turns precisely on this notion, as the protagonist, played by Gene Autry, is cleared of murder charges when the real killer's confession is caught on an experimental television receiver that is "tuned in" to his geographical location.

Works Cited

Boddy, William. *New Media and Popular Imagination: Launching Radio, Television, and Digital Media in the United States.* Oxford: Oxford University Press, 2004.

Corn, Joseph J., and Brian Horrigan. *Yesterday's Tomorrows: Past Visions of the American Future.* Baltimore: Johns Hopkins University Press, 1996.

Gelernter, David. *1939: The Lost World of the Fair.* New York: Avon, 1995.

Jones, Gwyneth. "The Icons of Science Fiction." In *The Cambridge Companion to Science Fiction*, edited by Edward James and Farah Mendlesohn, 163–73. Cambridge: Cambridge University Press, 2003.

Miller, Mark Crispin. *Boxed In: The Culture of TV.* Evanston, IL: Northwestern University Press, 1988.

Miner, Worthington. "Television: A Case of War Neurosis." *Fortune*, March 1946, 107–8.

Moseley, Sydney A., and H. J. Barton Chapple. *Television: Today and Tomorrow.* 4th ed. London: Pitman, 1934.

Sarnoff, David. *Pioneering in Television: Prophecy and Fulfillment.* New York: RCA, 1946.

Telotte, J. P. *A Distant Technology: Science Fiction Film and the Machine Age.* Hanover, NH: Wesleyan University Press, 1999.

Tichi, Cecelia. *Electronic Hearth: Creating an American Television Culture.* Oxford: Oxford University Press, 1991.

————. *Shifting Gears: Technology, Literature, Culture in Modernist America.* Chapel Hill: University of North Carolina Press, 1987.

Virilio, Paul. *The Vision Machine.* Translated by Julie Rose. Bloomington: Indiana University Press, 1994.

————. *War and Cinema: The Logistics of Perception.* Translated by Patrick Camiller. London: Verso, 1989.

SHADOWS ON THE CATHODE RAY TUBE

Adapting Print Science Fiction for Television

Lisa Yaszek

The early years of television were exciting times for science fiction authors, as broadcast versions of previously published short stories and novels promised to bring new audiences to their chosen genre. But the process of adapting the literature to television did not always go quite as authors expected. Consider, for instance, the case of *Tom Corbett, Space Cadet*. A wildly popular series aimed at a juvenile audience, *Tom Corbett* seemed to have everything a science fiction fan could want: it was based on a popular Robert Heinlein novel, it boasted rocket scientist (and science fiction author) Willey Ley as its technical advisor, and, best of all for viewers, from 1950 to 1955 it ran on all four major networks—sometimes simultaneously. But Heinlein himself was less than thrilled with the show: "I have written [Scribner's editor] Miss [Alice] Dalgliesh about the TV scripts. Did you read them? If so, you know how bad they are; I don't want an air credit on that show (much as I appreciate the royalty checks!) and I am reasonably sure that a staid, dignified house like Scribner's will feel the same way. It has the high moral standards of soap opera" (45).

To a certain extent, Heinlein's comments seem prescient. As Mark Bould explains, throughout its history in the United States, science fiction television (SFTV) has tended to "subjugate science to a blend of adventure, soap opera, topicality (sometimes even seriousness) and moralizing" (89). Furthermore, although children's series like *Tom Corbett* laid the foundations for this new narrative paradigm, Bould suggests, it was ultimately perfected by the adult-oriented science fiction programs developed for the prestigious, mixed-genre drama anthologies of the early 1950s.

In this essay I investigate Bould's claim by considering one particu-

larly significant made-for-TV science fiction event: the premiere broadcast of "Atomic Attack" on *The Motorola Television Hour* in 1954.
Based on the critically acclaimed novel *Shadow on the Hearth* (1950) by
Heinlein's contemporary Judith Merril, "Atomic Attack" seems to have
been just as dramatically changed in the process of adaptation as *Tom
Corbett*. Whereas Merril's novel explores how scientific thinking and
rational behavior might save Americans from the worst excesses of cold
war social and moral order, its televised counterpart insists that the
survival of the nuclear family depends on uncritical adherence to this
same order. But as we shall see, televisual adaptation has proved to be
more than a simple watering down of "good" print science fiction.
Rather, early SFTV programs such as "Atomic Attack" were the foun-
dational texts of a new visual science fiction storytelling tradition that
is related to, but not entirely congruent with, print science fiction. By
approaching "Atomic Attack" from this perspective, we can see how
SFTV emerged as a unique form thanks to three cultural forces: the
narrative traditions of print science fiction, the broadcasting imperatives of cold war television, and the aesthetic tradition of science fiction
filmmaking that directly preceded the development of SFTV itself.

The Early Years

As participants in a literary genre that emerged with the first television
broadcasts, science fiction authors have always been interested in the
scientific and social implications of TV. In 1926 Hugo Gernsback ushered science fiction into the modern era with the publication of *Amazing
Stories: The Magazine of Scientifiction*. Around the same time he
founded the experimental television station WRNY, which broadcast
postage stamp–sized images to the scanners of two thousand amateur
enthusiasts in the New York area in 1928–1929 ("Hugo Gernsback").
Not surprisingly, authors quickly realized that they could endear themselves to Gernsback by writing about television. For example, in 1927
Clare Winger Harris took third prize in an *Amazing Stories* contest for
a story that revolved around visual broadcast technologies, thereby
launching both a close friendship with Gernsback and a career that
spanned two decades (Donawerth 30).

When television became a staple of the average American home in
the late 1940s and early 1950s, audiences found that they had three

types of science fiction shows to choose from—and that science fiction authors were heavily involved with all of them. First, writers including Jack Vance, Walter Miller, and Robert Sheckley developed original scripts for juvenile series like *Captain Video and His Video Rangers* (1949–1955) and, of course, *Tom Corbett, Space Cadet.* While these series were wildly popular with children across America (indeed, television executives proposed resurrecting them immediately after the *Sputnik* launch in 1957), they were often dismissed as "too fluffy" for the serious viewing audiences that some early TV advocates hoped to cultivate.

Second, authors including Theodore Sturgeon, Henry Kuttner, and Arthur C. Clarke adapted their own, previously published work for adult-oriented science fiction anthology series including *Out There* (1951–1952), *Tales of Tomorrow* (1951–1953), and *Science Fiction Theatre* (1955–1957). In direct contrast to the juvenile series, these early science fiction anthology shows were celebrated by critics and science fiction authors for the faithfulness of their adaptations and the precision of their science. However, the same qualities that ensured these anthologies would appeal to print science fiction fans also limited their audiences, as many prime-time spectators found them too dry.

But the third trend in early SFTV—the production of stand-alone science fiction stories for mixed-genre drama anthologies—seemed just right to audiences and critics alike. The success of these shows may be attributed to the fact that the producers of drama anthologies (including *Westinghouse Studio One, Playhouse 90,* and *The Motorola Television Hour*) consistently chose to adapt previously published stories by authors, such as Ray Bradbury and Judith Merril, who had developed solid reputations both inside and outside the science fiction community.

Merril's writing was particularly well suited for the dramatic adaptations done on *The Motorola Television Hour.* Science fiction had become increasingly central to the American imagination after World War II because authors who had previously been dismissed for telling wild tales about nuclear science and technology suddenly seemed to be "prophets proven right by the course of events" (Berger 143). Merril's novel *Shadow on the Hearth* was very much in tune with the temper of this time, as it followed the adventures of an average suburban wife and mother grappling with the aftermath of nuclear war. This novel reinforced Merril's reputation within the science fiction community and secured her recognition by the larger literary world as well. In a 1950 book review, the *New York Times* compared *Shadow on the Hearth* to the cautionary works of H. G. Wells and George Orwell (Merril and Pohl-Weary, 99–100).

Parallel Views of the Nuclear Threat

The opening scenes of "Atomic Attack" hew closely to Merril's novel, which follows the story of Gladys Mitchell, a Westchester housewife and mother whose life is turned upside-down by World War III: her husband Jon is presumed dead in New York City, her daughters Barbara and Ginny are exposed to radioactive rain at school, and her son Tom, a freshman at Texas Tech, seems to have vanished. In this brave new world, even the most familiar aspects of suburban life suddenly become strange: basic utilities fail and men become monsters who abuse their power as civil defense officers to harass the women and children they are meant to protect. Thus *Shadow on the Hearth* fulfills one of the primary dictates of golden age science fiction as it was articulated by *Astounding* editor John W. Campbell: that authors should create stories that put a human face on the sometimes overwhelmingly abstract problems attending dreadful new sciences and technologies (Westfahl 184).

Writer David Davidson and director Ralph Nelson establish the dangerous impact of nuclear weapons on the nuclear family in "Atomic Attack" much as Merril does in her book, beginning with scenes of domestic tranquility that give way to chaos once World War III begins. Indeed, the opening chapters of Merril's novel were particularly well suited to Nelson's directorial needs. M. Keith Booker notes that early SFTV often failed to interest audiences because small budgets prevented screenwriters and directors from creating convincing science fictional sets and special effects (5). *Shadow on the Hearth*, however, takes place primarily in a suburban home, and by the mid-1950s set designers were experts at creating low-cost domestic interiors for sitcoms and dramas alike. Moreover, by 1954 Nelson was expert at filming such interiors, having already done so for the sitcom *I Remember Mama* and other anthology dramas, including *Studio One*, *ABC Album*, and *Medallion Theater* ("Ralph Nelson").

The few special effects that Merril's novel did require were also easily addressed within the constraints of a small budget. For example, Gladys survives the bomb with no ill effects because she virtuously turns down a lunch date with friends to do her daughter's laundry. Nelson underscores the drama of this moment in "Atomic Attack" by shooting Gladys and her washing machine in front of a window that enables the television audience (if not Gladys herself) to see the light from the nuclear explosion in distant New York City. The choice is an effective one, as it allows Nelson to illustrate the terrifying power of nuclear weapons rather than devoting extended screen time to belabored (and less viscerally powerful) descriptions of them.

Moreover, telling a story about the effects of nuclear war in the mundane setting of the suburban home enabled Nelson to capitalize on television's unique propensity for immediacy and intimacy. As Lynn Spigel explains, anthology drama directors generally followed the conventions of live theater, using "naturalistic acting styles, slice-of-life stories, and characterizations that were drawn with psychological depth" to make audiences "feel as if they were in the actor's presence, witnessing the events as they happened" (139). This is certainly true of "Atomic Attack," which begins with the Mitchell family sitting around the breakfast table, telling jokes and quibbling over chores. When Jon Mitchell throws down his paper to ask, "Why can't we be like other families? A nice, normal family?" Gladys breezily assures him, "We *are* normal. As oatmeal and apple pie!" Throughout this scene Nelson underscores this normalcy by centering the Mitchell family in harmonious medium-range shots, providing his audience with a perfectly composed view of the television family.

In subsequent scenes, Nelson uses a more jarring directorial style to convey the chaos of nuclear war. He devotes the most screen time to Gladys, using close-up shots to convey her confusion and terror and long shots to emphasize her physical isolation in the home. Gladys rarely takes center stage in the long shots; instead, Nelson positions her at either the far left or far right of the frame. Furthermore, whereas Nelson sets the opening breakfast scene to a lighthearted musical score reminiscent of those written for family sitcoms, post-bomb scenes unfold to either the sound of screaming sirens or deathly silence. Thus the audience experiences a disruption in its comfortable viewing habits parallel to the disruption that Nelson's protagonist experiences in her comfortable middle-class life.

Conflicting Views of Civil Defense

After establishing the danger of nuclear weapons, however, "Atomic Attack" diverges radically from *Shadow on the Hearth*. This departure reflects the different demands of writing for print and writing for television. Merril was a self-proclaimed leftist, feminist, and antiwar activist who chose a career in print science fiction because it seemed to be one of the few venues where progressive authors could freely express dissent from the cold war status quo. Indeed, she recalls writing this novel for just that purpose: "*Shadow on the Hearth* was a very political novel. It was written for political reasons, and one of the central characters was a physicist who understood about atomic warfare and what it [really] meant" (Merril and Pohl-Weary, 100). More specifically, *Shadow on the Hearth* reflects Merril's conviction that while nuclear weapons were bad enough in themselves, the conditions that enabled nuclear war would also enable new, repressive social and moral orders to be established in the name of national security.

Merril most clearly illustrates the danger of atomic age technocultural order with the character of local civil defense leader Jim Turner. Turner is a petty tyrant who uses his newfound power to abandon his family, tyrannize the men under his leadership, and extract sexual favors from the neighborhood women. For example, he promises to help Gladys and her family evacuate from Westchester County—but only "if we got to know each other a little" (185). When Gladys resists and offers to take evacuees into her own home instead, Turner vengefully denies her request: "I know it would be nice for the kids here, but you got to remember what I told you before. It wouldn't make things any easier to have a couple of extra kids here" (186). Turner's words certainly sound sympathetic, but discerning readers must wonder, Isn't the real problem here that a few extra children "wouldn't make things any easier" for Turner in his pursuit of Gladys's affections?

Gladys is aided by another stock science fiction protagonist: the visionary scientist. Garson Levy is a nuclear physicist turned math teacher under surveillance by the U.S. government for his highly publicized peace activism. At first Levy seems astoundingly ordinary: "He didn't look like a madman, or a hero either. He looked like a scholarly middle-aged man who never remembered to have his suit pressed" (143). But, much like Gladys, Levy rises to the occasion of World War III heroically, escaping from his government-imposed house arrest to make sure that his students' families are warned about the effects of radiation poisoning. Impressed with Levy's concern for others, Gladys invites this so-called public enemy to stay with her for the duration of the war. In return, the scientist helps Gladys fix her gas leak, defend her home from marauders, and secure medical attention for her daughters.

In the end, however, all this heroism seems to be for naught. One of Gladys's daughters remains ill; her son, who seemed to have disappeared, calls with the news that he has been drafted into the army; her husband returns home gravely wounded; and Levy is diagnosed with potentially fatal radiation poisoning. This ambivalent conclusion is key to Merril's project: If she depicted a postholocaust future where scientists could solve all the problems associated with nuclear war, then there would be no reason to protest that kind of war in the first place. But by demonstrating that even the heroic efforts of such women and men might not be enough to guarantee survival in a postnuclear future, she makes a strong case for peace activism in the present.

Conversely, "Atomic Attack" insists that families can and will survive nuclear war—and that they will do so precisely by embracing the principles of civil defense. Consider, for instance, Nelson's treatment of civil defense broadcast technologies. "Atomic Attack" is framed by four major radio announcements from CONELRAD, the emergency broadcast system established by President Harry S. Truman in 1951. Each broadcast includes information about the progress of the war and the actions that civil defense units have taken to secure America. In direct contrast to her print counterpart—who quickly dismisses civil defense broadcasting as a tissue of lies—the heroine of "Atomic Attack" takes great comfort in assurances that "our will to fight remains unbroken and already we have taken the offensive to pay the enemy back on his own terms."

Nelson underscores the benevolence of CONELRAD in two distinct ways: by casting popular newscaster John Daley as the voice of civil defense and by making the radio itself a central feature of key shots in which order is restored to the Mitchell household. Once CONELRAD starts broadcasting, Nelson returns to the measured pacing and medium camera shots that marked the opening scenes of "Atomic Attack," providing viewers with carefully composed images of the Mitchell women clustered around the radio at the kitchen table. Furthermore, whereas the actors playing Gladys and her daughters droop sadly over the radio during announcements about the devastation of America, they pull themselves upright and lift their chins proudly in response to Daley's concluding remarks about the country's unbroken spirit—a spirit they clearly share. Thus CONELRAD takes the place at the center of the family previously occupied by Jon Mitchell, suggesting that although nuclear war might split the family apart, civil defense will knit it back together again.

Political Influences on Science Fiction Adaptation

Why make these dramatic changes to Merril's story? One answer lies in the historical evolution of broadcast technologies. Before World War II the U.S. government did little more than regulate commercial rivalries and fund public service programs. During the war, however, government officials worked closely with radio producers to create programs to boost home front morale. These practices carried over into the cold war as the American government continued to use radio and, increasingly, television "to create consensus and support for its policies" (MacDonald 10). TV executives were quick to create partisan programming in part because they feared persecution by the House Committee on Un-American Activities, but also because they truly believed that television would enhance democracy.

This was a particularly useful state of affairs for the Office of Civil Defense, which defined civil defense as a public service and could therefore encourage broadcast executives to produce high-quality propaganda at low cost (Stocke 46–47). In many cases, this was a mutually profitable situation. The *Motorola Television Hour* producers made government involvement with "Atomic Attack" a central selling point of the show, announcing at the beginning that "the play you are about to see deals with an imaginary H-bomb attack on New York City—and with the measures that Civil Defense would take in such an event for the rescue and protection of the population in and around the city," and then giving profuse thanks to the Office of Civil Defense in the closing credits. The producers' move was strategic: the chance to feature real-world civil defense experts—much like the choice to cast real-world radio announcer John Daley as the voice of CONELRAD—seemed to enhanced the appeal of "Atomic Attack" as a speculative drama grounded in both scientific and social reality.

Given the attention that the Office of Civil Defense lavished on "Atomic Attack," it is no surprise that director Nelson depicts the character of Jim Turner (William Kemp) heroically. This Turner is no ignorant despot but a conscientious, well-trained official who takes his work seriously. When Gladys marvels at his efficiency in the face of disaster, the civil defense leader gravely replies, "Well, we trained for it long enough. Civil defense—some folks thought it was a kid's game. . . . Some game!" Nelson further underscores Turner's nobility by placing him at the center of every scene in which he appears, while the Mitchell women gather in close orbit around him. Much like the radio in earlier scenes, then, Turner represents both the benevolence of civil defense and its centrality to the nuclear family in the nuclear age.

As civil defense becomes increasingly heroic in "Atomic Attack," scientific freethinking, in the form of Garson Levy—renamed Lee in the broadcast version—becomes less so. The scientist still shows up at the Mitchell house in time to give a handy explanation of nuclear weapons and radiation poisoning, but the heroines of "Atomic Attack" hardly find this information comforting. Instead, it sends the Mitchell daughters into screaming hysterics and causes Gladys to soundly chastise Lee for "coming here and stirring us up like that." Worse yet, Lee's behavior threatens the entire nation. He spends much of his time hiding off screen because he believes that Turner wants to arrest him for his antiwar activities. In the end, viewers learn that Turner is looking for Lee because the government desperately needs his expertise. Thus Lee turns out to be something of a self-involved fool, and the message is made clear: scientific skepticism is all well and good, but only when it is used to support (rather than critique) the political status quo.

Aesthetic Influences on Science Fiction Adaptation

Although this celebration of military action over scientific inaction seems antithetical to the message of Merril's original story, it is very much representative of the cultural negotiations that have occurred whenever science fiction literature is adapted for visual presentation. Brian Attebery explains that whereas early magazine science fiction often lionized the character of the youthful scientist, who wins wealth, prestige, and love by dint of his ingenuity and scientific know-how, early science fiction film and television reduced this protagonist "to a foil for the cinematic action hero. No longer the hero, he is now just the guy in glasses who says, 'Don't shoot, this is a unique scientific opportunity' just before the alien eats him" (347). This tendency in visual science fiction goes a long way to explaining what happened when *The Motorola Television Hour* adapted *Shadow on the Hearth* for television. Levy, now Lee, no longer saves the day by exercising his intellect; instead, he is made subordinate to the action-oriented Turner, who wins Gladys's admiration by rescuing the scientist from his own monstrous misconceptions.

The shift in emphasis from the scientist-hero to his action-adventure counterpart also makes sense in terms of the economic forces brought to bear on much visual science fiction. Film and television producers are under immense pressure to turn profit on everything they create, and so when they "borrow SF's images and ideas about the future, they favor what has already been conceived of in terms of sci-fi" (Attebery 348). In the case of early SFTV producers, this frequently meant borrowing from the familiar action-oriented *Flash Gordon* and *Buck Rogers* film serials of the 1930s. While these serials offered viewers "thrilling images of other planets and other times," they depended primarily on "suspenseful plots" and "swashbuckling heroes" to keep audiences coming back for more (Booker 4).

And indeed, traces of this pattern are evident throughout "Atomic Attack"—especially in the revamped character of Gladys Mitchell herself. In direct contrast to her print counterpart, the televised Gladys finds herself repelled by Lee and almost ridiculously attracted to Turner. For example, when Turner gives her a survival manual, our heroine gratefully gushes, "Thank you. Vital facts for civilians, effects of radiation, community organization—you think of everything!" The message here seems clear: Lee is suspect because he demands that Gladys think for herself. Turner, however, knows how to treat a lady in distress—just offer her clearly defined guidelines for action, thereby alleviating the need for thought.

And of course, over the course of "Atomic Attack," Gladys becomes a feminine version of the swashbuckling action hero in her own right. First, she whips her own daughters into shape, literally shaking them out of hysterics while reminding them, "We've got to keep our heads together!" Later, she enforces quasi–military order on the refugee women who share her home, ordering them to "stop all this talk of dying. . . . [It] reminds me how frightened I am." Not surprisingly, Gladys's actions are highly effective: by the end of the film, her daughter has taken over the child care duties and the refugee women have taken over the daily operations of the Mitchell household, leaving Gladys free to participate in other aspects of civil defense.

And despite what she tells the other women, even death can't keep our heroine down for long. Upon learning of her husband's demise in New York City, Gladys faints and takes to her bed. However, when she reappears in the next scene, she is suddenly well rested and perfectly groomed, serenely announcing, "I know this now. We will oftentimes do things for others that we would never dream of doing for ourselves. . . . [And so] back to the kitchen!" Indeed, just in case viewers have missed the point, "Atomic Attack" ends with Gladys at the kitchen table, listening to John Daley announce the end of the war. When her youngest daughter asks if America has emerged victorious, Gladys clasps her child tightly and proclaims, like a postapocalyptic Scarlett O'Hara, "Not yet, but . . . I promise you . . . dear, we are *going* to win!"

The Triumph of a New Narrative Paradigm

Although viewers do not know for sure whether America ever wins the war against its unnamed enemy in "Atomic Attack," the subsequent development of SFTV confirms that the narrative paradigm structuring this story did indeed triumph on American television. Taking their cue from the success of the mixed-genre drama anthologies of the 1950s, the producers of subsequent SFTV anthologies, ranging from CBS's original *The Twilight Zone* (1959–1964) to the Sci-Fi Channel's more recent *Welcome to Paradox* (1998), have continued to adapt science fiction stories by well-known authors on topical subjects ranging from the dangers of nuclear war and a media-saturated society to the possibilities inherent in sexual liberation and virtual reality programming. Much like early stand-alone programs such as "Atomic Attack"—and in sharp contrast to their postwar predecessors—these science fiction anthologies do not dwell for long on the technoscientific conditions enabling the worlds they present. Instead, they focus on the social and moral dramas engendered by these conditions. As such, they both preserve the golden age dictate to put a human face on science and technology and modify it in ways that have historically guaranteed the largest broadest television viewing audience possible.

Similar patterns inform the stand-alone, made-for-TV movies that eventually replaced cold war mixed-genre drama anthologies. Heroes of PBS productions such as *The Lathe of Heaven* (1980) and *Overdrawn at the Memory Bank* (1983), adapted from stories by science fiction luminaries Ursula K. Le Guin and John Varley, are much like Gladys Mitchell of "Atomic Attack": they are average people who find themselves trapped in frightening technocultural situations beyond their control. Much like Gladys before them, the protagonists manage to survive in worlds that are suddenly terrifyingly changed beyond all recognition not by embracing intellectual reason or technical know-how (in both examples, misguided scientists are directly responsible for our protagonists' problems) but by affirming their emotional ties to others.

Finally, while government-sponsored science fiction programming all but vanished after 1960, the tendency to celebrate swashbuckling heroes engaged in militaristic derring-do is still very much a part of SFTV. This is particularly evident in action-adventure SFTV series. For example, whereas Martin Caiden's 1973 novel *Cyborg* sweepingly condemns warmongering governments eager to transform civilians into soldiers by any means necessary, the television show based on it—*The Six Million Dollar Man* (1974–1978)—transforms the reluctant cyborg warrior of Caiden's novel into a smooth government operator. More recently, the producers of *The Secret Adventures of Jules Verne* (2000), a twenty-two-episode show built around the clever premise that science fiction godfather Jules Verne actually experienced everything he wrote about, updated this formula to imagine Verne as part of a government-endorsed group sworn to do battle with the League of Darkness, an international terrorist organization. Inevitably, while Verne's group is led by a Victorian version of James Bond who relies on luck and fast talk to win the day, the League of Darkness is led by a villainous cyborg corpse bent on using advanced steampunk technologies to secure world domination. Taken together, these shows indicate the very real extent to which "serious" cold war SFTV, much like the "serious" cold war print science fiction upon which it was based, set the standards by which critics and audiences alike judge much science fiction storytelling in various media today.

Works Cited

"Atomic Attack." *The Motorola Television Hour*. Written by David Davidson. Directed by Ralph Nelson. ABC, 1954. DVD, International Historic Films, 2005.

Attebery, Brian. "Cultural Negotiations of Science Fiction Literature and Film." *Journal of the Fantastic in the Arts* 11 (2001): 346–67.

Berger, Albert I. "The Triumph of Prophecy: Science Fiction and Nuclear Power in the Post-Hiroshima Period." *Science-Fiction Studies* 3 (1976): 143–50.

Booker, M. Keith. *Science Fiction Television: A History*. Westport, CT: Praeger, 2004.

Bould, Mark. "Film and Television." In *The Cambridge Companion to Science Fiction*, edited by Edward James and Farah Mendlesohn, 79–95. Cambridge: Cambridge University Press, 2003.

Donawerth, Jane. "Illicit Reproduction: Claire Winger Harris's 'The Fate of the Poisedonia.'" In *Daughters of Earth: Feminist Science Fiction in the Twentieth Century*, edited by Justine Larbalestier, 20–35. Middletown, CT: Wesleyan University Press, 2006.

Heinlein, Robert. *Grumbles from the Grave*. New York: Del Rey, 1989.

"Hugo Gernsback." *NNDB*. 2007. http://www.nndb.com/people/ 381 /0000 45246/.

MacDonald, J. Fred. *Television and the Red Menace: The Video Road to Vietnam*. New York: Praeger, 1985.

Merril, Judith. *Shadow on the Hearth*. New York: Doubleday, 1950.

Merril, Judith, and Emily Pohl-Weary. *Better to Have Loved: The Life of Judith Merril*. Toronto: Between the Lines, 2002.

"Ralph Nelson." *The Internet Movie Database*. 2007. http://www.imdb.com/ name/nm0625680/.

Spigel, Lynn. *Make Room for TV: Television and the Family Ideal in Postwar America*. Chicago: University of Chicago Press, 1992.

Stocke, John Gregory. "Suicide on the Installment Plan: Cold-War-Era Civil Defense and Consumerism in the United States." In *The Writing on the Cloud: American Culture Confronts the Atomic Bomb*, edited by Alison M. Scott and Christopher D. Geist, 45–60. Lanham, MD: University Press of America, 1997.

Westfahl, Gary. *The Mechanics of Wonder: The Creation of the Idea of Science Fiction*. Liverpool: Liverpool University Press, 1999.

FROM BIG SCREEN TO SMALL BOX

Adapting Science Fiction Film for Television

Gerald Duchovnay

One of the key concerns of the nascent television networks in the United States in the late 1940s and 1950s was determining what kind of programming would attract audiences. One place they looked was movies. With a history dating back to Georges Méliès's *Voyage to the Moon* (1902); successful serials such as *Flash Gordon* (1936) and *Buck Rogers* (1939), themselves adaptations of comic strips and pulp fiction; and films such as *Destination Moon* (1950) and *The Thing from Another World* (1951), science fiction programmers had a "preconstructed and preselected audience" (Elsaesser 93). Considering the variety of demographics, the networks early on opted to air inexpensive science fiction programs, such as *Captain Video and His Video Rangers* (1949–1955) and *Tom Corbett, Space Cadet* (1950–1955), aimed largely at juvenile audiences, knowing that parents often watched with their children. Although these shows were primarily Earthbound and had minimal special effects budgets (visual effects were often performed in-camera), it was quickly demonstrated that there was a large audience for these shows, with *Captain Video* attracting as many 3.5 million viewers.

However, even with such early successes, network executives generally considered science fiction "a problematic genre in that its futuristic worlds and speculative storylines often challenged both the budgets and narrative constraints of the medium" (Sconce). By the early 1960s, though, with a thirst for diverse programming, networks were willing to gamble on science fiction shows. One way to lessen the networks' financial risk was to adapt to the small screen successful science fiction films that offered strong premises on which to construct continuing narratives and developing characters. While film and television are similar in many ways, adapting a work from the big to the small screen is especially complicated in the case of science fiction, thanks in part to, as Michele Pierson argues, its emphasis on an "aesthetic experience of wonder" (168) that always brings additional financial and technological considerations. Most critical discussions of filmed adaptations focus on the fidelity to the source or on the director's signature input. For the networks, however, the aim is to hire a creative force, generally a producer, to adapt a film to meet television's demands regarding technology, narrative, audience, and financing. Who is chosen often determines the success or failure of a series.

In 1973, a *New York Times* article by film historian and author Aljean Harmetz asked, "How Do You Pick a Winner in Hollywood?" The answer to the question is the same for television and film: "You Don't." This is amply demonstrated in the series (not including spin-offs and sequels) that have attempted to make the transition from film to television. Of the twenty science fiction television (SFTV) shows that have been adapted from films, nine ran for one season or less (*Beyond Westworld* holds the record for the shortest run, with only three shows broadcast), and four lasted just two seasons.[1] Why has there been such a high failure rate for SFTV? What follows is an examination of how producers, narrative patterns, visual effects, demographics, and financing impacted three adaptation series: the highly touted but failed *Planet of the Apes* (1974), the hybrid *War of the Worlds* (1988–1990), and the highly successful *Voyage to the Bottom of the Sea* (1964–1968).

A key difference between *Voyage to the Bottom of the Sea* and most other adaptation efforts is that this series had continuity and a controlling creative presence in Irwin Allen. Like the Emmy Award–winning producer-writer David E. Kelley today, Allen clearly had his finger on the TV viewer's pulse in the early 1960s. Prior to making the film *Voyage to the Bottom of the Sea*, Allen had worked in magazines, radio, and advertising and had then turned his attention to documentary films. He made several, including the Academy Award–winning *The Sea around Us* (1952) and a remake of *The Lost World* (1960).

The desire to keep audiences entertained through adventure and spectacle—an essential aspect of Allen's artistic credo—was probably much influenced by his love of reading adventure stories as a child and the adventure and spectacle in films such as *The Hurricane* (1937), *The Rains Came* (1939), and *Gone with the Wind* (1939), which were the rage when Allen moved to Hollywood in the late 1930s. During World War II, real-life disasters replaced those on the screen, but after the war, science fiction films focused on new forms of disaster: alien invasion and atomic apocalypse. Whereas many of these filmmakers looked to the skies, Allen looked to the seas. Tapping into his previous film experience, a national interest in the nuclear-powered submarine *Nautilus* and its top-secret crossing of the North Pole in 1958, and his childhood love of Jules Verne's *20,000 Leagues under the Sea* (1870), Allen wrote, produced, and directed *Voyage to the Bottom of the Sea*.

Later novelized by Theodore Sturgeon, the film focuses on Admiral Harriman Nelson's (Walter Pidgeon) attempt to use the atomic submarine *Seaview* to extinguish a fire in the Van Allen radiation belt. Nelson and Commodore Lucius Emery (Peter Lorre) believe that firing an atomic missile into the belt at a precise spot and moment will end the catastrophe, but scientists and members of the United Nations disagree and try to stop him. As Nelson attempts to carry out his plan, the *Seaview* loses its communication system; encounters a minefield, a hostile UN submarine, and a giant squid; overcomes a mutiny, a religious fanatic, and a saboteur; yet manages to launch the missile, extinguish the flames, and save the world. Added to the mix are a love relationship between Captain Crane (Robert Sterling) and Lieutenant Connors (Barbara Eden) and imaginative special effects (squid, submarine, fiery Van Allen belt) by L. B. Abbott. Although the plot is largely formulaic, Allen's desire was to awe the spectator with, as the film's trailer hyperbolically claimed, "The most exciting adventure film you have ever encountered."

With the box office success of *Voyage*, ABC invited Allen to produce a television series. Whereas early SFTV—such as *Captain Video, Buck Rogers,* and *Adventures of Superman*—was often faulted for being juvenile, shows such as *Tales of Tomorrow* (1951–1953) and *The Twilight Zone* (1959–1964) had suggested some adult possibilities for the genre. Allen, however, was less interested in whether his audiences found his science fiction shows thought provoking or attuned to political or ecological issues than he was in entertainment, broadly construed. On why he chose this project, Allen said, "I didn't sit down and think, 'Let's do a military show.' Instead I thought, 'Here's a popular movie. Thousands of people paid to see it in theaters; now why shouldn't it go on TV as a serial, why shouldn't it be as popular?'" (quoted in Gardner X21).

Fancying himself a showman in the mold of Cecil B. DeMille, Allen sought to offer entertainment with simple plots of good versus evil, easily identifiable characters, well-known supporting character actors, lots of action and spectacle, and innovative effects and gadgetry, but with modest production costs. As Brian Rose observes, "TV genres . . . are essentially commodities, manufactured for, and utterly dependent on, public consumption and support. While popular culture theorists may argue about the hidden needs and desires genres reflect and fulfill, the formulas that have endured are those which manage to yield a regular profit for their production" (5). Allen was able to flourish and survive in this environment by reusing sets, plots, and stock film footage, in the process bringing something of a cinematic look to his series on the small box.

Creator-producer Irwin Allen (center) prepares a scene with David Hedison (left) on the set of *Voyage to the Bottom of the Sea*. (Image provided by Jerry Ohlinger's Movie Material Store Inc.)

Allen's recycling of his own material becomes immediately apparent in the pilot episode of *Voyage*, "Eleven Days to Zero," in which the *Seaview* must set off a bomb in the Antarctic to prevent an earthquake that will devastate much of the world. On the way the submarine encounters a shark, a giant octopus, and an enemy agent. Even though the plot mirrors many aspects of the original film's plot and both interior and exterior shots of the *Seaview* were lifted from the film and reedited to fit this episode, the network executives and viewers were excited that Allen had brought his filmic sense to television by combining that already proven adventure plot with the aesthetic experience of wonder that marked the best science fiction cinema.

How much a show costs is obviously a determining factor in greenlighting any television series, but budget is especially important in adapting science fiction films, given all that is typically needed to create visual spectacles. Special effects take time and money to create, and most series try to shoot one episode a week. Noting the relative paucity of SFTV in the late 1950s despite the obvious cultural interest in space, Oscar Godbout explained that well-done visual effects simply cost too much and took too much time to complete. He suggested that "the ideal situation would be to have a series" whose action "could be integrated and matched to extensive and well-executed science-fiction footage from a stock-film library" (X9). And that was Allen's goal. In fact, Jon Abbott argues, *Voyage to the Bottom of the Sea* "only came to exist" because Allen and Fox Studios kept the film's submarine sets (11), which had cost $400,000 to create.[2]

A prime example of Allen's recycling aesthetic can be seen in the episode "Turn Back the Clock." Given up for dead, Jason Kemp (Nick Adams) reappears, telling a fantastic tale of escaping from a prehistoric lizard in a tropical anomaly in the Antarctic. Admiral Nelson tests some esophageal matter found on Jason's clothing that seems to come from a Mesozoic specimen, and when the specimen is shown to have been alive in the last year, Nelson sets out on the *Seaview* in a quest for answers, taking with him Jason and noted underwater photographer Carol Denning (Yvonne Craig). In a diving bell accident, Jason, Carol, Nelson, and Captain Crane find themselves swept up in a current and deposited in the Mesozoic jungle they were seeking, and there find giant lizards and spear-carrying natives who sacrifice humans to a fire god. Aided by a native girl, they free another scientist who is being held captive and eventually escape to an iceberg, where the *Seaview* rescues them just before the hidden world is destroyed.

The title of this episode not only captures the plot's subject but also describes Allen's reuse of shots and stock film footage. In fact, some viewers wrote in to *TV Guide* to complain about the thefts (Abbott 28). According to writer Sheldon Stark, "Allen was jumping up and down over this old earthquake footage he had. He asked me to write a story around it. For a writer to come in cold like that and find fuzzy earthquake footage waiting there was a help" (quoted in Phillips and Garcia 543). Critics have noted that many writers and directors are "all of a piece," repeatedly reworking the same theme and using the same character types, but Allen went a step further with his self-referential borrowings that were "adapted" via reediting and bringing back characters (such as the native girl) from earlier films. This approach worked for most of his TV audience and allowed Allen to spend his budget in other areas, thus making a series like *Voyage to the Bottom of the Sea* consistently look like a more expensive production than it was.

Another effective reweaving of previous material shows up in "The Sky Is Falling," which uses stock footage of panic in the cities when a flying saucer passes over Seattle, San Francisco, and Los Angeles before landing in the ocean. Sent to investigate, the *Seaview* picks up a passenger, Rear Admiral Tobin (Charles McGraw), nicknamed Trigger-Happy Tobin. When the *Seaview* finds the saucer, McGraw orders it to fire torpedoes at the ship, but Nelson hesitates, thinking the saucer may be trying to communicate with them. Subsequently, Nelson is taken aboard the spaceship, where he encounters an alien who appears to be his double (it notes that its real appearance would offend humans) and who explains that the alien craft, while studying Earth, has suffered a ruptured fuel line. Throughout, Tobin urges action, and military jets bomb the spaceship. Working as peacemaker, Nelson helps the aliens to refuel their saucer, which escapes Earth just in time to avoid another attack. When Crane says that the aliens will return and hopes that they remember they were treated as friends, Nelson wonders aloud "if we will."

Clearly in this, the series' first encounter with aliens, *Voyage to the Bottom of the Sea* was building on a long history of popular alien invasion films like *The Day the Earth Stood Still* (1951). The episode's script stresses a series of dualities commonly played up in such works—friend versus enemy and militarist versus humanist—that reflected contemporary cultural bifurcations and would permeate many of the subsequent episodes. At the same time, the episode effectively employs stock footage of the flying saucer and panic in the cities, which it combines with close-ups of the crew's desperate faces when the *Seaview* is threatened. These images would, in turn, become a new stock element, eventually resurfacing in subsequent shows.

My focus to this point has been on how Allen was able to rework formula and recycle footage to lower production costs, but as Larry Gianakos observes, Allen's early success with *Voyage* was also due to the highly creative professional team that he surrounded himself with, especially the "the technical . . . professionals, . . . the art directors, cinematographers . . . and musicians" (449), as well as writers who created interesting stories and actors who performed in a way that audiences could relate to. Although Allen, who coscripted the original film with Charles Bennett, did some of the writing (including the story and pilot), he hired many of the same writers for his shows. Bennett, who had worked with Hitchcock on seven of his films, early on shared with Allen his strategy of the "suspense-time limit angle" (Bennett 121): creating a situation in which a catastrophe will occur unless action is taken by a certain time. It would provide Allen with a flexible formula that he would effectively recycle numerous times during the series' run.

Instead of using the cast from the movie, Allen recruited new actors, including Richard Basehart (Admiral Nelson) and David Hedison (Captain Crane). Basehart had extensive experience in the theater and international cinema. As the series progressed, he wished for more demanding scripts and periodically tired of not being able to explore more facets of his character. Still, he understood the challenge of his role: "You take an undeveloped character and you have to make him alive. You take what's there, and you round him out. You see, the lack of time sharpens an actor's tools to razor-sharp edges. There's no time to study. You're on, and it's up to you to create the man, the mood, instantly" (Basehart 21). Using the money saved from recycling footage, Allen was able to hire well-known and highly talented guest actors for many of the episodes, including Robert Duvall, Eddie Albert, Lloyd Bochner, Jill Ireland, Richard Carlson, Ed Asner, George Sanders, and Malachi Throne.

Admiral Nelson (Richard Basehart) inspects a rescued Mercury space capsule in *Voyage to the Bottom of the Sea*. (Image provided by Jerry Ohlinger's Movie Material Store Inc.)

To David Hedison, whom Allen had worked with in *The Lost World* (1960) and had recruited intensely for the role of Commander (later Captain) Lee Crane, the "overall strengths of *Voyage* were the acting and the photo effects" (quoted in Phillips and Garcia 541). L. B. Abbott, head of 20th Century-Fox's special photographic effects department, brought to the project thirty-five years of experience with miniatures and in-camera effects. Without any of the sophisticated visuals associated with today's CGI or the luxury of George Lucas's Industrial Light and Magic, Abbott and his crew helped to establish the television show's own aesthetic experience of wonder through underwater photography and creative use of miniatures while meeting the harried time lines of a series and keeping within budget. He was aided by cinematographer Winton Hoch, production illustrator Maurice Zuberano (who did more

Captain Crane (David Hedison) mans the submarine *Seaview*'s periscope in *Voyage to the Bottom of the Sea*. (Image provided by Jerry Ohlinger's Movie Material Store Inc.)

than one thousand sketches for one episode alone), and supervising art director Jack Martin Smith (who designed the *Seaview*), all of whom had worked with Allen on the film.

Although many factors contributed to the show's success, the key was that Irwin Allen managed to combine the appearance of high production values with formulaic plots that audiences could follow and enjoy. With its alien encounters, crews trapped below the ocean's surface, prehistoric animals, and spectacular visual effects (spaceships, giant underwater spiders and squids, submarine-consuming whales, and an assortment of other dangerous underwater creatures) that were produced relatively inexpensively—or simply lifted from earlier films— *Voyage* upped the ante for SFTV special effects. Drawing on these assets, the series attracted a large enough audience to stay afloat for four years, a relatively long run for a science fiction show in a time when even the more challenging and thought-provoking *Star Trek* would last but three (1966–1969).

By the end of the second season, Allen had become fully engaged with a new series, *Lost in Space*, and was already preparing a third, *Time Tunnel*. As a result, he provided less attention and money to *Voyage*, the plots saw more and more monsters, and the creative energy seemed to disappear. The series began a slow slide downward, and by season four, some of the narratives practically seemed parodies of earlier shows.[3] However, as multiple fan Web sites attest, *Voyage*'s blend of likable characters, challenging external threats, and exciting effects (for the time) continue to appeal to many viewers.

As Harmetz notes, though, it is difficult to predict what will be a "winner"; such was the case with the 1974 television adaptation of *Planet of the Apes* (1968). The original film was adapted from Pierre Boulle's novel *La planète des singes*; scripted by Michael Wilson and Rod Serling; starred major actors, such as Charlton Heston, Roddy McDowall, Kim Hunter, and Maurice Evans; was nominated for two Academy Awards; and received an honorary award for outstanding achievement in makeup. More than thirty years later, in 2001, the Library of Congress recognized the film as "culturally significant" and added it to the National Film Registry. The film's appeal combined its freshness of theme with culturally rich allusions as it dealt with racism, power, knowledge, evolution, the Vietnam War, and a host of other significant cultural topics.[4] Just as significant, it inspired four sequels, resulting in a fan base that readily suggested to CBS executives that a TV series would be a sure thing (although it has been claimed that network president William S. Paley did not like the idea [Phillips and Garcia 253]). After Roddy McDowall agreed to reprise his role, success seemed assured. Yet despite this and other instances of cast continuity, a ready-made audience, diverse thematic options, a budget of $200,000–$300,000 per episode, and six days to shoot each ("How Much Milk" 6–10), the series collapsed in December 1974 after only thirteen of the fourteen episodes shot had been aired.

One element that was missing was the continuity provided by a creative force like Irwin Allen. Although Arthur Jacobs, producer of all the *Planet of the Apes* movies, had been working on a television series since 1971, he died of a heart attack in 1973, just as the series was taking shape, and that loss proved substantial. Anthony Wilson and Art Wallace became the writers, and Stan Hough, who had produced such relatively weak films as *Emperor of the North* and *Mrs. Sundance* (both 1973), took over as producer. This group worked with the executive producer, Herb Hirschman, to mold stories that, like the film, were intended to comment on contemporary society. As Hough offers, they felt that the show could "reveal truths and show things we could never otherwise get away with. Make social statements. About the violent side of human nature. About the horrors of the police state. About the blindness of prejudice" (quoted in "How Much Milk" 9–10). The trouble was that, as Wallace admits, "very little science fiction" remained, and eventually the decision was made to "soften" the tone of the original film, which was often satirical, bitter, and ironic, due in large part to Charlton Heston's character and dialogue. As a result, Wallace explains, "Instead of a weekly condemnation of mankind, the storyline gave humans the benefit of the doubt. If man were to ever regain control of his planet, perhaps he would be of a better, more tolerant breed" (quoted in Phillips and Garcia 250).

The pilot episode, "Escape from Tomorrow," draws on the basic premise of the original film as it recounts how three astronauts leave Earth in 1988, move through a time warp, and crash-land their spaceship on an unknown planet in 3085. Although one of the astronauts dies, Alan Virdon (Ron Harper) and Pete Burke (James Naughton) survive the crash and find themselves in a civilization ruled by apes. Much like the Earth they left, the ape civilization is marked by specific class distinctions, each embodied in an individual figure. Urko, for example, represents the military class, and Zaius the ruling class. Another ape, Galen (Roddy McDowall), befriends Virdon and Burke, helps them escape incarceration and certain death, and joins them as a fugitive and companion in adventure.

After a month-long publicity campaign, the pilot episode was fairly well received, earning a 34 share, although it was topped in its time slot by NBC's *Sanford and Son*, which earned a 46 share. In its second week, *Planet of the Apes* again finished second, this time behind a different comedy, *Chico and the Man* ("How Much Milk" 10), but its share remained high. However, in subsequent weeks the ratings noticeably dipped. Although it was considered the second-most-popular show among two- to eleven-year-olds, that audience was not the demographic

The principals in the failed *Planet of the Apes* series: Galen (Roddy McDowall), Alan Virdon (Ron Harper), and Pete Burke (James Naughton). (Image provided by Jerry Ohlinger's Movie Material Store Inc.)

that CBS executives like Fred Silverman anticipated, especially since a year earlier, a Friday-night airing of the original film had garnered the "phenomenal tune-in" of nearly 60 percent of all viewers (Doan A1).

The reasons for that shortfall were difficult to discern. As Eric Greene notes, the basic plot, with its obvious reflections of contemporary social angst, was a staple of a number of other science fiction shows in the 1970s that focused on "a group of fugitives or wanderers moving from place to place."[5] However, only two of those, *Space: 1999* and *The Incredible Hulk*, made it into a second season (157). Episode five of *Planet of the Apes*, "The Legacy," perhaps best illustrates why this adaptation failed to sustain an audience. Written by Robert Hammer, the episode opens with Galen, Burke, and Virdon coming upon a ruined city where they encounter other humans, although no one will talk to them. In a vacuum-sealed vault, they discover a machine that projects a hologram of an old man who explains how the world's knowledge was buried in this and other cities before the Great Destruction. When spotted by an ape patrol, they flee in different directions, but Virdon is captured, along with a native woman, Arne, and a young boy, Kraik (Jackie Earle Haley), and all are imprisoned. In prison Virdon becomes a source of wisdom for the boy, instructing him in the general rules he should live by: tell the truth, don't take things without permission. After escaping, they return to the city and reunite with Burke and Galen but find that the apes have set fire to the machine—evoking the Nazis' book burnings and the popular film *Fahrenheit 451*. Leaving Arne and Kraik safe at a nearby farm, Virdon, Galen, and Burke set out on the road once again.

What the episode offered audiences was a small morality play, one in which a boy begins to bond with adults, learns something of family life, and discovers the power—and danger—of knowledge. Supporting these lessons, Arne and Virdon discuss their past lives and the family ties that can never be reestablished (although Arne is always looking longingly at Virdon). Though most episodes focus on such human values rather than on technology, this one also offers the holographic machine that stores mankind's wisdom. Tellingly, though, the fugitives willingly abandon the technology, even though it might be Virdon and Burke's only means to learn how to return to Earth and their former lives and to ensure the safety of Arne and Kraik.

Heavily didactic, with some familiar conflict, rather unexciting chase scenes, and tepid dialogue (Virdon tells Arne, "You could meet another man," and she answers, "Yes, I didn't think so, but I do now"), this episode offers little creativity or inventiveness—in fact, little to play upon the key thrusts of the original film. Ron Harper generally agreed, describing *Planet of the Apes* as a one-joke show and adding, "Unless you have really good stories, you lose the suspense and the humor" (quoted in Phillips and Garcia 250). The acting was also problematic. McDowall's ape character occasionally served as a moral voice in this world turned upside-down, but for the most part he was relegated to turning his head, moving his nostrils, wrinkling his skin, and shifting his eyes to convey emotion. Although many have said that good acting often takes place in the eyes, an actor's eyes are generally part of a face that contributes to the total emotional context—all of which are here buried under layers of latex and makeup. Perhaps most important of all, there was little in the way of technology (apart from the holographic device, which looked like a vending machine) or thoughtful ideas that would appeal to science fiction enthusiasts, and after the pilot episode, the funding for visual effects was negligible.

Obviously, a number of hurdles are involved in putting on any television series, but especially one drawn from a strong and coherent prior text like *Planet of the Apes*. Television series and movies always start with scripts, and although it is not uncommon for more than one writer to work on a film's screenplay, that procedure is standard in television. Most often one or two writers create a particular show, or several writers meet to discuss and flesh out an episode. Even if there is a solid premise and consensus on a show's narrative arc, if the group consists of very different egos and ideas, the final product will probably be marked by inconsistency. On *Planet of the Apes*, no writer is credited with more than two episodes, and no director with more than three. Combine those circumstances with a limited budget for cast and special effects, excessively long shooting days (in addition to the hours spent each day applying makeup for many in the cast), and short deadlines to complete episodes, and the quality of the production had to suffer. Booth Colman, who played Zaius, noted that although the "props, costumes and actors were superior the material was decidedly inferior. It was rushed into production before stories could be properly prepared" (quoted in Phillips and Garcia 253).

An episode that aired in late November, "The Tyrant," written by Walter Black and directed by Ralph Serensky, further illustrates why the series attracted fewer and fewer viewers. It is a soporific reworking of the Robin Hood motif, with no adventure, no action, dreadful sets, and no humor. The episode is mostly talk: ape officials confiscate the humans' grain as "extra taxes" and Galen, Virdon, and Burke plot to get it back. With a weak, dialogue-intense script, a worn plot, and much of the episode devoted to apes talking to other apes, there is little to entertain children or adults. According to Serensky, at this point in the season, there was already talk of discontinuing the series, so there was no money for effects, they had to shoot fifteen pages of script in a day, and, as he notes, "When you're shooting talking apes, it doesn't necessarily make the best of drama" (quoted in Phillips and Garcia 256). And here too, a crudely moral tone pervades the episode, as we learn that corruption, greed, and bribery are bad in the hands of those in power, but the humans' stealing to get grain back is acceptable because they have been victimized by the evil apes.

A quick look at what happened to a third film adaptation, *War of the Worlds*, will further reinforce my basic premise that a producer or other creative force who shapes a TV series can determine whether the show is a success. Considered one of the seminal 1950s science fiction films, applauded in particular for its special effects ($1.4 million of a $2 million budget), *The War of the Worlds* (1953) was very different from its source material. H. G. Wells's work is regarded as an "encounter with our own future selves" and with "human insignificance" (M. Rose 100, 74), and, like the film *Planet of the Apes* and its novel source, both this film and the novel on which it is based open up to numerous social, political, and religious readings. Most science fiction fans and reviewers, however, have focused on the power of the film's special effects and dismissed the adaptation as less Wells and more producer George Pal in its weak character development, tepid love story, and emphasis on the power of religion. As David Wingrove notes, Pal's film has little fidelity to the original and makes "what was a story of genuine alien intrusion into a simple Atom Bombs and Tanks power struggle with a love interest and religious undertones thrown in for good measure" (257). John Baxter also contends that "atheist Wells would have cringed at the liberties scenarist Barré Lyndon took with his story," especially the "heavy religious motif" (149).

In the early 1970s, Pal developed an interest in adapting the film *The War of the Worlds* for television. Using pieces of the 1953 film, he created a promotional reel, describing a plot in which, after the battle against the aliens has gone on for many years, the aliens depart and are pursued by ships from Earth. According to one source, this promo footage suggests a linear rather than episodic plot (Gosling). The project was never approved, and it was not until October 3, 1988, that a syndicated television series premiered, using as a lead-in to each episode the title of the film, images of the spaceships and their destruction of Los Angeles, and a voice-over about the events in 1953 and the defeat of the aliens. The two-hour-long pilot "The Resurrection" does not reprise the film, and the cast, as is usually the case for such adaptations, is different, although a few links to the film remain: we learn that after his parents were killed by the aliens, astrophysicist Harrison Blackwood (Jared Martin) was raised by Clayton Forrester (Gene Barry in the film), and Ann Robinson reprises her film role, Sylvia Van Buren, in a few episodes of the first season.[6] These aspects, as well as the occasional use of some imagery from the 1953 film, offered solace to avid fans of the film, some of whom were disappointed in the television series, primarily because of changes implemented in the second season.

The creator of the initial season was writer-producer Greg Strangis. He realized that adapting or reprising the film would not be sufficient. Scientific knowledge about Mars had changed considerably. In addition, as a series creator for Paramount Television, he had to plan on a full season of twenty to twenty-two episodes. Strangis notes, "I made every effort to be respectful to the source material and still have the requirements of a continuing series" (quoted in Phillips and Garcia 560). During its first season, the show made a respectable showing and developed a growing fan base. The final episode, "The Angel of Death," opens with visuals of the solar system, star bursts, and a landing on Earth of another alien form, Katara. She is a Synth, a female android from Qar'To, who, though she omits one key motivating factor, confides to one of the main characters that her mission is to hunt down and kill the aliens who preceded her. Throughout the first season, constant threats to the principal characters, intriguing visual effects (including the original death ray of the spaceships), and an absence of the happy resolutions

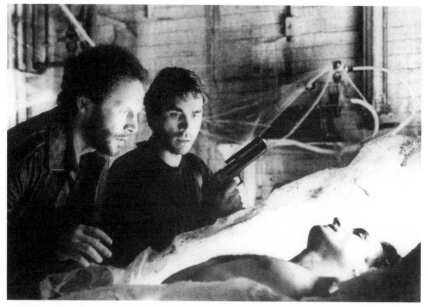

Blackwood (Jared Martin) and Kincaid (Adrian Paul) discover an alien body in *War of the Worlds*. (Image provided by Jerry Ohlinger's Movie Material Store Inc.)

that were so common to many of the *Planet of the Apes* episodes kept viewers tuned in.

However, after Frank Mancuso Jr. was hired to produce the second season, he broke a cardinal rule for established genre series: keep form and content consistent. Mancuso began by retitling the series *War of the Worlds: The Second Invasion*; then, in a move that surprised and baffled viewers, cast, and critics, he took the show in a new direction. In the first episode of the second season, two of the main characters are killed, a Rambo-like character is added, and the locale and enemy change. There are no explanations of what destroyed the "old world" or why it was replaced with a postapocalyptic, *Mad Max*–type environment. The changes to cast, plot, and setting were even more surprising given that the ratings for the first season of syndication had been among Paramount's highest for the year. With the death of two popular characters, a much darker turn to the story, plots that left many viewers frustrated, and the general loss of consistency, the ratings declined precipitously, and the show was canceled at the end of the second season.

Tim Brooks and Earle Marsh, echoing Harmetz's comments on picking a winner, observe,

> One lesson that producers never seem to learn is that a show spun off from a hit theatrical movie has no better chance of becoming a hit on TV than does any other new series. The elements that make money for a movie are quite different than those that make a series popular (broad audience appeal, likable characters, situations that can be taken in many different directions, etc.). And, of course, the stars and budget of the big screen are seldom available to TV. Nevertheless, every season brings new headlines about the latest theatrical blockbuster that's about to become a hit series. It seldom works. (1484)

But as we have seen, having the right producer or other creative head is a good start.

Making a television series is, like most successful ventures, a collaborative process. Writers, actors, directors, musicians, effects specialists, and other professionals all contribute. In television, the producer, who often has the power and responsibility for putting together all the pieces, is a crucial force. With *Voyage to the Bottom of the Sea, Planet of the Apes,* and *War of the Worlds,* that force was the primary factor that led to the success or failure of the series. *Planet of the Apes* is fairly representative of series that are poorly adapted from their films and lack a producer with the vision to understand what makes a unique project transfer to the small screen. The first producer of *War of the Worlds* knew how to update the original, whereas his successor ignored a dedicated and supportive audience when he chose to take the series in a radically different direction. As writer, director, and producer of the film *Voyage to the Bottom of the Sea,* Irwin Allen was able to successfully adapt the big-screen version to television because of his intimate knowledge of his source, his ability to assemble a professional team that could create effects for television based on their training in film, his skill in reusing previously shot footage, and his capacity to understand and implement what audiences wanted to see on the small box in their living rooms: intriguing and fast-paced narratives, unambiguous characters, adventure, and dazzling visual effects. Allen was the first to show us how the process of adapting science fiction film to television might succeed.

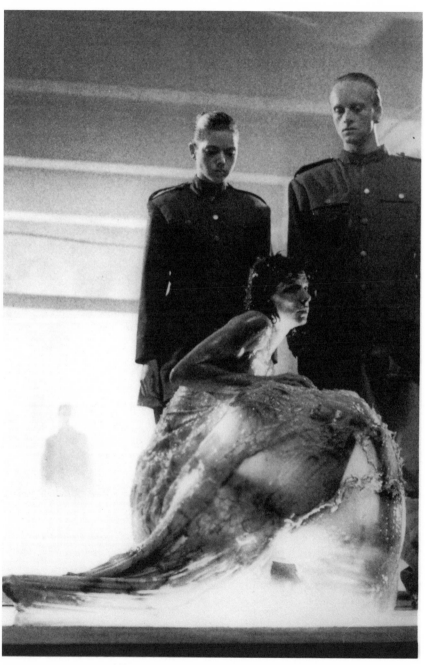

Aliens inspect a new human clone in *War of the Worlds*. (Image provided by Jerry Ohlinger's Movie Material Store Inc.)

Notes

I would like to thank Texas A&M University–Commerce for a faculty development leave that allowed me the time to research and write this essay, and J. P. Telotte for his editorial assistance.

1. I classify *Honey, I Shrunk the Kids* and *Weird Science* as comedy rather than science fiction. The following titles, culled from Morton, Brooks and Marsh, DVD listings, and Phillips and Garcia, are the key science fiction adaptations to television: *Buck Rogers*, April 15, 1950–January 30, 1951, and *Buck Rogers in the 25th Century*, September 20, 1979–April 16, 1981; *Adventures of Superman*, February 1953–December 9, 1957; *Flash Gordon*, 1954–1955; *Voyage to the Bottom of the Sea*, September 14, 1964–September 15, 1968; *Planet of the Apes*, September 13–December 27, 1974; *Logan's Run*, September 16, 1977–January 16, 1978; *The Amazing Spider-Man*, April 5–May 3, 1978 (a limited run, then seven special shows from fall 1978 to July 6, 1979); *Beyond Westworld*, March 5–March 19, 1980; *Starman*, September 19, 1986–September 4, 1987; *War of the Worlds*, October 7, 1988–May 7, 1990; *Alien Nation*, September 18, 1989–July 26, 1991; *Swamp Thing*, July 27, 1990–May 1, 1993; *Highlander*, 1992–1998, and *Highlander: The Raven*, 1998–1999; *Robocop: The Series*, 1994; *Stargate SG-1*, 1997–2007, and *Stargate Atlantis*, 2004–present; *Timecop*, September 22, 1997–July 18, 1998; *Total Recall 2070*, March 1999–January 2000.

2. Abbott, in what seems to be a misprint, says the cost was $40,000. All other sources, including the show's official Fox Web site and Allen himself, indicate a cost of $400,000.

3. Author and fan Mark Phillips explains in "Memories of Watching *Voyage to the Bottom of the Sea*" that, at the time, "a TV show had to maintain a baseline 16 rating for renewal and a 26 share. *Voyage*'s first year on Monday nights averaged a 21.5 rating, and 33 share, finishing #33 out of 100 shows for 1964–1965. Year two, now on Sundays, averaged a 17.1 rating and a 30 share, finishing 69th for the year. Year three kept that small but loyal audience, with a 16.7 rating, a 30 share, and placing 63rd. The fourth year began fairly well in the ratings but it fatigued by spring 1968, ending its season with a 14.6 rating and 25 share."

4. See, for example, Eric Greene's study Planet of the Apes *as American Myth*.

5. Shows with similar plots include *Starlost, Genesis II, Ark II, Space: 1999, Logan's Run, Fantastic Journey* (with Roddy McDowall), *The Incredible Hulk*, and *Battlestar Galactica*.

6. Steven Spielberg also employed Robinson for a cameo appearance in his 2005 version of the story.

Works Cited

Abbott, Jon. *Irwin Allen Television Productions, 1964–1970: A Critical History of* Voyage to the Bottom of the Sea, Lost in Space, The Time Tunnel *and* Land of the Giants. Jefferson, NC: McFarland, 2006.

"The Angel of Death." *War of the Worlds*. Written by Herbert J. Wright. CBS, May 15, 1989.

Basehart, Richard. Interview by Marian Dern. *TV Guide*, June 19, 1965, 19–22.

Baxter, John. *Science Fiction in the Cinema*. London: Tantivy Press, 1970.

Bennett, Charles. "The Jules Verne Influence on *Voyage to the Bottom of the Sea* and *Five Weeks in a Balloon*." In *Omni's Screen Flights/Screen Fantasies*, edited by Danny Peary, 120–23. New York: Doubleday, 1984.

Brooks, Tim, and Earle Marsh. *The Complete Directory to Prime Time Network and Cable TV Shows, 1946–Present*. 8th ed. New York: Ballantine, 2003.

Doan, Richard K. "'Apes' Capture Lion's Share of Initial Ratings." *TV Guide*, September 29, 1973, A1.

"Eleven Days to Zero." *Voyage to the Bottom of the Sea*. Written and directed by Irwin Allen. ABC, September 14, 1964.

Elsaesser, Thomas. Introduction to *Writing for the Medium: Television in Transition*, edited by Thomas Elsaesser, Jan Simons, and Lucette Bronk, 91–97. Amsterdam: Amsterdam University Press, 1994.

"Escape from Tomorrow." *Planet of the Apes*. Written by Art Wallace. Directed by Don Weis. CBS, September 13, 1974.

Gardner, Paul. "Drafted to Serve—On Land, Sea and TV." *New York Times*, September 13, 1964, X21.

Gianakos, Larry James. *Television Drama Series Programming: A Comprehensive Chronicle, 1959–1975*. Metuchen, NJ: Scarecrow, 1978.

Godbout, Oscar. "TV Blast-Off: A Slow Start." *New York Times*, August 3, 1958, X9.

Gosling, John. "The Historical Perspective." *War of the Worlds Invasion*. http://www.war-ofthe-worlds.co.uk/war_of_the_worlds_tv_pal.htm.

Greene, Eric. Planet of the Apes *as American Myth: Race, Politics, and Popular Culture*. Hanover, NH: Wesleyan University Press, 1998.

Harmetz, Aljean. "How Do You Pick a Winner in Hollywood? You Don't." *New York Times*, April 29, 1973, 135.

"How Much Milk Can You Get from an Ape?" *TV Guide*, December 7, 1974, 6–10.

"The Legacy." *Planet of the Apes*. Written by Robert Hammer. Directed by Bernard McEveety. CBS, October 11, 1974.

Morton, Alan. *The Complete Directory to Science Fiction, Fantasy, and Horror Television Series: A Comprehensive Guide to the First 50 Years, 1946 to 1996*. Peoria, IL: Other Worlds Books, 1997.

Phillips, Mark. "Memories of Watching *Voyage to the Bottom of the Sea*." *Mike's Voyage to the Bottom of the Sea Zone*. http://www.vttbots.com/phillips_part1.html.

Phillips, Mark, and Frank Garcia. *Science Fiction Television Series: Episode Guides, Histories, and Casts and Credits for 62 Prime Time Shows, 1959 through 1989*. Jefferson, NC: McFarland, 1996.

Pierson, Michele. *Special Effects: Still in Search of Wonder*. New York: Columbia University Press, 2002.

"The Resurrection." *War of the Worlds*. Written by Greg Strangis. Directed by Colin Chilvers. CBS, October 3, 1988.

Rose, Brian G. Introduction to *TV Genres: A Handbook and Reference Guide*, edited by Brian G. Rose, 3–10. Westport, CT: Greenwood, 1985.

Rose, Mark. *Alien Encounters: Anatomy of Science Fiction*. Cambridge, MA: Harvard University Press, 1981.

Sconce, Jeffrey. "Science Fiction Programs." *The Museum of Broadcast Communications*. http://www.museum.tv/archives/etv/S/htmlS/scienceficti/scienceficti.htm.

"The Sky Is Falling." *Voyage to the Bottom of the Sea*. Written by Don Brinkley. Directed by Leonard Horn. ABC, October 19, 1964.

"Turn Back the Clock." *Voyage to the Bottom of the Sea*. Written by Sheldon Stark. Directed by Alan Crosland Jr. ABC, October 24, 1964.

"The Tyrant." *Planet of the Apes*. Written by Walter Black. Directed by Ralph Serensky. CBS, November 22, 1974.

Wingrove, David. *The Science Fiction Film Source Book*. Essex, UK: Longman, 1985.

PART II

THE SHAPE OF THE SHIP

Narrative Vehicles and Science Fiction

TOMORROWLAND TV

The Space Opera and
Early Science Fiction Television

Wheeler Winston Dixon

Despite their veneer of innocent entertainment, early science fiction television (SFTV) series such as *Flash Gordon, Captain Video and His Video Rangers, Tom Corbett, Space Cadet, Space Patrol,* and *Rocky Jones, Space Ranger* tapped into America's fear of and wonder at the power of the atomic bomb, as well as the rapid technological developments ongoing in other fields, including television itself. Often produced on shoestring budgets, these series nevertheless excited the imagination of cold war viewers, who were increasingly uncertain about their future both at home and abroad. The message in all these series was often the same: the universe was in peril, and only the forces of the United States could put matters right. Early 1950s SFTV, particularly of the space opera variety, was fundamentally shaped by the social climate of the era and supported a key central idea: that America had to be first in the space race—and any other new scientific arena—to avoid imperiling our national freedom. At the same time, it balanced this sense of peril against the rich fantasy zone that it offered for young children and adolescents, as evidenced by the number of such series with a young boy as a continuing character. The resulting visions conjured up by these pioneering space operas arguably shaped much of what was to come in the 1960s and beyond in SFTV, setting up specific tropes, narrative frameworks, and character archetypes that have become fixtures in both SFTV and the American cultural imagination.

In considering these series, we should remember that, with a few exceptions, 1950s SFTV was aimed primarily at children and adolescents rather than adults. Yet far from naive narratives, as they are often described—and in which terms they are often dismissed from serious consideration, much as were early novels in this vein—the space operas by design inculcated cold war values into their young viewers and thus may have helped set the stage for a counterrebellion in the 1960s, when the normative values displayed in these programs gave way to more mature visions, such as those found in shows like *The Twilight Zone*, *The Outer Limits*, and the more sophisticated space opera narrative of *Star Trek*. Placing these series in this historical context gives us a better overview of the formative television era of the 1950s as it was actually lived by adolescent viewers and can help explain how the baby boom generation came to adulthood with a rich sense of nostalgia for the period, when social, economic, and political conflicts were presented in rather stark, black-and-white contrasts, appropriate in a medium that was itself black and white.

Space Patrol was emblematic of the concerns of many of these early series and was one of the first of the group to appear on television, debuting on March 13, 1950, as a daily fifteen-minute television series on KECA in Los Angeles. Set in the thirtieth century, the series chronicles the adventures of a group of intergalactic policemen from the Federation of the United Planets who patrol the galaxy to combat interstellar crime from a manmade planet, Terra, which orbits the sun between Earth and Mars. This ambitious premise was enthusiastically embraced by the public, and before the close of 1950, ABC had picked up the show for national distribution as a half-hour weekly series while continuing the live, local, fifteen-minute broadcast in Los Angeles. To add to the media saturation, ABC decided to run *Space Patrol* as a weekly half-hour radio series as well, utilizing the same cast members (Lucanio and Coville 196–97). The television series proved so popular that it ran for five years, from 1950 to 1955, chalking up 210 network episodes and 900 local fifteen-minute episodes in addition to the weekly radio broadcasts (Lucanio and Coville 200).

The plots of the episodes, which are often linked to each other in the manner of a soap opera or cinematic serial, are essentially formulaic, lending an impression of simplicity and cultural naivete. The central characters are Commander Buzz Corry (Ed Kemmer) and Cadet Happy, Corry's sidekick, played with gee-whiz enthusiasm by Lyn Osborn. Carol Carlisle (Virginia Hewitt), daughter of the secretary-general of the Federation of the United Planets, is Buzz's love interest. The series' principal antagonist is Prince Bacarrati (Bela Kovacs), who continually hatches plots to dominate the galaxy and thwart the law-and-order campaign of the Space Patrol. Formulism was essential, as scripts had to be pounded out quickly; with two national weekly series (radio and TV) and one local daily series, 82,000 words per week were required to keep the *Space Patrol* franchise up and running (Lucanio and Coville 197). But despite the formula-induced constant conflicts the series depicted, *Space Patrol* presents an essentially reassuring universe, one in which good always triumphs over evil. As series creator Mike Moser noted in a 1952 interview, "If we cause a single nightmare, we've failed in our purpose" (quoted in Lucanio and Coville 198). While this early entry into the science fiction landscape was designed to be a continuing cold war morality play, it is one in which the outcome is never in doubt. The United Planets (a stand-in for the United Nations), espousing recognizably American values, works to produce a hopeful future.

Rocky Jones, Space Ranger, which clocked in a mere thirty-nine episodes during its syndicated run in 1954, is equally colored by the cold war status quo but possesses far slicker production values than live efforts like *Space Patrol.* Shot on film in Hollywood in half-hour episodes (and designed with a linking story so that sets of three episodes could be turned into "instant" feature films after the series ended its TV run), *Rocky Jones* follows the adventures of its eponymous hero (Richard Crane) as he patrols the galaxy for the United Worlds of the Solar System with his credulous sidekick Winky (Scotty Beckett); nominal love interest Vena Ray (Sally Mansfield); Bobby (Robert Lyden), a young boy designed to encourage audience identification among younger viewers; and the sage Professor Newton (Maurice Cass), who advises Rocky on scientific matters. This distribution of roles, in which the performers become not so much characters as situations, drew on the movie serials of the 1930s and 1940s and is shared by much 1950s children's programming, no matter the genre. Thus *Rocky Jones* mimics *Space Patrol* in its plot structure and dramatis personae, but the use of film allowed the series to achieve a high gloss in the special effects sequences, particularly in the scenes involving the takeoff and landing of Rocky's spacecraft, the *Orbit Jet.* Like *Space Patrol, Rocky Jones* features one key antagonist, the evil Cleolanta (Patsy Parsons), who seeks to undermine the stability of the solar system through a variety of nefarious schemes. More than just a cardboard villain, in both her rhetoric and actions she evokes the specter of real-world cold war tensions from her obviously Soviet-styled domain. But as with *Space Patrol*, each episode of *Rocky Jones* ends with the forces of good triumphant and malefactors vanquished. Here too, the outcome of Rocky's adventures is never in question, despite that it often focuses on far more complex and com-

An alien commandeers the *Orbit Jet* with Rocky Jones (Richard Crane) and Winky (Scotty Beckett) at the controls. (Image provided by Jerry Ohlinger's Movie Material Store Inc.)

pelling social issues—the need for freedom of information, the problems of refugees, the nature of nationalism.

A bit less polished, the television version of *Flash Gordon* gained a rather curious prominence from that very characteristic—one that, in fact, underscores the real-world stage on which the action of the space operas played. The character of Flash Gordon has its origins in a syndicated comic strip created by Alex Raymond, which debuted on Sunday, January 7, 1934, as a full-color, lavishly illustrated adventure serial (Woolery 173). That character eventually inspired three serials by Universal Pictures (*Flash Gordon* [1936], *Flash Gordon's Trip to Mars* [1938], and *Flash Gordon Conquers the Universe* [1940]), all starring Buster Crabbe in the title role. But whereas the serial versions of *Flash Gordon* were produced with relatively lavish budgets, costs for the television series were cut to the bone, and production shifted from Hollywood to West Berlin and later Marseilles to wring every possible advantage from each production dollar. Universal's rights to the character had lapsed, and two former company executives, Ed Gruskin and Matty Fox, decided to take a gamble on the property. Fox had worked on the original serials at Universal and was well aware of the value and enduring appeal of the *Flash Gordon* character; with his new company, Motion Pictures for Television, Fox signed a deal with King Features, owner of the Flash Gordon character, to create the low-cost television series, making *Flash Gordon* one of the few 1950s science fiction series based on an existing character rather than an original creation (Lucanio and Coville 113), and one of the few shows shot outside the United States.

Budgeting $15,000 per episode for twenty-six half-hour segments, Gruskin turned to Wenzel Ludecke of Berliner Synchron, a West German postproduction and dubbing studio, to see if he would be interested in furnishing production facilities for the series at a bargain price (Worsley and Worsley 65). Ludecke, along with his partner Joe Nash, an expatriate American who would play Dr. Zarkov, Flash's scientific advisor, struck a deal to shoot the series in West Berlin in 1953. Veteran production manager Wallace Worsley Jr., whose father directed Lon Chaney Sr. in the 1923 *Hunchback of Notre Dame*, was offered the chance to make the jump to director and accepted a salary of $750 per week—two-thirds of which was deferred until all twenty-six episodes were complete (65). Arriving in Berlin in November 1952, Worsley discovered that preproduction for the series had fallen seriously behind schedule; it was not until May 1953 that shooting actually got underway. An abandoned beer hall in Spandau became the shooting stage for the series, with Worsley shooting one episode every three days. Only the principal actors (Steve Holland as Flash; Irene Champlin as Dale Arden, Flash's love interest; and Nash as Dr. Zarkov) spoke English; the rest of the cast and the crew spoke only German. As Worsley later described the torturous shooting process, "No matter what galaxy we explored, everyone spoke with a German accent. The use of German actors who could not speak English required us to use a lot of close-ups. I would stand behind the camera, correctly positioned for the actor's look, and read his or her line; the actor would then repeat the line, mimicking my pronunciation and emphasis" (69). Financing too was not as solid as Worsley had been led to expect; indeed, he had to shoot "the last three episodes in two days each" on two standing sets to bring the series to its first season conclusion (70). Not surprisingly, given the impoverished production circumstances, Worsley received only $1,000 of his $5,000 deferred salary when the episodes were completed; he refused to continue with the series until he was paid in full, which predictably never occurred (72). To shoot the second season, producer Edward Gruskin moved the entire company to Marseilles, where Gunther von Fritsch (who directed a portion of Val Lewton's *Curse of the Cat People* [1944]) took over the series, which now had a decidedly French look to it, completing the final thirteen episodes for a total of thirty-nine. *Flash Gordon* debuted on American television as a syndicated program on October 1, 1954.

Although, thanks to its comic strip and serial background, the series drew on a much earlier cultural context, its peculiar method of international coproduction, and particularly the shift from Germany to France so soon after World War II, gave the series an interesting new cultural dimension, even a perceptible air of a split cultural identity. Although *Variety*'s reviewer felt that "technical work on this series, filmed in West Berlin, is up to the demands of the script and the average [viewer] probably won't notice the differences in quality between this and home-grown produce" (*Daily* Variety), the copious stock footage and the numerous exterior sequences shot in the ruins of the bombed-out metropolis give *Flash Gordon* a distinctly ravaged look. German cultural historian Mark Baker is particularly struck by the resulting mise-en-scène, which

> really shows what Berlin looked like in 1953: the ruins still standing from WWII and the open areas where buildings used to stand. It is also like a little travelogue of Berlin, with all the major sites, including the "Funkturm" (radio tower), which looks like a miniature Eiffel Tower, the bombed-out ruins of the Reichstag, the Brandenburg Gate, the Siegessaeule (Victory Column), and the ruins of the Kaiser Wilhelm Memorial Church, which has been kept as a ruin as [a] war memorial until today. You can also see the main street of the former West Berlin, the Kurfuerstendamm, though it is hard to recognize, since many of the buildings are gone. . . .
>
> At the beginning of the episode "Flash Gordon and the Brain Machine," stock footage is used . . . to depict a rebellion on Neptune. After the obligatory 1950s shot of atomic bomb test footage, the next scene shows what would have been a very current event when *Flash Gordon* was being filmed in West Berlin. On June 17, 1953, workers in East Berlin began an open protest demonstration against the East German government. The center of the action was the Potsdamer Platz, which lay on the (then open) border between East and West Berlin. As the crowd of protesters began to swell and the East German government seemed paralyzed, Soviet tanks moved in (revealing who was actually in charge) and began firing at and killing demonstrators and bystanders alike. This is the scene, taken from West German newsreel footage, which is shown to illustrate the panic on Neptune.
>
> You can see people running wildly across a large open area, with some barely visible landmarks and signs for the Berlin S-Bahn (the elevated train in Berlin which runs underground at Potsdamer Platz) and people running past them, and probably into the stations to get out of harm's way. These are very recognizable images for Germans, since this uprising became iconic for West Germany, representing the horrible conditions for workers in the East, as well as showing the true nature of East Germany as a puppet state of the Soviet Union. . . . Maybe Americans watching on their TVs in the 1950s didn't realize what they were seeing, but these were very powerful and stirring images for Berliners of that era.

Although few viewers may have grasped the full implications of this cultural context, *Flash Gordon*'s visual internationalism and a sense of just what was at stake in the conflicts it depicted were readily apparent. The shift to the Marseilles facility for subsequent production must have created some confusion, as the German expressionist style of the West Berlin episodes was replaced with a more stylish, modern approach in the lighting, set design, costumes, and even the incidental music. Nevertheless, the series was an immediate hit with the public, and it remained in syndication throughout the 1950s and early 1960s as popular and eminently presold programming.

Despite their different looks, all of these 1950s series have a common, unifying theme: peace in the universe can be achieved only by dangerous efforts and the unilateral dominance of the Western powers. Within this context, the othering of Middle Eastern, Eastern European, and Asian cultures remains a constant visual and aural trope. *Captain Video and His Video Rangers*, the longest-running live series of the era and for many the prototypical television space opera, particularly capitalizes on this approach. First broadcast over the old DuMont network on June 27, 1949, and continuing until April 1, 1955, it starred Al Hodge as Captain Video (in all but a few episodes), battling a variety of intergalactic villains such as Hing Foo Sung, described in the program's script as "a wily Oriental" (Lucanio and Coville 100) and obviously suggesting the menace of a Communist China. The series was so influential that it spawned a theatrical film serial in 1951 from Columbia Pictures (101). It was so strongly perceived by some in the U.S. Senate as a potential menace to the minds of young and impressionable children that series star Hodge was required to testify before a Senate subcommittee on the possible deleterious effects of the series (100).

Commando Cody: Sky Marshal of the Universe, which premiered on NBC in the summer of 1955, was a filmed series from Republic Pictures based on its 1952 serial *Radar Men from the Moon*, which introduced the character of Commando Cody, played by Judd Holdren, although earlier versions of the character can be seen in the 1949 Republic serial *King of the Rocket Men* and the 1952 sequel to *Radar Men from the Moon*, *Zombies of the Stratosphere*. There was also a certain incestuousness in the casting of 1950s science fiction leading men, suggesting the emphasis on a thoroughly conventionalized heroic type. Holdren also played Captain Video in the 1951 motion picture serial based on the *Captain Video* television program, and in an odd twist, Cody, an agent for the Interplanetary Commission who is once again dedicated to preserving peace throughout the galaxy, is through most of

Captain Video (Al Hodge) instructs his fellow ranger (Don Hastings) behind one of *Captain Video*'s more elaborate sets. (Image provided by Jerry Ohlinger's Movie Material Store Inc.)

the series assisted by his easygoing associate Dick Preston, played by Richard Crane, who also patrolled the planets as Rocky Jones (Lucanio and Coville 108). *Commando Cody*, however, lasted a mere ten episodes on network television, and Republic itself shortly collapsed as a studio in the wake of television's onslaught, unable to adapt to a changing marketplace.

A number of other 1950s SFTV series, including *Rod Brown of the Rocket Rangers* and *Tom Corbett, Space Cadet*, similarly aimed at a juvenile audience while subtly imposing a simple cold war dynamic on space adventuring. But in this otherwise black-and-white moral universe, a few series would also point to the future, aiming their rather different sorts of science fiction narratives more squarely at adults as they overtly explored cold war culture. One was a 1958 British teleseries, *H. G. Wells' Invisible Man.* Ostensibly based on the character created by Wells, creator Ralph Smart's version has very little to do with the novel, the 1933 classic James Whale film from Universal, or even any of its many sequels for that company. In direct contrast to the source material, the hero of Smart's series, Dr. Peter Brady (whose identity Smart never revealed, as a publicity gimmick; the character was "voiced"

Aliens capture Commando Cody (Judd Holdren). (Image provided by Jerry Ohlinger's Movie Material Store Inc.)

by performer Tim Turner), lives in bourgeois luxury in the English countryside near Elstree with his sister, Diane Wilson (Lisa Daniely), and her daughter Sally (Deborah Watling). Unlike the protagonist of Wells's narrative, Brady becomes invisible by accident, while experimenting with refracted light. For the most part, the invisibility special effects are handled by wires holding various objects such as car keys, test tubes, and guns; more expensive effects, achieved with matte photography, are used very sparingly. Quite often, first-person camerawork from Brady's point of view lends artificial presence to his invisible "appearance" on screen. Brady's asynchronous voice and his transparent "look" thus replace all other personal physical characteristics. Like those of the space operas, these special effects are quotidian in the extreme but fittingly so, since they are not the series' real focus. Rather, it operates on the principle of the denial of spectacle. As the series progresses, Brady's invisibility becomes increasingly mundane and absolutely public. At one point, Brady lectures to his students at Oxford University in a partially invisible state, pointing to the blackboard with empty sleeves to press home a point, adroitly picking up a piece of chalk with his invisible hands. What interested producer-writer Ralph Smart much more than these feeble parlor tricks was the series' vision of the flagging hold of the British Empire on global politics and the various ways in which an invisible emissary could be used to reinforce British influence abroad.

In the first episode of *H. G. Wells' Invisible Man*, titled "Secret Experiment," Brady's sudden invisibility is explained as the result of a freak nuclear accident. Reflecting the period's pervasive paranoia, the authorities are immediately suspicious of what Brady will do with his newfound powers, and they imprison him. Eventually, the authorities promise not to confine Brady in the future, and he offers to use his special skills in various hot spots around the world, wherever the empire's interests might be threatened. Thus in subsequent episodes Brady is dispatched by Cabinet Minister Sir Charles to various mythical Middle Eastern, Eastern European, and African countries to foil gun-running schemes, attempted revolutions, atomic weapons smuggling, and the like, all with the consent and cooperation of the British authorities. In "The Gun Runners," American B actor Louise Allbritton uncovers a gun-smuggling operation in a wayward British colony, with Brady tagging along invisibly to assist her in uncovering the scheme. In another episode, "Man in Power," the young prince of an unstable Middle East monarchy is called home from his studies at Oxford (where Dr. Brady is one of his tutors) after his father is assassinated by a corrupt military dictatorship. Brady again acts as an invisible agent in service to the empire, unmasking the traitorous general responsible for the attempted coup and ensuring that the young monarch is properly crowned. In both episodes, much is made of the "moral obligation" these smaller countries have to uphold the political dominion of the West; even if they are not colonies, their interests are certainly seen as being allied with those of Great Britain and the United States.

In one of the most prescient and/or paranoid episodes, "The Big Plot," parts to produce a nuclear bomb are discovered in the wreckage of an aircraft crash. Confronted with the evidence, Brady concludes that an international gang of terrorists plans to plant nuclear devices in every major capital of the Western world and extort vast sums of money from capitalist countries to underwrite the activities of the Soviet regime. Further, Brady theorizes that these activities are being carried out under cover of an international peace organization. In a similarly fear-charged episode, "The Rocket," the decadent gambling habits of a defense plant employee lead to blackmail and a plan to hijack an experimental rocket for illegal export behind the iron curtain. Brady intervenes, the rocket is recovered, and order is restored. Finally, in the episode "The Shadow Bomb," Brady and his cohorts successfully create a land mine that is triggered by changing patterns of light, using a series of photocells; during an experiment, a technician is trapped next to a live bomb, and only the Invisible Man (who casts no shadow) can rescue the man from violent death. As soon as the rescue is effected, the technicians triumphantly test the bomb, which will then be exported to British colonies all over the globe to further enforce the aims of the British Empire. In all cases, Brady's invisibility is readily pressed into service for the empire's benefit. "I want you here right now, Brady—and invisible!" barks a cabinet minister at one point. Clearly, Brady's invisible agency in service of the colonial British Empire is seen as one of Whitehall's last lines of defense against a threatened and even crumbling status quo.

In the United States, another attempt at breaking out of the mold of the space opera and producing more adult science fiction was made with the half-hour series *Science Fiction Theatre*, one of the few 1950s television series shot in color. Each week it presented a new story exploring the wonders of science, which in most cases turn out to cause more harm than benefit. Hosted by Truman Bradley, the series racked up a total of seventy-eight episodes, with a first-run syndication period between 1955 and 1957. Produced by Ivan Tors (who had done substantial work in science fiction already, having produced films like *The Magnetic Monster* [1953], *Riders to the Stars* [1954], and *Gog* [1954]) and distribution impresario Maurice Ziv, with his brother Frederick Ziv serving as executive producer, each episode begins with Bradley demonstrating a scientific "trick" for the viewing audience and segueing into a story based on the possibility of science fact's extending into the realm of science fiction.

While many premises of the series are intriguing—such as those of "Time Is Just a Place," in which a husband and wife discover that their neighbors are time travelers who have fled the future to escape a repressive government, and "One Hundred Years Young," in which a man can seemingly live forever—the production values of the series were ultimately little better than those of the space operas of the era. And although *Science Fiction Theatre* was initially a success and arguably paved the way for such later series as *The Twilight Zone* and *The Outer Limits*, it is seldom revived today and has received scant critical attention. This oversight is somewhat surprising, since it employed some of the best directors then working in television, including William Castle and Tim Gries; featured screenplays by such genre luminaries as Jack Finney, Doris Gilbert, and Joel Rapp; and employed A-level stars, each usually for a single episode (since the series told a new story each week without any continuing characters), such as Zachary Scott, Vincent Price, Kenneth Tobey, Otto Kruger, and Gene Barry. Yet despite these factors, the series has a flat, perfunctory air and often seems hastily staged and shot, with minimal special effects. In short, *Science Fiction Theatre* remains more interesting in its concept than its actual execution. Nevertheless, it was one of the few adult science fiction series of the era, and just like its more juvenile counterparts, it reflects the air of mystery and unease that surrounded the world of 1950s science.

In rather stark contrast, we might consider the most paranoid yet mesmerically convincing space opera of the early 1950s, *Captain Mid-*

night. Based on a 1930s radio serial, *Captain Midnight* in its retuned cold war version starred Richard Webb as Jim Albright, a.k.a. Captain Midnight, sworn protector of freedom, justice, and the continually threatened American way of life. Character actor Sid Melton played the role of Ichabod "Ikky" Mudd ("Mudd with two *d*s," he invariably noted), Captain Midnight's mechanic, assistant, and comic foil. To bring the show into the atomic age, a new character was added, one Aristotle "Tut" Jones (played by Olan Soulé), a research scientist who supplies Captain Midnight with a seemingly endless array of gadgets, presaging the character Q in the James Bond films. A private citizen with a war hero record, Captain Midnight lives in a palatial estate with

Captain Midnight (Richard Webb) escapes from his captors. (Image provided by Jerry Ohlinger's Movie Material Store Inc.)

its own observatory and landing strip, and he heads an international network of Secret Squadron members who supply their leader with a bewildering barrage of tips, news leads, and suspicious rumors needing investigation. The television version of *Captain Midnight* is almost exclusively a boys' club, with Captain Midnight as a surrogate father figure, and its three central figures live out a fantasy existence of non-stop action, relentless pursuit, and almost unlimited power. And that power—like America's—is exercised on an international stage, for Captain Midnight is apparently recognized throughout the world as an emblem of law and order. In his state-of-the-art jet plane, the *Silver Dart*, he flies around the world, much as Rocky Jones and Captain Video patrol the planets, assisting "friendly governments" in the task of winning the cold war.

Hardly as idea oriented as the narratives of *Science Fiction Theatre*, the episodes of *Captain Midnight* are often violent beyond the standards of most children's television of the era. Episode titles such as "Murder by Radiation," "Electronic Killer," "Death below Zero," and "Doctors of Doom" suggest the series' unusually violent edge. In "Death below Zero," a young Secret Squadron member comes to headquarters with his sick dog, who is ill from eating outdated meat. Captain Midnight confronts the butcher who sold the boy the meat, accidentally uncovers a bank robbery scheme, and is nearly frozen to death in a meat locker as he tries to unravel the crime. In "Curse of the Pharaohs," the daughter of an eminent archaeologist appeals to Captain Midnight for help when her father is kidnapped. Tracking down the criminals responsible, Captain Midnight also uncovers and foils a plot to smuggle arms to "unfriendly" Arab nations in an effort to destabilize the Middle East. In "Top Secret Weapon," a young boy from the Soviet bloc infiltrates squadron headquarters, pretending to be a refugee looking for a new home. In actuality, the young boy, Stefan (Amelio Galli), has been "programmed" by Soviet spymasters to sabotage an experimental secret weapon in Captain Midnight's laboratory. Only the last-minute intervention of the captain and his associates prevents the young boy from carrying out his mission. At the end of the episode, Stefan is "deprogrammed" and adopted by an immigrant couple as a U.S. citizen, suggesting a proper solution to cold war tensions—literally, the Americanization of the Eastern European other.

As J. Fred MacDonald notes in his study *Television and the Red Menace, Captain Midnight* is one of the most politically loaded children's series of the era, challenging precisely because its ideological battles—like those of *Invisible Man*—are so openly played out. It takes place in then-present-day America, with much of the world presented as allied against America. Whereas the other science fiction programming discussed in this essay present a *universe* fraught with imminent peril, only *Captain Midnight* creates a *world* that young boys and girls might readily recognize and feel as if they genuinely inhabited (124). Furthering this context, the show makes Captain Midnight and his colleagues seem like actual people rather than fictional constructs, suggesting that, eventually, the captain might call upon any of his viewers for help. To cement this hold on the viewer's imagination, Captain Midnight does not possess superpowers (like Superman) or travel through space in some future time (like Rocky Jones, Flash Gordon, or Buck Rogers); his adventures are firmly anchored in the political and technological present. Even the captain's airplane, the *Silver Dart*, is an actual aircraft supplied by the Douglas Aircraft Corporation and the U.S. Navy (both credited at the end of each episode), thereby linking the captain to the military and the emerging military-industrial complex. Thus Captain Midnight, on the surface at least, does not inhabit a fantasy world; he seems a real-life hero (Dixon 21), enmeshed in the period's cultural dynamics—and its very obvious cultural perils.

Indeed, the 1950s was a zone of confusion for many viewers, one in which the lines of reality and fantasy were often blurred. Before 1945, who could have imagined a weapon with the power of the atomic bomb, other than a small group of scientists and a handful of prescient science fiction authors? Suddenly, Americans were living in the atomic age. Who was to say that such standards of the space opera as space travel, time travel, invisibility cloaks, teleportation, and the like would not soon be realities as well? If children's programming was often paranoid and freely used scare tactics to involve its viewers, what could one say about such "adult" films as *Red Planet Mars* (1952), in which God sends messages from Mars that bring about the collapse of the Soviet Union, or *Invasion USA* (1952), which depicts a Soviet invasion of the United States, including scenes of Manhattan being atomized by an enormous nuclear blast? Americans could also hear the voice of God on the radio in *The Next Voice You Hear* (1950), admonishing Earth's populace to slow down and smell the roses while remaining content in their social situation.

The political and social landscape of the 1950s was, throughout much of the media, presented like a war zone, a place of fear and contestation, a site of perpetual unease—in short, with the sort of exaggerated plotting and action typical of the space opera. In retrospect, one can see shows like *Captain Video*, *Space Patrol*, and *Rocky Jones* as reassuring influences in a world that subconsciously teetered on the brink of destruction; threats were well defined, relatively easily contained, and seldom did anyone really get hurt. The real world was a far more unsettled place. If one sees that space opera series of the early 1950s served, for the most part, as instructional media, then one might also argue that they presented, in necessarily simplistic terms, a microcosm of events that were then being played out on the world political stage. Whether shot on film for verisimilitude or broadcast live using the barest of sets and minimal special effects, the space operas and other science fiction series of the era served primarily as socializing agents for a new generation, coming of age in a world that even their parents often could barely comprehend themselves. In the 1960s, a plethora of SFTV series, especially *Star Trek*, would move media discourse forward into new realms of social negotiation, based not on force but on reason, favoring negotiation over violence. But the landscape of the 1950s was much more primitive, with everything seemingly at risk through the mere push of a button. In a world of such blanket uncertainty, some reassurance was required. The world of 1950s science fiction is thus a terrain marked by constant warfare, but one in which the victory of the just is inevitable.

Certainly, the children's-oriented space opera was not the most sophisticated mechanism with which to address and cope with such an unstable social environment, but in the newly complex world of the 1950s, most members of society sought an element of simplicity. The reassuring vision these series offered, of the world as a moralistic landscape of clear-cut choices, still seems attractive today, even as we realize it must be resisted as the nostalgic dream it surely is. There are no simple answers, and the programs discussed here ultimately demonstrate that fact. No matter how many times the Space Patrol, Captain Video, or

Rocky Jones came to the rescue of the galaxy, a new threat was always dimly visible at the horizon. Time and again, the dominant science fiction programs of the 1950s sought to demonstrate that eternal vigilance is the price of liberty. Peace, conflict, resolution, then the appearance of a new nemesis—the cycle continues in a self-fulfilling prophecy of constant threat and constant containment in a pattern that well suited the still formative world of series television.

Note

I wish to thank Mark Baker of the Freie Universität, Berlin; Todd Geringswald of the Museum of Television and Radio, New York; and Kristine Krueger of the Margaret Herrick Library, Center for Motion Picture Study, Academy of Motion Picture Arts and Sciences, Los Angeles, for their research assistance and guidance during the writing of this essay.

Works Cited

Baker, Mark. E-mail message to author, November 16, 2005.

Daily Variety *Television Reviews*. Vol. 1, *1946–1956*. New York: Garland, 1989.

Dixon, Wheeler Winston. *Lost in the Fifties: Recovering Phantom Hollywood*. Carbondale: Southern Illinois University Press, 2005.

Lucanio, Patrick, and Gary Coville. *American Science Fiction Television Series in the 1950s*. Jefferson, NC: McFarland, 1998.

MacDonald, J. Fred. *Television and the Red Menace: The Video Road to Vietnam*. New York: Praeger, 1985.

Woolery, George W. *Children's Television: The First Thirty-Five Years, 1946–1981*. Vol. 2, *Live, Film and Tape Series*. Metuchen, NJ: Scarecrow, 1989.

Worsley, Wallace, Jr., and Sue Dwiggins Worsley. *From Oz to E.T.: Wally Worsley's Half Century in Hollywood*. Lanham, MD: Scarecrow, 1997.

ANTHOLOGY DRAMA

Mapping *The Twilight Zone*'s Cultural and Mythological Terrain

Rodney Hill

Widely considered the first important science fiction television series for adults, the original *The Twilight Zone* (1959–1964) introduced mass audiences to the idea that the genre—which had previously been largely marginalized, especially on television—could present serious subject matter in a well-made dramatic format.[1] What most distinguishes the show from many others of the period is that it addresses political issues generally considered taboo for the medium at the time—racism, McCarthyism, the threat of nuclear war—by virtue of science fiction's seeming remove from reality. This element also helps explain *The Twilight Zone*'s extraordinary longevity: rather than presenting stories directly related to (and thus limited by) specific social concerns of the time, the show mythologizes those issues, fashioning broader, less time-bound tropes that still speak to the larger American culture of the mid- to late twentieth century. Typically overlooked, though, is the show's frequent reflexive turn, through which it examines the potential of genre TV as an agent of contemporary myth.[2] In all these ways, we may regard *The Twilight Zone* as a significant precedent for later, landmark series ranging from *Star Trek* to *Firefly* to the revival of *Battlestar Galactica*—and for what J. P. Telotte has identified as a tendency in recent media science fiction: "to provide us not so much with the sort of 'escape' . . . once ascribed to all genre productions, but rather with a mirror of and access to our increasingly complex cultural landscape" (203).

The Twilight Zone's creator, Rod Serling, made a name for himself as a television writer during the heyday of live TV drama. In 1953, the success of Paddy Chayefsky's *Marty*—which Erik Barnouw terms a "landmark in the history of anthology series and an inspiration to many writers" (157)—ushered in a host of dramatic anthology series, with no fewer than twenty-nine on the air that fall (Sander 82). That same year, Serling began a fruitful relationship with *Kraft Television Theatre*, to which he contributed dozens of scripts, significant among them "Patterns," a scathing indictment of the corporate world, broadcast in 1955. Serling biographer Gordon F. Sander characterizes 1955 as "an espe-

In "The Invaders," an old woman (Agnes Morehead) battles miniature aliens who have crashed into her house.

cially strong year for serious television," citing *See It Now*'s interview with Robert Oppenheimer, Mary Martin's performance in *Peter Pan*, and an adaptation of Herman Wouk's *The Caine Mutiny* among other examples. Yet "the most notable dramatic television event of the season was undeniably" Serling's production of "Patterns" (99), which the *New York Times* described as "one of the high points in the television medium's evolution" (quoted in Boddy 89).

One reason for this recognition was the social awareness and critique that "Patterns" offered, which was part and parcel of what Serling saw as the responsibility of all dramatic writing: "The writer's role is to menace the public's conscience. He must have a position, a point of view. He must see the arts as a vehicle of social criticism, and he must focus on the issues of his time" (quoted in Sander xviii). Serling made a similar point in a 1956 *New York Times* interview: "I think that of all the media, TV lends itself most beautifully to presenting a controversy. You can just take a part of the problem, and, using a small number of people, get your point across" (quoted in Sander 130).

And with the dramatic anthology series, writers like Serling, Chayefsky, and Gore Vidal found the opportunity for just this sort of free expression. According to Barnouw, "Unlike the formula-bound episodic series, the anthology series emphasized diversity. The play was the thing" (154). Except for length and certain technical requirements, anthology series like *Kraft Television Theatre* offered themselves as "carte-blanche invitations to writers—and writers responded" (156). As the 1950s wore on, however, dramatists found less and less openness on the parts of networks and sponsors to any political or "controversial" content. Sander describes this gradual decline in hard-hitting, socially relevant, live drama in the later 1950s, noting that a "small window of creative opportunity began to close, and TV playwrights were faced with increasing censorship from timorous ad agencies and broadcasting executives" (xviii). So even as Serling's star continued to rise, with such acclaimed programming as the Emmy-winning "Requiem for a Heavyweight" (1956) to his credit, he met with increased criticism and even censorship of the political content of the scripts he was contributing to the various anthology drama series. For example, the anticorporate sentiments found in "Patterns" prompted the *Wall Street Journal* to label Serling a Marxist—an accusation that could not be taken lightly in the immediate post-McCarthy era—and his 1956 teleplay "The Arena," which centered around Senate infighting, was rewritten almost beyond recognition (Sander 103, 116). In 1957, *Television Age* reported that Serling complained that "commercial TV programs won't buy a script which has 'the faintest aura of controversy' about it" and insisted that "the writer is constantly 'hamstrung' by 'taboos and imposed dogmas' that emanate from the sponsor" (quoted in Sander 130). Similarly, in a 1959 interview with Mike Wallace, Serling protested the difficulties facing serious television writers: "I think it's criminal that we are not permitted to make dramatic note of social evils that exist, of controversial themes as they are inherent in our society. I think it's ridiculous that drama, which by its very nature should make a comment on those things which affect our daily lives, is in a position, at least in terms of television, of not being able to take that stand" (quoted in Sander 143–44). It would seem that Serling had grown skeptical about the possibilities for television drama and the future of the anthology format.

Yet given his prior success with this form and the general critical praise for it, Serling sought to work out a new approach, one that drew on the flexibility and emphasis on dramatic quality that was part of the anthology tradition while couching its challenging subject matter in a popular mythology, that of science fiction. In an oft repeated but perhaps apocryphal quotation, Serling observed, "A Martian can say things that a Republican or Democrat can't" (quoted in Javna 16). That comment speaks to another element of the new form that would come to mark *The Twilight Zone*, namely, a keen awareness of carefully working within a formula and format—how it might work best, how far one might go. The result was a self-consciousness that would surface throughout the series, always conveying a sense of Serling's uneasy accommodation to the new television climate and its restricted possibilities.

When Serling proposed a science fiction–oriented series, CBS considered the idea "déclassé," and Mike Wallace blithely dismissed the genre by asking Serling if he had given up on doing the sort of serious television that was associated with the anthology show format (Sander 130). Sander cites a "widespread perception on the part of critics and interviewers that by doing *The Twilight Zone* Serling was somehow debasing himself" (150). Although these attitudes may have further stoked Serling's concerns about what might be accomplished in television's changing context, he also recognized that the ghettoization of the genre would enable him to follow the tactic of keeping the series' serious subject matter under the radar of network executives, sponsors, and some critics, and thus to more easily address various cultural problems: the threat of nuclear war, the red scare, and the ever present danger that suburban conformity might deteriorate into fascism.

A chief character found in all these issues is fear. As a genre that often deals with speculation about the future, science fiction (like other genres of fantasy) is familiar with and particularly well suited to address our various fears: of technological and cultural change, of the future, of the unknown—all rife in the rapidly changing post–World War II American culture. One of the best-known *Twilight Zone* episodes, "Nightmare at 20,000 Feet," explores precisely this climate of fear. In it, Bob Wilson (William Shatner), a nervous airline passenger, becomes convinced that a creature is attempting to sabotage the plane midflight. We learn that Bob previously had a similar in-flight panic attack that landed him temporarily in a mental hospital. Bob describes the creature to his bewildered wife Ruth, specifically identifying it as a gremlin, a mischievous, mythical creature often blamed for mechanical failures and accidents on planes during World War II. That reference links Bob's anxiety to a fear that the technology itself will fail. Counterbalancing Bob's fear is Ruth's apparently unconditional trust in science, as she reassures her husband, "If you weren't well, Dr. Martin just wouldn't let you fly. . . . It's just that simple." Ironically, Bob finally uses another piece of technology—a pistol he has pilfered from a sleeping policeman—to shoot through the plane's window and ward off the gremlin. Upon landing, Bob is wheeled away on a stretcher, presumably back to the mental hospital, but the mise-en-scène—as well as Serling's closing narration—shows us evidence of the gremlin's attack and suggests that, despite their desire to dismiss his fantastic narrative, the others will eventually come to accept Bob's story. Of course, we know that Bob's fears, as well as his efforts to warn the other passengers, were justified, and that knowledge clearly resonates with Serling's own situation as fantasist, as someone who saw his work as serving a similar warning function for a culture caught up in its own fears, those of the cold war.

From the mysterious, even mystical aspects of the sky, it was but a short conceptual leap to another mysterious realm, unexplored space. In an amazing bit of prescience, "And When the Sky Was Opened" depicts the first space shuttle flight, during which two astronauts (Rod Taylor and Jim Hutton) encounter events they cannot make sense of—in fact, in a nod to the restrictions of television, we learn that the events cannot even be represented visually. Unable to articulate what he has seen, each man gradually loses his memory of the encounter and finally fades from memory himself, so that to the rest of the world, it is as if he never existed. Like "The Odyssey of Flight 33" and "The Last Flight," this episode is a cautionary tale not only about the dangers of the unknown but also about problems of communication and the effects of repression—the failure of one and the success of the other making those who see and know too much disappear.

Another episode dealing with space exploration, "People Are Alike All Over," specifically addresses the fear of the unknown, in this case, the fear of alien life forms. In the opening scene, Sam Conrad (Roddy

Bob Wilson (William Shatner) confronts this nightmarish gremlin in "Nightmare at 20,000 Feet."

McDowall), a biologist sent on the first mission to Mars, expresses his fears about the mission, but the pilot Warren Marcusson (Paul Comi) reassures him, offering his optimistic philosophy that people, wherever they are, are bound to be alike and should not be feared. Injured during the landing, Marcusson desperately wants to see the Martian landscape before he dies and pleads with Conrad to open the hatch, but Conrad, frightened by tapping sounds from outside the ship, refuses. After Marcusson dies, Martians, who do in fact have human form, force the hatch open. The astonished Conrad initially strikes an aggressive posture, making threatening gestures with a weapon, before his situation sinks in and he exclaims, "You're people . . . just like I am!" He quickly comes to trust his hosts and is soon housed in a facsimile of a terrestrial apartment home. Ultimately, though, Conrad realizes that his domicile is actually a cage in a zoo, where he is on permanent, public display for the citizens of Mars, who regard him with fascination and apprehension. The episode ends with Conrad's final, ironic observation: "Marcusson, you were right! People are alike everywhere." Much scholarship has pointed out the tendency in science fiction films of the era to metaphorize communism through aliens; of course, this was simply a version of the broader tendency of "othering," of projecting the negative, repressed aspects of the self, either individually or collectively, onto other people or cultures, thereby demonizing them. Conrad's mistake is underestimating his own shadow qualities (irrational fear, the impulse to use violence before reason) even as he projects the shadow onto the Martian other. Thus he fails to predict the Martians' ultimate projections onto him (reinforced, of course, by his own aggressive actions), as the tables are turned and he finds himself in the position of other. But in becoming the exhibit of otherness, he also serves to point up the rather problematic nature of our common cultural stories, particularly the simple narratives of the other that abounded in both science fiction cinema and television of this period.

Indeed, *The Twilight Zone* often points out that perhaps the greatest thing we have to fear is ourselves. Exemplary in this regard is the classic "The Monsters Are Due on Maple Street," in which an idyllic, all-American suburban neighborhood turns into a mob scene in the span of a few hours. On a sunny Saturday afternoon, the residents of "Maple Street, USA" hear a strange roar overhead, accompanied by a bright flash of light. Immediately, all technology ceases to function, from stovetops to radios to automobiles. An imaginative teenage boy offers a rather outlandish narrative, that the trouble is the product of alien invaders—creatures who probably look just like humans. Initially the adults seem amused by these farfetched stories, but sentiments shift when one man's car starts, making him suspect in the eyes of his neighbors. Despite the best efforts of the one seemingly rational man in the neighborhood (Claude Akins), full-blown panic soon sets in, and wilder and wilder accusations erupt into violence and pandemonium. At the close of the episode, our point of view shifts to that of the aliens who have, in fact, landed nearby and have been manipulating the cars and lights on Maple Street, and who now watch coolly as the residents destroy each other. One alien says to the other, "They pick the most dangerous enemy they can find, and it's themselves."

For the most part, other series of this era tend to shy away from such internal cultural struggles, preferring simple conflicts that externalize the evil. As Barnouw observes, "Telefilms rarely invited the viewer to look for problems within himself. Problems came from the evil of other people, and were solved—the telefilm seemed to imply—by confining or killing them" (214). By contrast, *The Twilight Zone* seems to interrogate and criticize that very process of othering, reminding us that evil exists within all men (and, by extension, all societies). But it drives that point home by opening up a further dimension on such situations—in "The Monsters Are Due on Maple Street," by framing its events within a metanarrative, a story about the effect of a boy's unsettling story, and a populace watching for aliens that finds it is being watched by those same aliens. More than just an ironic turnabout, that narrative dimension again suggests the critical self-consciousness that Serling brought to the series. In this case it is one that reflexively produces a most effective illustration of the ease with which we are manipulated by those commonplace stories of the evil other and of our reluctance, even inability, to see ourselves as the subjects of such narratives. In so doing, it extends the scope of its critique from the personal to a broader cultural level. More than being simply about the shadow aspects of individual characters, this episode, like so many others of *The Twilight Zone*, thereby helps us see some of the darker aspects of the American shadow, in fact, of what we might term the sociocultural "show."

Just as "People Are Alike All Over" and "The Monsters Are Due on Maple Street" self-consciously address the processes of othering and show making, still other episodes take on the very matter of cultural mythology (which, as Joseph Campbell points out, is often enacted through archetypal characters), implying the centrality of myth to the health and survival of society while warning of its potential misuse. One notable example is the episode "On Thursday We Leave for Home." Here, William Benteen (James Whitmore) leads a colony that has been stranded on a remote, barren planet for thirty years, unable to communicate with Earth, which many of the colonists are too young to remember or even to have seen at all. Their will to survive has been sustained by stories about Earth told by "Captain" Benteen (as he insists on being called), in which he emphasizes the home planet's lush greenery, blue waters, and cool darkness of nightfall—all foreign in this parched world of perpetual daylight sustained by two suns. In fact, Benteen exerts a rather heavy-handed authority, apparently drawn from his ability to hold the people's imaginations through these stories. After years of silence, though, a competing "story" intrudes—a radio signal from Earth, announcing that a spaceship has been sent to bring everyone back home. When the rescue party arrives, Benteen finds his control suddenly challenged by the mission's leader, Colonel Sloane (Tim O'Conner), as the colonists begin planning their lives back on Earth—the real Earth rather than Benteen's fictional one. Addicted to the authority forged by his illusions, Benteen elects to stay on the planet (and urges his former followers to do so as well) rather than surrender the power he has gleaned from his own mythmaking. As all the colonists leave their former figurehead behind, Serling delivers Benteen's epitaph: "William Benteen, who had prerogatives: he could lead, he could direct, dictate, judge, legislate. It became a habit, then a pattern and finally a necessity. William Benteen, once a god—now a population of one, in the Twilight Zone." This coda clearly strikes at the abuse of power while pointing to the need for those cultural myths that produce power to remain firmly grounded in reality.

These musings echo many other episodes that warn about the problems of power while examining the influence and function of myth and, more generally, storytelling. Nowhere are these concerns more apparent than in "The Old Man in the Cave," set in a postapocalyptic 1974 in which nuclear bombs have "set the clock back a thousand years." A small community of survivors is led by Mr. Goldsmith (John Anderson), a self-proclaimed keeper of the legend, protector of the fables, and a vital medium for the people. For it is his task to deliver instructions for survival from a mysterious old man in a cave, whom no one has ever seen. Like Moses bringing the commandments down from the mountain—or even like a television narrator who submits tales "for your perusal"—Goldsmith tells the people what food they may and may not eat (much of it has been contaminated with radiation), which fields are safe for planting, and how to live in this very dangerous world, all based on information he supposedly receives from the cave. Enter Major French (James Coburn), leader of a rogue band of militants, who arrives to impose his own rule of law—and censorship—on the community while helping himself to their limited resources. French seeks to replace Goldsmith's myth-based authority with fascistic order and discipline, urging the people to disregard the cave's instructions and to doubt the very existence of the old man. French demands that Goldsmith take everyone to the cave so that they can see the old man for themselves. When a stone door slides away and the crowd enters, they discover that the "old man" is actually a powerful computer, which Goldsmith has been using to formulate survival strategies, to produce the narratives that will allow the culture to move forward. French incites the mob to violence, they destroy the computer, and they then eat all of the forbidden cans of food, despite Goldsmith's pleas. Within hours, everyone but Goldsmith lies dead.

Several aspects of this episode encourage us to read it simply as a religious or mythical allegory. We easily recognize the "old man" as a symbolic, patriarchal deity, complete with his proscription against "forbidden fruit"; the cave, with its stone rolled away, calls to mind the tomb of Christ, as well as Plato's cave. Yet perhaps most intriguing is its fundamental notion that the computer-as-god, representing all that remains of human knowledge and science, must be mythologized if its truths are to be communicated and accepted in a post-technological, relatively primitive age. Years in the story are designated "after the bomb" rather than "anno domini," and a few lines of dialogue call to mind biblical passages: for instance, "Man doesn't live by bread or canned food alone." French also specifically invokes the ancient Greek myth of Jason and the Golden Fleece, often seen as an allegory of royal power and its legitimacy. This reference, combined with the name of our protagonist, Goldsmith, may remind us of a familiar trope in various myths, described by Campbell in *The Power of Myth*: that of the hero who emerges from the wilderness bearing gold (divinely inspired wisdom), only to have it turn to ashes (representing the followers' inability to see). Elsewhere, Campbell points out that in certain myths, gold symbolizes "the mysterious creative energy of God" (130n). That golden, even vital, knowledge, though, here goes unheeded because of the people's inability to accept its manner of presentation.

In this way, "The Old Man in the Cave" not only interrogates mythology directly but also foregrounds two other concerns that would increasingly prove central to *The Twilight Zone*. One is the threat of all-out nuclear war and its devastating effects, obviously one of the most pressing political problems of the time and one that would benefit from being framed within a science fictional context. We might note that Rod Serling was an active member of Citizens for a Sane Nuclear Policy (Sander 155). The other concern is with the difficulty that was faced—implicitly by media workers and mythologists like Serling himself—in trying to communicate such dangers. For with the need to couch even the most vital messages—for example, about the very survival of Western culture—in a broadly generic or mythic form, Serling clearly felt some anxiety about the ability of television and thus of his own series to communicate the dangers effectively to a popular audience.

Numerous other episodes of *The Twilight Zone* deal explicitly with the theme of nuclear devastation. It figures prominently in the celebrated "Time Enough at Last," an episode that also emphasizes the difficulties of common communication. Here Henry Bemis (Burgess Meredith), a bookworm, fortuitously survives a hydrogen bomb, having sequestered himself in a bank vault to read during his lunch hour. Emerging after the blast, he finds no other survivors (no other readers) and quickly concludes that there is little reason to go on living. Yet just as he is about to commit suicide, he notices the remains of a public library, with thousands of books scattered on the ground—a discovery that gives him new purpose in life. Yet as Bemis plots out his reading schedule for months and years to come, his thick-lensed eyeglasses fall off and shatter, rendering his treasure trove of books useless.

While this and other *Twilight Zone* episodes may be best remembered for their twist endings, their narrative cleverness is inextricable from their thematic thrust and a certain self-consciousness that is usually overlooked. When seen through the prism of that ironic twist, "Time Enough at Last" obviously emerges as a critique of 1950s American conservatism, conformity, and anti-intellectualism. At the bank, Bemis's boss (Vaughn Taylor) constantly berates him for reading, which apparently does not fit the mold of the ideal corporation man. "Forget reading," his boss admonishes, "and get back to your cage!" If Bemis is imprisoned in an overly rationalized, compartmentalized system at work, he finds little respite at home, where his wife (Jacqueline DeWit) ridicules him for being inept at the "art of conversation," by which she means the idle talk that stands in for real communication. She too harangues Bemis for his absorption in books, going so far as to cross through, in heavy black marker, every line on every page of one of his books of modern poetry. Despite his problematic relationships, Bemis constantly tries to connect with other people, including his customers at the bank, but no one can relate to his enthusiasm for literature and ideas. When Bemis sits down in the bank vault to read his newspaper, we glimpse a one-second foreshadowing of the nuclear blast, apparently unseen and unheeded by everyone, in the shape of an admonitory headline: "H-Bomb Capable of Total Destruction." Serling's argument seems clear enough: a world where ideas are suppressed, where knowledge is devalued, where people do not read, where communication itself is problematic, is doomed. In this light, the episode's ironic coda takes on added weight beyond being simply a cruel twist of fate: the time for ideas is past, for now there is no one with whom to share them.

This sort of double critique crops up time and again in *The Twilight Zone*, often in settings of quasi-Orwellian, fascistic dystopias where messages of conformity and the modes of those messages become equally significant. In the futuristic "Number Twelve Looks Just like You," a teenage girl is reluctant to go through her "transformation," an apparently universally accepted, coerced process of plastic surgery and media brainwashing that makes everyone uniformly beautiful and complacent. A similar theme is explored in the classic "Eye of the Beholder," in which the main character is a woman seen only in bandages for most of the episode. Several previous attempts at plastic surgery have failed to make her look normal, and this is her last chance before being consigned to a colony for undesirables. When the bandages come off, her doctors bemoan that there has been no change in her appearance. In the quint-essential *Twilight Zone* twist ending, we see that the woman (Donna Douglas) is actually quite beautiful, while the "normal" people, whose faces we have not seen before, appear as hideous, piglike monstrosities. Chief among them is a televised Hitler-esque figurehead, whose speeches of intolerance we have heard broadcast throughout the episode.

The power of television plays an even more specific and pivotal role in another episode depicting a fascist future scenario: "The Obsolete Man." In a reprise of his Henry Bemis role from "Time Enough at Last," Burgess Meredith portrays a librarian named Romney Wordsworth, who has been deemed obsolete in a totalitarian society where books and religion are banned. Put on trial, Wordsworth—whose name evokes not only the poet but also the worth of words—defiantly faces the chancellor (Fritz Weaver), who sits in judgment, and when sentenced to death he asks only two things: that he be allowed to choose the time and manner of his execution and that his death be televised (the latter of which is particularly agreeable to the chancellor). Wordsworth lures the arrogant chancellor to his home and holds him prisoner, informing him that he has chosen to be killed by a bomb, set to go off in just a few minutes. As the appointed time draws near, the automated television cameras observe coldly as the chancellor panics, begs for his life, and finally exclaims, "In the name of God, let me out!" Wordsworth responds with a smirk, "Yes, Chancellor, in the name of God, I *will* let you out." Having tricked his adversary into invoking the forbidden concept of God—on television, before an observant and judgmental national audience—he is satisfied and releases the chancellor, just moments before the bomb goes off. However, because of his actions, which have been exposed on television before the nation, the chancellor is himself condemned as obsolete and put to death. Serling's narration concludes, "He was obsolete. But so was the state, the entity he worshipped. Any state, any entity, any ideology that fails to recognize the worth, the dignity, the rights of man—that state is obsolete."

It is tempting to read the revelatory role of the TV cameras in this episode as one of the most telling reflexive elements in the series. Certainly, it seems a thinly veiled reference to the televised Army-McCarthy hearings of 1954, which helped strip Senator Joseph McCarthy of his political clout. The junior senator from Wisconsin embodied many of the problems in 1950s American culture that *The Twilight Zone* repeatedly addresses: paranoia, guilt by suspicion, anti-intellectualism, and a hunger for power. And significantly, Burgess Meredith was one of many artists identified as being suspect in this period. Serling told Mike Wallace in 1959 that his dream project was to write a play about McCarthyism (Sander 144). However, the episode's observation of television's power to reveal and to draw out public opinion seems just as significant as its commentary on human dignity and rights—in fact, perhaps more of an insight into what the series was able to accomplish within its anthology format.

If we see those cameras in Wordsworth's monastic abode as reflexively attesting to Serling's awareness of television's power and its ability to effect social change, then we can better gauge why *The Twilight Zone* matters so much. Serling and his collaborators seem to have understood the power of both science fiction and the new medium of television well indeed, recognizing in the former a tool for creating important, socially critical drama in a form that would not incur the wrath of network executives, advertising agencies, corporate sponsors, or congressional committees, and in the latter a powerful tool for helping people to see the real shape of their culture. With a fine grasp of psychological, mythological, and cultural structures and a well-honed understanding of how they might be effectively worked into the flexible structure of the anthology drama format, Serling and company employed them time and again in a determined—and arguably quite successful—attempt to transform the American cultural landscape for the better.

Notes

1. Mark Bould cites a few serious science fiction endeavors on TV in the mid-1950s, including the "Man in Space" (1955), "Man and the Moon" (1955), and "Mars and Beyond" (1957) episodes of the *Disneyland* television series (88), but the long-range impact of such isolated programs pales alongside that of *The Twilight Zone*, and their approach was generally more speculative and informational than dramatic.

2. Here I mean "myth" in its more positive connotation, as laid out by Joseph Campbell and other scholars, not in the pejorative sense of reinforcing nationalist and bourgeois values of the status quo, as described by Roland Barthes.

Works Cited

"And When the Sky Was Opened." *The Twilight Zone.* Written by Rod Serling and Richard Matheson. Directed by Douglas Heyes. CBS, December 11, 1959.

Barnouw, Erik. *Tube of Plenty: The Evolution of American Television.* 2nd ed. New York: Oxford University Press, 1990.

Barthes, Roland. *Mythologies.* Translated by Annette Lavers. New York: Hill and Wang, 1972.

Boddy, William. *Fifties Television: The Industry and Its Critics.* Urbana: University of Illinois Press, 1990.

Bould, Mark. "Film and Television." In *The Cambridge Companion to Science Fiction,* edited by Edward James and Farah Mendlesohn, 79–95. Cambridge: Cambridge University Press, 2003.

Campbell, Joseph. *The Hero with a Thousand Faces.* 2nd ed. Princeton, NJ: Princeton University Press, 1968.

"Eye of the Beholder." *The Twilight Zone.* Written by Rod Serling. Directed by Douglas Heyes. CBS, November 11, 1960.

Javna, John. *The Best of Science Fiction TV.* New York: Harmony, 1987.

Joseph Campbell and the Power of Myth. Prod. Joan Konner and Alvin H. Perlmutter. Perf. Joseph Campbell and Bill Moyers. 1988. DVD. New York: Mystic Fire, 2001.

"The Last Flight." *The Twilight Zone.* Written by Richard Matheson. Directed by William F. Claxton. CBS, February 5, 1960.

"The Monsters Are Due on Maple Street." *The Twilight Zone.* Written by Rod Serling. Directed by Ron Winston. CBS, March 4, 1960.

"Nightmare at 20,000 Feet." *The Twilight Zone.* Written by Richard Matheson. Directed by Richard Donner. CBS, October 11, 1963.

"Number Twelve Looks Just like You." *The Twilight Zone.* Written by Charles Beaumont and John Tomerlin. Directed by Abner Biberman. CBS, January 24, 1964.

"The Obsolete Man." *The Twilight Zone.* Written by Rod Serling. Directed by Elliot Silverstein. CBS, June 2, 1961.

"The Odyssey of Flight 33." *The Twilight Zone.* Written by Rod Serling. Directed by Justus Addiss. CBS, February 24, 1961.

"The Old Man in the Cave." *The Twilight Zone.* Written by Rod Serling. Directed by Alan Crosland Jr. CBS, November 8, 1963.

"On Thursday We Leave for Home." *The Twilight Zone.* Written by Rod Serling. Directed by Buzz Kulik. CBS, May 2, 1963.

"People Are Alike All Over." *The Twilight Zone.* Written by Rod Serling. Directed by Mitchell Leisen. CBS, March 25, 1960.

Sander, Gordon F. *Serling: The Rise and Twilight of Television's Last Angry Man.* New York: Dutton, 1992.

Telotte, J. P. *Science Fiction Film*. Cambridge: Cambridge University Press, 2001.

"Time Enough at Last." *The Twilight Zone*. Written by Rod Serling. Directed by John Brahm. CBS, November 20, 1959.

ANIMATION, ANIME, AND THE CULTURAL LOGIC OF ASIANIZATION

Dennis Redmond

The study of contemporary Japanese science fiction television (SFTV) is a lot like the classic science fiction story wherein intrepid scientists discover space aliens have landed on Earth. The trouble is that no one believes them. Why? The proof aliens are here is precisely that everything is so terrifyingly normal. Similarly, many of the core elements of Japanese SFTV—thermonuclear lizards, giant robots, and cartoon mascots—were once viewed as either outrageous oddities or exclusively Japanese obsessions. Yet nowadays Godzilla, Evangelions, and Pokémon have become almost as iconic and ubiquitous as Mickey Mouse and the NBA. The more popular the exotic world of Japanese SFTV has become, the less world audiences think of it as exotic or alien—or recognize its real cultural significance.

The paradox deepens when we consider just how drastically that world audience has changed since the end of the cold war. Today our planet has 2 billion cell phones, 500 million computers, and a truly multinational consumer culture (International Telecommunication Union). No single nation-state dominates the mass media, the world economy, or global geopolitics anymore. Put another way, the enormous impact of Japanese SFTV on our media-savvy and multinational twenty-first century cannot be explained simply by reference to Japan's specific national identity or culture. In fact, some of the most interesting works of Japanese SFTV are shockingly un-Japanese in terms of aesthetic style as well as narrative content.

One of the main reasons Americans have failed to assess this cultural significance is the unique historical context of Japanese SFTV. Whereas American SFTV draws much of its content from the plentiful archives of U.S.-based pulp fiction, comic books, television, and science fiction cinema, Japanese SFTV is dependent on multinational media. The latter's two most significant influences are the cultures of anime (Japanese-style animation) and 3-D video games. Although the earliest forms of anime and video games emerged in Japan and the United States during the 1960s, they quickly escaped their national spawning grounds. Today, South Korea, North Korea, Taiwan, Hong Kong, China, France, and the United States are all significant producers of anime, while India, China, Russia, and many of the countries of the European Union have become powerhouse 3-D video game producers.[1]

Both anime and video games have rich histories of multimedia innovation and cross-cultural borrowing. Anime artists such as Akira Toriyama and Hayao Miyazaki drew inspiration from classic Disney films such as *Fantasia* (1940), as well as live-action works such as Jan Svankmajer's *Alice* (1988), a mordant retelling of *Alice in Wonderland* in a Czech turn. At the same time, video game franchises ranging from Square Enix's legendary *Final Fantasy* series to Hideo Kojima's magnificent *Metal Gear Solid* routinely cite sources as diverse as Western European auteur cinema and the Hong Kong action blockbuster.

The upshot is that Japanese SFTV, video games, and anime reciprocally influence each other in powerful and productive ways. The anime culture played a particularly important role in diffusing the innovations of Hong Kong action films within Japanese SFTV, ranging from the balletic editing sequences of the *wuxia* (Chinese martial arts) films to John Woo's slow-motion "bullet-time" camera technique. The anime culture also developed a varied vocabulary of stylized effects capable of generating rich characterization and emotional complexity from simple visual materials. The exaggerated eyes of anime characters have become standard in world animation, and the stylized confrontations and complex geopolitical themes of anime series such as Akira Toriyama's *Dragonball Z* raised the bar for future action franchises.

Video game culture played an equally important role in revolutionizing the elements of music, sound editing and voice acting. Kojima's *Metal Gear Solid 3*, for example, features elaborate cut scenes, complex characters, a gripping musical score, and the superb voice acting of David Hayter and other talented actors. Contemporary video game culture is dominated by franchises and organized in terms of episodic content. The typical game requires ten to twenty hours of play-through time, an investment of time comparable to watching a season of a television series.

Anime and video games also provided a venue for sophisticated meditations on identity politics and post–cold war geopolitics. Rumiko Takahashi's anime series *Ranma ½* (1988–1992) delivers a rip-roaring satire of the foibles of Japanese gender roles, identity politics, and consumerism during the height of the Japanese bubble economy. Square Enix's *Final Fantasy 12* (2006) is a fusion of mythological fantasy, role play, post–Iraq war geopolitics, and science fiction.

This extraordinarily rich narrative environment has had two significant effects on Japanese SFTV. First, it has contributed a vast archive of characters, story lines, editing styles, and visual innovations on which to draw. Second, it has allowed Japanese SFTV to follow in the footsteps of American SFTV. Historically, American SFTV has been profoundly influenced by the political imaginary of the U.S. empire. It could not be otherwise, given the overwhelming influence of the U.S. economy over its cold war competitors. In 1945, the United States generated half the industrial output of the planet and began to bankroll the recovery of Japan and Western Europe; for the next four decades, it fielded the richest and most technologically advanced consumer culture in the world. There is nothing in the annals of Japanese SFTV comparable to the opening of the classic *Adventures of Superman* (1953–1957), where the Man of Steel stands on Earth as if it were the front lawn of America Inc. Nor is there anything like the benevolent neocolonialism of the *Star Trek* franchise, with its wide-eyed NASA-esque idealism backed by murderous Pentagon-like firepower. This is not to argue that Japanese SFTV is free of the toxic racism, sexism, militarism, and xenophobia that afflict all media cultures, only to underline that at some point in the 1970s, Japanese SFTV broke from the U.S. imperial script and has never looked back.

In retrospect, two key geopolitical events conspired to make this breakout possible. The first was Japan's post–World War II demilitarization. Japan's postwar boom was founded on civilian industries, epitomized by Toyota engineering, Sony style, and Canon creativity.[2] In contrast, the high-technology sector of the United States was the recipient of vast subsidies from the Pentagon, Silicon Valley was largely financed by defense contracts, and aerospace giant Boeing is now one of the largest military contractors in the world.[3] It should not be surprising that American SFTV gravitates toward the U.S. military-industrial complex, whereas Japanese SFTV gravitates toward consumer electronics.

The second event was Japan's role in jump-starting the economic boom of east Asia. Beginning in the mid-1980s, formerly autarkic economies like China and Vietnam, colonial antagonists like South Korea and Japan, and cold war enemies like Taiwan and China shelved their real and imaginary grievances to invest in—and trade with—each other. After much trial and error, these countries adopted variations of Japan's highly successful developmental model to accelerate their own economic growth.[4] The result has been one of the most impressive economic expansions in world history. Today, east Asia is linked by dense networks of capital flow, commodity exchange, and media broadcasts. Total trade between China and Japan is now larger than total trade between Japan and the United States, and the countries of east Asia have accumulated well over $2 trillion in currency reserves (Stetser).

This economic boom has been paced by equally impressive flows of people, ranging from mass tourism to internal and external labor migration. In 2005, the World Tourism Organization estimates, 31 million Chinese, 16.5 million Japanese, 10 million South Koreans, and 2.7 million Thais traveled as outbound tourists, visiting mostly other Asian destinations (Nawaz).[5] Tens of millions of Chinese citizens are moving from China's countryside to its cities each year in search of better lives. Millions of Filipinos and Indonesians work in Malaysia and Singapore, and a million Koreans live and work in Japan (*World Migration* 106–7).

Over time, the vast east Asian market exerted an increasingly powerful effect on Japan's media culture. In the 1960s, painful memories of Japanese imperialism in World War II meant that Japanese media artists could not follow in the footsteps of American SFTV and depict a benevolent colonialism. In the 1970s, anti-imperial sentiment was solidified by the object lesson of the U.S. neocolonial war in Vietnam. To be sure, Hollywood and American consumer culture remained enormously popular in Japan. By the 1980s, however, Japanese media artists began to find they had more in common with the makers of Hong Kong films and China's fifth-generation directors than with filmmakers in Hollywood. At some point in the early 1990s, the bullet train of east Asian community left the station, and it has been gathering speed ever since. The sheer scale and scope of regional integration foreclosed any recrudescence of Japanese imperialism, in the same way that Germany's integration into the European Union consigned German expansionism to the history books, but it did much more. It made possible new types of multinational cultural exchange: a cultural logic of Asianization.

The concept of Asianization is meant to complement Koichi Iwabuchi's useful notion of the "popular Asianism" of the Japanese mass media (548). "Asianism" highlights specifically binational forms of cultural exchange between Japan and its east Asian neighbors, whereas "Asianization" refers to the sum total of the multinational media flows throughout the entire region—the simultaneous exchange of music, film, television, and game narratives across multiple national borders.

The rapid proliferation of broadband Internet and media-capable cell phones throughout east Asia has kicked both Asianism and Asianization into high gear. Today, Japan imports Korean TV serials, such as *Winter Sonata* and *Jewel in the Palace*, as well as films and "Cantopop" (Cantonese popular music) from Hong Kong. Korean online video games and Japanese anime are hugely popular in China, while Japanese anime series and films are hits throughout east Asia and, indeed, the world.

Japanese SFTV has acknowledged the process of Asianization in two ways. First, it has critiqued the pervasive techno-Orientalism of mainstream U.S. and European mass media, as well as its indigenous Japanese counterparts.[6] Second, it has begun to consider the utopian possibilities of a larger east Asian community of nations based on multilateral diplomacy, equal exchange, and mutual respect. It has done this by critiquing east Asia's own homegrown traditions of xenophobia, colonialism, and militarism, including those elements within its own cultural history.

Hideaki Anno's anime series *Neon Genesis Evangelion* (1995) is one of the first significant examples of this new cultural logic. The initial episode of the series seemed to be a straightforward *mecha* cartoon in which giant robots piloted by teenagers have to stop an alien invasion of Earth. The mecha has been a staple of Japanese SFTV from *Mazinger Z* (1972–1974) and *Mobile Suit Gundam* (1979–1980) to *Super Dimension Fortress Macross* (1982). However, *Evangelion* turns the theme of alien invasion on its head. Its twenty-five episodes enthralled audiences with a mixture of pulse-pounding action and thoughtful and unexpected meditations on natural history, social responsibility, and adulthood. As the series progressed, Anno repudiated the latent militarism, sexism, and xenophobia of the mecha by accessing an extraordinary array of Japanese, American, and European media forms. Most of all, the series broke new ground by showcasing powerful, complex female characters, unlike anything in the annals of anime. In fact, one of these characters, Asuka Langley, a young girl of half-German, half-Japanese descent, is the first credible multinational character in the history of Japanese SFTV.

The result was a double-barreled critique of Japan's indigenous identity politics of gender, race, and sexuality, as well as the rapacious economic agenda of its *keiretsu* business elites.[7] There is a similar double-edged critique at work in the literal translation of the Japanese title of the series, *Shin Seiki Evangelion*: "Gospel of the New Century." The creators of the series apparently wished to simultaneously evoke and subvert the theological implications this title would have in English-speaking countries. They therefore crafted a translation that points away from a potentially fundamentalist theology and toward the electronic biology, as it were, of consumer capitalism. More specifically, *Evangelion* critiques the production and reproduction of bodies in late capitalism by showing that the giant robots are neither simply ciphers of Japanese electronic engineering nor symbols of a militarized, colonialist masculinity. They are full-fledged subjects, embodiments of a progressive east Asian collective consciousness.[8]

A few years later, the TV series *Cowboy Bebop* (1998–1999), created by Hajime Yatate and directed by Shinichiro Watanabe, would push *Evangelion*'s achievement still further. The main characters are four cash-strapped, space-traveling bounty hunters in flight from a ruined Earth. Spike is a laconic martial arts expert with a shady past, Ed is a quirky female computer hacker, Faye is an independent-minded pilot, and middle-aged Jet is a tough-minded mercenary with a philosophical streak (video game fans will note Jet's resemblance to the incidental character Reddas in *Final Fantasy 12*).

None of these characters follow their respective mass cultural conventions, nor is any one tied to a definable national identity in the way Anno's characters are. The only obvious geographic reference in the series is to Faye's hometown, which resembles contemporary Singapore, that is to say, a multinational entrepôt. Watanabe skillfully balanced the underlying anomie of the plot with moments of slapstick hilarity, and film noir visuals with martial arts mayhem. The quick-witted scripts and ironic endings gently tweak many of the more egregious conventions of Japanese SFTV, such as out-of-control robots, mad scientists, corrupt police forces, and renegade *yakuza* (Japanese mobsters).

Watanabe would later translate this sensibility to another key series, *Quack Experimental Anime Excel Saga* (1999), a wild and woolly satire of every Japanese and American SFTV cliché ever made, plus a few that hadn't been invented yet. The series is loosely based on Koushi Rikudo's *manga* (the generic Japanese term for "comic book"), which was once considered impossible to translate into television because of its scandalous content as well as the sheer density of its inside jokes about Japanese manga and anime culture. Wisely, Watanabe avoided a literal transcription of the manga. Instead, he allowed the science fiction narratives and visuals to carry the story. The delirious pacing, over-the-top sight gags, and deft scriptwriting are complemented by satires of Japanese, U.S., and European animation traditions. For example, Excel, the main character, parodies the *Evangelion* character Asuka Langley, underlining the degree to which Anno's series has become embedded in the landscape of contemporary Japanese SFTV. There is also Pedro, a Brazilian-Japanese character who is played mostly for laughs but whose very presence points to the fast-growing immigrant communities of contemporary Japan (significantly, at the end of the series, Pedro's family moves to Japan).

The most noteworthy recent work of Japanese SFTV is Satoshi Kon's *Paranoia Agent* (2004). This series represents a change of pace for Kon, who is best known as the director of visually stunning, thought-provoking anime feature films such as *Millennium Actress* (2001) and *Tokyo Godfathers* (2003). Fortunately, Kon did not compromise the quality of his work in transitioning to the small screen. *Paranoia Agent* is a fusion of media genres—the crime thriller, the film noir, the mystery, the role-playing video game, the giant robot adventure, the horror movie, Nintendo's *Paper Mario* (2001)—along with Japanese SFTV motifs too numerous to count, into a parable of the arrival of multinational media politics in east Asia. *Evangelion* created a hyperspace junction between Japanese SFTV and the multinational SFTV of the future; *Paranoia Agent* travels through that junction.

The main characters of the story are two police officers, the hard-bitten Keiichi Ikari and his younger, less conventional partner, Mitsuhiro Manwa. Their names are not accidental. "Ikari" hints at the two Ikaris, father and son, who star in Anno's *Neon Genesis Evangelion*; "Manwa" suggests "manwha," the term for Korea's thriving cartoon and animation culture. This twin reference to Japanese anime and its Korean analogue not only brackets two of east Asia's most prominent animation cultures but also nods in the direction of the Hallyu, or Korean wave, the imported Korean television melodramas that have become huge hits in contemporary Japan.

Paranoia Agent's Ikari and Manwa are investigating a series of criminal assaults. Citizens are being struck down by an unknown teenager on roller blades, armed with a golden bat. The media quickly dubs the attacker *shonen batsu* (literally "bat boy"; the English translation is "li'l slugger"). At first, the attacks are nonfatal and even a bit comic, but they quickly escalate into savage beatings, gruesome mass murders, and finally a full-scale war. The search for Li'l Slugger quickly turns into an allegorical tour of the toxic, dehumanizing effects of multinational consumerism, ranging from schoolyard bullying to endemic sexual violence, from repressive identity politics to the collective madness of xenophobia and war. Eventually, Ikari and Manwa resign from the police force, choosing to unravel the mystery of Li'l Slugger on their own as private detectives. This shift not only abolishes the coordinates of national space latent in the crime thriller but also points to the arrival of explicitly multinational aesthetic forms. During one episode, the characters have to battle their way through a 3-D console video game, replete with slapstick boss battles and less than helpful nonplayer characters. During a later episode, Ikari crashes through a simulacrum of a cartoon world rather like *Paper Mario*. Other episodes show Manwa searching through the shortwave radio spectrum to track Li'l Slugger's movements and battling against the constantly mutating monster.

As it turns out, Li'l Slugger's reign of terror has been triggered by an innocent-looking cartoon mascot called Mellow Maromi, a stylized pink dog that is also the linchpin, within the narrative world, for a best-selling television and toy franchise. Maromi's creator is a young woman named Tsukiko Sagi, a highly successful anime artist whose company has put her under crushing deadline pressure to create a commercial sequel to Maromi. When she begins to fall apart under the stress, Maromi takes on a deadly life all its own.

This clever rewriting of Mary Shelley's *Frankenstein* (1818) for the multinational era concludes with a plot twist worthy of the finale of *Evangelion*. In Anno's series, the audience discovers that the alien invaders were merely ciphers of humanity's neocolonial and economic violence against itself. *Paranoia Agent* goes further by naming the central agent of that violence. This agent mutates constantly, is not limited to any national space, and inhabits all cultural spaces simultaneously. This monster is nothing less than multinational capitalism itself, a system that, the series suggests, if left to its own devices, will destroy individual subjects as ruthlessly as it is wrecking the ecology of our planet.

Yet Kon does not counsel despair in the face of the overwhelming might of this system. Instead, he points to new forms of collective resistance. The model for this response is the final alliance among Sagi, Manwa, and Ikari to bring the multinational monster under control. Sagi's artistic creativity, Manwa's tracking skills, and Ikari's force of will turn into symbols of multinational aesthetics, theory, and social movements. Their alliance represents the prototype of a new kind of east Asian solidarity, capable of resisting the worst impulses of keiretsu capitalism and Wall Street neoliberalism on their own multinational terrain.

The need for such solidarity is not simply a rhetorical ploy. Economic interdependence has brought undreamt-of prosperity to East Asia, but it has also made cross-cultural dialogue and multicultural understanding urgent necessities for the region's citizens and communities. Environmental protection and consumer safety require cross-border regulations. Singapore and Malaysia have become as dependent on mass labor migration as Switzerland and France.

We can find a striking confirmation of Satoshi Kon's vision in the field of Korean science fiction. One of the first Korean animated series to be exported, *BASToF Syndrome* (2001) adopts many of the conventions of the mecha and Japanese SFTV, including giant robots piloted by teenagers, adolescent growing pains, and video games that seem more real than reality. Five years later, Korean science fiction had matured enough to produce its first multinational masterpiece, Joon-ho Bong's film *The Host* (2006). It cleverly rewrites the Godzilla narrative, showing how a ravenous monster is spawned by a combination of U.S. cold war intervention and neoliberal hubris. What ultimately defeats the monster is not a national scientist or Pentagon superweapon but a combination of an Olympic-level archery competition, prodemocracy media mobilization, Korean cell phone acumen, and a creatively reconfigured traffic pole—in effect, multinational media and industrial infrastructures, which anticipate some form of east Asian cultural and political community.

We do not yet know what political forms this community will take. Perhaps regional organizations such as the Association of Southeast Asian Nations will continue to deepen their scale and scope. Alternatively, entirely new forms of multinational democracy may emerge, on the model of the European Union.

One of the most significant long-term effects of Japanese SFTV is its enormous influence on east Asia's booming video game culture. Japanese publisher Enterbrain estimates that game software sales in 2006 reached $815 million in China and $2.24 billion in Korea ("Online Gaming" 3). These totals compare favorably with Japan's game market ($4.42 billion), and if current growth rates hold, China and Korea will soon rival the other two major game markets in the world, Europe ($7.43 billion) and the United States ($7.83 billion). More remarkable still, total video game sales throughout east Asia are now higher than the sum total of cinema box office receipts and DVD sales and rentals in the region (Brightman; Ihlwan; Schilling, "Japanese Films"; Schilling, "Japan Home Entertainment"). Animation, anime, and Japanese SFTV are leading the way in a seismic shift in media production and consumption throughout east Asia and indeed the world while forming one of the most important public spaces, where the contradictions and possibilities of east Asian integration can be debated, narrated, and shaped.

Notes

1. Although the exact numbers are difficult to determine, most analysts estimate the 2005 total sales of the world animation industry (the sum of media broadcasts, films, DVD sales, toys, and other merchandising) at $40 billion. Japan probably makes up about a fifth of this total. The animation market in China reportedly reached $2.5 billion in 2006 (Chung). Based on reports from individual national markets and press releases from the NPD Group (see http://www.npd.com), I estimate that world video game revenues amounted to $36 billion in 2006.

2. Japan remains the world's single largest producer of machine-tools, the machines that make all other machines ("Producers").

3. Military spending composed 10.2 percent of the U.S. economy in the 1950s, 8.5 percent in the 1960s, 5.8 percent in the 1970s, and 6.0 percent in the 1980s (Coen and Hickman 55–56). After shrinking during the 1990s, U.S. military spending exploded after 2001. In 2006, the United States accounted for 47 percent of all military spending on the planet. Together, the democracies of the world account for 80 percent of world military spending. The only nondemocratic country with a large military is China, with an annual budget of $122 billion. However, China's population is 4.5 times larger than that of the United States; thus annual U.S. military expenditures are $2,147 per U.S. citizen, whereas annual Chinese military expenditures are $90 per Chinese citizen (Sharp; Stockholm International Peace Research Institute).

4. The east Asian boom had nothing to do with neoliberal ideology or privatization and everything to do with sophisticated industrial policies and heavy public investment in education and infrastructure. For Japan, see Michael Gerlach's *Alliance Capitalism* and David Friedman's *The Misunderstood Miracle*. For South Korea see Alice Amsden's *Asia's Next Giant*. For Taiwan, see Robert Wade's *Governing the Market*.

5. As late as 2001, Chinese mainlanders could visit only 18 other countries and regions. Today they can visit 132 countries and regions. According to data from Zhang Guangrui, director of the Tourism Research Center at the Chinese Academy of Social Sciences, 4.5 million Chinese traveled abroad in 1995 and spent $3.7 billion during their trips. In 2005, the number increased to 31 million and total spending skyrocketed to $21.8 billion. For more information, see "Outbound Tourism Sector" and Arlt.

6. All too many Western accounts of east Asian mass media are informed by technologized versions of Orientalism: the rewriting of the colonialist fictions of the noble savage, the barbaric tribal horde, and the benevolent settler-colonist in a consumerist turn. As late as the mid-1980s, mainstream U.S. journalism alternately applauded and condemned the Japanese as rigidly collectivistic or irrationally individualistic, mystically Eastern or robotically Western, wildly oversexed or icily frigid. In short, the Japanese were as stereotyped as Japan's high-tech export goods.

7. The keiretsu are gigantic corporate networks that produce about one-third of the entire output of the Japanese economy. These are not centralized monopolies but rather diffuse, overlapping networks of ownership and control. Unlike in the United States, where individuals still own half of all the stock of publicly traded companies, stock ownership in Japan is overwhelmingly concentrated in the hands of banks and corporations. Typically, a keiretsu bank and each of its affiliated companies own a small stake (usually less than 5 percent) of the stock of other affiliates. Each stake is small, but they add up to effective group control of the firm. Interestingly, there are roughly analogous

modes of corporate governance in Taiwan, Singapore, and South Korea. The keiretsu model is also spreading rapidly in China and Vietnam. For more information, see the *Japan Company Handbook* (Summer 2005).

8. For a more complete analysis of *Neon Genesis Evangelion*, see chapters 6 and 7 of my book *The World Is Watching*.

Works Cited

Amsden, Alice. *Asia's Next Giant: South Korea and Late Industrialization*. New York: Oxford University Press, 1989.

Arlt, Wolfgang Georg. *China's Outbound Tourism*. London: Routledge, 2006.

Brightman, James. "Japan: 2006 Sets Record for Video Game Industry." *GameBiz Daily*, January 12, 2007. http://biz.gamedaily.com/industry/feature/?id=14943.

Chung, Olivia. "China Draws on Cartoon Cat's Success." *Asia Times*, May 15, 2007. http://www.atimes.com/atimes/China_Business/IE15Cb03.html.

Coen, Robert M., and Bert G. Hickman. "Macroeconomic Impacts of Disarmament and the Peace Dividend in the US Economy." In *The Peace Dividend*, edited by Nils P. Gleditch, 55–56. New York: Elsevier, 1996.

Friedman, David. *The Misunderstood Miracle*. Ithaca, NY: Cornell University Press, 1988.

Gerlach, Michael. *Alliance Capitalism*. Berkeley: University of California Press, 1992.

Guangrui, Zhang. "China's Outbound Tourism: An Overview." Paper presented at the University of Surrey Tourism Business Frontiers Forum, London, November 8, 2006. http://www.som.surrey.ac.uk/WTM/GuangruiWTM ChinaOutboundTourism2006text.pdf.

Ihlwan, Moon. "South Korea: Video Game's Crazed Capital." *Business Week*, March 26, 2007. http://www.businessweek.com/globalbiz/content/mar2007/gb20070326_937184.htm.

International Telecommunication Union. *Yearbook of Statistics 2004*. Geneva: ITU, 2004.

Iwabuchi, Koichi. "Nostalgia for a (Different) Modernity: Media Consumption of 'Asia' in Japan." *Positions* 10 (2002): 547–73.

Omar, Nawaz. "Asian Outbound Tourism Takes Off." *World Tourism Organization*. June 2006. http://www.world-tourism.org/newsroom/Releases/2006/june/asianoutbound.html.

"Online Gaming Helps Lift Game Software Sales across Globe." *Nikkei Weekly*, June 4, 2007, 3.

"Outbound Tourism Sector on Rise in China." *Asia Times*, February 9, 2006. http://www.atimes.com/atimes/China_Business/HB09Cb02.html.

"Producers." *2007 World Machine Tool Output and Consumption Survey*. http://www.gardnerweb.com/consump/produce.html.

Redmond, Dennis. *The World Is Watching*. Carbondale: Southern Illinois University Press, 2003.

Schilling, Mark. "Japanese Films Win Box Office Battle of 2006." *Variety Asia Online*, January 1, 2007. http://www.varietyasiaonline.com/content/view/535/53/.

———. "Japan Home Entertainment Sales Dip." *Variety Asia Online*, March 12, 2007. http://www.variety.com/article/VR1117961012.html?categoryid=20&cs=1.

Sharp, Travis. "The Bucks Never Stop: Iraq and Afghanistan War Costs Continue to Soar." Center for Arms Control and Non-proliferation. August 27, 2007. http://www.armscontrolcenter.org/policy/securityspending/articles/bucks_never_stop/.

Stetser, Brad. "Almost Unimaginably Large (2006 Global Reserve Growth)." *Roubini Global Economics Monitor*. March 30, 2007. http://www.rgemonitor.com /blog/setser/186728/.

Stockholm International Peace Research Institute. Military Expenditure Database. http://www.sipri.org/contents/milap/milex/mex_database1.html.

Wade, Robert. *Governing the Market*. Princeton, NJ: Princeton University Press, 1990.

World Migration Report 2005. Geneva: United Nations and International Organization for Migration, 2005.

PART III

WHAT FUELS THESE FLIGHTS

Some Key Concerns
of Science Fiction Television

"DREAMS TEACH"

(Im)Possible Worlds in Science Fiction Television

Christine Mains

In "Absolute Power," a fourth-season episode of the long-running science fiction series *Stargate SG-1*, the character Daniel Jackson (Michael Shanks) is placed into a dream state by an alien who wishes to show him the corrupting consequences of technological power. "Dreams teach," the alien tells his team, who are unaware that in the hours they watch him sleep, Daniel lives a year as a brutal dictator who becomes responsible for their imprisonment and death. Of course, this sort of immersion of characters in alternate worlds of dream or delusion is a staple of science fiction television (SFTV), one of several tropes that explore the act of constructing possible worlds in narrative. Spurred on in part by increasing scientific interest in quantum mechanics, science fiction narratives in all media have conjured a variety of such parallel universes, alternate realities, possible worlds. SFTV has often reflected on the dazzling confusion of the multiverse it can visualize; most often, it presents viewers with two worlds in one, representing what narratologist Lubomír Dolezel terms a "dyadic world" (128). This dyadic approach is at the heart of episodes that place characters who inhabit a fantastic world into a "normal" environment to suggest that the fantastic world is a lie, a delusion for which the characters spend much of the episode being treated. They are eventually forced into making a choice to resolve their inner conflict and return to the world that they—and we—think of as familiar and normal. Such two-world models explore SFTV's construction of heroic characterizations and even the conventions of storytelling within the episodic format.

SFTV typically follows what Robin Nelson terms a "flexi-narrative" format (24), meaning that it combines stand-alone episodes, in which the story is resolved by episode's end, with a continuing narrative arc or thread that runs through an entire season or series. After several seasons of watching characters deal with their personal issues and struggle against enemy forces, viewers come to know the characters and the world they inhabit quite well. Over time, viewers become accustomed to entering what David Herman terms the "storyworld," the set of "reconstructed timelines and inventories of existents" that constitute this particular fantasy narrative (570). The storyworld is the primary narrative world, constructed by viewers episode by episode, the characters' "real" world, with a history, geography, and natural laws of its own.

We usually accept SFTV's storyworlds as real, despite that they may include beings and situations not found in our world, because it is essential to do so. For as Jan Johnson-Smith explains, the genre's narratives not only use the tools and strategies available to all storyworlds but "must also distinguish themselves from the realities of our everyday world by creating new or different rules by which their realities function" (19). The viewer caught up in the storyworld little cares whether the rules for the impossible are technological or magical, whether the characters fight aliens or vampires; "for a genre like sf, not only must the world be plausible, but a strong degree of estrangement from the mundane world is also vital. Whether in verbal or visual form, sf must break with everyday reality" (20). In *Smallville*, a young Clark Kent (Tom Welling) comes into his powers as the future Superman, defender of the American way, already beset by enemies. In *Charmed*, a trio of sisters draw on their family inheritance as witches to fight demons and save innocents. Buffy Summers (Sarah Michelle Gellar) of *Buffy the Vampire Slayer* is the chosen one, the one girl in the world with the strength and agility to slay vampires and demons. The storyworld of *Stargate Atlantis*, a spin-off of *Stargate SG-1*, includes present-day characters who fight vampiric aliens and robots from their base in a distant galaxy. *Star Trek: Deep Space Nine*, the third series in the *Star Trek* franchise, set on a space station centuries in the future, recounts the characters' war against technologically advanced and hostile aliens. These storyworlds are plausible to the viewer despite the estranging presence of the unfamiliar or impossible because the characters seem like real people with real relationships and real emotional issues.

That the impossible storyworld is the characters' real world complicates Dolezel's conception of "alethic dyadic worlds," his term for the formation of two-world narratives generated by contrasting alethic modalities of possibility.[1] Alethic modalities are those governing conditions of possibility, necessity, and contingency, the conditions bound up in "what if" statements. Narratives generated by such modalities focus on conditions of possibility, on what is considered logically possible or impossible. In the dyadic world model, there is "a unification in one fictional world of two domains in which contrary modal conditions reign" (128); in other words, in the storyworld, two domains, one possible according to the loci logic of the storyworld and one not, are juxtaposed, often for thematic purposes. Dolezel's own example of an alethic dyadic world is that of mythology, which contrasts the natural world, a world like the actual world, with a supernatural world containing gods, miracles, and metamorphoses (128–29). Dolezel further notes that, in some cases, the "alethic contrast between the natural and the supernatural is bridged by intermediate worlds. Dreams, hallucinations, madness, drug-induced altered states" (117) may be offered as explanations for the presence of the impossible in a storyworld that imitates the actual world. But what explanation can be offered to a character who, though his storyworld normally contains the impossible, is suddenly faced with only the possible?

Most SFTV series, if they run more than a few years, produce at least one episode in which a character wakes up in a psychiatric hospital to be told that the life he or she has been living, the life that viewers have been watching unfold, is nothing more than a delusion. In *Smallville*'s "Labyrinth," *Buffy the Vampire Slayer*'s "Normal Again," *Charmed*'s "Brain Drain," and *Stargate Atlantis*'s "The Real World," lead characters Clark, Buffy, Piper Halliwell (Holly Marie Combs), and Dr. Elizabeth Weir (Torri Higginson) find themselves in exactly this situation. Benjamin Sisko (Avery Brooks) of *Star Trek: Deep Space Nine* undergoes a slightly different but related experience in "Shadows and Symbols": he receives a vision of himself as Benny Russell, a 1950s writer for *Incredible Tales*, scribbling on the walls of a mental institution where he has been confined since his breakdown shown in a previous episode, "Far beyond the Stars." In all of these examples and others, the characters face a difficult choice: believe what they are told, that their lives have been nothing more than delusions that they must abandon to return to sanity and health, or fight against what, according to the dyadic logic of the storyworld, must be a hallucination of sanity that they must overcome to return to the struggle against evil enemies that has been their destiny. They must choose between the storyworld, which is their reality despite its impossibilities, and an "asylum world" that cannot be true, even though it makes more sense according to the laws of the normal world.[2]

This depiction of an asylum world has recurred often enough in the genre to produce a familiar pattern. It is not only the progression of the plot that evokes this sense of a formula but also the features of the verbal and visual forms noted by Johnson-Smith. The various shows' creators have at their disposal a repertoire of images and visual effects that help to advance the narrative's plot and themes, both establishing the formula of the asylum world and departing in some ways from the conventions. The physical appearance of the institutional set, for instance, generally includes codified spaces: a small confined room for the patient, complete with a narrow bed in the corner; a barred window through which the outside world might be glimpsed; a locked door with a small, grilled security window; a long hallway down which doctors and orderlies can stride menacingly or patients can be dragged kicking and screaming; a large room for group therapy or recreational activities, from which the patient can attempt escape; and a private office in which the doctor can meet with the patient and provide rational explanations for the patient's presence in the asylum world.

Another common visual feature is the appearance and performance of an actor portraying the doctor, an authority figure who can occasionally be threatening but is more often wise, kindly, paternal, dressed in sober clothes or a white coat, often with a trim beard or goatee (in none of these examples is the kindly doctor a woman). The projection of authority and gentle wisdom is important reassurance both to the character within the narrative and to the viewers outside the narrative; the character is naturally shocked and upset at the turn of events, and the viewers are also concerned not only for the character with whom they identify but also, depending on the nature and the timing of the entry into the asylum world, for the disruption of the familiar storyworld. A question arises, no matter how fleeting, about the truth of the doctor's initial statement that the storyworld does not exist, has never existed, that the character has been residing in the mental institution for as many years as the show has been on the air. In a sixth-season episode of *Smallville*, for example, Dr. Hudson (Matthew Walker) tells Clark that he suffered a psychotic break more than five years earlier. In "Normal Again," late in the sixth season, Buffy's psychiatrist tells her that she was admitted six years before, suffering from schizophrenia. In an episode early in the show's third season, the soft-spoken Dr. Fletcher (Alan Ruyk) informs Elizabeth Weir that the two years she believes she has resided in the alien city of Atlantis exist only in her mind, as she was admitted following a breakdown only three days prior to waking up in a hospital on Earth. In effect, the doctor erases every event that the character has experienced and the viewers have witnessed.

The doctor's explanation also accounts for why the delusions suffered by the character involve fantastic and impossible events, an explanation that makes sense to the character and to the viewers familiar with the medical and psychological jargon so much a part of the late twentieth and early twenty-first centuries. Elizabeth's creation of the technologically advanced city of Atlantis where she commands a military and scientific expedition is, according to Dr. Fletcher, an extension of her childhood dreams of becoming an astronaut; such childhood fantasies "offer a peaceful refuge from the harsh realities of adult life" where, she has been told, her fiancé recently died in a car accident. Dr. Hudson tells Clark that his delusion results from the traumatic death of his natural parents when he was a small child, an event that has left him feeling helpless, with no control over his environment: "You created an alternate universe in which you feel safe and secure. In a world where you have no power, you choose to give yourself superpowers." The creation of amazing powers by the powerless patient echoes in other shows centering on young protagonists: *Charmed*'s Piper is informed bluntly, "You don't have powers, you're not a witch, you don't save innocents, you never did." And Buffy's doctor tells her that she has created a world in her mind in which she and her friends have superpowers that they employ in "great, overblown conflicts" against vampires, demons, and even gods. But she is beginning to break free of the delusion, he tells her, pointing out that her current "illusory" enemies are no longer gods but merely a trio of hapless high school bullies. It all sounds perfectly plausible, certainly more plausible than amazing powers and impossible events. After all, as Buffy's friend Xander (Nicholas Brendon) observes from the storyworld where she shares her experiences of the asylum world, "You think this isn't real just because of all the vampires and demons and ex-vengeance demons and the sister that used to be a big ball of universe-destroying energy?" Summed up so bluntly, the premises of the storyworld do seem incredible.

Adding to the confusion about which world is real are the rational explanations offered by other characters in the storyworld as to why the hero is experiencing the hallucinatory asylum world. In "Brain Drain," exposition is provided by the sisters' nemesis, the Source (Peter Woodward), who takes on the form of her doctor in the asylum world, announcing to another character and thus to the viewers that he is using magic to enter her mind; visually, this exposition is supported by a cut from Piper in the asylum to Piper lying on an altar surrounded by crystals and candles, while the Source leans over her menacingly. Buffy first experiences her alternate world when a demon she is fighting stabs her in the arm with its sharp spine, an event followed by a cut to a cowering Buffy in hospital pajamas, being held down by orderlies who inject her; her friend Willow (Alyson Hannigan) later explains to her and to the audience that the demon is known for its hallucination-producing venom. "The Real World" opens on an asylum world and does not allow the viewers to enter the storyworld until more than halfway through the episode, when the camera zooms in for an extreme close-up on the sleeping Elizabeth in her room and zooms out on an unconscious Elizabeth lying on a scanning bed in Atlantis; the other characters then discuss the presence of Replicator nanites in her body, although they do not know exactly what the nanites are doing to her. The longtime viewer familiar with the storyworld of the *Stargate* universe, however, knows that one of the Replicators' tactics is to produce a dream state in which the victim experiences an alternate life, a tactic used on other members of the team in the preceding episode. While Clark is in the psychiatric hospital, he is informed by another patient who claims to be from Mars that an alien from the Phantom Zone has taken control of his mind, that "the entity will gain control of your body with all its powers" and that control will "allow the Phantom Zone to enslave mankind"; the audience familiar with the extended storyworld of superhero comics knows that this man is not just another patient suffering from his own delusions but is rather the first appearance of another superhero, the Martian Manhunter.

On the one hand, we encounter a paternal authority figure who rationally accounts for the deluded creation of an impossible world by a confused patient who is feeling troubled by a lack of control over his or her environment. On the other hand, we meet concerned friends, trusted by both character and longtime viewers, with explanations that seem irrational according to the premises of the real world but perfectly in keeping with a storyworld where encounters with vampires and aliens are everyday events. Who and what is the character to believe? If the friends are right, then they exist and so does the storyworld; the character is no longer powerless, true, but that power comes with the burden of fighting a long struggle against enemy forces. If the doctor is telling the truth, then the storyworld can be dismissed, and with it friends and enemies alike. In the asylum world lies the possibility of treatment and a return to a normal life, an escape from the burdens of power and destiny. Thus we can see that a key feature of this alternate world formula is the dramatization of the character's inner conflict, leading to the choice that restores both the character's commitment to the fight against evil and the storyworld's privileged position of narrative reality.

There would, of course, be no inner conflict if there were no question, if the characters were able to assert the reality of their storyworld and deny that of the asylum world. However, the character's faith is shaken by what seems to be incontrovertible evidence that the storyworld is a lie, that the kindly doctor is telling the truth. One key piece of evidence is the absence of other characters from the storyworld. Often, other regular characters who might be expected to appear in the asylum world are notably missing; in their place are the guest actor who plays the kindly doctor and, occasionally, infrequently recurring characters who are not normally part of the storyworld. In *Stargate Atlantis*'s "The Real World," for instance, the only storyworld character who appears in Elizabeth's asylum world is General Jack O'Neill (Richard Dean Anderson), who, though he is an essential element of the *Stargate* universe, is not a regular on the spin-off. The only storyworld characters who appear in Buffy's asylum world are her parents, yet in the storyworld, her father abandoned the family before the start of the series and her mother Joyce has recently died. When other regular characters are present, they tend to support rather than undermine the asylum world, appearing in other, more normal forms or confirming the rational explanation of insanity. Dr. Wykoff in *Star Trek: Deep Space Nine*'s "Shadows and Symbols" is played by the same actor who plays an enemy Cardassian military leader, and in the earlier "Far beyond the Stars," the episode that details the breakdown that sends Benjamin Sisko's alter ego Benny Russell into the institution, the regular and recurring actors on the show appear without their usual prosthetic makeup, playing employees and writers at the offices of *Incredible Tales* or the waitresses, baseball players, and cops who inhabit Benny's 1950s asylum world. In *Charmed*, Piper's sisters are also patients, sharing in her delusions; their nemesis the Source takes on the role of the kindly doctor advising her; and her husband is a doctor who wants her to accept treatment so that they can be together without breaking the ethical rules against patient and doctor involvement, reflecting the restrictions imposed on their relationship in the storyworld. And on *Smallville*, Clark escapes from the psychiatric hospital to return home, where he confronts his friends and family, all of whom inform him that he is indeed delusional. Some of their claims can be explained away as part of a plot against him: Lana (Kristin Kreuk), who tells him that they have been in love since childhood and will be together as soon as he is cured, is in the storyworld engaged to his enemy Lex Luthor (Michael Rosenberg). Clark's mother is supposedly married to Lex's father, and the pills she claims to be for her allergies might be drugs used to control her. But there is no way to explain away the obviously long-abandoned coffee shop or Lex's amputated legs. When Clark tries to assert that his asylum world is all a trick perpetrated by Lex, the wheelchair-bound man screams, "Open your eyes, you crazy son of a bitch! Does this look like a trick to you?!"

Further evidence that the asylum world may be real is the absence of the character's superpowers, the impossible, supernatural forces that are normally found in the storyworld. It is Buffy's slayer abilities, Clark's superpowers, Piper's witchcraft that mark their storyworlds as supernatural rather than natural, that distinguish them from the actual world inhabited by the viewer. Such powers are not an element of the actual world, and it is resemblance to the actual world that defines the possible world as natural in Dolezel's dyadic model. Although these powers are

The rest of *Smallville*'s cast gathers around principals Lana Lang (Kristin Kreuk), Clark Kent (Tom Welling), and Lex Luthor (Michael Rosenbaum).

normal for the character in the storyworld, their impossibility is acknowledged intradiagetically, as something special that sets the character apart from the rest of the world. Buffy, Clark, and Piper all keep their superhero identities secret from the world at large, and *Stargate Atlantis*'s Elizabeth, though she has no enhanced abilities of her own, commands an expedition that is kept secret from most of the world. In their asylum worlds, the secret knowledge that marks a special status in the storyworld becomes instead proof of insanity. If the character were able to exercise that power, it would prove that the alternate world is the delusion, but within the alternate world that power is not in evidence. Buffy, who normally has the physical strength and agility to fight entire gangs of vampires and demons, is easily overpowered by a couple of human orderlies. Piper's magic simply does not work; at one point, she escapes from the hospital into the street, where she chases a purse snatcher into the path of an oncoming car. Her attempt to use her freezing power to stop the car fails, and she wakes again in the institution, bearing the bruises and scrapes that serve as physical reminders of her lack of supernatural power. Clark Kent, the young Superman, not only cannot fly or see through walls or leap tall buildings in a single bound—although to be fair, he does not try to—but he also is no longer affected by kryptonite exposure. And when Elizabeth asks to contact General O'Neill, he seems puzzled by her claims of a secret government operation called Stargate Command and informs her that her work is to negotiate treaties involving nuclear proliferation.

The visual register typically provides more evidence that calls into question the reality of the storyworld that the character clings to. Special effects made possible by advances in technology are the normal tools of directors and editors working to create SFTV, allowing them to convey what the world might look like not only to those with supernatural abilities but also to those losing touch with reality or "seeing things." Thus Elizabeth's attempts to convince herself and her doctor that Atlantis is not a delusion are sabotaged by visual anomalies: as she speaks with General O'Neill, for instance, she is shaken when his head appears to wobble rapidly from side to side, although he is unaware of any such trauma. She sees a shadowy figure attempting to reach her through a wall that melts, and her reflection in her bathroom mirror has no face. At one point, she opens a closet door to find the blue puddle of the Stargate event horizon.[3] In "Far beyond the Stars," Benny Russell is disturbed by changes in the appearance of his fellow writers at the magazine; as he speaks with K. C. Hunter,[4] for instance, the woman in the 1950s-era dress suddenly sports a shorter hairstyle and the nose ridges that are a distinguishing feature of the Bajoran Kira Nerys (Nana Visitor). In addition to CGI and other special effects, odd camera angles, movements, and rapid cuts between scenes can also suggest disorientation. In one very effective scene, the camera cuts rapidly between Benjamin Sisko dancing with freighter captain Kasidy Yates in his quarters on the space station and Benny Russell dancing with waitress Cassie in his 1950s apartment; the dizzying movement of the camera around the dancing couples and the rapid cuts suggest the confusion of the two worlds. And, of course, simple dramatic technology like props and costuming can produce similar effects. Benjamin Sisko's entrance into the asylum world is marked when he sees a man in a baseball uniform walking through the space station, and Clark's insistence that the asylum world is a delusion shatters when the camera, acting as his eyes, pans quickly around the doctor's office to spot normal everyday objects bearing the names he knows from his storyworld: a nurse named Raya, a magazine titled *Phantom Zone*. Such evidence makes the doctor's explanation that he has constructed his hallucination from the bits and pieces of the real world entirely plausible.

Ultimately, it is their life stories, their narrative situations in the storyworld, that tempt the characters to surrender to the accumulation of evidence. SFTV, after all, is not about the mundane lives of ordinary people going about their daily business but about the actions of extraordinary people who often must sacrifice themselves for the greater good. The heroes of these stories bear the secret burden of keeping the world safe from disaster and, often, ignorant of its danger. How tempting, then, to be offered respite from the responsibility, to lay down the burden and live a normal life. Buffy may be the chosen one, but she is also a very young woman whose mother has recently died, leaving her alone to care for a teenage sister who didn't even exist until the year before. Slayer by night, burger flipper by day, a college dropout who has to balance paying the bills with saving the world, angry at her friends for dragging her out of heaven after a well-deserved end to her struggles, angry at herself for becoming sexually involved with the very kind of monster she is supposed to be slaying—is it any wonder that Buffy wants to go home with her parents? Piper has always been the sister most resistant to developing her magic powers; her older sister has recently died in the battle against the Source, and she is ready to give it all up to spend time with her nonmagic friends, to work as a chef, to have children with her husband. She's looking for "an opportunity to get out of the demon-fighting business." In "Labyrinth," Lana points out to Clark that if his hallucination of the storyworld is real, then in that world, not only does he not have her love, but he is also responsible for a lot of pain and tragedy. He can stop fighting, she tells him, and live a normal life: "Your destiny isn't to save the world, Clark. It's to be with me." Benjamin Sisko is also nearing the end of his rope, after years of commanding a space station during a time of war.[5]

Thus the asylum episode typically dramatizes the character's inner conflict, resolved only in the climax, when the character must finally choose whether to surrender to the asylum world and embrace the refuge it falsely offers or to reject a seemingly safe haven and return to the fight. Sometimes this choice is staged so as to evoke the character's position as torn between two worlds, placing the character between two sets of characters, each representing one of the worlds. Piper makes her final decision in a wheelchair in a hospital garden, her false doctors on one side, exhorting her to finish reading the "poem" that represents the spell to relinquish all her magic, and on the other side her sisters, who have used magic to transport into her asylum world, pleading with her to stop. In "The Real World," Elizabeth exits a hospital elevator to find herself in the winding tunnels of the Stargate Command; she is trapped in the middle of a hallway, with General O'Neill at one end reminding her that she is experiencing a hallucination, and at the other, Atlantis's military leader, John Sheppard (Joe Flanigan), who has found his way into her asylum world by breaching the quarantine barriers that protect everyone else from nanite infection. Sheppard tells her bluntly what is happening to her in the storyworld and encourages her to run to the Stargate and safety. The choice between different worlds might be even more clearly depicted by a visual blurring of the boundaries between them. For example, in "Normal Again," storyworld Buffy crouches under the stairs in her basement, where her friends are fighting for their lives against the demon she has unleashed against them, while asylum world Buffy crouches in a corner of her hospital room, urged by her mother and her doctor to kill off the imaginary friends who keep dragging her back every time she has a chance for recovery. Similarly, in "Shadows and Symbols," Benjamin Sisko, on a desert planet far from Earth, hesitates to open an alien object that could prove useful in their war when he has a vision that he is Benny Russell, scribbling his stories about Sisko on the walls of his hospital room while Dr. Wykoff urges him to paint over the words to symbolically erase his delusion. And sound can prove as useful as visuals to convey the breaking of barriers between storyworld and asylum world. Thus the constant irritating hum that plays in the background of every scene in "Labyrinth," occasionally rising to a crescendo of indeterminate noise, resolves into the growling and barking of Clark's dog, standing guard over him in his barn while one alien invades his mind and another tries to help him escape.

Obviously the flexi-narrative format of SFTV requires that the character choose to return to the fight, the real focus of the narrative arc. Heroes do not quit when the going gets tough, and Clark, Buffy, Piper, Elizabeth Weir, and Benjamin Sisko wouldn't be the heroes we have embraced if they surrendered more than briefly to their desire for a normal life. Proponents of theories regarding parallel universes—theories exposited by the characters in these television shows—argue that for every choice made, a new universe branches off. But in the actual world, bound and limited by human sensory perceptions, we experience only one world, in a linear progression from beginning to end. Storytelling is all about the road not taken, the cost of a decision, the impact of acting and reacting upon the characters, but we want a sense of closure, of lessons learned, a satisfying resolution to a plot. Life in the actual world may end with a whimper, with a quiet return to health and normalcy, but life in a storyworld has to end with a bang.

As for the extradiagetic viewer, exploring the narrative possibilities might be intriguing for a single episode, but that episode must ultimately advance the narrative arc, not end all arcs with no hope of a return to the familiar—and entertaining—storyworld. But what if the series were ending anyway? What if the asylum world formula were employed in the series finale? It is highly unlikely, especially in these days of cultural franchises, that any producer would adopt the Bob Newhart approach; "It was all a dream" might work for a sitcom, but not for a cult television program with the potential to generate spin-offs, comic books, fan fiction, and convention appearances. The alternate world must be proved a lie, the storyworld a reality, resolving the ontological tension experienced, at least to some extent, by the viewer. Usually this resolution is unambiguous, the privilege of the storyworld restored through extended tag scenes in which the characters discuss their experiences and confirm the explanation offered within the storyworld: alien influence, demon possession, a vision. "Brain Drain," for instance, spends the first third of the episode in the storyworld and offers a fairly long tag scene at the end. "Labyrinth" enters the asylum world within the first minute or so of the episode but ends with several scenes in which Clark speaks with the Martian Manhunter, with Chloe, and with Lana and Lex in the coffee shop, restored to its former glory. "The Real World" opens on the asylum world, but the penultimate scene shows Elizabeth walking through the Stargate as her doctor morphs into the Replicator who has invaded her mind. The final tag scene, a dialogue between Elizabeth and Sheppard, however, raises a few gentle questions, as Sheppard jokes that maybe now they are both infected.

More interesting, however, is the rarer occurrence, when a television show plays deliberately with an ambiguous resolution to these alternate world storylines. "Normal Again" ends not in the storyworld but in the asylum world, surrendering the power of the last word. The doctor shines a penlight into Buffy's unresponsive eyes and declares her lost in a permanent catatonic state, while her parents weep over her unmoving body. True, in the storyworld, she has not yet taken the antidote and thus could be experiencing another hallucination. But in her catatonic state, asylum world Buffy is "seen" rather than "seeing." The power of the final scene, especially in light of her earlier account, in which she confided to Willow that her parents had admitted her to a psychiatric hospital when she began seeing vampires, cannot but raise a few doubts for the viewer.[6] A similar ambiguity arises in the final scenes of "Far beyond the Stars." In the asylum world, Benny Russell suffers a nervous breakdown, screaming, "It exists in here, in my mind. I created it. It's real!" He is talking about his stories about a futuristic space station and a Negro commander named Sisko. Back on *Deep Space Nine*, Benjamin Sisko ponders his experience. "What if all of *this* is the illusion," he speculates. "Maybe Benny isn't the dream. Maybe we're nothing more than figments of *his* imagination." At these words he moves to see his reflection in the glass and sees, instead of his uniformed self against the backdrop of stars, an image of Benny Russell. This closing scene itself mirrors an earlier scene set in the asylum world, in which Benny, imagining the world of the story he is currently writing, looks into his apartment window and sees a uniformed Sisko against the city skyline. Who is the dreamer and who the dream?

Of course, the extradiagetic power of the storyworld, clearly confined within the box of the television set, generated by both the economics of production and the imaginations of its creators, will always guarantee its privileged position as the "real" world, no matter how writers and directors may play with the possibilities. It is unlikely that any SFTV series will be daring enough to extend the alethic dyadic model much further than it already has been. But such episodes continue to be produced and find fan favor, precisely because they comment so intriguingly on the conventions of storytelling and exploit the power of fantastic narratives to create worlds of imagination. "Dreams teach," the alien Shifu tells Daniel. And indeed, the impossible storyworlds of SFTV are dreams created by writers, directors, and actors that teach the viewing audience to question reality rather than blindly accept the voice of authority, to keep on fighting the good fight.

Notes

1. Possible worlds semantics has migrated from philosophical discussion to literary theory, notably in the work of Lubomír Dolezel and Marie-Laure Ryan. In *Heterocosmica: Fiction and Possible Worlds*, Dolezel describes a four-modal system of possible worlds semantics that generates the construction of narrative worlds: the alethic modalities, which govern the possibility or impossibility of fictional worlds; the axiological modalities, relating to the valuing of fictional elements as good or bad, desired or feared; the epistemic modalities, which concern knowledge and ignorance; and the deontic modalities, controlling what is prohibited or prescribed in fictional worlds. These systems can interact in various ways, including the dyadic contrast of opposing poles of any particular modality: the MirrorVerse of *Star Trek* or the WishVerse of *Buffy the Vampire Slayer*, for instance, is an axiological dyadic world, formed by the contrast between good and evil.

2. I have chosen the term "asylum world" for a couple of reasons: to name the imagined world after the physical place in which such episodes are often set and, more important, to evoke synonymically the concepts of refuge, haven, and sanctuary thematically central to the story lines of such episodes.

3. Not only is this visual special effect a signature image of the *Stargate* universe, but this particular scene is also a callback for fans of *Stargate SG-1*: in a fourth-season episode of the parent show, Daniel Jackson, under alien influence but believed to be suffering from paranoid schizophrenia caused by too much

'gate travel, is institutionalized after seeing a Stargate event horizon form in his bedroom closet.

4. The character is said to be modeled on D. C. Fontana, a writer for the original *Star Trek* series, and on pulp author C. L. Moore; all of the writers at *Incredible Tales* are based on well-known writers of golden age science fiction stories.

5. Elizabeth Weir does not face this kind of inner struggle for both intradiegetic and extradiagetic reasons. Although in the storyworld she commands the expedition, she is seldom on the front lines of battle. And, unlike the other series under discussion, *Stargate Atlantis*'s asylum episode aired at the beginning of the third season, rather than several years into its run.

6. Episode writer Diego Gutierrez and director Rick Rosenthal discuss the possibility on the DVD commentary, where they agree that they and series creator Joss Whedon did everything narratively and cinematically possible to enhance the ambiguity of the interpretation, desiring not to signal the privileging of one reality over the other.

Works Cited

"Absolute Power." *Stargate SG-1*. Written by Robert G. Cooper. Directed by Peter DeLuise. Showtime, January 19, 2001.

"Brain Drain." *Charmed*. Written by Curtis Kheel. Directed by John Behring. WB, November 8, 2001.

Dolezel, Lubomír. *Heterocosmica: Fiction and Possible Worlds*. Baltimore: Johns Hopkins University Press, 1998.

"Far beyond the Stars." *Star Trek: Deep Space Nine*. Written by Ira Steven Behr and Hans Beimler. Directed by Avery Brooks. UPN, February 11, 1998.

Gutierrez, Diego, and Rick Rosenthal. "'Normal Again': DVD Commentary." *Buffy the Vampire Slayer* season 6. DVD, 20th Century-Fox Home Entertainment, 2004.

Herman, David. "Storyworld." In *Routledge Encyclopedia of Narrative Theory*, edited by David Herman, Manfred Jahn, and Marie-Laure Ryan, 569–70. London: Routledge, 2005.

Johnson-Smith, Jan. *American Science Fiction TV: Star Trek, Stargate and Beyond*. Middletown, CT: Wesleyan University Press, 2005.

"Labyrinth." *Smallville*. Written by Al Septien and Turi Meyer. Directed by Whitney Ransick. CW, January 25, 2007.

Nelson, Robin. *TV Drama in Transition: Forms, Values, and Cultural Change*. Basingstoke: Macmillan, 1997.

"Normal Again." *Buffy the Vampire Slayer*. Written by Diego Gutierrez. Directed by Rick Rosenthal. UPN, March 12, 2002.

"The Real World." *Stargate Atlantis*. Written by Carl Binder. Directed by Paul Ziller. Sci-Fi Channel, August 18, 2006.

"Shadows and Symbols." *Star Trek: Deep Space Nine*. Written by Ira Steven Behr and Hans Beimler. Directed by Allan Kroeker. UPN, October 7, 1998.

FRAKING MACHINES

Desire, Gender, and the (Post)Human Condition in *Battlestar Galactica*

Susan A. George

> Cyborg imagery can suggest a way out of the maze of dualism in which we have explained our bodies and our tools to ourselves.
> —Donna Haraway, "A Manifesto for Cyborgs"

> Love is a strange and wonderful thing, Chief. You should be happy you experienced it at all, even if it was with a machine.
> —Gaius Baltar, *Battlestar Galactica*

The Sci-Fi Channel's updated, reenvisioned series *Battlestar Galactica* (2004–present) has generated considerable attention from both the popular press and media scholars, and for many reasons. First, it takes science fiction seriously and, as the popular press has noted, is heavily informed by the events of 9/11. In addition, unlike other successful Sci-Fi Channel programs, such as *Stargate SG-1*, that consistently show the worst bringing the best out in the human race, *Battlestar Galactica* consistently addresses hard human issues, such as drug and alcohol abuse in the military, the sacrifice of human lives to preserve a way of life, a technophobia that manifests itself as a new form of racism, and even the justifiable use of suicide bombings. As Admiral William Adama (Edward James Olmos) comments in the episode "Final Cut," it shows humanity, embodied in the crew of the *Galactica* and the fleet it guards, "warts and all."

Moreover, at no point does *Battlestar Galactica* offer pat answers or cleanly resolve its problems in sixty minutes. Quite to the contrary, as Adam Rogers notes: "There's no single political subtext. The show has all the subtexts at once." What the series says about identity, the feminine, masculinity, desire, and technology is consistently both ambiguous and—perhaps because of that very ambiguity—at times disturbing, as if the series were, in its own parlance, "fraking with" our heads. The two epigraphs opening this essay point to some of the tensions, concerns, and anxieties it evokes, particularly in relation to the human-looking Cylons, pejoratively called, as in Ridley Scott's acclaimed science fiction film *Blade Runner* (1982), "skin jobs." While on the surface these new Cylons fulfill some of the promise evident in Donna Haraway's vision of cyborg identity, the Cylons, especially the female models, also embody our culture's fear and love of technology, producing a conflicted vision that intersects in a central issue of contemporary science fiction narratives: our problematic attitude toward both gender and technology.

Practically since the invention of film and television technology, this troubled relationship has been the subject of much media science fiction. One of the hallmark efforts of early science fiction cinema, Fritz Lang's *Metropolis* (1927), visualized many of the industrial and scientific concerns troubling Western culture in the 1920s and brought them into focus through the figure of the robotic Maria. U.S. science fiction films produced during the height of the cold war, particularly efforts like *Attack of the 50 Ft. Woman* (1958), *She Demons* (1958), and *The Wasp Woman* (1959), frequently linked our technological advances in less than positive ways to woman and the power of female sexuality. And this same connection has been developed more recently in works like *Eve of Destruction* (1991), *Steel and Lace* (1991), and *Terminator 3* (2003). Another reason *Battlestar Galactica* has attracted so much attention is that it has brought this concern into mainstream science fiction television (SFTV), framing its discussion of technology by directly connecting it to the feminine and desire. To unravel the complex construction of gender and desire as embodied in the human-form Cylons on *Battlestar Galactica*, this essay looks at relations among the representation of technology, the female Cylons, the men who love them, and the "real" women in the series. The various stories, both progressive and residual, that emerge regarding gender and desire clearly reflect a contemporary world struggling to cope with the identity-transforming possibilities of technology in a world teetering on the brink of what some call a posthuman future.[1]

The key cast members of the new *Battlestar Galactica* gather around a Viper fighter. Clockwise from upper left: Starbuck (Katee Sackhoff), Captain Lee Adama (Jamie Bamber), *Galactica* Sharon (Grace Park), Caprica Six (Tricia Helfer), Gaius Baltar (James Callis), Admiral William Adama (Edward James Olmos), and President Laura Roslin (Mary McDonnell).

In *Technopoly: The Surrender of Culture to Technology*, Neil Postman reminds us that "technology, in sum, is both friend and enemy" (xii). While it typically "makes life easier, cleaner, and longer," it is also a friend that "asks for trust and obedience"; in fact, "there is a dark side to this friend. . . . The accusation can be made that the uncontrolled growth of technology destroys the vital sources of our humanity. It creates a culture without moral foundation," what Postman terms a "technopoly" (xii). Though Haraway and robotics researcher Hans Moravec see utopian possibilities in the merging of human and machine, the historical evidence repeatedly shows that new technologies generate fear and anxiety as well as excitement and hope.

This conflicted attitude quickly surfaces when the *Galactica* is being decommissioned. The secretary of education, Laura Roslin (Mary McDonnell), later to become the president of the colonies, suggests to Adama that the *Galactica*'s computer systems be networked and made more user friendly, since the ship is going to be a museum used for teaching purposes. The following exchange results:

> Adama: It is an integrated computer network and I will not have it aboard this ship.
>
> Roslin: I heard you're one of those people. You're actually afraid of computers.
>
> Adama: No, there are many computers on this ship, but they're not networked.
>
> Roslin: The computerized network would simply make it faster and easier for the teachers to be able to teach . . .
>
> Adama: (*interrupting*) Let me explain something to you. Many good men and women lost their lives aboard this ship because someone wanted a faster computer to make life easier. I'm sorry that I'm inconveniencing you or the teachers, but I will not allow a network-computerized system to be placed on this ship while I'm in command. Is that clear?

In the narrative logic of the miniseries, this exchange establishes why the *Galactica* looks so "antiquated to modern eyes," with "phones with cords, awkward manual valves, computers that barely deserve the name"; it hints at how the Cylons used human technology against their "masters" before; and it foreshadows the new Cylon attack. It also directly articulates the issues that Postman raises about technology's being both friend and enemy and the rise in technocracies that has resulted.

Postman observes, "In a technocracy, tools play a central role in the thought-world of the culture. Everything must give way, in some degree, to their development. . . . Tools are not integrated into the culture; they attack the culture. They bid to *become* the culture" (28). Before the Cylon war, the twelve colonies were technocracies, and one of those tools created to make life easier, the Cylon centurions, literally attacked the culture, playing out the worst-case scenario for the future of any technocracy. If, as Postman suggests, the United States is a technopoly in which "all forms of cultural life [submit] to the sovereignty of technique and technology" (52), then *Battlestar Galactica*'s stance regarding technology becomes a cautionary tale about our dependence on and acceptance of technology. In view of the bloody war already fought and the coming attack, the "antiquated" design of the *Galactica* is not just a postmodern nod to nostalgia and the earlier television series, and Adama's refusal to allow computerized networks on the ship is not just the raving of a technophobe. Instead, these elements are the series' response to the current cultural moment and the nation that is desperately trying to find a balance between two "world views—the technological and the traditional" (48).

Just as quickly, the series establishes a more complex connection between the dangers of technology and the feminine. The three main female Cylons of the first two seasons, the tall, blonde, usually scantily clad Caprica Six (Tricia Helfer) and both Caprica Sharon and *Galactica* Sharon (Grace Park) recall the various science fiction tales concerning synthetic women and their relations with men and to patriarchy. The observation Anne Balsamo has made about the nature of the cyborg woman ultimately proves true for female human-form Cylons: "These female-gendered cyborgs inhabit traditional feminine roles—as objects of man's desire and his helpmate in distress" (151).

The first such Cylon model introduced in the series is the Number Six. After the first human-Cylon war, we learn, "a remote space station was built where Cylon and human could meet and maintain diplomatic relations. Every year, the colonials send an officer. The Cylons send no one." The 2003 miniseries that launched the revamped *Battlestar Galactica* starts when the Cylons finally send a representative. The aging colonial officer seems bored and tired as he does his job, awaiting the Cylon representative that he figures will never come. Just as he begins to doze off, the unexpected happens. A long shot from the officer's point of view shows the two large metal doors of the chamber open and two centurions enter and come halfway down the chamber's ramp. A long shot shows them taking up positions on either side of the ramp. While shots of the inscrutable centurions' faces continue, showing their red visual sensors moving from side to side, the sound of heels on metal is heard. A shot from the knees down of human-looking legs in brown suede boots cuts to a long shot from the officer's point of view of Number Six in a form-fitting red suit. She moves around the desk to the officer's side, perches on the edge, and in close-up studies his face. Leaning forward, now only inches from his face, she asks, "Are you alive?" to which he replies in close-up, "Yes." The camera cuts back to a close-up of Number Six, who replies, "Prove it," as she starts to kiss him repeatedly. When the attack begins, the colonial officer tries to pull away from her, but she holds his head in her hands, saying, "It has begun," and then resumes kissing him as the scene shifts to the outside of the station now under attack.

From these opening moments, several things are quickly established. First, the series continues what Claudia Springer has described as "a misogynistic tradition, exemplified by *Metropolis*, of associating technology with women's bodies to represent the threat of unleashed female sexuality" (114). In Lang's dystopic vision of a world strictly divided between the haves, who live in idle luxury aboveground, and the have-nots, workers who toil and live belowground and keep the city running, a key figure is Maria. A good and kind daughter of a worker, her prophecies of a coming mediator give the workers hope that their suffering will soon end. When Joh Fredersen, the master of Metropolis, feels that his authority over both his son and the workers is threatened by Maria, he enlists the help of Rotwang, who sends an android in the form of Maria to incite the workers to rebellion. To make sure she can pass not only as human but as female, they take her to a club where she literally performs gender by dancing an erotic striptease for upper-class men, who are instantly enthralled. Once released upon the workers, the seductive female figure easily incites a revolt. The link between technology and the destructive power of female sexuality established by Lang's film, which has resurfaced powerfully in later science fiction, becomes especially prominent in *Battlestar Galactica*.

In several ways, Number Six's function is similar to that of android Maria. A Number Six is sent to seduce the womanizing Gaius Baltar (James Callis) so she can "poke around" in colonial navigation and defense systems. Through him she gains "access to the defense mainframe . . . communication frequencies, deployment schedules, [and] unlimited access to every database." Her expertise with and as technology allows her to build in back doors to disable the defenses of the colonies and, as Lieutenant Gaeta (Alessandro Juliani) explains, "to use [Baltar's] navigation program to disable [colonial] ships." Like Maria, then, she is thoroughly established as the quintessential double threat—as both technology and female sexuality run amok.

Throughout the series, the Number Sixes, especially Caprica Six, are hypersexualized both in action and dress. She is usually shown wearing

Cylon as sexual seductress: Caprica Six (Tricia Helfer).

extremely revealing, even see-through, clothing. In scenes highly unusual for SFTV, she is shown naked in a hot tub and in the brig, although most often she parades around the ship in heels and a red, form-fitting halter dress. As in the opening sequence detailed above, Number Sixes are often shown seducing or sexually toying with human men. On occupied Caprica, a Number Six catches Lieutenant Karl C. "Helo" Agathon, a member of the *Galactica* crew, and as in the opening sequence asks him if "he is alive" and then begins kissing him. Before the attack on Caprica, Caprica Six is shown touching, undressing, and having sex with Baltar. Even after the attack, she remains visible, though only to Baltar, and continues her seduction, deciding to initiate sex in the most awkward places, such as the command deck of the *Galactica*. Exactly how or why she appears to Baltar remains unclear. She may be a manifestation of his guilt for his part in the attack on Caprica, a hallucination, or even a religious vision. But whatever she is, she uses her sexuality to exert a powerful and negative impact on events and the remaining human population, as she repeatedly seduces Baltar into doing her bidding and betraying his fellow humans.

In addition to evoking other synthetic women such as Maria, Number Six functions as a technological version of film noir's femme fatale. Janey Place has observed that the iconography of the femme fatale "is explicitly sexual, and often explicitly violent as well" (44–45)—both features fundamental to Number Six. Like many other femmes fatales, she is blonde, has perfect makeup, and is often "characterized by her long lovely legs" (45). As Baltar puts it, she is "little more than [a] toaster with great looking legs." Number Six is also overtly sexual in her behavior and, when necessary, "explicitly violent." For example, the Six on occupied Caprica appears to take great pleasure in her physical strength, as her vicious and sadistic beatings of both Caprica Sharon and Starbuck (recast as a woman in the new series) demonstrate. Baltar's Caprica Six hallucination gives him pleasure, but she is not above using physical force to convince him to agree with her whenever necessary. In the episode "Litmus," after an unsuccessful Cylon bombing on board the *Galactica*, Baltar fears he has become their target. While walking down a corridor, he tells Six that he is going to destroy his Cylon detector so the Cylons will have no reason to kill him. She slams Baltar against the corridor wall face first, turns him around, pins him to the wall by his neck, and in close-up tells him—as she applies pressure—"No, you won't. You're going to complete the detector just as I told you." When he replies, "Or what?" she answers—quoting David Banner as the Hulk—"Don't make me angry, Gaius. You wouldn't like me when I'm angry." Then she kisses him, reinforcing the mix of sadism and eroticism so characteristic of the femme fatale. However, she has no need for the femme fatale's key "iconography of violence (primarily guns)" that is a "specific symbol . . . of her 'unnatural' phallic power" (Place 45); her stronger, better body is itself a formidable weapon and symbol enough.

I should note there is a significant postmodern—even posthuman—twist to Number Six's revisioning of the femme fatale. Place notes, "The ideological operation of the myth (the absolute necessity of controlling the strong, sexual woman) is . . . achieved by first demonstrating her dangerous power and its frightening results, then destroying it" (45). This is not the case with Number Six. Because of her technological construction, she cannot die or be easily contained; even if her current body is destroyed, she will simply "wake up somewhere else in an identical body"—with her consciousness, her body, and the threat they represent intact. Therefore, the relative state of equilibrium and reestablishment of patriarchal order achieved at the end of most film noir with the death or imprisonment of the disruptive female never occurs in *Battlestar Galactica*, offering a far more complicated and challenging image of the strong and sexual woman.

Although *Galactica* Sharon is not sexualized to the extent Number Six is, she is also an object of desire and one that breaks rules, putting her lover, Chief Tyrol (Aaron Douglas), repeatedly at risk. Their romantic and sexual relationship is itself a violation of the colonial code of military conduct. When she starts having "blackouts" and when missing items such as G-4 detonators end up in her possession, she goes to Tyrol for help. Their clandestine meeting in "Litmus" almost leads to his complete ruin. After the bombing incident, Adama asks the master of arms, Sergeant Hadrian, to investigate how anyone could get aboard the ship undetected. During the tribunal Hadrian convenes, Tyrol's loyal crewmembers offer various alibis to conceal his secret rendezvous with Sharon at the time a Cylon agent was accessing a nearby weapons locker. When it looks as if Tyrol nevertheless will be accused of "aiding and abetting the crime through conspiracy and collusion with the Cylons," a junior crewmember takes the blame, even though he is stripped of his rank and sent to the brig. Moved by guilt, Tyrol ends the affair, his comments to *Galactica* Sharon echoing those of many victims of traditional femmes fatales: "I put everything on the line for you. I cover for you. I protect you. I risk my career, my freedom, my integrity."

Although Tyrol is not completely destroyed as the men in noir frequently are, his reputation and position aboard the *Galactica* are adversely affected. And though she is certainly not the archetypal femme fatale that Number Six is in terms of dress and sexual aggressiveness, *Galactica* Sharon remains a disruptive and destructive feminine force who seemingly cares little about what happens to others. She is also presented as dangerous, as big a threat as Number Six to male authority and the hierarchical command order of the *Galactica*. This threat is made most explicit in the episode "Kobol's Last Gleaming, Part 2." While on a mission, *Galactica* Sharon literally comes face-to-face with her Cylon identity when she encounters multiple copies of herself. After successfully completing her mission and returning to *Galactica*, she attempts to assassinate Adama, throwing the ship into a crisis as the alcoholic Colonel Tigh (Michael Hogan) is pressed into the command role.

The Caprica version of Sharon also starts out as a deceiver whose mission is to become pregnant by seducing Helo, who has been stranded on occupied Caprica. Although she manages to seduce him, she also falls in love with him. Consequently, the Cylon plan to push them together becomes more than a plot as Caprica Sharon turns away from the Cylons and starts working to protect herself, Helo, and their unborn child. In the two-part episode "Home" she helps President Roslin and her group find the Tomb of Athena and destroys centurions in a firefight to protect the humans. In season two's "Flight of the Phoenix," while she is a prisoner on *Galactica*, her actions save the ship. Earlier, in "Scattered," when Adama is in critical condition, Tigh allows Gaeta to network the ship's computers, and the Cylons take the opportunity to plant a "logic bomb" in its system. To combat this subversion, Sharon deploys her bionic construction to purge the ship of the Cylon virus. After cutting her hand, Sharon pushes the fiber optic comlink that will allow her to "broadcast to all frequencies and have direct contact with the mainframe" up into her arm. As the *Galactica*'s systems come back online, Sharon, as planned, sends a virus back to the Cylon Raiders, disabling them and leaving them easy prey for the colonial Vipers, whose pilots hoot and holler about payback and destroying "toasters." Sharon has no obligation to help, the process clearly causes her physical pain, and in assisting the humans she betrays her own kind, yet she gains no gratitude from the humans. Adama looks at her and orders "the thing" be taken "back to its cell."

By the series' third season, Sharon has been integrated into the crew. However, she is still not completely trusted. Her allegiance is repeatedly questioned by all but Helo, to whom she is now married, and she remains acutely aware that she must constantly prove herself to her new human community. Where her allegiance will lie now that she knows that Roslin and Dr. Cottle lied when they told her that her child, Hera, had died, will ultimately define her role in the series. In this season, though, she seems to have become an exemplary helpmate, not only to her man but to the human race in its distress. So, like the female-gendered cyborgs discussed by Balsamo, Sharon seems to gradually shift valence, eventually settling into a traditional representation of the feminine, even if at a great cost.

While these female Cylons might suggest a return to stereotypes, they also reveal some interesting things about masculinity in the *Battlestar Galactica* universe. All of the men who love or have sex with synthetic women in the series are younger, of a different generation than Adama and Tigh, and far less suspicious of technology. This point is made most evident in "Six Degrees of Separation" when "Shelley Godfrey," actually a Number Six, comes to the *Galactica* and implicates Baltar in the attack on Caprica. While having a drink in Adama's quarters, she tries to work her erotic magic on him. The scene is shot almost entirely in close-up with low-key lighting. Putting her head on his shoulder and sobbing, she tells him, "There are times I feel so alone now." While Adama keeps his head forward, she puts her face close to his and adds, "Times when I just want so much to be held again." She continues, "There must be times when you feel alone, when the thought of another body next to yours seems like something out of a dream." When she moves in and kisses him, he does not respond in any way; he only gives her a curious look as he gets up. The scene cuts to him telling Tigh, "Do not under any circumstances allow Shelley Godfrey to leave this ship. Put her under surveillance discreetly."

Perhaps what makes him suspicious is that her attempted seduction is too good. Repeatedly, humans in the series note that the Cylons have a way of "fraking with your head," and her comments may have been a little too close to the mark. In any case, Adama is not seduced into fraking this machine. Although he has no way of knowing for certain she is a Cylon, he rejects her advances and tries to contain "a robot shaped like a woman" that "represents technology's simultaneous allure and powerful threat" (Springer 56) by putting her under surveillance. As with his refusal to network the computer systems on the *Galactica*, Adama combats "fears of overpowering technology" (56) by trying to contain it or to make it serve the needs of the fleet, not allow it to use the fleet for its own purposes.

In contrast to Adama, both Baltar and Chief Tyrol are technophiles who, as Postman offers, "gaze on technology as a lover does on his beloved, seeing it as without blemish and entertaining no apprehension for the future" (5). Early in the miniseries, an interviewer describes Baltar as a "media cult figure currently working as a top consultant at the ministry of defense on computer issues" and notes that he has "controversial views on advancing computer technology." In response, Baltar summarizes his views: "The ban on research and development into artificial intelligence is, as we all know, a holdover from the Cylon wars. Quite frankly, I find this to be an outmoded concept. It serves no useful purpose except to impede our efforts . . ." Six enters, and as his voice trails off, the scene cuts to Baltar and Six against the wall, passionately kissing and undressing each other on their way to the bedroom. This cut underscores his love for and interest in artificial intelligence, shows his mind-set as predisposed to the good offered by technology, and literally embodies his seduction by its—her—charms. Thus, although he acts shocked when he finds out he has been sleeping with a Cylon for two years, he quickly and easily recovers, subsequently showing no compunctions about having virtual sex with her and actual sex with another Caprica Six during season three.

As chief engineer, Chief Tyrol is naturally fond of technology as well, and an assortment of scenes show him working on, designing, and caressing various ships in the bay. In one very telling scene, the chief is alone examining a damaged Viper. Various close-ups show him running his hand along the body of the ship, crosscut with a similar series showing him caressing *Galactica* Sharon. One close-up of his hand running down the length of the ship match cuts to his hand moving down Sharon's arm. The crosscutting continues until he realizes that the Viper is beyond repair, and he slaps an "unserviceable scrap" sticker on the cockpit glass. Significantly, this episode is the one in which he tells Sharon that their affair is over. Upon discovering that she is a Cylon, he is far more disturbed than Baltar, although later, when one of his crew "kills" that copy, he goes to her and she dies in his arms, revealing his lingering tenderness for this "fraking machine."

Both Baltar and Tyrol are men in love with technology more literally than they think, and for both it makes sense. It has been forty years since the Cylon war, and Tyrol and Baltar have come to maturity in a different time, when the bias against technology seems outmoded and unnecessary. Tyrol's love of machinery clearly echoes the traditional notion of the American male's love for muscle cars. Baltar believes that lifting the research ban would enhance his professional career and "cult status." Helo is not as directly linked to technology as Baltar and Tyrol; he tries to kill Caprica Sharon when he discovers she is a Cylon, though he eventually manages to adjust and to accept Sharon and the love he feels for her. A large part of his acceptance has to do with their child, but he also seems to be able to judge her on the basis of her actions, not her construction—just as, the narrative suggests, we may eventually come to do with the technological components of our own world.

The men's reactions to the female Cylons, then, suggest several things. First, they underscore the familiarity of, reliance upon, and acceptance of the technological that pervades postmodern culture. Technology has become ubiquitous, and, as Postman notes, people want to love and trust it. For not only is technology everywhere, but people believe that it makes their lives better and that, almost like some loved one, they cannot live without it. Devices such as personal computers, cell phones, and PDAs have become so commonplace it is considered odd not to have them. In true technopoly fashion, people have become so accepting of the technology around them that they no longer question or think about it. Within this framework the generational divide between the men who love and those who reject Cylon women is not surprising; it parallels a divide evident in our culture. The young, it seems to suggest, are far more willing to accept new technologies and ways of thinking—or are simply more easily seduced by its lures. The series pointedly leaves open both possibilities.

Second, if "we are all cyborgs," as Haraway claims (50), and still sexual beings who desire each other, then is it such a stretch to think that humans would desire synthetic lovers? Helo's desire and love for Caprica Sharon suggest it is at least possible. The rise in digital sex and cybersex Web sites like Throbnet and Sleazenet prove that technology, in this case computers, has "seduced some users away from face-to-face romantic interactions altogether" (Springer 54–55). Mark Dery calls this phenomenon "mechano-eroticism," observing that "the only thing better than making love *like* a machine, it seems, is making love *with* a machine" (quoted in Springer 55). For Helo this desire becomes a reality, and one presented as not entirely negative. Helo and Caprica Sharon have apparently found common ground; they acknowledge their love and even reproduce, ensuring the survival of both human and Cylon in a new hybrid form that may be better suited for the future than either human or Cylon.

However, because of their histories and belief systems, neither the human nor the Cylon culture is able or willing to face the future suggested by Helo, Sharon, and their child. Through the men who accept and those who reject machines, the series shows technology as "both friend and enemy," with all the ambivalence that the issue raises in contemporary U.S. culture. For Adama, the domesticated technology of the *Galactica*, with its "antiquated" phones and computers, is familiar and safe, while the Cylons represent uncontained technology that threatens military order, patriarchy, and, most important, human survival. For Helo, as for Haraway, embracing Cylon technology, with its ability to bridge the gap between human and nonhuman, may be a positive step, rendering obsolete Western culture's long history of dualist thinking, which has formed an indelible line between us/good and other/bad and fostered a history of violence and intolerance. In this way the series stages the hopes and excitement as well as the fears and anxieties that are bound up in these new and unpredictable technologies.

And yet the humans have very good reason to distrust the Cylons, who want to eliminate the human race or at least reduce it to a "manageable" size. Although the human-form Cylons briefly discuss trying to peacefully coexist with humans when they occupy New Caprica in season three, such accommodation has never been part of their plan. Even in a possibly hybrid future, the role of biological men and women seems little more than that of reproduction. Though Helo and Sharon's relationship has unexpectedly become something more, it is important to remember that it started out as a Cylon experiment, with Helo as the lab rat. The Cylons had been unsuccessful in their attempts to reproduce biologically; thinking the missing piece might be love, they put into motion the scheme to make Helo fall in love with Sharon.

A far more disturbing and darker vision of reproduction in the post-human future appears in the episode "The Farm." After finding the Arrow of Apollo on Caprica, Starbuck (Katee Sackhoff) and Helo encounter a resistance movement. While on maneuvers with them, Starbuck is wounded; she wakes up in a hospital, where a Dr. Simon does a pelvic exam and tells her she has a cyst on one of her ovaries that he needs to keep an eye on. He then tells her, "We got to keep the reproductive system in great shape. It's your most valuable asset these days. . . . Finding healthy, childbearing women your age is a top priority of the resistance and you will be happy to know that you are a very precious commodity to us." Though Starbuck notes she is "not a commodity" but a "Viper pilot," he insists that having children is her "most valuable skill right now." Starbuck eventually discovers that Simon is a Cylon and that the "hospital" is a Cylon reproduction lab filled with women in beds, legs up as if in gynecological stirrups, with a variety of devices, tubes, and sensors attached to them. Horrified, she recognizes one of the women and tries to detach her, but the woman surprisingly begs her to cut the power, even though it will kill them all: "Cut the power. Can't live like this. We're baby machines." And Starbuck, sobbing, complies.

Of course, Simon did not lie; Starbuck and the rest of the women in the hospital are indeed valuable assets, both to the resistance and to the Cylons. The future for Starbuck and the rest of the fertile women left on occupied Caprica—and presumably on a larger scale if the Cylons have their way—is, by comparison to the planned exploitation of Helo as a baby-making machine, much more gruesome and oppressive. There is no illusion of love, no autonomy, only pain and involuntary reproduction here. The human women simply become another part of the machine, if a biological one. In the Cylons' posthuman future, women on a large scale are completely oppressed, reduced simply to wombs, sustaining "the ideology of woman-as-fetal-incubator" long promoted by Western science and culture (Bordo 81).

While the Cylons offer some appealing advantages—strength, instant information transfer, virtual immortality, and even the lure of eternal youth—they are not simply "a creation in a postgender world," as Haraway might hope (51), but, as the Number Sixes and Sharons prove, are distinctly gendered. They are not so much without an "origin story in the Western sense" (Haraway 51) as they are bound by it. As with other issues the series raises, there are no simple answers. What *Battlestar Galactica* offers on all fronts is a grim vision of humanity struggling, as Howard P. Segal puts it, "to live sanely and humanely in [a] pervasively technological society" (9). At times the humans succeed, at others they fail, while in their ambiguous representations the Cylons invariably frake with their heads. But what both humans and Cylons dramatize is the difficult negotiations required to remain human in a universe that is, apparently, moving toward a posthuman condition. As both Postman and Segal would argue, the world of *Battlestar Galactica* is not so removed from our own, and the battle that both its humans and Cylons fight is disturbingly similar to the one facing contemporary culture.

Note

1. For my purposes here, "posthuman" primarily denotes a time when humans will have undergone such radical changes through genetics, physical merging with technology, and so forth that the classification *Homo sapiens* will no longer apply. These new sentient beings, the posthuman, would, most theorists believe, exceed human capabilities and possibilities, becoming a new apex on the evolutionary scale. For more on this subject, see N. Katherine Hayles's *How We Became Posthuman*.

Works Cited

Balsamo, Anne. "Reading Cyborgs Writing Feminism." In Kirkup et al., 148–58.

Bordo, Susan. "Are Mothers Persons? Reproductive Rights and the Politics of Subject-ivity." In *Unbearable Weight: Feminism, Western Culture and the Body*, 71–97. Berkeley: University of California Press, 1993.

Haraway, Donna J. "A Manifesto for Cyborgs: Science, Technology, and Socialist Feminism in the 1980s." In Kirkup et al., 50–57.

Hayles, N. Katherine. *How We Became Posthuman: Virtual Bodies in Cybernetics, Literature, and Informatics.* Chicago: University of Chicago Press, 1999.

Kirkup, Gill, Linda Janes, Kath Woodward, and Fiona Hovenden, eds. *The Gendered Cyborg: A Reader.* New York: Routledge, 2000.

Moravec, Hans. "The Age of Robots." Field Robotics Center, Robotics Institute, Carnegie Mellon University. June 1993. http://www.frc.ri.cmu.edu/~hpm/project.archive/general.articles/1993/Robot93.html.

Place, Janey. "Women in Film Noir." In *Women in Film Noir*, edited by E. Ann Kaplan, 35–67. London: BFI, 1980.

Postman, Neil. *Technopoly: The Surrender of Culture to Technology.* New York: Knopf, 1992.

Rogers, Adam. "Captain's Log: Want to Understand *Battlestar Galactica*? Eavesdrop on Its Writers." *Slate*, November 29, 2006. http://www.slate.com/id/2154625.

Segal, Howard P. *Future Imperfect: The Mixed Blessings of Technology in America.* Amherst: University of Massachusetts Press, 1994.

Springer, Claudia. *Electronic Eros: Bodies and Desire in the Postindustrial Age.* Austin: University of Texas Press, 1996.

SPACE VEHICLES AND TRAVELING COMPANIONS

Rockets and Living Ships

Samantha Holloway

Humans explore. It's what we're good at. When modern humans appeared on the planet, their skill at finding new places and surviving the journey made population of the globe possible. Once we had mapped and inhabited the globe, we began to feel that we needed new space—and what could be more tempting to this human urge to travel, to discover, to conquer than a new planet, a new solar system, or even a whole new galaxy?

To go places faster, we domesticated horses—and then replaced them with cars. Airplanes soon became pervasive because they could go places cars could not, places without connecting roads. But the next logical need was for something to take us completely elsewhere—to other planets—and do it quickly. And what better place to showcase this technology's development than through another device for near instantaneous transportation: the television.

Enter the Spaceship

To look in more detail at how we have addressed this need, I want to begin with a definition. A spaceship is any self-contained, self-propelled vehicle that can travel interstellar distances. It is a broad definition but useful for launching this discussion. Because of its broadness, it allows us to look at the great variety of ships and conveyances of science fiction television (SFTV) to compare them and see how they have changed from simple rockets to more innovative forms—ships that interact with their crews like humans, even living ships. In constructing such ships, television has allowed us to visualize our very human urge to travel out into space and the future, and through that to show us a variety of possible consequences: we could explore space in huge starships, we could wind up stranded in space by our own creations, we could live peacefully in space on borrowed technology, we could find ourselves interacting, like equals, with fully living ships. We might well think of SFTV's various representations of the starship as themselves different screens on which we have projected for cultural contemplation these and other possible scenarios of our human destiny.

The idea of a spaceship is not new. In his 1865 novel *From the Earth to the Moon*, Jules Verne envisioned one, a bulletlike contraption with space for a few passengers who would not mind being shot from a giant cannon and crashing into the surface of the moon. Though not self-powered, as per our definition, it is self-contained enough to be a step along the path that leads to the starships that flash across our screens today. Before television, the image of the spaceship appeared in film adaptations of Verne's novel, in various other science fiction movies, and in the film serials that imprinted the idea on an entire generation who grew up watching them. The spaceship was a way to get off Earth and onto other worlds, and it was a seed that helped generate the explosion of science fiction literature and, eventually, that of SFTV as well.

However, the spaceship only really took off—pardon the pun—when that other vehicle for travel, television, entered the home. Here was a visual medium that anyone could see, that children could grow up watching every morning and evening, that families could bond around while seemingly traveling anywhere. And true to their nature as vehicles for exploring the unknown, spaceships moved here too, both in cinematic serials, shrunk down for home viewing, and in new shows born for television and its "passengers," such as space operas like *Captain Video and His Video Rangers* and *Space Patrol*. Television became popular because postwar America was rich enough to afford it—and the dreams it envisioned—but the political environment in which we watched was full of fear, thanks to the cold war climate of Communist paranoia.

However, spaceships could transport us away from the troubles of home to a place where enemies were easily recognized and easily defeated, a place where American ingenuity and resolute hometown values always stopped the foreign-looking villains before they could take over Earth. The spaceship provided both a thrill and a comfort in a period of stress and possible doom. The ships of these early shows were direct ideological descendents of the rockets that had starred in the previous decade's war: V-2s, tall, sleek, phallic, the cutting edge of rocket science, and, of all the vehicles known at the time, perhaps the most likely to get a man away from here, into space. In the early years of television, spaceships were almost always like them—sleek, silver, involving vertical liftoffs and fire shooting out of the engines far below the cockpit. Although they were often modified from the rockets everyone knew from World War II—by an added tail fin, perhaps, or a pair of short wings—they were still essentially rockets. Thus in *Rocky Jones, Space Ranger*, although Rocky's (Richard Crane) ship is called the *Orbit Jet*, it is not, in fact, a jet. Jets propel themselves by compressing and directing air or exhaust, but in space, where there is no air, there can be no jets. The orbit jet is just a rocket, like those used by Germany to deliver bombs and those the Russians would soon use to send dogs and satellites into orbit and fear into American homes.

The *Orbit Jet* from
Rocky Jones, Space Ranger.

Rockets are fairly simple and entirely mechanical—mainly controlled explosions and a payload of some kind. Kids in the 1950s built them for science projects. The rocket ships of early SFTV were equally simple in idea if not in depiction: they were typically cylinders with a rocket engine and a nose cone, built for vertical liftoff from a support structure of some kind, though these had habitable cockpits and impressive weaponry and lacked the breakaway segments of many larger rockets. The *Orbit Jet* is one of these extrapolated rockets, a logical next step from the ones already in production at the time. It is little more than a vehicle; though Rocky and Winky can fight in it, its main purpose is to get them from one place to another. Similar vehicles are central to *Space Patrol*, *Captain Video*, *Tom Corbett, Space Cadet*, and other early series wherein a man flies to rescue beautiful women and save Earth from enemies who are not so different from those of the United States at the time. These simple ships were a plot device more than anything, a way to get the hero from one place to another, occasionally to be stolen and recovered, but nothing to live in or to speak to. They were not characters.

Living in Space

After President Kennedy decided to make space travel a reality in the 1960s, we started moving into space, just as we had been on television for more than a decade. Because of advances in rocket science and the birth of computers smaller than warehouses, man could live and work in outer space, free of the surface of the planet but not free from competition, as cold war enemies still strove against each other. Cooperation among nations wouldn't come until later, but the ideal of intergalactic peace was already there; *Star Trek*'s Kirk (William Shatner) had an immensely diverse crew, including a Russian man, a Japanese man, an African American woman, and even a half-human alien, the ultimate blending of two worlds. The *Enterprise* proved a new kind of ship, a home as well as a vehicle. Built for long missions, she was, unlike her rockety forebears, more than just a way to get from one place to another—she was a place in and of herself and a first step to personification.

Of course, while largely computer controlled, *Enterprise* was not self-aware. The idea of an artificial intelligence hadn't yet pervaded

The Robinson family's *Jupiter 2* spacecraft from *Lost in Space*.

popular culture and was still a theory in the laboratories, where no one had yet challenged what it meant to be sentient.[1] However, in a new twist, the shipboard computer allowed the *Enterprise* to be spoken to and to respond like a human, even if in stilted approximation, bringing spaceships as a whole one step closer to independent life. But she was meant specifically to enable the exploration and expansion humans had evolved for—in a time of lingering stress and social unrest, the *Enterprise* showed us how to work with our enemies and return to the things that humans do best: finding new places and making them our own.

After the 1970s' dearth of space-based science fiction, in the 1980s the space opera again became a prominent science fiction form, and that reappearance inevitably brought a new diversity in spaceships. The decade saw the demise of rocket-based space travel in the real world and the rise of the space shuttle—so the ships portrayed in SFTV began to take on shapes resembling the shuttle. They became space planes, flown like fighter jets or cargo liners. It is an influence we can easily see in a

Blake's renegade ship *The Liberator* from the BBC production *Blake's 7*.

show like *Buck Rogers in the 25th Century*, an updating of the comic strip and serial plot of a modern man frozen in space and recovered in the far future. This Buck (Gil Gerard) is a smirking, irreverent, testosterone-laden man who brings the natural fight and wit of the 1980s present into a much calmer and balanced future that badly needs his help to defeat space pirates and world conquerors. Although Buck doesn't join the military, he works with the crew of the *Searcher* to teach them fighting skills. While in spirit the show is very much a throwback to the serials, it tackles issues of the 1980s like environmental collapse and world-spanning warfare, nuclear holocaust and chemical weapons, all interspersed with Buck's saving beautiful women and flying his ship like a jet. The ships of this series are either personal-sized fighters or the massive military city ships that house them (a pattern also seen in the original *Battlestar Galactica* series[2]), though most of the action centers on the small fighters. They are sleek, sharp vehicles with the performance characteristics of fighters, and they have the ability to jump past light speed to avoid the long flight between planets and keep the pacing of the series from lagging whenever they go from one solar system to another. And the aliens and pirates have different-looking ships, each designed to suit their own aesthetics and needs, differentiating them from the good guys as only design can. However, these ships are still just conveyances, if rather flashy ones, and the only AI is that of robots, which are everywhere.

The end of the 1980s brought us *Star Trek: The Next Generation*, the first and arguably most successful of the many spin-offs from the original 1960s series. *The Next Generation*'s *Enterprise*-D was the fleet's flagship, the top of the line of ships produced in the timeframe of the show. It was more than three times the size of the original *Enterprise*, was much roomier, and added the concept of a detachable saucer section to the basic shape of its predecessor, a special effect used many times in the first two seasons but almost forgotten in the subsequent five. This ability to decouple the saucer section emphasized the basic flying saucer–ness—and alien kinship—of the ship's design and effectively made two ships of one, allowing the fleet's most advanced and powerful ship to become almost a small fleet in itself when its shuttlecraft were also in flight.

Appropriate to its new capacities, the *Enterprise*-D was given an expanded, ongoing mission, as opposed to the original's five-year mission, that required the ship itself to become more of a home. Thus many crewmembers brought their families with them, and the quarters were more spacious and apartmentlike. In effect, the *Enterprise*-D is a small city in flight, complete with a saloon of sorts; recreational facilities, including the often malfunctioning holodeck that, rather like television itself, can take you anywhere you wish to be; and several specific labs to tackle any problem the ship encounters as it seeks new life and new civilizations. It is a shining example (literally shining in the opening sequence, silvery white against the blackness of space) of how well-adjusted and emotionally sophisticated humans can work together to advance the species as a whole and continue our species-wide drive to find new places. Like its 1960s predecessor, it was meant to convey Gene Roddenberry's hopes for a better future, one in which humanity is united as a species, but it is also a warship, having powerful weapons that are used whenever the crew's safety is at stake. In fact, the *Enterprise* uses her weapons often enough that her claim to be on a peaceful mission sometimes seems suspect. The *Enterprise* collects data, runs experiments, and contacts new alien species and civilizations, but it also fights old enemies and new, both in defense and in offense, and when diplomacy fails, it is almost always the stronger force, blasting its way out of dangerous situations just as wild and irresponsible Buck Rogers and Flash Gordon do. The reason is simple: even a projection of an ideal future also reflects the present, a rather violent and forceful present that fought its way through the Gulf War and survived the fallout from the fall of the iron curtain and communism. So while *The Next Generation* attempts to show us what we can be, it also shows us what we were at the time it aired, what we still are today, and the streamlined new *Enterprise* takes special prominence since it is the screen on which we are shown.

Though the *Enterprise*-D is not inherently alive, it is obviously more advanced than its predecessors and more interactive than any ship portrayed on television up to that point. The crew does encounter a living ship on more than one occasion, most notably in the third-season episode "Evolution," when a nanomachine virus infects the *Enterprise* itself rather than the more commonly infected crew, and its side effects are a new intelligence in the ship's own systems—one that interferes with the crew's ability to live comfortably and effectively on their ship. We then learn that the *Enterprise* has biological components behind her sleek, metal-paneled walls, and this is how the virus has infected her. However, the series never mentions these aspects of the ship again, nor are they investigated further, and as the new intelligence is expunged with the infection, the ship is restored and reset to its starting status, leaving behind the intriguing notion of a living ship. The *Enterprise* is not alive, despite all its updates of earlier models' technologies and its new ideas and purposes, and it must stay nonliving for the show and the crew to continue as they were meant to be. Several episodes each season deal with the concept of a living ship, since the idea is an interesting plot device and speaks to the public awareness of advances in computer technology and the real possibility of artificial intelligence. However, it was apparently considered not suitable for a setting—it remains external to the show and the ship that stands at its center.

New Ships, New Possibilities

By the 1990s, the concept of a spaceship had become far more sophisticated, and the ships themselves began to take on new characteristics. *Babylon 5*, for example, introduces a veritable cornucopia of ships, since the setting is a space station where beings from all over the galaxy stop off on their travels. Almost all of the ships we see are more advanced than the human ships: those of the Minbari are sleek and clean; those of the Centauri rich, decadent, and oddly Napoleonic; those of the Narn built for fighting and warfare. The most unusual are the Shadow Raiders. Barely seen through much of the series' five-year run, these ships are more alien than any of the others—insect- or spiderlike, as much biological as mechanical. The Shadows are treated as the ultimate unknowable enemy, and the biological character of their ships is just one more indication that they are different, truly alien, aberrant.

This same emphasis on ship diversity also shows up in *Star Trek* spin-offs such as *Deep Space Nine* and *Voyager*, where the great variety of alien ships reflects the variety of the universe. Among these diverse types we might note (in addition to the human-built Federation ships) the Romulan Bird of Prey, shaped as its name implies; the Klingon war cruisers; and the Cardassian battleships. However, the chief innovation in the concept of the starship shows up in the Borg ships. They are not at all aerodynamic, for they have no need to travel through air, as the others often do, and they are entirely functional, existing only to further the Borg missions of destroying and assimilating. There are no creature comforts on a Borg ship, since the Borg are simply parts of the ships and parts do not need special accommodations. The only species the Borg have been unable to assimilate is Species 8472, beings whose technology is entirely biological—including the most biological ships encountered in any of the *Star Trek* spin-offs—who are immune to Borg technological nanoprobes and are thus irreversibly alien.

The birth of *Andromeda* in 2000, only a year before the end of *Voyager,* envisioned a new possibility for interaction with the *Andromeda Ascendant.* It was a top-of-the-line starship when built but is three hundred years out of date when the pilot episode finds it caught in a black hole's event horizon, and it is salvaged after everything it knows and stands for has fallen. *Andromeda* includes an AI, a holographic interface that can project itself anywhere on the ship, and an android body to allow that consciousness both to leave the ship and to experience life somewhat as a human does, interacting with the crew more efficiently and with more understanding. Although she is fully intelligent, the intelligence is entirely artificial. The ship itself is a warship with no claims to be anything else, but she is also an antique, an old hero trying her best to restore order to the universe. The show treats this mission as a noble one, but it is always an uphill and perhaps impossible battle: time cannot be reset; things change. Even a rebuilt empire will be different, as the ship and her crew learn when, in the third season, the fragments of the new order prove to be flawed. But most important, she reflects the impulse to put things right, to restore ancient values while proving that change is inevitable. In our species' need to move outward, the *Andromeda Ascendant* suggests, we also tend to look back, try to fix previous misdeeds, remake things once made wrong. In these respects she effectively reflects the complex dimensions of our human nature.

More recently, *Stargate SG-1* has also introduced a great variety of starships, all of them of alien origin—even those built by humans, since they have been made from retroengineered alien technologies, usually captured after one of Stargate Team 1's rather destructive world-saving missions. What is perhaps most interesting about the series is that it is set in the present; ordinary humans, not emotionally advanced, future humans with better education and technologies, have to build these ships, fly them, and defend Earth. And when these ships are retroengineered into human technology, they are often clunkier, uglier, and more utilitarian, an experimental appropriation, not a pure design, reflecting our own current level of technology and suggesting just how far we have to go before we are a fully space-faring, starship-born civilization.

The majority of the starships in *Stargate SG-1*'s lengthy run are the Goa'uld ships, all variations on Egyptian architectural themes and aesthetics, and so they are very different ships than we generally find in SFTV. These ships are often pyramidal, their inside walls slanting and their deck plates and bulkheads formed to look like sandstone and granite. But the ships' internal structures, the mechanics and the computers, are really new: there are no circuits and wires as in our computers, but instead crystals of various lengths and colors that must be arranged in specific orders within banks of other crystals. When they are correctly aligned, they glow and the ship functions; when they are damaged or incorrect, the human scientists and engineers have to move them around and realign them to bypass the damaged systems. There are no diagrams, no resemblances to human technologies, highlighting our own limited understanding of advanced technology. Less populous in this show's galaxy, but more as we expect a starship to be, are the Asgard ships: silvery, streamlined, technologically advanced, and full of holograms, giant view screens, and curved walls in graceful interiors. At the other end of the spectrum are the Ori ships of the final seasons. Instead of projecting the image of highly advanced technology, they appear to be more like medieval fortresses than ships, especially when viewed from the inside.

Stargate SG-1 also establishes that alien technologies can download a mind into a ship's computer core, as we see when the gray alien Thor (Michael Shanks) of the Asgard must leave his body and exist in the wiring of a ship for survival. But as we have seen in other series, this situation presents us with an external intelligence, not one inherent in the ship. In a show in which minds are frequently taken over and moved around—by the Goa'uld, by alien computer viruses, by old artifacts that download libraries into brains and overwrite them—it was probably only a matter of time before a ship was taken over in a like manner. But this hybrid circumstance falls short of being a living ship.

Ships Come Alive

Farscape, created by Rockne S. O'Bannon, the same man who brought us the sociopolitical *Alien Nation* and the sea- instead of space-based *SeaQuest DSV*, both involving new takes on science fiction standards, gives us the first truly living ship that is not a one-shot or an alien oddity. The Leviathan ship *Moya* is a fully realized character as much as she is a ship, and even as she provides her crew with all the amenities—housing, atmosphere, transport—she carries on her surprising life as a living, interacting creature. She communicates through the symbiotically bonded Pilot (voiced by Lani Tupu) and during the first season she even becomes pregnant and gives birth to a hybrid gunship named Talyn. Talyn, however, suffers the fate of most external intelligences in science fiction. Created by Peacekeeper tampering in the Leviathan genetic code, he is not fully either but is a new sort of threatening presence—powerful, born with the weapons Leviathans do not naturally have, and ready to fight. In the end, he sacrifices himself to save his "friends" and his mother, thus ending his anomalous existence and putting the idea of a living ship back where it belongs: with the nonthreatening Leviathans or not at all.

The more recent series *Firefly* renders its central ship not only nonthreatening but welcoming, in a rather old-fashioned way. *Serenity*, though she is far advanced from current technological possibilities, seems pointedly outdated, only a jury-rig or two away from falling apart. This is intentional. An antique ship is generally overlooked or underestimated by others—as by the Alliance, whom the *Serenity*'s crew is trying to avoid at best and to actively oppose at worst. Unlike the *Enterprise*, *Serenity* is not a symbol of peace or democracy; she is just a home to rebels, fugitives, and smugglers and is therefore a projection of those who have lost a good fight and refused to fall in line with a socialist "utopia"—a society that remains perfect only by controlling the lives of all those within it, limiting their ability to fly away from its rule. *Firefly* shows us the downside of the shining and advanced societies of science fiction, a downside that some will not just give themselves over to. Some—like the antique ship itself—will fight to stay alive and free, preserving the inherent wisdom of those who hunt and gather to survive and to keep moving on. If those attitudes seem a bit antique, they are fundamental to the very notion of the spaceship and aptly embodied in her.

The last *Firefly* episode, "Objects in Space," does explore another dimension for *Serenity*, albeit one that still embodies that rather outmoded spirit. As a result of her government conditioning, River Tam (Summer Glau) is a new kind of human who finds herself out of the loop often enough to identify more closely with the inert technology of the ship than with her crew. Upon hearing that she is thought dangerous and is unwanted on *Serenity*, River makes herself disappear by "becoming" *Serenity*, hacking into the communication system and effectively transforming herself into the intelligence the ship doesn't have, the voice of the antique starship they all live on but can't speak to. That temporary "haunting," though, only points up the abiding suspicion of a self-directed, "human" technology, and she must eventually return to her own identity to find acceptance. While River-as-*Serenity* is an intriguing hybrid creation, in the end she is just another in the long line of external intelligences imposed on the nonliving ships so prevalent in SFTV.

The Sci-Fi Channel's updated version of *Battlestar Galactica* envisions a far more complex sort of technological development, partly illustrated in the variety of its spaceships. The series' namesake *Galactica* is one of a small fleet bearing all that remains of humanity, as in the original series, but she is rare even there, where most of the ships are technologically far more advanced. However, they are also far more susceptible to Cylon computer attacks than is the *Galactica*, since they were designed and built more recently. *Galactica* is, in its own way, as much an antique as *Serenity* is, and here too that antiquity proves its saving grace. Its older communication system, for example, is too simple for Cylons to infiltrate, and its nonintegrated systems can be isolated from each other, allowing them to stand relatively impervious. At the beginning of the series, *Galactica* is about to be decommissioned and turned into a museum. When the Cylons attack, however, this older ship is left as the only protection for humanity's remnants—and she proves a most effective bulwark.

But in contrast to this ancient ship are the really interesting craft in the series, those of the Cylons. The Cylons themselves are a mechanical-electronic-organic hybrid, with specialized models that perform specialized functions. Cylons as a group do not differentiate between those that appear human and those that appear mechanical, between the Centurions, who do most of the land fighting, and the shiplike Raiders. Thus in the second season we discover that Raiders do not have pilots but are entities unto themselves, with hard metal exteriors protecting soft, membranous biological interiors, somewhat like *Farscape*'s *Moya*, and even imbued with independent intelligence, though they are "like an animal, trained to fight," according to the Cylon infiltrator Sharon (Grace Park).

The bigger ships—the battleships, mother ships, and resurrection ships that allow the human-form Cylons to live indefinitely—are presumably as biological as the Raiders. They serve as homes and conveyances to the human-forms, though they are sparsely decorated, since even a very humanlike robot is still a robot and does not need a lot of furniture and decoration.[3] And like the Borg, Cylons are part of the whole, but they are more sophisticated in design. The Borg are living creatures turned mechanical; the Cylons are mechanical creatures that have gained life. The human-forms can interface with the ships through consoles full of a gel that connects their brains and the brain of the ship—a brain that is itself a hybrid, allowing them all to interact with each other and function as one race, one entity. These complex technological creations are projections of the underlying fear of technology that plagues us, as computers advance faster and faster, as they get worked into everything we spend our lives with, even into our bodies, and they pose the ultimate question bound up in such developments: will they eventually prove smart enough to take over? In *Battlestar Galactica*, they apparently are, and they want to wipe humans out and take their place in the galaxy. The ship *Galactica* suggests that lowering the level of technology might help save us, and the Cylons are an example of why it could be a good idea to do so. Built on the framework of a show created just as computers were becoming public and pervasive, the new version of the series takes that fear, extrapolates it into a world full of haunting mistakes, and forces humans to walk a thin line between the technology that might help us advance and continue our journeys and the technology that could kill us all.

Sometimes a spaceship can itself seem like a whole world, as in the original *Star Trek* series when the *Enterprise* comes across a ship bearing a people who believe they are on a planet. It is a nicely suggestive situation, one that should remind us that a spaceship—again, like television itself—is inevitably a microcosm of the world we live in: what we see as well as our thoughts, our fears, our hopes, our philosophy about the world, potentially everything about us in an era, all that is taking us somewhere. Spaceships, after all, are not simply technology; they are us. And we project onto them—like the narrative screen of television—what we feel, hope, and dream for ourselves, or we let them battle what we want to avoid. New ideas and new issues will continue to cause our imagined ships, these crafts of narrative, to change just as we do, to keep pace not so much with science as with what we hope for and what we want to avoid as we move through the murky edges of what constantly shifts from science fiction into human history.

We have seen how television's starships evolved from glorified rockets to glorified cities in flight, from purely mechanical vehicles to computerized machines and then to living beings in their own right—and we're only beginning. The starship is the perennial symbol for the future, the hope that we can avoid destroying ourselves as a species and can leave the shelter of Earth to survive the rigors of space and find new places to go, new lands to be the first people to set foot on, new frontiers as enticing as the ridge of the next hill was to our ancestors as they left Africa and Europe and spread out across the spaces of the globe. Humans travel. Humans explore. It's what we do. And we construct the sorts of spaceships—in our minds and on our screens—that let us see and do what must be done.

Notes

1. *2001: A Space Odyssey*, which appeared at approximately the same time, imprinted popular culture with the notion that an AI could kill. However, the computer on the *Enterprise* seems intended to prove how people can work together for all mankind; a computer that might go mad and kill would be counterproductive.

2. The series also borrowed old sets from the earlier show, which is perhaps why there is something of a *Battlestar Galactica* look to the series, even though *Buck Rogers* is pointedly campier and played largely for laughs.

3. These ships are, however, still more decorated than the Borg ships in *The Next Generation*. The Borg have no interest in their human side and are in fact kept from realizing that they were once human at all, whereas the Cylons know they were created in humanity's image and wish to prove they are better than their creators. They are, in effect, upgrades, more modern, and their ships' aesthetic reflects this notion.

PART IV

THE BEST SIGHTS "OUT THERE"

Key Series

THE POLITICS OF *STAR TREK*

M. Keith Booker

The original *Star Trek* television series, which ran on NBC from 1966 to 1969, is arguably the best-known single work in the history of science fiction media. It was certainly one of the most important works of American popular culture in the 1960s, even if its true importance did not emerge until later, when its showings in syndication greatly increased its audience and influence, enabling it to become the inspiration for a long string of other television series, feature films, novels, and merchandise that carried the *Star Trek* brand name into the twenty-first century. The *Star Trek* franchise has exerted a powerful influence on a number of other works of science fiction, especially those on television, and has become the gold standard for science fiction television (SFTV) series. Though very much a product of its time, *Star Trek* addresses such big issues, including those of gender, race, and class, that its relevance extends well beyond the 1960s. It projects the ultimate fulfillment of the dreams of the Enlightenment and, in so doing, demonstrates not only the strengths but also some of the essential weaknesses that have informed Western culture throughout the modern era.

This broad relevance might explain some of *Star Trek*'s staying power, but the reasons for the success of the series are many. With very little in the way of impressive special effects to offer audiences, the original series became strongly focused on characterization and on the exploration of compelling interpersonal relationships among the major characters. It also often featured thoughtful and thought-provoking subject matter, and, after two cold war decades in which much of American science fiction was dominated by pessimistic postapocalyptic narratives and xenophobic alien invasion tales, it was refreshingly upbeat in its vision of the potential for better living through technological and ethical advancement. In an era of American history generally marked by diminishing expectations, *Star Trek* and its successors have from the very beginning been unabashedly optimistic, consistently (if sometimes naively) confident in the ability of human beings to overcome all obstacles. The voyages of the starship *Enterprise* represent exploration and discovery on a grand scale unavailable on Earth since the days of Columbus—or at least since the exploration and subsequent taming of the American West. Thus it is no accident that the notion of *Star Trek* as "*Wagon Train* to the stars" (as creator Gene Roddenberry pitched the series to NBC, even if he never really saw it that way himself) has had such long currency. *Star Trek* is a very American series, and parallels between the exploration of the galaxy and the exploration of the American West are inescapable. The American flavor of excitement and discovery that informs the original *Star Trek* can be seen in its famous declaration of space as the "final frontier," both echoing the importance of the western frontier in American history as a whole and quite directly recalling President John F. Kennedy's then recent characterization of his visionary program for revamping American society (in which the space race played a central role) as a "new frontier." But this emphasis on exploration has been central to Western culture since the voyages of Columbus helped to usher in the modern era—along with a history of colonial exploitation and other ills.

In *Star Trek*, interstellar travel has led to the establishment of a vast United Federation of Planets, presumably a benevolent and voluntary alliance of advanced planetary civilizations (the most important criterion for advancement is technological, in particular the achievement of warp drive engines for interstellar travel) that have joined to promote peace, cooperation, and the pursuit of scientific knowledge. The *Enterprise* is an advanced starship that has set out on a mission to explore uncharted parts of the galaxy and to recruit new members for the Federation from among any advanced civilizations encountered, but presumably always observing the Prime Directive, a fundamental anticolonialist order that forbids the crew from interfering in the development of the less advanced civilizations they meet. Yet the rhetoric with which the series openly declares the United Federation of Planets to be an anticolonialist enterprise is made problematic by its very connection to the taming of the American frontier, with its associated legacy of racism and genocide.

Similarly problematic (though also highly attractive) is *Star Trek*'s central conceit of a utopian future in which scientific and technological progress has solved virtually all social and economic problems (at least on Earth), leaving each human being free to explore his or her full potential as an individual—and leaving the human race free to explore the cosmos. However, this future is not perfect, and the series insists, in the best Enlightenment tradition, that human potential can be realized only in the face of struggle and conflict. Although universal automation and affluence have seemingly made most human labor unnecessary, *Star Trek* remains informed by a powerful Protestant work ethic, even if most workers are skilled professionals whose work is challenging, rewarding, and almost entirely nonalienating. Indeed, however freed individuals might be from the necessity to work for a living, the series provides a very American endorsement of professionalism, and its main characters are strictly identified with the work they do aboard the *Enterprise*. Surprisingly, though, there are no real working-class characters (presumably because technology has replaced the working class with machines, producing an essentially classless society on Earth), although the disposable "redshirts" who fare so badly in *Star Trek* landing parties might be consigned to that class.

The captain of the *Enterprise*, James T. Kirk (memorably played by Canadian actor William Shatner), is a walking icon of Americanism, and we eventually learn that he hails from Iowa, in the American heartland. Leonard McCoy (DeForest Kelley), the ship's irascible doctor, is similarly all-American, though his obvious southern roots do add a regional note, suggesting that there is some room for diversity in the America of the future. Of course, the diversity of the *Enterprise* crew is nearly legendary, including prominent roles played by the African communications officer Uhura (Nichelle Nichols) and the pan-Asian helmsman Sulu (portrayed by Japanese American actor George Takei), though one could argue that these characters demonstrate the ability of the Federation's all-encompassing ideology to absorb various cultures rather than the ability of these cultures to maintain their own identities. The *Enterprise* even includes a prominent Russian crewmember, though that crewman is the young and naive Pavel Chekov (Walter Koenig), who often seems sadly (if comically) misinformed, having apparently been indoctrinated during his upbringing with a false sense of the centrality of Mother Russia to world history. Among the major characters, only First Officer Spock (Leonard Nimoy) seems to offer any real challenge to an American ideology, but then the half-Vulcan Spock is not entirely human.

Star Trek's multicultural cast, here gathered on the bridge of the *Enterprise*, was genuinely groundbreaking. (Image provided by Photofest.)

Yet this seeming respect for diversity, both on the *Enterprise* and within the Federation, is tempered by the fact that one criterion for Federation membership is that a member planet have a single world government that can speak for it. This insistence on world governments has venerable roots in science fiction (H. G. Wells was one of the first to see world government as a prerequisite to any utopia), but it also suggests that the Federation is willing to deal only with limited diversity within individual societies. It is certainly the case that the future consensus society of Earth projected by *Star Trek* is one based on a thoroughly Western vision of the importance of material wealth and technological modernization. Indeed, although the original *Star Trek* series shows us little of future Earth, its social problems seem to have been solved largely by achieving unanimous support for this vision, which presumably means that all non-Western-style societies have, by the twenty-third century, been swept away (along with the working class) into the ashcan of history.

What is left after this process, of course, is a thoroughly American-ized global culture, and it is not all that difficult to imagine the sanitized globalization (which then moves toward galacticization) of *Star Trek* as the end point of American-dominated globalization currently under way in our own world. Indeed, a closer look at *Star Trek* shows that its vision of the future is far more thoroughly informed by American ideals than the internationalism of the crew of the *Enterprise* might first sug-gest. Of course, the very name *Enterprise* inescapably suggests "free enterprise," despite the stipulation of *Star Trek* that capitalism has become obsolete in the twenty-third century. And although the "U.S.S." that precedes the name of the *Enterprise* presumably means "United Star Ship," the use of the designation for United States Ship that has long preceded the names of American naval vessels is all too obvious. Moreover, the name *Enterprise* belongs to a long line of distinguished American naval vessels, dating back to the original, which started out as the H.M.S *George III* but was then commandeered by the Continen-tal navy (by a force led by Benedict Arnold, no less), eventually to be used in service against the British in the American Revolutionary War. A second, more obscure, U.S.S. *Enterprise* also saw service in the Revo-lutionary War. However, the name does not carry an inherently antico-lonial aura, for the third *Enterprise* patrolled the Caribbean in 1799 to help assert U.S. hegemony there and then served extensively, under the command of Stephen Decatur, in the Mediterranean in attacks on the Barbary pirates of Africa. The fourth *Enterprise* saw service in the Far East but was used primarily to patrol the coast of Brazil to protect U.S. interests there. Later, the seventh *Enterprise*, an aircraft carrier, saw extensive service in the campaign against Japan and was the most deco-rated U.S. warship of World War II. The eighth *Enterprise*, launched in 1960 and still in service as of this writing, was the world's first nuclear-powered aircraft carrier, a major emblem of U.S. global power during the cold war. In short, the name *Enterprise* is substantially associated with the assertion of U.S. military power in various parts of the globe, an association that the makers of *Star Trek* could hardly have missed.

In this context, it is also telling that the (heavily armed) *Enterprise* is under the command of Kirk, who declares unapologetically in one episode that he is a soldier, not a diplomat, his profession (like that of McCoy as a doctor or Spock as a scientist) providing the central component of his identity and determinant of his actions. And, given the supposedly peaceful nature of the *Enterprise*'s mission, the ship and its crew surprisingly often find themselves engaged in various forms of combat—presumably to add drama to the show, but also serving as an inadvertent endorsement of militarism. Still, as Bruce Franklin has demonstrated, *Star Trek* becomes less consistently hawkish as time goes on, perhaps showing the impact of contemporary protests against the American involvement in Vietnam. As Franklin notes, the series displays a general suspicion of pacifism in the episode "City on the Edge of Forever" and continues in this manner with "A Private Little War," an allegorical vision of U.S. involvement in Vietnam as a dirty but necessary intervention to halt the spread of tyranny. But in "The Omega Glory" *Star Trek* offers a more suspicious take on the U.S. effort in Vietnam—and on the cold war as a whole. In this same vein, we might note that, in the first-season episode "Errand of Mercy," violent conflict between the Federation and the rival Klingon Empire is prevented only through the intervention of an advanced alien race of energy beings. However, by the third season's "Day of the Dove," the Federation and the Klingons actually resist the efforts of malevolent aliens to pit them against one another.

Still, though set in the twenty-third century (when Earth has presumably moved beyond such things), *Star Trek* remains saturated with the binary us-versus-them logic of the cold war, which was itself an outgrowth of the binarism of the colonialist tradition.[1] The Federation-Klingon opposition is obviously part of a general allegorizing of the cold war in *Star Trek*, as is the rivalry between the Federation and the cunning Romulans (offshoots of the ultracivilized Vulcan race who have opted for aggression rather than diplomacy as their central mode of dealing with other societies). Other episodes address the cold war even more directly, as in "The Omega Glory," where the *Enterprise* discovers a planet torn by senseless strife between the rival Yangs and Kohms (Yanks and Communists). In many cases, the clashes between the Federation and its rivals generate plots that recall cold war spy dramas, as in the classic (and comic) Klingon episode "The Trouble with Tribbles" and "The *Enterprise* Incident," an espionage thriller in which Kirk and Spock manage to steal a Romulan cloaking device. The echoes of the cold war in the ongoing clashes between the (presumably anti-imperialist)

Federation and these rivals (both tellingly described as empires) are inescapable.

Further, if the United Federation is clearly an extension of the United States, the violent, warlike Klingons and sophisticated Romulans together extend the bifurcated depiction of the Soviets generated by the often contradictory rhetoric of cold war America. In this rhetoric, Soviets in particular and Communists in general were alternately depicted as hopelessly backward bumpkins with a tendency toward mindless violence and as diabolically sophisticated (and devious) intellectuals. Thus, though capitalism and communism were both products of the Enlightenment, the Soviets had somehow both failed to achieve the rationalism so valued in Enlightenment thought and taken that rationalism to a dangerously cold-blooded extreme. *Star Trek* solved the dilemma of this vision by splitting these contradictory stereotypes, linking the Klingons with a violent primitivism and showing the Romulans as extending the rationalism of the Federation (especially the hyperlogical Vulcans) in exaggerated and harmful directions.[2]

This negative depiction of the Romulans is not surprising, for despite its seeming endorsement of Enlightenment rationalism, *Star Trek*, in keeping with science fiction tradition, always maintains that passion is at least as important as intellect as a tool for dealing with the world. Thus, while the cerebral Mr. Spock has long been hugely popular with the geekier *Star Trek* fans (who identify with both his logic and his status as a social outsider, which sometimes adds a touch of emotion even to his characterization[3]), the volatile and action-oriented Kirk is the central carrier of the series' "official" ideology.[4] And the Klingons serve to mark what happens when this preference for passion over intellect goes too far. What is particularly interesting, however, is that this depiction of the emotional Klingons is part of a general constellation of characteristics that closely adheres to so many of the racist Orientalist stereotypes that *Star Trek* is supposedly above and beyond. By often failing to transcend such stereotypes, the series demonstrates just how deep-seated stereotypical thinking can be. In particular, while the imperialistic Klingons supposedly stand as emblems of colonialist aggression, the series as a whole depicts the Klingons via an array of Orientalist stereotypes (including irrationality, violence, and excessive devotion to tradition and ritual) of the kind described by Edward Said in *Orientalism*. Said powerfully demonstrates how racist stereotypes about colonized peoples were originally developed in the Enlightenment West to justify the West's various efforts at colonization and exploitation.

Given the close parallels between this discourse of Orientalism and the rhetoric of cold war America, it should come as no surprise that the Klingons are central to the Orientalism of *Star Trek*, which renders the anticolonialism of the show (if not the Federation itself) a bit suspect. Still, a directive of nonaggression and noninterference with regard to less advanced civilizations is certainly admirable, and many episodes of the original *Star Trek* take (or at least attempt to take) the Prime Directive quite seriously. In "Friday's Child," for example, Kirk and his crew travel to Capella IV, a planet where generous deposits of a rare mineral needed for outer space life-support systems have recently been discovered. The Capellans apparently have a relatively "undeveloped" culture, but the Federation has not considered taking the mineral by force, however valuable it might be. Instead, it has sent the *Enterprise* to Capella IV to negotiate for trade rights, with instructions to respect Capellan cultural practices. These negotiations (helped along by McCoy, who was earlier stationed on the planet and is thus familiar with Capellan culture) are eventually successful, though only after Kirk, Spock, and McCoy convince the Capellans that the Federation will respect their autonomy—unlike the imperialistic Klingons, who are also attempting to negotiate, less honestly, for mineral trade rights.

"Friday's Child" never explains why the Capellans cannot trade with both the Federation and the Klingons, especially as the two powers are not formally at war. But the simple assumption that the Capellans must cast their lot with either the Federation or the Klingons seems to indicate the extent to which *Star Trek* is shot through with the either-or mind-set of the cold war. In light of this mentality, it becomes clear that the Federation is not prepared to take Capella IV by force largely because the Klingons would not stand for it—and vice versa, just as both the Soviets and the Americans were extremely limited in their ability to take military action because of the fear of coming into conflict with the rival power. From this point of view, the Prime Directive sometimes looks suspiciously like propaganda, designed to help convince "third galaxy" planets that they would be better off to side with the Federation than with the Klingons—much in the way the United States and its allies vied with the Soviet Union and its allies in the 1960s to see which could make a more compelling case for itself as the legitimate foe of colonialism and friend of international liberation.

Certainly, *Star Trek* wants to identify the Federation as such a friend on a galactic scale. Indeed, in "Errand of Mercy," the first episode that features Klingons, the Federation directly steps in to try to save the seemingly backward planet of Organia from an anticipated Klingon invasion there. Since the planet is "strategically located," this intervention does not seem entirely altruistic, but we recognize that the Federation has the Organians' best interests at heart. Yet in the episode the *Enterprise* fails to prevent the Klingon invasion, partly because the Klingons reach the planet with an entire fleet whose firepower far exceeds that of the *Enterprise*, and partly because the peaceful and seemingly slow-witted Organians refuse to take any action to defend themselves. Once the Klingons are in power, their colonial governor Kor proves himself a conventional Oriental tyrant, imposing a stern rule marked by violence. He also underscores the parallels between the Klingons and their Soviet counterparts on cold war Earth when he emphasizes the collective nature of their society. The Klingons are strong, he declares, "because we are a unit. Each of us is part of the greater whole."

As a Federation fleet warps its way toward Organia to engage the Klingons, all-out war seems inevitable. However, the episode takes a revealing turn when the Organians suddenly show themselves to be ultra-advanced energy beings, whom Spock characterizes as being as far above humans and Vulcans on the evolutionary scale as humans and Vulcans are above the amoeba. The Organians, acting like the galactic robot police in *The Day the Earth Stood Still* (1951), then impose a treaty that requires the Federation and the Klingons to remain at peace, despite that the Organians too are in principle opposed to interfering in the affairs of others. Although the Federation effort is presumably designed to preserve Organia's sovereignty in the face of the Klingon threat and so does not violate the Prime Directive, the episode's portrayal of the Organians ultimately endorses the intervention of more advanced cultures in the affairs of less advanced ones.

What is perhaps most interesting about "Errand of Mercy," however, is its suggestion of the difficulty in determining which societies are more advanced than others, given that the Organians are, to all appearances, both socially and technologically backward. That the ultra-advanced Organian society is stagnant gains resonance when one considers how often Kirk tends to interpret the Prime Directive to mean that he and his crew cannot interfere in the "normal" development of less advanced societies but that they are perfectly justified in intervening to set "abnormal" or "stagnant" societies on a course toward normality and potential membership in the Federation. Thus, in "Return of the Archons," Kirk leads a radical intervention in the society of Beta III precisely because it seems to be stagnant and not progressing normally. When the *Enterprise* landing party arrives on Beta III, they discover a culture that seems to live in complete tranquility, though this tranquility has been achieved through a suppression of all individuality and creativity. The society is strictly ruled by an entity known as Landru, which turns out to be a powerful supercomputer built six thousand years earlier by a scientist who had hoped to guide his increasingly violent society toward peace. Kirk manages to cause the computer to destroy itself, thus "liberating" the Betans and allowing them to pursue the evolution of their culture without computerized interference. Yet, as the *Enterprise* prepares to depart, we learn that they are leaving behind a "team of experts" to "help restore the planet's culture to a human form." Of course, "human form" here means one that suits the values of the Federation and twenty-third-century Earth.

Spock does point out that to destroy Landru violates the Prime Directive, but Kirk dismisses his concerns, arguing that the Prime Directive does not apply in this instance because this is not a "living, growing culture." Apparently, for Kirk, the Prime Directive forbids interference only in cultures that are not already developing in directions of which he approves—an attitude that, as we have seen, is questioned in "Errand of Mercy." As "Return of the Archons" ends, Spock wonders if allowing the inhabitants of the planet to pursue their individuality is really an improvement, since it probably means they will often resort to violence and achieve their individual goals at the expense of others. After all, we have learned that, with Landru in charge, there was "no war, no disease, no crime," and that Landru was programmed to seek "tranquility, peace for all, the universal good." Spock thus declares Landru a wonderful feat of engineering and dismisses Kirk's complaint that the computer lacked a "soul" as "predictably metaphysical"; the scientist Spock says he prefers "the concrete, the graspable, the provable." He then notes "how often mankind has wished for a world as peaceful and secure as the one Landru provided." However, Kirk, as usual, has the last word: "Yes, and we never got it. Just lucky, I guess."[5]

In such moments Kirk is at his most American, espousing the notion that struggle against obstacles is itself a virtue. For the cold warrior Kirk, a utopia (recall that "utopia" was often negatively associated with communism) would be inherently dehumanizing. In the episode "This Side of Paradise," the *Enterprise* encounters on a distant planet a colony of humans who have achieved what seems to be perfect bliss through inadvertently inhaling drugs that grow naturally on the planet. When his crew (including the ultrarational Spock) falls under the drugs' influence and deserts the *Enterprise* to join the colonists, Kirk proceeds to destroy the whole setup—regarding it, once again, as abnormal. This episode typifies a general suspicion of utopian ideals that is a crucial part of the *Star Trek* ethos, which tends to value struggle as central to the definition of "human." As Kirk muses at the end of the episode, "Maybe we weren't meant for paradise. Maybe we were meant to fight our way through. Struggle. Claw our way up. Scratch for every inch of the way. Maybe we can't stroll to the music of the lute. We must march to the sound of drums." Yet Spock is not so sure, dismissing Kirk's speech as nonregulation "poetry" and pointing out that the situation on the planet was not unequivocally bad. "For the first time in my life," he notes of his experience while under the drug's influence, "I was happy."

Spock's point is potentially a highly subversive one, both in its rejection of capitalist competition and in its approval of drug-induced happiness. Indeed, his frequent tendency to endorse the very utopianism of which Kirk is so suspicious sometimes makes him sound dangerously receptive to communistic ideals, an attitude that would become even clearer in his communalist insistence, in the second *Star Trek* movie, that logic dictates that the needs of the many outweigh those of the few. Again, Spock's view is portrayed in *Star Trek* as that of someone who is only half human (and likes to think of himself as all Vulcan), so it can hardly be taken as representative of *Star Trek*'s view of the human condition. And ultimately, the bulk of *Star Trek* tends to suggest not only that the expansionist-colonialist impulse is natural (in the mode of the old doctrine of manifest destiny) but that it represents the finest aspects of Western human nature: the willingness to struggle and a capacity to grow.

Several decades after the making of the original *Star Trek*, it is easy to criticize the colonialist impulses that inform the original series,[6] just as the ubiquitous short skirts of the female crew members now seem sexist, despite the series' occasional gestures toward gender equality.[7] However, the staying power of *Star Trek* sometimes makes us forget that the series is a product of the 1960s, when anticolonial, antiracist, and antisexist ideas were only beginning to percolate to the surface of American consciousness. *Star Trek*—like all television, film, and litera-ture—is very much a product of its time, in terms of both its lingering acceptance of longtime American myths and its attempts to struggle against the prejudices and imaginative limitations to which it is heir. And as such, these ideological rifts only show most clearly at a dis-tance.

As we have seen, *Star Trek* goes out of its way to stipulate that the United Federation of Planets is not a colonialist or imperialist undertak-ing. It further suggests that oppression based on race and gender will be eliminated in future society. That the series then frequently falls into much of the same stereotypical thinking that is central to both racism and sexism is testimony more to the power of these stereotypes than to the series' weakness. That *Star Trek* is unable to break free of certain assumptions (especially regarding the superiority of the masculine and of a worldview drawn from the Enlightenment) illustrates how easily Western culture has accepted them. Further, it is certainly the case that the original *Star Trek* was more political (and liberal) than typical tele-vision programs of its time, and the subsequent entries in the franchise have shown an increasing awareness of cultural attitudes toward race and gender.

The same cannot be said for class, which *Star Trek* (like the opposi-tional political movements of the 1960s) never manages to deal with in a substantive way. Granted, *Star Trek*'s vision of the obsolescence of the working class (and thus of capitalism itself) in the future is potentially radical, and at least one late episode, "The Cloud Minders," strongly criticizes a society that is marked by extreme class divisions of the kind that once existed on Earth. Indeed, Kirk and his minions violate the Prime Directive to stop the brutal exploitation of workers in this society. Nevertheless, the potential of *Star Trek*'s vision of a postcapitalist society is not realized because the obsolescence of class-based oppression is carefully depicted not as the fall of capitalism but as its ultimate success. In the twenty-third century, we learn, capitalism has made universal affluence possible and has replaced the working class with machines, so that all humans have become members of a universal leisure class. That these wealthy, privileged individuals still desire to explore and colonize the galaxy, not for economic reasons but simply because it is there, once again conveys the message that, by their nature, human beings need to struggle against obstacles—even other sentient beings.

Nevertheless, *Star Trek* does posit that class-based oppression is not necessary for the economic success of a technologically advanced society—and that doing away with this oppression is a natural (and desirable) consequence of genuine civilization. Part of the optimism that makes *Star Trek* so special is its apparent belief that capitalism itself will naturally evolve to the point where this oppression simply disappears. While *Star Trek*'s heart may, in this instance, generally be in the right place, the series does not appear to appreciate that class fundamentally differs from gender and race. Racial and gender equality, after all, are not structurally incompatible with capitalism, whereas capitalism must maintain class-based inequality to survive. By assuming that race and gender are more relevant than class as categories of social and economic inequality, *Star Trek* misses an opportunity to boldly go where American culture had seldom gone before. Then again, had the series launched a genuine assault on capitalism, we might never have seen it. And that, despite the series' various limitations, would be a great loss for the history of SFTV.

Notes

1. See Pietz for an argument that the rhetoric of the cold war was a "substitute for the language of colonialism" (55).

2. For an alternative suggestion, that the Klingons represent the Soviets while the Romulans represent the Chinese, see Worland.

3. It is telling that Spock's most popular episode is "Amok Time," in which he is driven by a biological imperative to seek sexual release on his home planet.

4. Kirk often breaks rules and disobeys orders, but that is a marker of the (very American) official espousal of the importance of individualism by the Federation.

5. See Lagon's argument that Kirk's willingness to intervene in the histories of "abnormal" societies is intended as a critique of American interventionist policies around the world. For Lagon, incidentally, Spock's point of view represents that of the series. He may be giving the series too much credit, however. Although Spock often voices an important counter opinion, I believe it is Kirk (as captain and as a human) whose point of view is more fundamentally that of the series.

6. Among the critiques of the racism and colonialism that creep into the various incarnations of *Star Trek*, the most extensive is probably Daniel Leonard Bernardi's book Star Trek *and History*.

7. In the series pilot, the *Enterprise* featured a female first officer, a daring move that the network quickly vetoed.

Works Cited

Bernardi, Daniel Leonard. Star Trek *and History: Race-ing toward a White Future*. New Brunswick, NJ: Rutgers University Press, 1998.

Franklin, H. Bruce. "*Star Trek* in the Vietnam Era." *Science-Fiction Studies* 21 (1994): 24–34.

Lagon, Mark P. "'We Owe It to Them to Interfere': *Star Trek* and U.S. Statecraft in the 1960s and the 1990s." In *Political Science Fiction*, edited by Donald M. Hassler and Clyde Wilcox, 234–50. Columbia: University of South Carolina Press, 1997.

Pietz, William. "The 'Post-Colonialism' of Cold War Discourse." *Social Text* 19–20 (Fall 1988): 55–75.

Said, Edward. *Orientalism*. New York: Random House, 1979.

Worland, Rick. "Captain Kirk: Cold Warrior." *Journal of Popular Film and Television* 16, no. 3 (1988): 109–17.

SCIENCE FICTION TELEVISION IN THE UNITED KINGDOM

Mark Bould

This essay considers a range of science fiction programs produced over the last half century in light of two key concerns: the nature of British broadcasting's institutional and industrial structures and practices and the British experience of postwar modernization, as empire increasingly gave way to a contested position within the consolidating world market and traditional social structures within the United Kingdom rapidly changed.[1] It is hardly surprising that a genre concerned with historical change—with the futures that might stem from the present and what those futures reveal about the historical moment we inhabit—frequently focuses on the dialectical struggle between the premodern and the modern, between tradition and innovation. What most seems to distinguish British science fiction television (SFTV) is its development within a national context of imperial decline following World War I. This shift was felt particularly strongly after World War II, as British colonies, which once constituted a quarter of the world's landmass and population, won their independence. This experience sharply contrasts with the U.S. ascendance, particularly since 1945. As this essay will demonstrate, British SFTV has often evoked these anxieties about the end of empire and the concomitant decentering of the United Kingdom within a globalized economy—while celebrating the erosion of traditional privilege and authority in the world of consumer capital—by foregrounding changing class relationships and gender roles.

On January 1, 1927, the BBC, established by royal charter, began radio broadcasting in the United Kingdom. Operating with relative autonomy from commercial imperatives and direct government control, it remains publicly funded by an annual license fee levied on its audience rather than by advertising. Its public service "remit" obliges it to inform, educate, and entertain all of the British Isles, provide political balance, and maintain editorial independence. The history of the institution is perhaps best understood as an ongoing negotiation of these require-

209

ments (amid growing commercial competition) from a generally conservative, middle-class, and (southeast) English perspective. Similarly bound by these stipulations, the BBC Television Service was launched on November 2, 1936. The first high-definition television broadcasters in the world, the BBC could reach a radius of up to one hundred miles from Alexandra Palace in North London and the four hundred households in that area with televisions. Among those early programs was the first-ever instance of SFTV, a heavily abridged adaptation of Karel Capek's *R.U.R.* broadcast live on February 11, 1938. By 1939, when the service closed down for the war's duration, the audience had increased to almost twenty thousand households. Restarted in 1946, the service rapidly spread to Birmingham, Manchester, Bristol, Scotland, and Wales, returning to science fiction subjects with a fuller adaptation of *R.U.R.*, broadcast twice in 1948, and an hour-long adaptation of H. G. Wells's *The Time Machine* in 1949. As the number of television licenses rose from 750,000 in 1951 to 9 million by 1958, Conservative politicians backed by various business interests lobbied for commercial television. Their opponents argued that such competition would inevitably turn to lowest-common-denominator programs and an insidious "Americanization," forcing the BBC to lower its standards and abandon its public service role. However, the supporters of commercial television won the debate, and Independent Television (ITV) was launched in 1955 and by 1962 had spread across the United Kingdom. It was overseen by the Independent Television Authority, which charged the regional franchises to provide a public service, not dissimilar in aims from the BBC's, but typically interpreted rather differently.[2] It was in this context that British television produced its first major science fiction programs.

Early drama at the BBC was conceptualized in terms of intimacy: families gathered in their darkened living rooms watching nine- or fifteen-inch screens; actors crafting live performances, as on stage, but with the cameras bringing them into close-up. One producer to rebel against these dialogue-driven, intimate dramas was Rudolph Cartier, who collaborated with author Nigel Kneale on the groundbreaking, controversial, and popular six-part serials *The Quatermass Experiment* (1953), *Quatermass II* (1955), and *Quatermass and the Pit* (1958–1959), and a two-hour adaptation of *Nineteen Eighty-Four* (1954). Their emphasis on fast-paced drama and on opening up the action—*Quater-*

mass II makes especially effective use of location footage filmed at the Shell Haven oil refinery and inserted into the live broadcast—would become increasingly important as the BBC faced ITV's competition. The *Quatermass* serials[3] capture a sense of postimperial melancholy, as the eponymous professor's British Experimental Rocket Group struggles to create a British space program. Each serial begins in failure (the first manned space mission crashes to Earth with two of its crew missing; the first nuclear-powered rocket explodes on the launchpad; Quatermass loses control of the group to the military) but ends in muted triumph as good men die to save the planet. The serials allude to British technological feats—radar, the Jodrell Bank Observatory, the Comet jet passenger plane, the Windscale nuclear facility, which provided the plutonium for the first British atomic bomb—but populating the Britain their middle-class heroes inhabit are rural and working-class stereotypes who seem stuck in a prewar past. WWII, already deeply mythologized, hangs heavy over these serials: enlisted men and noncommissioned officers symbolize some fundamental British decency that prompted the nation to stand firm against Hitler, while the Blitz is invoked as a symbol of indomitable national unity.[4] *The Quatermass Experiment* (of which only two episodes survive) ends with the no-longer-human astronaut, transformed into a vegetal monster, persuaded to commit suicide (live on national TV from Westminster Abbey, where Elizabeth II had been crowned, her televised coronation providing a major impetus to the extension of television's role in British culture).[5] *Quatermass II* parallels the creeping bureaucratization of daily life with both radioactive fallout and contagion by body-snatching aliens. It is critical of the continuation of the wartime security state and its arbitrary exercise of power in peacetime and of the demolition of old communities and their replacement with prefabricated housing and new towns. The program also suggests Britain's precarious position in a global economy while offering a general critique of empire, as Britain is threatened with subjugation by a group-mind "colonial organism."

This critique becomes more explicit in *Quatermass and the Pit*. The British government had been negotiating the transition from the British Empire to the British Commonwealth of Nations since the 1920s, but after WWII more and more of these nations were demanding independence. The 1950s saw a series of crises throughout the former empire (e.g., the Mau Mau uprising in Kenya [1952], the South African demolition of Sophiatown [1955], the Suez fiasco [1956], the Ba'athist revolution that overthrew Iraq's puppet monarchy [1958]). At the same time, immigration into Britain from the Indian subcontinent and the Caribbean increased, and as Kneale was preparing his script, mobs of white Britons attacked black communities in Nottingham and London.[6] Something of this cultural context surfaces in the series—a radio news broadcast speaks of "terrorist activity in Nigeria" and "race disturbances" in Birmingham; a solitary West Indian, for whose presence Kneale had to fight, plays a construction worker—while the story reveals that humankind is the result of a genetic experiment conducted on hominid apes by Martians 5 million years ago. An ancient ceramic-organic Martian spacecraft, initially mistaken for an unexploded German bomb, is uncovered and releases residual "psionic" powers that trigger in humans ancient and destructive Martian instincts. After defeating this threat, Quatermass powerfully rejects the notions of racial and national purity circulating in real-world calls for immigration controls, noting that "we are the Martians. If we cannot control the inheritance within us, this will be their second dead planet."

Similar concerns surface in the seven-part serial *A for Andromeda* (1961; a single episode and fragments survive) and its six-part sequel, *The Andromeda Breakthrough* (1962), both devised by astronomer Fred Hoyle. In the near future, a message from two hundred light years away, detected by British radio telescopes, gives instructions for building a supercomputer that then teaches biologists to synthesize DNA to produce a biosynthetic embodiment called Andromeda (virtually identical to Christine, a lab assistant the computer has murdered). As the ministries of Science and Defense struggle over control of the machine, spies from Intel, a multinational corporation, infiltrate the project. The computer enables British experts to build an independent missile defense, prompting a break from the Western Alliance and visions of a return to the "halcyon days of Queen Victoria": with this "new and . . . finer industrial revolution," the prime minister boasts, "we're going to be a great little country again." Dr. Fleming, who believes that "whenever a higher intelligence meets a lower one, it destroys it," considers the computer a fifth column from another world. He seduces the emotionless and amoral Andromeda away from the computer's influence, educating her into humanity and enlisting her in the machine's destruction. The sequel is set primarily in the Middle Eastern republic of Azaran, a country newly independent from Britain and in the process of cutting the final ties of empire: British oil interests and trade agreements. Recognizing that the world market is replacing imperial power, Azaran provides Intel a secure site to construct and operate its replica of the computer, while the corporation secretly supports a military coup to replace the democratic civilian government. Although both serials present a range of competent women, Andromeda is part of a postwar tendency, especially evident in British science fiction films, to link the threats and promises of modernization with women who push at the boundaries of constraining gender roles. Christine dies because she gets too close to the machine; Andromeda is threatening and in need of "salvation" because she identifies with the machine completely. Traumatized by her near death at the end of *A for Andromeda*, Andromeda must again be drawn away from the influence of the machine and freshly rehumanized. Meanwhile, Intel director Mademoiselle Gamboule increasingly identifies with the machine and its alien modernity. Driven to hysterical megalomania, she brings the threat of total destruction down on the world in hope of gaining power in a new, ordered, postcatastrophe society.

By the late 1950s, ITV competition reduced the BBC's audience share to less than 30 percent. To counter this decrease and justify its continued public funding, the BBC adopted various strategies, including the recruitment of successful ITV personnel, such as Sidney Newman, producer of the prestigious drama anthology *Armchair Theatre* (1956–1968) and the children's science fiction series *Target Luna* (1960), *Pathfinders in Space* (1960), *Pathfinders to Mars* (1960–1961), and *Pathfinders to Venus* (1961).[7] Appointed BBC head of drama in 1962, Newman quickly sought to develop a Saturday teatime science fiction series aimed at children ages eight to fourteen and the adults who might watch with them.[8] Composed of serials that would normally last for four to seven twenty-five-minute episodes, *Doctor Who* would run throughout the year and each episode would climax with a cliff-hanger (and have a midpoint cliff-hanger to facilitate overseas sales to broadcasters needing commercial breaks). The series premiered on November 23, 1963, and ran for 695 episodes, until December 6, 1989.[9] Whereas early seasons ran for 40 or more weekly episodes, the number dropped to around 25 in 1970. Having lost its familiar Saturday evening slot in 1982, *Doctor Who* experimented with just 13 episodes in 1985, although they were expanded to forty-five minutes each, and in its final four seasons, ran for only 14 twenty-five-minute episodes.

"An Unearthly Child," the first *Doctor Who* narrative, opens in contemporary London with fifteen-year-old Susan Foreman, an enigma unfathomable to schoolteachers barely a generation older than she. Susan loves British pop music and possesses a surprisingly detailed grasp of history, as well as scientific knowledge far in advance of 1963. However, curious gaps in her cultural knowledge, like forgetting that Britain does not have decimal currency, lead her teachers to wonder whether she is foreign, perhaps American. These puzzles initially displace the key question at the center of the series (Who is the Doctor?) and establish the boundaries for the adventures to follow, as the Doctor and his companions travel in time and space. At the end of the first episode, the Doctor whisks Susan, as well as her science and history teachers, Ian and Barbara, back ten thousand years, where they encounter a tribe of cavemen struggling to recover the secret of fire in the face of an advancing ice age. The story establishes the adventure format of separation/reunion, capture/escape, pursuit/evasion that will dominate the next twenty-six years, as well as the program's consistent advocacy of the BBC's political and social liberalism. Faced with a cavewoman who does not understand kindness or friendship, Ian and Barbara attempt to educate her in these humanity-defining qualities and later give lessons in democracy (a tyrant is not as strong as the whole tribe acting collectively) and in the desacralization and redistribution of knowledge, arguing that everyone in the tribe, not just the leader, should know how to make fire. Ian and Barbara normalize certain liberal values as universally superior even as they perpetuate a gendered hierarchy of appropriate masculine and feminine behavior and introduce retributive justice.[10]

Because initial plans called for alternating historical and science fiction adventures (and despite injunctions against "bug-eyed monsters," which were perceived as being a distinctly American lowest common denominator), "The Daleks," written by Terry Nation,[11] was selected as the second narrative. In "An Unearthly Child," a wise woman, seeing that the quest for fire threatens her tribe's existence, warns, "We will end in fire." Building on this image, the Doctor next finds himself on devastated, postapocalyptic Skaro, five hundred years after a neutronic war. Effortlessly gliding over the featureless surfaces of their metal city, the warlike Daleks, grating away in electronic monotone, suggest the triumph of an inhuman modernity. In contrast, the pacifist, pastoral Thals must be prodded into violent action against the Daleks before their priggish attitudes—normally indicative of middle-class English decency and BBC liberalism—can guarantee their future. Less than favorable audience responses to "An Unearthly Child" and escalating production costs prompted the BBC chief of programs to cancel *Doctor Who*, but the Daleks, immediately and immensely popular,[12] saved the series. By the time Dalekmania died down, *Doctor Who*'s emphasis had changed significantly from the quasieducational aims Newman initially proposed, with the historical adventures dwindling and disappearing by 1967.

The longevity of *Doctor Who* is often attributed to its format's flexibility, with seasons composed of different-length serials, each of which could be set anywhere and anytime, and with a cast, including the protagonist, that could be changed at regular intervals. Typically, commentaries on the series emphasize how changes in personnel, whether of the seven actors who played the Doctor or of producers and script editors, changed the tone of the series or privileged certain kinds of stories. But equally important are the continuities across which these variations developed. For example, during Jon Pertwee's years as the Doctor (1970–1974), the character's adventures are mostly restricted to contemporary Britain and are often instigated by the problems British industry faced in the global marketplace. Invaders gain footholds through businessmen (and colluding government) seeking advanced plastics or new power sources, while industrial pollution breeds monsters. When the Doctor does venture off Earth, he encounters striking miners. Such events continue the concern with appropriate governance but shift from abstract certainties preached to cavemen to more direct and less assured considerations of how parliamentary democracy struggles to work.

However, the series never really strays from the BBC's agenda of liberal neutrality nor shifts from an institutionalized, conservative reformism. The 1970 episode "Inferno," for example, sees a driven sci-

The fourth incarnation of Doctor Who (Tom Baker) and his companion Romana (Lalla Ward) are surrounded by Dalek enemies.

entist recklessly pursuing geothermal energy to free Britain from dependence on imported oil. Official support for the project means that even when its dangers are revealed, the government-appointed supervisor cannot halt it without first reporting to an oversight committee, and the military forces guarding the installation cannot intervene without orders from above. In a freak accident, the Doctor is thrown into an alternate Earth, in which Britain has become an Orwellian state whose rigidity prevents any intervention in its parallel project, resulting in global destruction. On his return, the Doctor stops the project without official sanction, but it is nonetheless implied that, whatever its faults, British democracy is still the best available system of government. In 1975, "Genesis of the Daleks" simplified these concerns somewhat. On a fog-shrouded battlefield, the slow-motion deaths of two soldiers recall a Vietnam-era antiwar poster, while the gas-attacked trenches of this "army of boys" allude more specifically to World War I. The ultramodern domed cities of the Thals and Kaleds contrast with the ragtag uniforms and ancient weapons of their soldiers, as the very modern condition of the perpetual warfare state reveals the barbarity underpinning it. The Kaled scientific elite and officer class, whose costumes and salute are modeled on those of the SS, demonstrate their fundamental lack of decency by failing to offer the Doctor a cup of tea. Their leader, Davros, dismisses democracy as an ineffectual form of government based on compromise among a thousand viewpoints, and preaches a doctrine of racial purity. To perpetuate the Kaleds, he strips mutated test subjects of their emotions and houses them in mobile units called Daleks. These perfect killing machines might signify the pinnacle of an inhuman modernity, but to ensure racial purity they must become completely other, as a result of which they are incapable of recognizing Davros as one of their own, and they kill him. By once more imagining the Doctor's archenemies as Nazis, the series utilizes the mythos of World

Davros, the creator and controller of the Dalek menace in *Doctor Who*.

War II as a just war against tyranny to give a degree of moral certitude to the Doctor's genocidal mission to prevent the Daleks' creation. It also revisits that key moment of twentieth-century British self-mythology—the isolated stand against evil that cost an empire—to disavow Britain's ongoing history of colonial violence, oppression, and expropriation.

Before joining the BBC, Newman also initiated *The Avengers* (1961–1969), which exemplifies in various ways ITV's approach to science fiction in the 1960s. In the late 1950s, Lew Grade's Incorporated Television Company (ITC) pioneered a mode of independent production in the United Kingdom that targeted international—and particularly U.S.—sales, first with historical series like *The Adventures of Robin Hood* (1955–1959) and then with contemporary adventure series like *The Invisible Man* (1958–1959), *Danger Man* (1960–1961, 1964–1967), and *The Saint* (1962–1969). Science fiction elements were not uncommon in ITC's adventure series, especially *The Prisoner* (1967–1968) and *The Champions* (1968), and ITC also backed Gerry and Sylvia Anderson's science fiction marionette and live-action series (*Supercar* [1960–1962], *Fireball XL5* [1962], *Stingray* [1963], *Thunderbirds* [1965–1966], *Captain Scarlet and the Mysterons* [1967], *Joe 90* [1968], *UFO* [1969–1970], and *Space: 1999* [1975–1977]). Early successes and continuing relationships with U.S. networks ensured that ITC producers would have significantly larger budgets than BBC producers, bringing increasing attention to production design, especially with the move to shooting on film and in color (at a time when color televisions were not even available in the United Kingdom).

Although it was not produced by ITC, *The Avengers* developed in a similar way, being shot on black-and-white film from 1964 to 1967 and in color thereafter, and selling to the United States. Starting off as a gritty thriller series, it rapidly transformed into the increasingly stylish and stylized format for which it is best remembered: the dapper John Steed and his equally fashionable but modern, independent female partners—most significant among them Cathy Gale and Emma Peel—combating outlandish villains and bizarre plots across a fantastical English landscape of country houses, quiet villages, and archaic institutions in which all kinds of modern and absurd innovations might be concealed. Sometimes the threat derives from an attempt to invoke past times, as in the 1966 "Small Time for Big Hunters," and sometimes from a too-determined pursuit of the modern, as in 1965's "The Cybernauts." Playing out the dialectic of tradition and modernity in a rather more playful tone than the *Quatermass* and *Andromeda* serials, *The Avengers* reveled in the passing of postwar scarcity and the emergence of postmodern consumer culture. Whereas BBC dramas typically saw science fiction as a genre, albeit a quite permeable one, to *The Avengers* it was just another pop element to incorporate, along with Savile Row suits, Bentleys, Lotuses, sword canes, miniskirts, and kinky boots. For many, the series epitomized swinging London and social mobility, although it maintained a distrust of foreigners and the working class. (For example, in the 1967 episode "Who's Who?" a pair of working-class assassins use brain transplant technology to take over the bodies of Steed and Emma, but, surrounded by conspicuous luxury, their uncouth manners and greedy consumption betray them.)[13]

A similarly conflicted tone marks *The Prisoner.* The opening sequence shows the unnamed protagonist racing a Lotus Seven past the Houses of Parliament, a modern, democratic institution housed in self-consciously archaic architecture and, in the House of Lords, preserving aristocratic privilege. Likewise, his apartment contains trophies of colonial rule, as well as brochures for international tourism. After resigning as an agent, he is abducted to the Village, given the name Number 6, and subjected to elaborate schemes to break his will. Beneath the Village's simulacral Italianate architecture, traversed either on penny-farthings or in Mini Mokes, lies an austerely modern realm, whose operators try to persuade Number 6 that the political differences between East and West are meaningless epiphenomena overlaying a shared project of social control. Despite his appealing resistance to the forces of domination, Number 6 is also shown to be arrogant, misogynistic, calculating, and ruthless. He escapes the Village several times, only to find himself returned, and when he permanently escapes, it is only to see the mechanisms of control extending into the world beyond his prison.[14]

In contrast, Gerry Anderson's science fiction series consistently depict a utopian future benefiting from world government, high technology, ethnic diversity, and a generally positive sense of Americanization.[15] They articulate the commonly made connection between technological developments and economic prosperity most famously

Mark Bould

expressed in soon-to-be prime minister Harold Wilson's 1963 desire to forge a new Britain from the "white heat" of reformist socialism and scientific revolution. Central to Anderson's vision are not only fabulous vehicles and cities but also a commitment to fashion, most evident in *Captain Scarlet*'s beautiful, multiethnic, female Angel fighter pilots and in the silver miniskirts and purple wigs of *UFO*'s female moon-base crew. The tensions in Anderson's multicultural pluralism become most evident in the secondary roles played by capable women, the jingoistic defense of Earth in *Captain Scarlet* and *UFO*, *Joe 90*'s recurrent stereotyping of Asians and Arabs, and the xenophobia characterizing Commander Koenig's encounters with aliens in *Space: 1999*.[16] The endless wandering of Koenig's moon base, blasted out of Earth orbit and into the depths of interstellar space, captures something of the early 1970s' sense of instability, as anticolonial struggles continued, oil prices rose, and global recession set in.

The BBC's *Moonbase 3* (1973), which attempted a brand of realistic, hard science fiction rarely seen on television, pushes this sense of technocratic utopian failure even further, imagining a European lunar outpost full of cultural and personal conflicts and marked by a suffocating confinement that matches the characters' sense of depression, isolation, and psychological repression. Expressing similar concerns as *Doctor Who* about pollution and the limits to economic and population growth, *Doomwatch* (1970–1972) follows a government agency battling vested interests and economic imperatives in the form of manmade viruses, embryology research, chemical weapons, electronic surveillance, nuclear power, noise pollution, pesticides, genetic engineering, designer drugs, urban neuroses, rabies, lobotomies, refugees, and, best of all, a contraceptive lipstick that is also an aphrodisiac. Equally grim in tone are *Survivors* (1975–1977) and *Blake's 7* (1978–1981). In the former, an accident in a Chinese laboratory releases a deadly virus that eradicates 95 percent of the human race, leaving a deserted Britain where a group of middle-class characters, freed from the unwashed masses, struggles to build a sustainable future. Resonating with the faddish self-sufficiency movement, it also returns to the question of proper government, with a problematic democracy fending off dictatorships of various sorts before finally attempting to unite the country through the self-consciously deceitful mythologizing of one of their number. *Blake's 7* represented an attempt by the BBC to produce a space opera that could hold its own in a post–*Star Wars* era, when ITV was importing big-budget series like *Battlestar Galactica* (1978–1980) and *Buck Rogers in the 25th Century* (1979–1981). After coproduction deals fell through, the BBC pressed on with *Blake's 7* with a much reduced budget, depicting a totalitarian interstellar federation against which the eponymous handful of rebels struggles; as the federation falls apart, so do the rebels, losing Blake and limping on to a finale in which they are all killed. Even as the series' fascination with the strong, sexually confident Servalan hints at the mood of a nation prepared to elect Margaret Thatcher, its dismal tone and perpetual sense of defeat can be understood as an ironic admission of the BBC's inability to compete with U.S.-produced science fiction spectacles.[17]

In the 1980s, as new effects technologies enabled increasingly spectacular science fiction cinema and as importing U.S. productions became relatively economical, British-produced series became less common. In

Three of the renegade heroes of *Blake's 7*: Jenna (Sally Knyvette), Blake (Gareth Thomas), and Cally (Jan Chappell).

fact, while the six-episode television version of *The Hitch-Hiker's Guide to the Galaxy* (1981) consumed the entire 1980 special effects budget of BBC Light Entertainment,[18] its parodic exploitation of science fiction conventions suggested an exhaustion of the genre—as if in the absence of the evolving production values of U.S. efforts, ideas, characters, and stories were no longer sufficient to hold an audience.[19] Moreover, after MTM Enterprises and Tandem succeeded in establishing a tradition of content-led "quality" television in the United States, in the 1980s an expectation of stylistic "quality" followed, adding a further range of production costs British TV could not easily match.[20] For example, the eponymous star of Channel 4's *Max Headroom* (1985) could become an iconic 1980s figure only after Lorimar spun off a multimillion dollar adventure series of the same name for ABC in 1987–1988.

As the long decline of *Doctor Who* dragged on through the 1980s, British SFTV became increasingly a matter of one-off dramas or short serials, with notable adaptations of *The Day of the Triffids* (1981), *The Invisible Man* (1984), *Chimera* (1991), *Stark* (1993), and *Black Easter* (1995), as well as such "quality" dramas[21] as the *Play for Tomorrow* series (1982),[22] *The Black and Blue Lamp* (1988), *A Very British Coup* (1988), *Yellowbacks* (1990), and *Cold Lazarus* (1996). This "quality" tradition, developed out of 1960s radical drama, was often profoundly critical of Thatcherism—of policies that sold off nationalized industries and essential public services, increased the tax burden on the poorest, dismantled the welfare state and social security networks, tied defense and foreign policy to U.S. imperialism, and fashioned a reactionary, jingoistic, antiworker, "dread of difference" culture. This development is nowhere more evident than in the antinuclear dramas broadcast in the mid-1980s, including *Z for Zachariah* (1984) and *The War Game* (filmed in 1965 but banned from broadcast until 1985; see Seed). The surreal paranoia of *Edge of Darkness* (1985) critiques a commitment to nuclear power that often seemed to be primarily concerned with breaking the strength of the mineworkers' union. *Threads* (1984) follows the lives of two families in the northern industrial city of Sheffield in the days leading up to and years after a massive nuclear exchange between the United States and the USSR. Its opening narration argues that our lives are inextricably interwoven, a refutation of Thatcher's proclamation that there is no such thing as society, only individuals.

Throughout the 1990s, which were dominated by U.S. productions, only three science fiction series achieved any longevity. *Goodnight Sweetheart* (1993–1999), a time travel sitcom whose protagonist shuttles between two lives and loves in contemporary and WWII Britain, uses its science fiction premise for little more than a strangely neutered farce about relatively guilt-free infidelity. Far more adept as science fiction is *Red Dwarf* (1988–1999), which, like the revitalized British literary space opera of Iain M. Banks and Colin Greenland, is relentless in its drive to devour every possible science fiction device. The three main characters, revived 3 million years in the future, after everything they know has passed away, are selfish and self-obsessed but nonetheless find themselves caring for each other and forming a community. This melancholy setup is, however, generally swamped by an anxious masculinity's turn to boyish humor, typical of British popular culture in the 1990s, in which an ironic posture allowed for the return of an unrestrained sexism (as in such comics and magazines as *Viz*, *Loaded*, and *FHM*). Still, *Red Dwarf* is significant in that it was able to utilize high-quality special effects and develop a distinctive televisuality.[23] *Bugs* (1995–1999), which follows a group of freelance (and then government-employed) high-tech adventurers, was an attempted return to the adventure series of the 1960s. In a Bond-like world of villains with fantastic new technologies, the protagonists tackle unscrupulous arms dealers, a rogue artificial intelligence, hijackers, assassins, blackmailers, other assorted criminals, and cheats, weaving science fiction gadgetry into an increasingly soap opera–ish series of formulaic adventures. It lacks the stylishness, fun, and humor of its models from thirty years earlier but nonetheless played a similar role in articulating a new vision of Britain, emphasizing a cool, consumer modernity as a marker of Britain's imagined place in a post–cold war world. In particular, *Bugs'* recurrent use of London's Docklands development—Canary Wharf and the iconic tower of One Canada Square appear in every episode of the first series, with an under-construction Millennium Dome cropping up in later episodes—seems like an affirmation of Thatcher's vision, taken up wholeheartedly by Tony Blair's New Labor, of a post-imperial London retaining global significance through its role as a financial center. Indeed, in several episodes, the team is directly involved in securing currency and international banking systems and in preventing the subversion of technologies that enable the functioning of global capital.

Of the small, late-1990s resurgence in SFTV, the most notable example was *Ultraviolet* (1998), in which vampires plot to genetically engineer a substitute for human blood and then to destroy human life through escalating climate change. Drawing more on the conventions of realist police drama than gothic horror, it casts the vampires as a shadow nation, existing unseen in the interstices of global capital and threatening the complete breakdown of national boundaries. Like *Invasion: Earth* (1998), *The Last Train* (1999), and especially the visually inventive and CGI-heavy *Randall and Hopkirk (Deceased)* (2000–2001), it also attempted to develop a distinctive televisuality. In this respect at least, this resurgence prepared the ground for the relaunch of *Doctor Who* in 2005, the centerpiece of the current revival of British SFTV.[24] The British political and institutional landscape underwent significant change in the 1990s. In 1997, after eighteen years of Conservative governments, New Labor won a landslide victory by successfully articulating a continuation of Thatcherism through a "cool Britannia" image and a commitment to a frequently invoked, and always euphemistic, modernization. This was promptly followed by a limited distribution of power to Scottish, Welsh, and Northern Ireland legislatures, institutionalizing a set of colonial relations between center and periphery not unlike those governing the relationship between the BBC in London and these "national regions." While the drama departments in Northern Ireland and Scotland scored major successes with *Ballykissangel* (1996–2001), *Hamish Macbeth* (1995–1998), and *Monarch of the Glen* (2000–2005), uncontroversial dramas that packaged stereotypical Irish and Scottish identities in terms of heritage culture and London's sense of a British national identity and audience, BBC Wales failed to produce a drama series deemed to have national appeal (see Blandford). That changed with the recommissioning of *Doctor Who*, which BBC Wales produced in collaboration with the Canadian Broadcasting Corporation, starting with thirteen forty-five-minute episodes. Significantly, only two of these episodes are set in Wales, though Cardiff streets sometimes stand in for London and Welsh actors for Londoners. Rather, this successful blend of the melancholy often associated with BBC science fiction and the modern, global Britain more often associated with ITV science fiction emphasize a London skyline that not only includes such traditional icons as the Houses of Parliament and the Tower of London but also such distinctive recent additions as the London Eye, One Canada Square, city hall, and the Swiss Re Tower, with the second season's "Fear Her" featuring the 2012 London Olympics in a not-yet-rebuilt Wembley Stadium.[25]

The new *Doctor Who*'s canny allusions to British popular culture (from Charles Dickens to Ian Dury and the Blockheads, from *Muffin the Mule* to *Big Brother*), its gently satiric approach to government- and media-led moral panics (about everything from terrorism, immigration, and weapons of mass destruction to hoodies, antisocial behavior orders, and school meals), and its casting of many familiar dramatic and comic actors (as full-fledged characters rather than in the novelty cameos that occurred in the 1980s *Doctor Who*) ensure its success with a Saturday evening audience. Its often humorous, sometimes wistful nostalgia for the *Doctor Who* of the 1960s and 1970s, as well as the Doctor's decision in the second series to dress like a mod, firmly locate the show within the culture's retooling of that image of Britain for a new millennium.

The series is also marked by a sense of loss and separation (which sometimes seems a rebuke to the BBC for allowing the original series' decline and cancellation). The Doctor is reimagined as the last surviving Time Lord, wracked by survivor guilt. His companion, Rose, mourns for her dead father, while her mother and boyfriend are bereaved by her repeated departures. The Doctor, consequently, becomes a curious blend of lover and father, but the reappearance of an old companion from the 1970s, Sarah Jane Smith, in the 2006 episode "School Reunion" presages the loss that Rose must ultimately accept. These Oedipal tensions are mirrored by a structural conflict between the series' tacit multiculturalism—captured by omnisexual Captain Jack Harkness, who exemplifies an exogamous future humankind that goes to the stars to "dance" with every species they meet—and the drive to reunite the nuclear family, even though it requires "impossible" transitions between alternate universes.

These tensions within *Doctor Who* recapitulate the dynamics that have always shaped British SFTV: the desperate maintenance of permeable borders between nations, ethnicities, classes, and genders; the longing for a return to the golden afternoon (probably Saturday teatime) of empire and the security of family and hierarchy; the desire for something new, different, and other than the tradition that mires us, and the thrill of fluid, unanchored possibility; and the BBC's uniting a nation in its viewing habits by fending off commercial broadcasting while embracing a commercial role in the global media. Like the very best of British SFTV, *Doctor Who* offers a clear image of what a postimperial power (and a noncommercial broadcaster), struggling with its history and its possible futures, looks like.

Notes

1. A major omission in this account is non–United Kingdom science fiction broadcast in the United Kingdom, which has primarily been U.S.-produced. Programs from Australia, Canada, Japan, and New Zealand have also proven successful, and there have been a significant number of United Kingdom coproductions with North American, European, and Australasian companies. For details of such programming, see Evans.

2. BBC2 was launched on April 20, 1964, with the commercial Channel 4 and Channel 5 following on November 2, 1982, and March 30, 1997. Cable services became widely available in the United Kingdom after 1983, with satellite broadcasting following in February 1989. Useful overviews of this history can be found in Crisell, Williams, and Buscombe.

3. There was a belated ITV sequel, *Quatermass* (1979).

4. WWII, and especially the Blitz, plays a significant role in British SFTV, including *Timeslip* (1970–1971), *Goodnight Sweetheart* (1993–1999), *Invasion: Earth* (1998), and *Doctor Who* (2005–present). *Torchwood* (2006–present) pointedly reminds viewers that London was not the only city to be heavily bombed, setting an episode in the Cardiff Blitz.

5. The 2006 *Doctor Who* episode "The Idiot's Lantern" makes this point explicit.

6. On these and related contexts, see Mellor. On the *Quatermass* serials, see Johnson and Chapman, "*Quatermass*." On Kneale, who also wrote *The Road* (1963), *The Year of the Sex Olympics* (1968), *The Stone Tape* (1972), and *Kinvig* (1981), see Murray.

7. Newman also produced the opening installment of the science fiction anthology series *Out of This World* (1962), whose thirteen teleplays included adaptations of works by Isaac Asimov, Philip K. Dick, and John Wyndham. Irene Shubik, the creator of *Out of This World*, later produced a similar series for the BBC, *Out of the Unknown* (1965–1971), adapting fiction by Asimov, Wyndham, J. G. Ballard, Ray Bradbury, John Brunner, Cyril Kornbluth, Henry Kuttner, Frederick Pohl, Robert Sheckley, Clifford Simak, William Tenn, and Kate Wilhelm.

8. There is a strong tradition of British children's SFTV, the earliest example of which is *Stranger from Space* (1951–1952). Whereas younger viewers have enjoyed the likes of *Space Patrol* (1963–1964), *The Clangers* (1969–1972, 1974), and *Teletubbies* (1997–2001), dramas for older children have included *Timeslip*, *The Tomorrow People* (1973–1979, 1992–1995), *The Changes* (1975), *Children of the Stones* (1977), *Chocky* and its sequels (1984–1986), *Dark Season* (1991), *The Demon Headmaster* (1995–1998), *Aquila* (1998), and *The Sarah Jane Adventures* (2007–present). On *The Demon Headmaster*, see Messenger Davies.

9. On *Doctor Who*, see the studies by Tulloch and Alvarado, Tulloch and Jenkins, Britton and Barker, Bignell and O'Day, Bignell, Cull, Newman, and Chapman, "Inside." On the 1996 movie *Doctor Who*, a U.S.–United Kingdom coproduction, see Wright, "Intertextuality."

10. If *Star Trek* in its various guises can be considered as revealing "the limitations of liberal discourse" in the United States (Bould, "Film" 90), *Doctor Who* performs a similar role in the United Kingdom, particularly in terms of the BBC's shifting understanding of its public service remit.

11. In addition to contributing scripts to *Out of This World*, *The Avengers*, *Out of the Unknown*, and *The Champions* (1968–1969), Nation adapted Asimov's *Caves of Steel* for *Story Parade* in 1964 and later devised *The Survivors* and *Blake's 7*. See Bignell and O'Day.

12. The audience rose from 7 million to 10.5 million over the seven episodes, and there were soon more than 130 items of Dalek-related merchandising.

13. On *The Avengers*, see Miller; O'Day; Chapman, *Saints*; and Britton and Barker.

14. On *The Prisoner*, see Britton and Barker; Bould, "This"; Johnson; and Short. The protagonist of *Adam Adamant Lives!* (1966–1967), developed by Newman at the BBC in response to *The Avengers*, cuts an affected dash somewhere between Steed and Number 6. An Edwardian gentleman adventurer revived from suspended animation, he overtly comments on the mores of consumerist modernity.

15. To help sell these expensive series, they were often intended to appear American.

16. Gerry Anderson's other science fiction series include *Terrahawks* (1983–1984), *Space Precinct* (1994–1995), and the CGI *New Captain Scarlet* (2005). On *Thunderbirds*, see Osgerby.

17. The impact of international coproduction on production values is perhaps most evident in the sex role–reversal sitcom-adventure series *Star Maidens* (1976), made in the United Kingdom with German financing and British, French, and German stars. The series' main, multilevel arcade set is clearly in a different league from anything the BBC could afford to build. On *Survivors*, see Bignell and O'Day and Sawyer. On *Blake's 7*, see Bignell and O'Day and McCormack. The somber time travel–ghost stories in ITV's *Sapphire*

and Steel (1979–1982), which champion order over chaos, seem also to resonate strongly with Thatcher's election and first term in office (see Wright, "Echoes").

18. This is often cited as the reason that the long-established BBC comedy series *The Goodies* (1970–1982), which contained significant fantasy and science fiction elements, moved to ITV. Few other British science fiction sitcoms succeed as sitcoms and as science fiction, the most notable exceptions being *Red Dwarf* (1988–1999) and *Hyperdrive* (2006–present).

19. A further trend, typified by the imported *Star Trek: The Next Generation*, was the soap opera turn of science fiction. In the United Kingdom, for example, *Star Cops* (1987), created by *Blake's 7* veteran Chris Boucher, offered a slightly less pessimistic view than *Moonbase 3* of human expansion into the solar system, modeling stories and character interactions on the soapish detective series for which he had also written, such as *Shoestring* (1979–1980), *Juliet Bravo* (1980–1985), and *Bergerac* (1981–1991). *Jupiter Moon*, a children's soap opera set on a satellite orbiting Jupiter, ran for 108 twenty-five-minute episodes, 3 per week with a weekend omnibus edition, on the short-lived British Satellite Broadcasting in 1990.

20. On televisuality, see Caldwell; in relation to science fiction, see Johnson.

21. In this context, "quality" refers to the single-play tradition of British TV drama, identified with such anthology series as *The Wednesday Play* (1964–1970) and *Play for Today* (1970–1984), and with such figures as Dennis Potter, Alan Bleasdale, David Hare, Stephen Poliakoff, David Mercer, Tony Garnett, Ken Loach, and Troy Kennedy Martin. See Caughie.

22. The plays in this series were Caryl Churchill's *Crimes*, Peter Prince's *Bright Eyes*, Tom McGrath's *The Nuclear Family*, Stephen Lowe's *Shades*, Graham Reid's *Easter 2016*, and Michael Wilcox's *Cricket*.

23. On *Red Dwarf*, see Helford's studies.

24. In addition to two spin-off series, the adult *Torchwood* and the children's *The Sarah Jane Adventures*, this miniboom includes *New Captain Scarlet*, *Hyperdrive*, the time slip police drama *Life on Mars* (2006–2007), the satirical pseudodocumentary *The Time Trumpet* (2006), and the time travel adventure *Primeval* (2007), as well as remakes of *The Quatermass Experiment* (2005) and *A for Andromeda* (2006). *Doctor Who*'s success has fueled rumors that the BBC will also relaunch *Blake's 7*, and new film and television versions of *The Prisoner* are in development. Classic British SFTV has also become attractive to filmmakers, with cinema adaptations of *The Avengers* (1998), *Thunderbirds* (2004), and *The Hitchhiker's Guide to the Galaxy* (2005), none of which have proven successful.

25. "Boom Town," set in present-day Cardiff, generally eschews older architecture, replacing a sense of historical specificity with the 1990s Cardiff Bay redevelopment and the Wales Millennium Centre, forlornly recreating the

Welsh capital as a modern, global city. The Cardiff-set spin-off series *Torchwood* rarely goes much farther afield, although its title sequence, not without irony, treats the bay area like Las Vegas in *CSI*'s opening credits.

Works Cited

Bignell, Jonathan. "Space for 'Quality': Negotiating with the Daleks." In Bignell and Lacey, 76–92.

Bignell, Jonathan, and Stephen Lacey, eds. *Popular Television Drama: Critical Perspectives*. Manchester: Manchester University Press, 2005.

Bignell, Jonathan, and Andrew O'Day. *Terry Nation*. Manchester: Manchester University Press, 2004.

Blandford, Steve. "BBC Drama at the Margins: The Contrasting Fortunes of Northern Irish, Scottish and Welsh Television Drama in the 1990s." In Bignell and Lacey, 166–82.

Bould, Mark. "Film and Television." In *The Cambridge Companion to Science Fiction*, edited by Edward James and Farah Mendlesohn, 79–95. Cambridge: Cambridge University Press, 2003.

———. "This Is the Modern World: *The Prisoner*, Authorship and Allegory." In Bignell and Lacey, 93–109.

Britton, Piers D., and Simon J. Barker. *Reading between Designs: Visual Imagery and the Generation of Meaning in* The Avengers, The Prisoner, *and* Doctor Who. Austin: University of Texas Press, 2003.

Buscombe, Edward, ed. *British Television: A Reader*. Oxford: Oxford University Press, 2000.

Caldwell, John Thornton. *Televisuality*. New Brunswick, NJ: Rutgers University Press, 1995.

Caughie, John. *Television Drama: Realism, Modernism, and British Drama*. Oxford: Oxford University Press, 2000.

Chapman, James. *Inside the Tardis: The Worlds of* Doctor Who. London: Tauris, 2006.

———. "*Quatermass* and the Origins of British Television SF." In Cook and Wright, 21–51.

———. *Saints and Avengers: British Adventure Series of the 1960s*. London: Tauris, 2002.

Cook, John R., and Peter Wright, eds. *British Science Fiction Television: A Hitchhiker's Guide*. London: Tauris.

Crisell, Andrew. *An Introductory History of British Broadcasting*. London: Routledge, 1997.

Cull, Nicholas J. "Tardis at the OK Corral: *Doctor Who* and the USA." In Cook and Wright, 52–70.

Evans, Jeff. *The Penguin TV Companion*. 2nd ed. London: Penguin, 2003.

Helford, Elyce Rae. "'OK, Homeboys, Let's Posse!' Masculine Anxiety, Gender, Race and Class in *Red Dwarf*." In Cook and Wright, 240–62.

———. "Reading Masculinities in the 'Post-Patriarchal Space' of *Red Dwarf*." *Foundation* 64 (Summer 1995): 20–31.

Johnson, Catherine. *Telefantasy*. London: BFI, 2005.

McCormack, Una. "Resist the Host: *Blake's 7*—A Very British Future." In Cook and Wright, 174–91.

Mellor, David Alan. "'The Monstrousness That Reigns Here': *Quatermass* and 'The Anglicisation of Outer Space.'" In *Alien Nation*, edited by John Gill, Jens Hoffmann, and Gilane Tawadros, 69–87. London: ICA, 2006.

Messenger-Davies, Máire. "'Just That Kids' Thing': The Politics of 'Crazyspace,' Children's Television and the Case of *The Demon Headmaster*." In Bignell and Lacey, 125–41.

Miller, Toby. *The Avengers*. London: BFI, 1997.

Murray, Andy. *Into the Unknown: The Fantastic Life of Nigel Kneale*. London: Headpress, 2006.

Newman, Kim. *Doctor Who*. London: BFI, 2005.

O'Day, Marc. "Of Leather Suits and Kinky Boots: *The Avengers*, Style and Popular Culture." In *Action TV: Tough Guys, Smooth Operators and Foxy Chicks*, edited by Bill Osgerby and Anna Gough-Yates, 221–35. London: Routledge, 2001.

Osgerby, Bill. "'Stand-By for Action!' Gerry Anderson, Supermarionation and the 'White Heat' of Sixties Modernity." In *Unruly Pleasures: The Cult Film and Its Critics*, edited by Xavier Mendik and Graeme Harper, 121–35. London: FAB, 2000.

Sawyer, Andy. "Everyday Life in the Post-Catastrophe Future: Terry Nation's *Survivors*." In Cook and Wright, 131–53.

Seed, David. "TV Docudrama and the Nuclear Subject: *The War Game*, *The Day After* and *Threads*." In Cook and Wright, 154–73.

Short, Sue. "Countering the Counterculture." In Cook and Wright, 71–92.

Tulloch, John, and Manuel Alvarado. Doctor Who: *The Unfolding Text*. New York: St. Martin's, 1983.

Tulloch, John, and Henry Jenkins. *Science Fiction Audiences: Watching* Doctor Who *and* Star Trek. London: Routledge, 1995.

Williams, Kevin. *Get Me a Murder a Day! A History of Mass Communication in Britain*. London: Arnold, 1998.

Wright, Peter. "Echoes of Discontent: Conservative Politics and *Sapphire and Steel*." In Cook and Wright, 192–218.

———. "Intertextuality, Generic Shift and Ideological Transformation in the Internationalising of *Doctor Who*." *Foundation* 92 (Autumn 2004): 64–90.

MAINSTREAMING MARGINALITY

Genre, Hybridity, and Postmodernism in *The X-Files*

Lacy Hodges

When it premiered in September 1993, Fox's *The X-Files* (1993–2002) was an anomaly in a primetime lineup then consisting mainly of sitcoms and cop shows. The series, which chronicles the adventures of FBI agents Fox Mulder (David Duchovny) and Dana Scully (Gillian Anderson) as they investigate various paranormal phenomena and wade through murky government conspiracies, developed a small following in its first two seasons and emerged as a mainstream television hit by its third. Taking a cue from earlier series such as *The Twilight Zone* (1959–1964) and *Kolchak: The Night Stalker* (1974–1975), *The X-Files* deals with the connection between the fantastic and the real. Though highly invested in maintaining a clear connection to recognizable reality, it utilizes many of the familiar narrative tropes and themes of science fiction and horror—aliens, monsters, and mutants. Furthermore, *The X-Files* was one of the few science fiction, fantasy, or horror genre "cult" shows to achieve mainstream success, paving the way for shows like ABC's *Lost* (2004–present) and NBC's *Heroes* (2006–present).[1] To explain why the series and its characters became such important and pervasive pop culture icons, we might consider the ways *The X-Files* mixes elements of science fiction, horror, and detective fiction to create a popular postmodern type of televisual text. Rather than conform to the conventions of only one genre, *The X-Files* incorporates tropes from numerous genres—both mainstream (detective fiction and police procedurals) and marginalized (science fiction and horror). This genre hybridity allowed the series to occupy a liminal space between the mainstream and the margins and to find a success that was previously unavailable to most science fiction shows. The hybridity and liminality of *The X-*

Files—in terms of genre, visual aesthetic, and narrative progression—reflected the paranoia and instability of the 1990s zeitgeist, and this confluence of politics and pop culture helped create the most successful and popular science fiction television (SFTV) show of the decade.

Like most science fiction, *The X-Files* exploits society's simultaneous obsession with and distrust of science and technology and the inevitable changes technological progress brings. In addition, the public's distrust of the American government, which gained strength in the post–World War II climate of McCarthyism and the cold war, became even more widespread as the century progressed. The Kennedy assassination, Vietnam, Watergate, the Iran-Contra scandal, and the *Challenger* explosion all added to the country's paranoia and the development of a conspiracy culture. *The X-Files*, coming at the end of a half century of distrust and paranoia, merely made explicit the thoughts that dominated the cultural imaginary. While popular police shows such as *NYPD Blue* (1993–2005) and *Law and Order* (1990–present) and political dramas such as *The West Wing* (1999–2006) purport to offer audiences a glimpse of the "reality" behind authoritarian structures, they often do so in a way that ennobles the government. Because their heroes (cops, lawyers, or, in the case of hospital dramas such as *ER* [1994–present], doctors) are often members of these dominant ideological systems, they tend to reassure viewers that authority is generally honorable and right. The stance of these police/law/hospital procedurals carries over into much other genre television as well, including SFTV. Spaceship captains, paranormal investigators, and secret agents (usually male) tend to uphold dominant ideological structures, defeating (literally) alien others in the name of progress, heroism, and white patriarchy.

Although not all television series portray dominant ideologies without question or concern, series that seriously challenge such structures tend to be couched in an antirealist mode that often tempers their critical effectiveness. In order to understand the appeal and importance of *The X-Files'* postmodern thrust, we might briefly recall one of its key antecedents, David Lynch's *Twin Peaks* (1990–1991), a series that shared many of *The X-Files'* themes and ideologies but lacked its long-term popular success. Like *The X-Files*, *Twin Peaks* has an FBI agent hero and deals with themes such as mysticism, spiritualism, and the supernatural. Unlike *The X-Files*, *Twin Peaks* had a rather short lifespan, running for only two seasons (a total of thirty episodes). Some explanation for *Twin Peaks'* inability to maintain popular and critical success can be found in its failure to conform to mainstream televisual aesthetics and narrative structures. In his essay "The Peaks and Valleys of Serial Creativity: What Happened to/on *Twin Peaks*," Marc Dolan offers two popular explanations for *Twin Peaks'* decline: "(a) the show went on too long and its plots spun out into needless complexity, and (b) the show took itself so seriously that it became, as one writer . . . put it, 'a self parody'" (31). Essentially, the series' structure and aesthetics were so far outside mainstream televisual codes that it left many viewers frustrated and alienated. *Twin Peaks'* reliance on dream sequences, mysticism, and spiritualism to investigate a "real" crime that is never satisfactorily solved resulted in a muddled mess; as Robin Nelson offers, the "de-centering tendencies of *Twin Peaks*, its refusal to accommodate the desire for followability or allow comfortable viewing positions are precisely those features which a regular audience rejects" (239).

Where *The X-Files* most differs from its predecessor is in its use of narrative realism to tell its stories, a difference that accounts for the series' longer success and perceived relevance. In *TV Drama in Transition*, Robin Nelson argues that "critical realism" (realism that "constructs fictional narratives based on specific aspects of the historical world") proves itself the most "valuable amongst realisms by offering the most usable stories in the foreseeable operational context of TV" (113, 119). Though Nelson cites *Twin Peaks* as an example of critical realism, by the show's second season its link to the "historical world"— to recognizable reality—became tenuous and unclear, precipitating its rapid decline in popularity. In other words, by the second season, *Twin Peaks* no longer seemed invested in the real, having become heavily reliant on the fantastic to tell its stories.[2] Critical realism's potential for mixing fantasy and realism is tapped much more effectively in *The X-Files*. Though the series incorporates themes and narratives similar to those used in Lynch's show, it does so with a more concrete connection to the "real world." Narratives involving aliens, monsters, and mysticism are tempered with rational science; fantasy is tempered with realism. Because it is willing to question and undermine dominant ideological structures within a consistently realist framework, *The X-Files* is the most successful SFTV series to effectively explore the paranoia and confusion that dominates the post–WWII American cultural imaginary.

The X-Files' use of critical realism is also fundamentally related to the series' ability to take advantage of the space between mainstream and genre television. Much like its thematic liminality, the series' ability to straddle the line between respectable mainstream drama and marginalized serial, while both conforming to and breaking from standard television narrative and aesthetic strategies, is crucial to its popularity and importance. Though some SFTV (notably the Star Trek franchise) gained critical respect by the 1990s, SFTV was still seen by many critics as less important than genres that worked within the normal constraints of realism. Many simply saw SFTV as "kid stuff." Spaceships, aliens, and robots weren't taken seriously as narrative components, so series that dealt in them were often critically neglected in favor of more realistic fare, such as dramas set in police departments, hospitals, and law firms, like NYPD Blue, ER, and L.A. Law (1986–1994). These were seen as respectable and important, while those set in the future or outer space were merely amusing diversions.[3] By utilizing the detective story tradition as the basis for many of its science fiction and horror stories and situating its narrative in the real world, The X-Files was able to appeal to mainstream audiences without being labeled as just a genre show. In fact, by combining these two traditions, it was able to use the tropes of science fiction while maintaining its mainstream legitimacy, thereby integrating into the mainstream science fiction traditions that had been largely marginalized in other TV series.

A reflection of this hybridity can be seen in the series' basic division of its narrative into two types of episodes: "mytharc" and "monster-of-the-week." The mytharc is a continuous story line about the government's involvement in a plot to cover up the presence of extraterrestrials on Earth. The monster-of-the-week episodes are stand-alone shows that operate much like standard detective or horror stories. In these episodes, a case is presented, investigated by Mulder and Scully, and then solved. These stand-alone episodes best illustrate the series' ability to integrate different genre traditions to create a more mainstream science fiction text, since they owe a large debt to traditional detective and police procedural narratives.

From Dragnet (1951–1959) and The Untouchables (1959–1963) to

Hill Street Blues (1981–1987), *NYPD Blue*, and the *Law and Order* and *CSI* (2000–present) series, police and detective stories have long been a staple of television culture. Whereas early series tended to rely heavily on the "just the facts" mentality of *Dragnet*, the 1980s saw a rise in the popularity of "buddy-cop" narratives such as *Miami Vice* (1984–1989) and *Moonlighting* (1985–1989). These shows often mix humor with drama and feature a pair of law enforcement agents who seem incompatible opposites but work well together to get the job done, even while bickering and trading snappy banter.[4] These narratives reflected the growing postmodern trend toward playful self-parody and pastiche in serious dramas, and the buddy-cop pairing stood in contrast to the traditionalism of earlier series. *The X-Files* took this tradition and added aliens and monsters to the usual mix of drug dealers and domestic terrorists. Working on the margins of the FBI, Mulder and Scully are an odd-couple buddy-cop pairing. Mulder is a male FBI agent, a believer who spends his life trying to prove the existence of supernatural phenomena. Scully is a female FBI agent and medical doctor, a skeptic about UFOs and the paranormal. Like all buddy-cop pairings,

The scientist Scully (Gillian Anderson) skeptically listens to Mulder (David Duchovny) spin his theories of conspiracy and alien invasion in *The X-Files*.

Mulder and Scully complement each other, banter, and occasionally humorously clash because of their different worldviews, although they do so while looking for aliens and liver-eating mutants. Mulder needs Scully to inject rationality into his insanity and to ground his forays into the unknown, while Scully needs Mulder to help her recognize the truth of the paranormal. And as in *Moonlighting*, the sparring between this odd couple is always spiced with a potential for romance.

What separates *The X-Files* from other police procedurals and buddy-cop shows is the series' ability to utilize conventional story lines and television aesthetics in unusual and novel ways. Unlike traditional television series that rely on ideologically and artistically conservative aesthetics, *The X-Files* "questions, undermines, and subverts conventional television codes, providing its own set of aesthetic pleasures" (Kellner 164). According to Douglas Kellner, early television series (partly because of the technology of the small, grainy, black-and-white screens of television sets, as well as the lack of variety in the networks producing series) were often "aesthetically impoverished and ideologically conservative" (163). As television technology advanced and more venues appeared, television aesthetics changed as well. The 1980s and 1990s saw an increase in experimentation in television: series such as *Hill Street Blues*, *NYPD Blue*, and *Homicide: Life on the Street* (1993–1999) began utilizing handheld cameras, and other series, including *The X-Files*, experimented with lighting techniques and employed various filming strategies to create an innovative televisual aesthetic. The days of the brightly lit soundstage were not altogether abandoned, but for shows striving for realism and a postmodern aesthetic, grittier filming techniques were an answer.

According to Jan Delasara, *The X-Files*' aesthetic, which depends on "the softening or negating of polarities," reflects the narrative's themes, as does its adherence to film noir and cinema verité visual styles (123). Though the series relies on creating an atmosphere of contemporary reality (the events of the show occur in real places, since the narrative uses real-world current events to tell its stories), it also aims to scare its viewers with vampires, ghosts, and other fantastic creatures. Because the series is at times intended to be both a horror text and a realistic depiction of FBI investigations, it must realistically portray not only contemporary reality but also the fantastic. Obviously, this task creates some aesthetic and technical difficulties, such as how to make the unreal seem real, as well as how to create believable special effects on a weekly television show's budget. The solution to these problems is often to conceal the more fantastic creatures, which are usually backlit and appear as silhouettes or shadows, half-hidden in darkness. Another solution is to have human monsters—if a liver-eating mutant looks like a human being with yellowish eyes, then the monster appears to be more real. Furthermore, *The X-Files* often relies on dark and hazy atmospheres to render fantastic events visually believable and compelling. *The X-Files* thus combines a critical realist aesthetic with the visual effects of horror and science fiction both to increase the realism of the events and to create a blurred and disorienting visual atmosphere.

In addition to adopting a postmodern look, the series works within the thematic structures of postmodernism, questioning the validity of the truths of its own narrative and occasionally adopting a tone of ironic self-mockery. The result is a text that frequently "leaves its central characters and its viewers in a hermeneutic limbo" (Knight 49), sometimes answering the questions it presents but just as often contradicting, denying, or mocking these same answers and the impulse to find them. This almost absolute absence of clarity, a result of both aesthetic and thematic subversions of traditional themes and tropes, results in an "infinite regress of interpretation" for viewers (49). In other words, the "truth" that the series claims is "out there" is never fully illuminated; instead, it is forever questioned, doubted, and rendered mutable. Since clear answers to the questions it asks remain elusive, viewers stay hooked because they are always guessing. This ambiguous atmosphere manifests itself in various ways—from narrative structure to lighting and set design—and speaks to both the genre hybridity of the series and its place in a postmodern television aesthetic. In his essay "Postmodernism and Television," Marc O'Day outlines the key attributes of this aesthetic: "Postmodern TV is characterized by a high degree of excess, fragmentation, heterogeneity, hybridization, aestheticization, stylization, intertextuality, recycling, bricolage, self-referentiality, and parody and pastiche. Postmodern programmes are often ontologically unstable, playfully foregrounding production contexts and environments (never doing this in the sober and revelatory fashion of the modernist text), shifting between realistic and fantasy worlds without comment, blurring the boundaries between fact and fiction or past, present and future, and casually using computer graphics and special effects to warp or wipe out televisual worlds" (117–18). *The X-Files* successfully employs all of these practices in telling its stories.

Though any given episode utilizes some of these techniques, the third season's "Jose Chung's *From Outer Space*" provides one of the most effective and successful examples of a postmodern story line and visual aesthetic. In this episode, Jose Chung, an author attempting to write the first "nonfiction science fiction" book, interviews Scully to get her version of events relating to the alien abductions of two teenagers, an aspiring screenwriter, and two Air Force pilots. The episode is framed by Scully's telling her story to Chung and utilizes flashbacks (told from the points of view of Scully, Chung, local law enforcement officials, the abductees, and various witnesses) to recount one of the abduction cases. As Scully begins her story, Chung assures her that he is not looking for the "real" truth from her, since "truth is as subjective as reality," but rather is interested in what she *believes* happened. Throughout the narrative, Chung interrupts her to share with her others' versions of the same events that seem to contradict her own. For example, though Scully claims that Mulder interviewed one of the Air Force pilots in a local diner, Chung informs her that the diner owner denies such an encounter ever occurred. Another witness claims that Scully (who, according to the witness, was really a man disguised as a woman) threatened to physically harm him, whereas she denies any such encounter. Both Scully's and the witness's versions of events are shown, visually suggesting that neither reality is more real than the other and commenting on the notion that nothing on TV is truly real. In this way the episode directly speaks to the overall themes of the series, telling the audience that the revelation of some absolute truth will never happen—that there is no truth, or rather, that the truth changes depending on who is telling it. This condition is at the core of the series' postmodernism, as it promises answers that viewers will never have access to and mocks the idea that reality and fantasy are anything other than the same.

Another important dimension of this aesthetic is the way in which the series crosses audience gender boundaries. Science fiction, whether in literature, film, or television, is often considered a masculine genre

(Roberts 3)—a perception that has hampered SFTV in finding a wider audience. The reasons for this gender division are twofold. First, most SFTV series are created, written, and produced by men. They star male leads and tell stories about what have been traditionally seen as masculine concepts: science, rationality, and action-adventure. Second, they often fall into what John Fiske calls masculine narrative forms. According to Fiske, television produces texts aimed toward one of two gendered audiences: shows made for the feminine audience are open ended and likely to "resist narrative closure" (179), whereas shows produced for the masculine audience "are structured to produce greater narrative and ideological closure" (198). The difference in audiences' needs for narrative closure, Fiske argues, results from the fact that the masculine audience does not need to resist dominant ideologies (198). Certainly, many early science fiction and fantasy series would seem to fall under this rubric. The episodic narratives of such series as *Star Trek*, *The Twilight Zone*, and *Kolchak* provide audiences with a clear sense of narrative closure at the end of each episode. Because of its strong ties to science fiction, horror, and detective fiction, *The X-Files* would seem to fall quite easily into the masculine category, and yet, because it relies on an ever evolving mythology and questions dominant ideologies, *The X-Files* also links with what Fiske terms feminine texts, such as soap operas, which rely on an "ongoing, serial form with its consequent lack of narrative closure" (180). In mixing elements of traditionally masculine and feminine television shows, *The X-Files* becomes a text that works as both a series of weekly fantasy shows and a continuous, nine-year-long science fiction soap opera. And through this hybrid masculine-feminine narrative structure, *The X-Files* was able to occupy a space in popular culture that had been largely inaccessible.

In combining the openness of the continuous serial narrative with a closed narrative structure, *The X-Files* also furthers its thematic liminality. For example, in the ongoing mytharc of the series, the question of whether there are actually visitors from outer space or aliens are just a hoax perpetrated by the government is never satisfactorily answered. Of course, this lack of clarity became frustrating for audiences after six or seven seasons and was one of the series' most cited downfalls, but it was also necessary for *The X-Files* to achieve the success and importance that it did. Because the show relied on never fully answering the questions it posed, like a soap opera, viewers needed to keep watching if they wanted to know the fates of the characters. Furthermore, because there was seldom one specific case that Mulder and Scully were attempting to solve, the series could stretch mysteries out for several seasons without having to provide complete answers. The mythology of the show, as we have seen, is built on the conceit that the questions it poses can never be fully answered. Yet here too the series reaches for a balance with its monster-of-the-week episodes, which usually do provide some sort of narrative closure at the end of the forty-two-minute episode. In these nonmythology episodes, audiences could appreciate that, although Mulder and Scully could never quite uncover the big Truth, they found other truths week after week.

The X-Files further challenges genre conventions by creating a narrative in which the fantastic can often be explained through scientific means and, even more subversively, in which the female character is the one who deals in science and rationality. Though Mulder's theories of paranormal activity often direct the agents' investigations, solving the cases typically depends on Scully's scientific expertise. Thus episodes usually follow a similar format: a strange and seemingly unsolvable crime is committed, Mulder and Scully arrive to investigate, and Mulder offers a crazy theory—blaming aliens, vampires, or fat-sucking mutants—at which Scully scoffs. As the agents investigate, Scully performs autopsies and other scientific tests and offers a rational explanation, Mulder applies her science to his theory, and they solve the case. Furthermore, since it is real science—not futuristic science or the physics of a faraway galaxy—that proves necessary, *The X-Files* explores both the limits and the possibilities of human knowledge and understanding.

The liminal space between reality and fantasy that is represented by such scientific-supernatural investigative methods is clearly laid out in the series' pilot episode. A title card at the beginning of this episode claims that "the following story is inspired by actual documented accounts."[5] Following this title, a scene depicts a young woman being chased into a clearing and then caught by a young man who offers her up to a bright light that appears from the night sky above him. The episode situates this fantastic event—seemingly an alien abduction— within the mundane realism of a criminal investigation. Mulder, Scully, and local law enforcement examine evidence and interview witnesses to uncover the perpetrators, who are apparently from outer space. However, the absurdity of this determination is tempered by the realism of other events here. By blurring the line between fantasy and reality, the episode thus suggests that its science fiction aspects are real. Though the series never again uses the "inspired by actual documented accounts" opening, it does continually refer to real times, events, and places, particularly through the time stamps that appear onscreen during most episodes, thereby constantly situating fantastic events within reality's constraints.

In addition to the reality afforded to the show by its use of place and time indicators, the presence of the FBI, an organization that exists in the reality outside the show, in a series about the supernatural, underscores *The X-Files*' investment in the liminal. Like earlier mainstream television dramas that take much of their realism from following real people—cops, doctors, lawyers—*The X-Files* centers on members of an authoritarian bureaucracy. But unlike many other television cops, Mulder and Scully explicitly critique the institution in which they work; Mulder especially refuses to follow the rules of FBI investigative methods and often challenges the authority of his superiors. Many of the series' major narrative conflicts occur when Mulder and Scully refuse to listen to their superiors and pursue their own investigations (using FBI resources, of course) to discover the Truth. In "Squeeze," the third episode of the series, a fellow agent asks Scully—but not Mulder—to assist in his investigation into a series of murders involving victims whose livers are violently removed from their bodies. Scully explains to Mulder that he has been excluded because other agents don't want to hear his "spooky" theories, pointing to his basement office as proof of the FBI's lack of support for his paranormal investigations. Mulder concedes the point but observes that Scully is in the basement with him. The implication is that it is not only Mulder whom the FBI wants hidden from view but Scully as well, since she supports his investigations into the paranormal. The suspect in the case, a long-lived genetic mutant who can stretch his body to any length and who rips out and then feasts upon the livers of his victims, is caught by the FBI during the course of the non–X file investigation, but because the "traditional" agents can't accept that a seemingly young man could be "a hundred-year-old serial killer . . .

with ten-inch fingers," they are unable to solve the case. It is not until Mulder and Scully pursue an "out there" theory, unassisted by any other agents, that the case is finally resolved. Throughout this episode, it is made clear that Mulder and Scully, hidden away in the basement and viewed as embarrassments, are the better agents; the FBI agent who plays by the book and is on the bureau fast track is characterized as rigid, obtuse, and ignorant.

Clearly, the key to successfully investigating an X file is an ability to move beyond traditional, rational, bureaucracy-approved thinking to a more open, marginalized, supernatural-infused investigative method. Mulder and Scully are empowered by their governmental connections—they can investigate cases in the first place only because they are members of the FBI—but are at the same time condemned by the bureaucratic conservatism of the very agency that gives them their power. To investigate the aliens, mutants, and government conspiracies that make up these cases that, in the words of one of their superiors, "fall outside the bureau mainstream," Mulder and Scully must function both inside and outside the FBI's bureaucratic rules and regulations. While they are FBI agents and thus agents of the dominant ideological and governing system, they are also othered from this system of power by their status as rogue agents and thus relegated to the basement. In this way, Mulder and Scully become "a part of the very structure [they] attempt to resist" (Kubek 172), and their status as such is fundamental to the series' emphases on liminality and hybridity.

Though Mulder and Scully's status as what we might term liminal agents could, as one critic suggests, point to a "loss of faith in the national government that the [FBI] represents" (Cantor 118), their continued associations with the markers of bureaucratic power—everything that identifies them as FBI agents—reaffirms the series' ultimate alignment with mainstream ideologies. Season seven's "X-Cops," an episode that follows Mulder and Scully as they investigate a case being filmed for the reality television show *Cops* (1989–present), illustrates this point. The episode humorously places the agents in the midst of a street investigation in south central Los Angeles, where they search for a suspect who is at various times described as a giant wasp, a werewolf, a local pimp, and Freddy Krueger. The pseudodocumentary nature of the episode highlights Mulder and Scully's place as figures of bureaucratic law and order even as they approach the ever blurred line between fantasy and reality. The *Cops* format is designed to underscore for viewers the difference between law enforcement officers and civilians, and accordingly, Mulder and Scully are shown to be more in line with the other police officers than with the victims and witnesses they are interviewing. They are filmed as FBI agents and are clearly marked as such—they are well dressed, articulate, and, though Mulder insists on telling the camera crew that their suspect is a "contagion of fear," appear to be traditional figures of a government agency. "X-Cops" illustrates that while Mulder and Scully (much like the show itself) are interested in pursuing ideas outside the conservative world of the FBI, they still exist very much within an environment of mainstream constraints. The episode also shows that Mulder and Scully's liminal status within the law enforcement world is tied to the liminality of realism within the show itself. For the television series *Cops* functions as a marker of reality in two key ways: in its documentary format and in its status as a real show that exists outside *The X-Files'* narrative universe and within the audience's experience. By seamlessly inserting Mulder and Scully into an episode of a real series, the show both undermines and exploits the idea that any television show can accurately depict reality. In other words, the reality of reality television proves to be just as much an illusion as the reality of a giant wasp monster or a werewolf terrorizing south central L.A. Through this metanarrative, "X-Cops" effectively illustrates how *The X-Files* utilizes the space between mainstream police dramas and marginalized SFTV to create a successful genre hybrid.

By combining tropes of traditional genres such as police dramas with marginalized genres such as science fiction and horror, *The X-Files* challenges both the aesthetics and logic of mainstream television while offering an intriguing alternative. Like many prior series, it utilizes familiar science fiction tropes and images, such as the spaceship, the alien, and the mutant, to critique dominant ideologies, but it manages to do so in a way that prevents its being dismissed as merely a fantastic diversion. As a result, *The X-Files* is, in many ways, the ultimate postmodern series, and its success and influence can still be felt in television culture today. A number of series have attempted to mimic its aesthetic and narrative structure and have proved short lived—obvious examples are *Dark Skies, Profiler,* and *Millennium*—but other, more successful efforts clearly show the influence of *The X-Files*. ABC's *Lost*, for example, utilizes a similar narrative structure, combining an ongoing, conspiracy-related story line with more accessible, episodic plots. Although *The X-Files* was by no means the first series to employ a postmodern aesthetic, the buddy-cop pairing, or genre mixing, in its effective combination of these elements it proved both successful and significant, staking out a liminal position that increasingly seems crucial to an evolving SFTV.

Notes

1. In "Rewriting Popularity," Jimmie L. Reeves, Mark C. Rodgers, and Michael Epstein trace the evolution of *The X-Files* from cult sensation to mass appeal series and specify particular aspects that help to make a series a cult hit—particularly an avid, active fan base.

2. In "Family Romance, Family Violence, and the Fantastic in *Twin Peaks*," Diane Stevenson analyzes the relationship between the fantastic and the natural in the series, concluding that "*Twin Peaks* is a story that remains fantastic to the very end" (70).

3. Each of these series was awarded the Emmy for best dramatic series at least once: *L.A. Law* in 1987 and 1989–1991, *NYPD Blue* in 1995, and *ER* in 1996.

4. Though buddy-cop narratives existed before the 1980s, the decade saw a rise in their popularity in both television and film. *Miami Vice* and the *Lethal Weapon* films were among the most popular of these texts. Though buddy-cop narratives often feature two male partners, women are sometimes included. *Cagney and Lacey* (1982–1988) features a female duo, and *Moonlighting* adds another twist by casting a male-female couple as the leads.

5. These "actual accounts" seem to be the accounts of Betty and Barney Hill, a couple who claimed to have been abducted by aliens on September 19–20, 1961, in Portsmouth, New Hampshire. Details of their story—most notably the claim that they experienced missing time and had small metal objects implanted into their bodies during the abduction—are used in the pilot to describe the effects of alien abductions on human subjects.

Works Cited

Cantor, Paul A. *Gilligan Unbound: Pop Culture in the Age of Globalization.* Lanham, MD: Rowman and Littlefield, 2001.

Delasara, Jan. *PopLit, PopCult, and The X-Files.* Jefferson, NC: McFarland, 2000.

Dolan, Marc. "The Peaks and Valleys of Serial Creativity: What Happened to/on *Twin Peaks*." In Lavery, 30–50.

Fiske, John. *Television Culture*. New York: Methuen, 1987.

Kellner, Douglas. "*The X-Files* and the Aesthetics of Postmodern Pop." *Journal of Aesthetics and Art Criticism* 57 (1999): 161–75.

Knight, Peter. *Conspiracy Culture*. New York: Routledge, 2000.

Kubek, Elizabeth. "'You Only Expose Your Father': The Imaginary, Voyeurism, and the Symbolic Order in *The X-Files*." In Lavery, Hague, and Cartwright, 168–204.

Lavery, David, ed. *Full of Secrets*. Detroit, MI: Wayne State University Press, 1995.

Lavery, David, Angela Hague, and Marla Cartwright, eds. *"Deny All Knowledge": Reading* The X-Files. Syracuse, NY: Syracuse University Press, 1996.

Nelson, Robin. *TV Drama in Transition*. New York: St. Martin's, 1997.

O'Day, Marc. "Postmodernism and Television." In *The Routledge Companion to Postmodernism*, edited by Stuart Sim, 112–20. New York: Routledge, 2001.

Reeves, Jimmie L., Mark C. Rodgers, and Michael Epstein. "Rewriting Popularity: The Cult *Files*." In Lavery, Hague, and Cartwright, 22–35.

Roberts, Robin. *A New Species: Gender and Science in Science Fiction*. Chicago: University of Illinois Press, 1993.

Stevenson, Diane. "Family Romance, Family Violence, and the Fantastic in *Twin Peaks*." In Lavery, 70–81.

BABYLON 5

Our First, Best Hope for Mature Science Fiction Television

Sherryl Vint

Although not as long-lived as shows in the *Star Trek* franchise, J. Michael Straczynski's *Babylon 5* (1994–1998) has had a significant if sometimes unrecognized impact on American science fiction television (SFTV). Innovatively conceived as a novel for television—with a distinct beginning, middle, and end to its five-year story arc—*Babylon 5* demonstrates the capacity for television to tell complex stories and to allow characters and situations to change with time.[1] The show's five-year production span matches that of the events it chronicles from 2258 to 2262. Much of the pleasure in watching it comes from the elaborate narrative and the unity of its vision, a reflection of Straczynski's involvement with almost all aspects of production, including writing the vast majority of scripts. Although Straczynski has repeatedly described *Babylon 5* as a novel for television, another narrative form—the epic—might better capture the series' contribution to SFTV. In *Reading Television*, John Fiske and John Hartley argue that television serves a social function consistent with that of the bard of epic poems, conveying a culture's dominant values and constructing its self-image. Reading *Babylon 5* as a skillfully crafted contemporary heroic epic that also innovates upon tradition provides insights into its strengths, its weaknesses, and its influential place in contemporary SFTV.

Babylon 5 tells the story of four races—humans, Centauri, Minbari, and Narn—and their intersecting fates in a war between the Vorlons and the Shadows. The main cast includes Delenn (Mira Furlan) from Minbar, G'Kar (Andreas Katsulas) from Narn, Londo Mollari (Peter Jurasik) from the Centauri Republic, and four human characters, originally Jeffrey Sinclair (Michael O'Hare), Susan Ivanova (Claudia Christian), Michael Garibaldi (Jerry Doyle), and Stephen Franklin (Richard

Biggs). One of the show's key strengths is its willingness to put story ahead of other considerations (such as the star system), which led to the replacement of Commander Sinclair in season two by Commander Sheridan (Bruce Boxleitner). Aware that actors might leave, Straczynski outlined his five-year story with "trap doors" for each major character, enabling him to continue the narrative in a slightly modified way were he to lose one of his actors (Usenet [Google Groups], comment posted April 24, 1996).

Epics concern the heroic deeds of people who "enhance our belief in the worth of human achievement and in the dignity and nobility of man" (Bowra 121), and they typically assume "a social relation between gods and men, as between men and monsters" (Bayley 65). Indicative of its hybrid status as epic in form but science fiction in genre features, *Babylon 5* does not turn to the supernatural but instead includes god-like aliens, the Shadows and the Vorlons. Epics generally concern "action set in the period of the historical or quasi-historical past during which the struggle for the formation of *imperium*, the laying of geographical, genealogical, cultural and moral foundations, takes place" (Fichter 164), often representing the "fall of one civilization" and the "rise of another" (Merchant 124). Again consistent with its science fiction genre identification, *Babylon 5* is set in the future, not the past, but a future figured as historical in its opening monologue, as "the dawn of the third age of mankind," the new civilization born in the events narrated by the series. Similar to television itself, epics are often episodic in nature, requiring the poet "to think in narrative units that could be detached and would be intelligible and reasonably self-contained in recitation" (Mueller 176), but these units always form a single vision, thematically tied to "the wholeness of the epic vision" (Winnifrith 115). Most epics are collaborative efforts, orally composed and performed by bards who may not be their original authors. Similarly, *Babylon 5* is united by Straczynski's vision, but each episode is a collaborative work also made by directors and actors.

As a hybrid of epic and science fiction, *Babylon 5* revises and revitalizes both forms. Much of this value emerges from the complexity of its vision of the future as compared to the static visions typical of many other science fiction programs. This is not a future in which—as a character newly awakened from cryogenic storage naively anticipates—we

Babylon 5 begins a new era in television special effects: a Vorlon spaceship.

have "outgrown violence" ("The Long Dark"). Instead, this future is filled with flawed human (and other) beings who struggle with alcoholism, drug addiction, failed loved affairs, greed, weakness, fear, selfishness, and the like. At times, consistent with its epic framing, the series drifts toward myth and glorifies characters, such as Sheridan and Delenn, but for the most part its characters are full and complex. Even Bester, a Psi cop almost invariably characterized as a sociopath, has his sympathetic moments. The action unfolds in a similarly complex world, as we see when a labor strike is resolved by allocating part of the military budget to maintenance ("By Any Means Necessary"), underscoring that the series' conflicts are not only life-or-death confrontations with ancient forces but also familiar struggles with Senate subcommittees and resource allocation.[2] An intricacy also informs the texture of daily life on *Babylon 5*, which includes multiple social classes and helps, as Jan Johnson-Smith argues, to direct "the sense of wonder . . . away from technology and out into the sublime universe, into our experience of it" (236). It is partly through such a complexly imagined world that *Babylon 5* helped promote more serious SFTV, such as the reimagined *Battlestar Galactica* series (2004–present), often praised for its flawed and thus human characters, long narrative arcs, and focus on political as well as military struggle.[3]

Change, which is crucial to the innovations introduced by the series, is another feature that links to the epic form, which often traces a hero's life and thus includes moments of growth and change. G'Kar comments in season one, "No one here is exactly what he appears" ("Mind War"), and the multilayered characters implied in that observation help produce psychologically and socially complex stories. That *Babylon 5* was outlined as a whole enabled the series to use foreshadowing much more extensively than television typically does, demonstrating the narrative value of long story arcs. Prophecy and flashbacks are both characteristics of the epic form that help to create consistency in an episodic narrative (Winnifrith 115). *Babylon 5* is exemplary in its use of such techniques, gratifying fans with the pleasure of seeing how pieces fit together, such as the revelation that Sinclair is really Valen, the famed "Minbari not born of Minbari" ("War without End"), or the sight of Londo viewing Shadow ships flying over Centauri Prime, footage first seen in season one but not fully understood until season three. Yet the emphasis on foreshadowing and a thematic concern with destiny do not prevent the series from containing surprises, such as the prophesied destruction of Babylon 5, which proves to belong to an avoidable future, or Londo's recurring dream of his death in combat with G'Kar that is not the mutual destruction of antagonists we have expected but instead cooperation between characters who have come to be allies, perhaps even friends. While *Babylon 5* is filled with elements of prophecy, as Garibaldi comments, its vision is "the future: some assembly required" ("Hunter, Prey"), and one of its major themes is our responsibility to make that future through moral actions.

Like the characters, *Babylon 5*'s themes are also sometimes not what they seem to be. Initially the Vorlons appear to be creatures of light, benevolently helping the "younger races" defeat the Shadows, positioning the series within a typical epic scenario of the struggle between good and evil. Indeed, such metaphors recur through much of the first three seasons, and the religious parallels with Satan and God become explicit in the season two finale, "The Fall of Night," when the Vorlon Kosh finally emerges from his encounter suit. Everyone sees "a being of light" who conforms to his or her own religious tradition (humans see an

angel). Yet the season three finale, "Z'ha'dum," challenges those perceptions, as we learn that the struggle might be construed otherwise. The
Vorlons desire order and so take a firm hand in guiding younger races,
restricting them from certain kinds of knowledge,[4] while the Shadows
prove to be not nearly as malevolent as we have assumed. Since they
believe that strength comes through chaos, they have encouraged the
younger races to fight among themselves, predicting those who survive
will emerge stronger.

The major climax of the Shadow war, then, is not the epic defeat of
darkness by light. Instead, Sheridan and Delenn force a direct confron-
tation between the older powers, arguing that their battle is "about
ideology" rather than morality, since each wants to prove it is right
("Into the Fire"). Neither is helping the younger races, they insist, but
instead both are refusing to make way for these younger races and to
face the fact that they "don't need you anymore." In this context, the
Vorlons no longer appear as benevolent beings of light but as manipula-
tive tyrants who have interfered in others' development, convincing the
younger races that they are gods the better to control them. Such a revelation rewards long-term viewers, exposing that somewhat uncomfortable earlier moments—such as Delenn's torture by Sebastian in "Comes
the Inquisitor"—were hints that things did not sort simply into light and
dark. In this story line, *Babylon 5* resists some of the more conservative
aspects of epic narrative, in which the right and wrong moral sides
(however one might determine the shifting target of rightness) are clearly
indicated and right is always victorious. Conventional epic narratives
tell the deeds of exceptional heroes, "surpassing the dimensions of realism" (Merchant 1), but this series strives instead to fuse the sense of
wonder attendant upon epic narrative with a grittier, more realistic
vision of the future.

In fact, *Babylon 5* never reduces things to a binary of good and evil,
instead offering a complex analysis of how the category of "right" can
be constructed to serve any end. Londo begins his descent into greed
and power—which culminates in a renewed war between Narn and the
Centauri Republic—by telling the Shadow representative that he wants
to see the Centauri "reclaim their rightful place in the universe" ("Signs
and Portents"). Although his sense of right seems unacceptable, the
more sympathetic G'Kar similarly fantasizes about the destruction of

the Centauri, something that later proves a barrier when he wants to recruit allies, since they distrust how far he and his people will go in seeking a "rightful" victory. The allies he seeks, similarly, have more than one definition of "right." One of the most emotionally powerful moments in the series is the look of hope on G'Kar's face when he believes the Ministry of Peace representative may be willing to intervene on the Narn's behalf, a prospect the audience already knows is unlikely. The narrative shows the Ministry of Peace and its militant Night Watch patrol to be negative forces, as they refuse support for the Narn because Earth has nothing to gain. At the same time, however, some individuals honestly believe that they are doing the right thing, including the minister who proudly proclaims "Peace in Our Time" after signing a nonaggression pact with the Centauri ("The Fall of Night"). *Babylon 5* refuses a straightforward binary of good and evil through such characters who do things that ultimately have "evil" results but might nonetheless be motivated by good intentions (preserving peace on Earth). Unlike conventional epic, which conflates individuals' morality with that of their nation or race, *Babylon 5* thus contrasts characters such as the minister with other representatives of Night Watch who seem more clearly driven by personal power.

The allusion to World War II is difficult to miss, and much of the overall structure of *Babylon 5* loosely evokes the breakdown of the League of Nations leading up to World War II and the later establishment of the United Nations. This extended comparison to World War II is analogous to the extended similes that are a stylistic feature of epics. The heavy reliance on such parallels points to the tension between the series' desire to offer complex, realistic stories of political struggle and a simultaneous desire to tell a heroic story of how daring individuals can change history. World War II is often understood to be the least morally ambiguous war, and the tendency to see it as a fight between good and evil informs the parallels throughout *Babylon 5*, particularly in the President Clark story line. Unlike the Vorlons and Shadows story, this narrative arc relies on quite simple binaries between Clark's corrupt and "evil" forces and Sheridan's liberating "good" ones, while it also points to the American inflection of *Babylon 5*'s mythology in its revolutionary rhetoric about throwing off an unjust ruler through military action to return power to the people.[5]

Epic narratives often express "a strong sense of national identity and destiny" (Merchant 22), and the President Clark story line represents *Babylon 5*'s least reconstructed use of this epic convention, moving away from the more realistic characters and themes of the Vorlons and Shadows story line and toward a more mythologized account of events and legendary heroes. *Babylon 5* struggles with its simultaneous desires to be a novel for television—including characteristics of the novel such as complex and flawed characters—and its epic narrative arc, which conventionally requires glorification of the hero and a clear victory for the right side. In "A Late Delivery from Avalon," King Arthur appears to have returned, and G'Kar comments about the desire to believe in Arthur's mythic struggle, a conflict in which there is "no moral ambiguity, no helpless battle against ancient and overwhelming forces." *Babylon 5* understands the appeal of such just conflicts and sometimes tends toward myth, but overall it insists on a world of ambiguous struggle.

That ambiguity is particularly foregrounded when Sheridan takes actions or makes decisions that prompt us to question him even as the narrative continues to present him heroically, as in his decision to use telepaths altered by the Shadows in the liberation of Mars ("Endgame"). Although his choice seems necessary, only scale separates it from the rationale the Centauri Republic uses to justify devastating the Narn home world with mass drivers (and reminding us of the justification for the nuclear attacks on Japan). Similarly, the monstrous Emperor Cartagia plans the genocide of his own people, arguing, "Some are always sacrificed for the greater good" ("Whatever Happened to Mr. Garibaldi?"). Cartagia's assessment bears an uncanny resemblance to a phrase G'Kar experiences as an epiphany: "Some must be sacrificed so that all might be saved" ("Dust to Dust"). In *Babylon 5* context matters: Cartagia's phrase "the greater good" is open to political manipulation and can be defined as anything the speaker highly values (he defines it as himself), while G'Kar's emphasis is on the collective—"all might be saved"—not merely some "greater" portion.

Although the epic dimensions of *Babylon 5* dominate in its characterization of Sheridan and ensure that we see him as heroic,[6] the series nonetheless demonstrates its complexity by offering spaces for reflection and critique. When he needs the other races to agree to border patrols by the White Star fleet, he convinces them there is an "invisible enemy" from whom they demand protection ("Conflicts of Interest"), a strategy similar to Clark's use of the threat of the Shadows to convince people to give up civil liberties. If at times the series seems too willing to fall into binaries of truth and falsehood, at others it readily diagnoses those situations as the symptoms of ideology. As an example, in the season four finale, "The Deconstruction of Falling Stars," we learn of an attempted holographic reconstruction, five hundred years in the future, of the main characters for the sake of contemporary propaganda—a reconstruction that turns Franklin into a Mengele-like figure and Sheridan into a monomaniacal tyrant. That revision is valiantly resisted by the holographic Garibaldi, who not only protects the truth of their legacy but also thwarts an attempted coup. Here the epic qualities of the main characters dominate, as the story suggests not only that Sheridan's coup and the formation of the Interstellar Alliance will be the lynchpins for all history that follows but further emphasizes the extraordinariness of Sheridan and those around him, as even in holographic form they protect true freedom and the civilization they have created better than do its inhabitants.

The more realistic tone of the narrative and the ambiguities in Sheridan's character are most evident in his interactions with the telepath colony in season five. Fleeing the Psi Corps, the rogue telepaths seek political asylum and a home world of their own. Their leader, Byron, a charismatic figure, insists on a strategy of nonviolence, and his passion converts Lyta Alexander, the resident telepath, to his cause. Lyta has been an ally of Sheridan and the others, using her telepathic abilities at crucial moments, and without her interventions victory would have been impossible. However, when the crises are over, Sheridan and the others disregard and even mistrust her. They seem unaware of her financial struggles because of Psi Corps and at one point ask her to move because she can no longer pay rent. When Byron offers her respect and love, she has little difficulty accepting, even describing him in terms that recall earlier descriptions of Sheridan: "If Byron asked me to follow him into hell, I'd do it gladly with a smile on my face because I believe in him" ("Secrets of the Soul"). Lyta's version of Byron glorifies his leadership and casts him as a heroic figure who rightfully defies the unjust status quo, similar to the construction of Sheridan by those who supported his rebellion against Earth.

But unlike Sheridan, Byron never becomes a hero and is increasingly an outcast, eventually a martyr. Tired of waiting for the nontelepaths to acknowledge what he feels is his legitimate demand for a home world, Byron instructs the telepaths to gather the ambassadors' secrets to use as leverage, predictably resulting in panic and persecution. Even Sheridan, troubled that Byron's threat has worsened conflicts among the Alliance worlds, withdraws his support. He explains, "On a strictly idealist level it is understandable but they did it the wrong way, the inconvenient way" ("A Tragedy of Telepaths"). It falls to Delenn to remind him that the new president of Earth similarly characterized his war of liberation. Whereas Sheridan was presented as doing the right things for the right reasons, Byron does the wrong things for the right reasons, thereby losing control over the colony. Trying to prevent Byron from killing himself and the remaining telepaths when it appears they will be taken into custody by Psi cops, Sheridan tells him, "You are a symbol to these people," to which Byron responds, "So are you. You should remember that" ("Phoenix Rising"). Sheridan does not seem to understand that he might appear an oppressor to those not liberated by his Alliance, and he later threatens to kill Lyta when she resists arrest ("The Wheel of Fire"), although her illegal activities in support of the telepaths are as understandable as his. Lyta's fate is another example of *Babylon 5*'s complex engagement with moral problems and its willingness to let resolutions remain ambiguous.

Lyta's relationship with Byron, like Delenn's with Sheridan, is also important to the series' unconventional treatment of gender. In this respect the series strays most significantly from the epic model, which narrates the exploits of male heroes, mostly relegating women to the roles of seductress and faithful wife. Downes argues that the epic is "the exemplary genre of patriarchy" (206), but *Babylon 5* offers a vision of gender equality that anticipates that of the reimagined *Battlestar Galactica*, including women in the heroic warrior roles usually reserved for men. For example, the series resists turning Ivanova, female second in command, into a sex object. Only rarely do we see her out of uniform, and, unlike that of Deanna on *Star Trek: The Next Generation* (1987–1994), her uniform does not differ from those worn by her male colleagues. She speaks with authority, is taken seriously by those under her command, and never functions merely as a secretary to the male commander; in fact, she even commands the fleet that defeats Clark's elite forces. However, the effort to avoid turning her into a sex object does present her life as almost sterile. She seems consumed by her work, while other human characters have a fuller social being: Sheridan his great romance with Delenn, Garibaldi the reunion with Lisa, and Franklin a series of short-lived relationships. In contrast, Ivanova has only an ex-lover who comes to the station seemingly to rekindle his romance but in reality to promote the Earth First agenda ("The War Prayer"), the unrequited and never-consummated love of Marcus (Jason Carter), and the suggestion of a sexual relationship with the station's first telepath, Talia Winters (Andrea Thompson). While one might praise *Babylon 5* for depicting a lesbian relationship and a bisexual person, elements still inadequately represented in SFTV, it does heavily penalize both women. Talia turns out to be a sleeper agent whose personality is destroyed when her submerged persona takes over, and, more disturbing, this persona taunts Ivanova, telling her that it pursued the relationship solely to aid its spying. In the series finale, set twenty years in the future, only Ivanova seems to have a life bereft of human companionship. Although *Babylon 5* resists the tendency to sexualize a main female character, it achieves this only by removing any possibility of romance or sexuality.

Delenn, however, suggests other possibilities in the series' treatment of gender and sexuality, perhaps because her half-human, half-Minbari status makes her strength less threatening. The power of Delenn and Sheridan's leadership comes from their romantic partnership, but the series demonstrates in a number of ways that it is a bond from which they equally draw strength. For example, Delenn requires an image of Sheridan's power to overcome her depression and continue their political work when she believes he is dead, and he similarly finds her image gives him the strength to choose life on X'ha'dum and later to withstand torture on Mars. Just as the series refuses to sexualize Ivanova, it refuses to reduce Delenn's power and make her simply into a wife once she is romantically linked to Sheridan, as writers Anne M. Schofield and Nickianne Moody point out.[7] Instead, it produces a careful balance, as when both characters resolve the problems on their own worlds: Sheridan the war of liberation from Clark and Delenn the Minbari civil war. Both retain their independence and the power they had before becoming a couple, a fact emphasized when Delenn gently reminds Sheridan—

who urges her to stay home and send Lennier on a dangerous mission—that he should "never forget who I was, what I am, and what I can do" ("Lines of Communication").

Despite these many strengths, *Babylon 5* remains problematic in two ways. The first is its tendency to reinforce the idea of human exceptionalism that shapes much science fiction. *Babylon 5* is better than most SFTV in balancing its depiction of nonhumans and humans: three of the other races are represented in the recurring characters, and the plot does not focus exclusively on the problems of Earth and humans. The Minbari civil war, the rivalry between the Narn and the Centauri Republic, and the political machinations of the Centauri royal court are as important to the overall narrative as the liberation of Mars and the fight to free Earth from President Clark. The series usually presents the other races as complex rather than monolithic, struggling among themselves and sometimes demonstrating internal differences, such as the Minbari caste system. Yet the series occasionally slips. For example, in "The Parliament of Dreams," each of the other races demonstrates its dominant belief system, but Earth requires various denominational representatives. Other episodes, though, show an uncommon respect for different values, as in "Believers" when Dr. Franklin insists upon applying his moral standards to the treatment of a nonhuman child and tragedy results. Less positive is *Babylon 5*'s repetition of the outworn science fiction trope that humans have some special lesson to offer the universe, in this case the importance of bringing people together in a common cause despite their differences. Delenn says, "No one else would ever build a place like" Babylon 5 ("And Now for a Word"), and Londo convinces the League of Non-aligned Worlds to support Sheridan when he is imprisoned on Earth by arguing, "The humans have become the glue that holds us together" ("Between the Darkness and the Light"). In this way the series allows its thematic treatment of community to give way to one of science fiction's overused truisms by linking it too closely with humanity.

A second problem is *Babylon 5*'s depiction of a future that takes for granted the continued existence of capitalism.[8] Certainly, some capitalist social relations are critiqued: the dock workers' need to strike, the corporations' funding research expeditions for the sake of patenting technology,[9] and the presence of the homeless in the undeveloped part of the station called Downbelow. This last example is particularly sharp: The Lumati finally agree to open trade and diplomatic relations with Babylon 5 when their representative sees Downbelow and is impressed by the "will to isolate the genetically inferior part of your own species" ("Acts of Sacrifice"), paralleling the Lumati's tenet of segregating themselves from inferior species. As they observe, Downbelow allows the station to "create a workforce without a power base to challenge [them]." The people in Downbelow are described as those who come to Babylon 5 "looking for a new life, a new job," but become trapped "when they don't find it [and] they can't afford passage home" ("Grail"). The language evokes the promise of America as the New World and implicitly connects the lure of expansion and new opportunity with the frontier mythology of America and the human expansion into space, as well as with the imperium-building aspect of epic narrative. Despite such overt criticism of the economic consequences of capitalism, *Babylon 5* never acknowledges the degree to which the Interstellar Alliance is associated with capitalist social organization.

In "Rising Star" Delenn explains that the Alliance will "promote trade and stop aggression," because "the gains you will achieve by working with those in the Alliance far outweigh what you may gain by force." She also promises technology in exchange for joining, tying economic advantage to the commitment to peace. She notes, "Strength comes from a multitude of voices brought together in common cause"; while the common cause is not named, the language of "gains" suggests it is profit. What is left unsaid, seemingly unthought, is that capitalism cannot unite everyone in common cause, since its social relations rely on extracting surplus labor, necessarily excluding some from its brighter future. Thus, although *Babylon 5* critiques capitalism and offers a far more realistic and complex future vision than that popularized by *Star Trek* (whose replicators magically overcome scarcity), it never recognizes the material foundation of its vision. The Alliance is as much a trade network as a political one. Although G'Kar's Declaration of Principles for the Alliance tells us, "The universe speaks in many languages, but only one voice. . . . It is the small still voice that says we are one" ("The Paragon of Animals"), Delenn's farewell speech is offered in English, "the human language of commerce" ("Rising Star"). Whereas G'Kar speaks the series' thematic language, Delenn reveals its material base in commerce.

At times Straczynski acknowledges the importance of economics, as when he discusses network interest in the show based on its low production costs. He has begun production of direct-to-DVD releases, collectively titled *The Lost Tales*, that continue the story past 2262. These episodes expand on the series' embrace of the capitalist values of expansion but also demonstrate Straczynski's close relationship with fans, an important part of the *Babylon 5* phenomenon, successfully reproduced by other series creators such as Joss Whedon.[10] Straczynski, himself a fan of science fiction, includes many elements of what Damien Broderick terms the science fiction "mega-text" in his work and explicitly identifies his series as a response to the "undisguised and unmitigated" (7) disregard for the science fiction community that, he believes, other producers of SFTV have demonstrated. That status as both fan and writer also makes his relationship to the production of other media somewhat different from the more recent expansion of genre television into "authorized" extras beyond the broadcast, such as the online comic books

A "best hope" for humanity: *Babylon 5*'s multispecies Interstellar Alliance.

produced by NBC for *Heroes* (2006–present) and the Sci-Fi Channel's Webisodes of *Battlestar Galactica*. However, there are similarities too. Henry Jenkins was quick to see *Babylon 5* as a precursor to our era of media convergence where "the most profitable forms of popular culture are those that move fluidly across different media, gathering diverse audiences and alternative markets along the way" (xviii). Although Straczynski's motivation might be other than generating larger markets, the material consequences of his innovations exceed his intentions because *Babylon 5* and its merchandise exist as commodities. Thus Straczynski is both part of the fan culture he extols and an exemplary marketer. These two aspects need not be seen as contradictory, however: the series' merchandise is similar to the Alliance, which really does promote cooperation and peace yet also really does further the expansion of capital into new markets.

Traditional epics, as expressions of a culture's dominant values, circulated in face-to-face encounters and did not need to concern themselves with questions of marketing and media. Straczynski is not so fortunate, and some of the episodes of the series demonstrate his concern with the power of broadcast media to shape perception. He argues, "Television is a powerful medium, the mightiest conceivable, and like any great weapon it needs to be controlled, bent toward enlightening and ennobling and uplifting its audience . . . by people who understand the medium, and the craft of storytelling" (18). Clearly, he thinks of himself as one of these people, and in *Babylon 5* he reflexively queries the dangers of media misuse. "36 Hours on B5," for example, takes the shape of a news report in 2258. The perspective provided by the focus through Interstellar Network News prompts us to think about how the media shape political realities, an insight made all the more chilling, in the post-9/11 era, when we watch an argument about whether a destroyed Narn cruiser was carrying medical supplies or "weapons of mass destruction." However, other episodes suggest the power of truth to shine through, regardless of the degradation of the medium, as when Ivanova broadcasts the Voice of the Resistance to counter Clark's propaganda. But once we have watched "The Illusion of Truth"—an episode in which we first see the cast go about their business while being recorded by a news crew and then watch the distorted broadcast of those events—how can we believe in news objectivity? *Babylon 5* avoids pursuing the full implications of its critique—that any story, including its own narrative, is ideology from an interested position—preferring instead to assert a firm binary relationship between truth and propaganda.

Similarly, *Babylon 5* avoids pursuing the full implications of its epic narrative form, which posits Babylon 5 as the major turning point for a new civilization and—in "The Deconstruction of Falling Stars," which imagines the world one, one hundred, five hundred, and one thousand years after the formation of the Alliance—suggests that even when the solar system ends it will be important to preserve the Babylon 5 story. Such ambitions to colonize the future suggest the American and capitalist values from which *Babylon 5* emerges. Marx argues that capitalism, as part of its endless and inevitable drive to increase surplus value, must constantly strive "to go beyond its quantitative limit" (270), including the limit of sites for consumption. "Just as capital has the tendency on the one side to create ever more surplus labour," Marx explains, "so it has the complementary tendency to create more points of exchange" (408). The epic, as an exemplary form of empire, fits well with the tendency toward expansion, and so the epic aspects of *Babylon 5*'s narrative are consistent with its expansion into merchandise, the expansion of its story line into a future far beyond the series' nominal end, and the expansion of capitalism into the galaxy as a consequence of the Alliance's formation. At the same time, however, the major theme of *Babylon 5* is the need for community, the ideal that we are one despite surface differences of race, religion, nation, and class.

Babylon 5's epic form is thus in tension with its most overtly stated theme. Straczynksi consciously designed *Babylon 5* for our fragmented, postmodern era, which, he believes, "lacks for a mythology—there is nothing that brings us together. There is so much which pulls us apart and fractionalizes us. [*Babylon 5*] pulls people together" (quoted in Sharkey 28). This vision is appealing, but despite the many pleasures of *Babylon 5*, it remains a product of its cultural location in 1990s America. *Babylon 5* might pull people together in fandom, but in epic fashion it also emphasizes heroic individualism and capitalism, both of which conflict with its thematic emphasis on community. *Babylon 5* is, in fact, at its strongest when it defies epic and science fiction convention, emphasizing moral ambiguity over clear right and wrong, portraying complex and fallible characters instead of grandiose epic heroes. In effect, the series has two identities: mature, realistic SFTV and conventional, nation-building, hero-centered epic.

In season five, after his writings become the foundation of a new religion, G'Kar is enraged by a statue of his likeness, which he rejects as a fixed object that replaces the questing, spiritual impulse with ritual observation of a religious rule. This essay has described the many ways in which *Babylon 5* might be understood as an epic narrative, but to reduce the series to epic is to similarly make it into a static thing. Instead, *Babylon 5*'s strength comes from its refusal to embrace epic convention without revision. By setting its reconceived epic matter in the future rather than the past, it challenges us to make a better world by accepting our "obligation to society, to each other, and to the future" (Straczynski 15).

Notes

1. The planned arc was disrupted by Warner Bros.' canceling the series after its fourth season. It was picked up for a fifth season by TNT, resulting in a rather rushed pace during season four and a melancholy tone in season five, which often looks back to earlier events.

2. Another episode, "A View from the Gallery," is told from the point of view of two maintenance men, with the usual main cast appearing only in moments when these two characters overhear their fight to repel an invasion of the station.

3. *Babylon 5* is the first science fiction show to use CGI extensively, also influencing the future of SFTV.

4. For example, in season one's "Deathwalker," Kosh tells them, "you are not ready for immortality" before killing a scientist who has found a way to prolong life.

5. Clark became president by assassinating his predecessor (under Shadow influence) and retains power by suppressing the media, attacking civilian dissenters, and using Night Watch and a version of the FBI to spy on citizens, eroding civil liberties and eventually declaring martial law.

6. The series ends with Sheridan's death prompting a reunion. When he dies, the station is also taken offline (although the timing appears coincidental). This structure is consistent with the epic form, which narrates the life, adventures, and death of the main hero: Odysseus, Aeneas, Beowulf. Sheridan journeys to the underworld during his death and rebirth with Lorian, another typical event in the life of the epic hero.

7. The most problematic aspect of their romance is the reason offered in

"Atonement" for allowing Delenn to wed a non-Minbari. Unwilling to admit that Minbari "blood" is not pure but contains human elements, her clan leaders insist that she give as reason for wedding Sheridan an old custom of offering a woman from the winning side of a conflict to wed someone from the losing side as a symbol of new life and hope. Those who stand for purity and isolation over connection and community are generally not endorsed by the show's themes, mitigating to a degree the problematic nature of this gesture.

8. Although Kevin McCarron, Andy Sawyer, and James Brown all note that the series takes for granted the continuation of capitalism in its future, they say nothing specific about the ways in which this happens. More important, no one addresses the crucial point that this fact exists in problematic tension with the series' thematic emphasis on community and unity.

9. This plot strand might have been further developed had Commander Sinclair remained a major character in seasons two through five, as his girlfriend was involved in such expeditions.

10. Lancaster's 2001 *Interacting with* Babylon 5 calculates that Straczynski had posted seventeen thousand replies to fan queries and comments about the show at that date (2). Straczynski continues to interact with fans today, including discussing *The Lost Tales*, the first installment of which, "Voices in the Dark," appeared in July 2007.

Works Cited

"Acts of Sacrifice." *Babylon 5*. Written by J. Michael Straczynski. Directed by Jim Johnston. Prime Time Entertainment Network (PTEN), February 22, 1995.

"And Now for a Word." *Babylon 5*. Written by J. Michael Straczynski. Directed by Mario DiLeo. PTEN, May 3, 1995.

Bayley, John. "The Epic Theme of Love." In Winnifrith, Murray, and Gransden, 64–79.

"Believers." *Babylon 5*. Written by David Gerrold. Directed by Richard Compton. PTEN, April 27, 1994.

"Between the Darkness and the Light." *Babylon 5*. Written by J. Michael Straczynski. Directed by David Eagle. PTEN, October 6, 1997.

Bowra, C. M. "Some Characteristics of Literary Epic." In Draper, 121–30.

Broderick, Damien. *Reading by Starlight: Postmodern Science Fiction*. New York: Routledge, 1995.

Brown, James. "Cyborgs and Symbionts: Technology, Politics and Identity." In James and Mendlesohn, 110–29.

"By Any Means Necessary." *Babylon 5*. Written by Kathryn Drennan. Directed by Jim Johnston. PTEN, May 11, 1994.

"Comes the Inquisitor." *Babylon 5*. Written by J. Michael Straczynski. Directed by Mike Vejar. PTEN, October 25, 1995.

"Conflicts of Interest." *Babylon 5*. Written by J. Michael Straczynski. Directed by David Eagle. PTEN, May 5, 1997.

"Deathwalker." *Babylon 5*. Written by Larry DiTillio. Directed by Bruce Seth Green. PTEN, April 20, 1994.

"The Deconstruction of Falling Stars." *Babylon 5*. Written by J. Michael Straczynski. Directed by Stephen Furst. PTEN, October 27, 1997.

Downes, Jeremy M. *Recursive Desire: Rereading Epic Tradition*. Tuscaloosa: University of Alabama Press, 1997.

Draper, R. P., ed. *The Epic: Developments in Criticism; A Casebook*. Basingstoke: Macmillan Education, 1990.

"Dust to Dust." *Babylon 5*. Written by J. Michael Straczynski. Directed by David Eagle. PTEN, February 5, 1996.

"Endgame." *Babylon 5*. Written by J. Michael Straczynski. Directed by John Copeland. PTEN, October 13, 1997.

"The Fall of Night." *Babylon 5*. Written by J. Michael Straczynski. Directed by Janet Greek. PTEN, November 1, 1995.

Fichter, Andrew. "The Dynastic Epic." In Draper, 164–71.

Fiske, John, and John Hartley. *Reading Television*. London: Methuen, 1978.

"Grail." *Babylon 5*. Written by Christy Marx. Directed by Richard Compton. PTEN, July 6, 1994.

"Hunter, Prey." *Babylon 5*. Written by J. Michael Straczynski. Directed by Menachem Binetski. PTEN, March 1, 1995.

"The Illusion of Truth." *Babylon 5*. Written by J. Michael Straczynski. Directed by Stephen Furst. PTEN, February 17, 1997.

"Into the Fire." *Babylon 5*. Written by J. Michael Straczynski. Directed by Kevin Dobson. PTEN, February 3, 1997.

James, Edward, and Farah Mendlesohn, eds. *The Parliament of Dreams: Conferring on* Babylon 5. Reading: Science Fiction Foundation, 1998.

Jenkins, Henry. Foreword in Kurt Lancaster, *Interacting with* Babylon 5, xv–xxii. Austin: University of Texas Press, 2001.

Johnson-Smith, Jan. *American Science Fiction TV: Star Trek, Stargate and Beyond*. Middleton, CT: Wesleyan University Press, 2005.

Lancaster, Kurt. *Interacting with* Babylon 5. Austin: University of Texas Press, 2001.

"A Late Delivery from Avalon." *Babylon 5*. Written by J. Michael Straczynski. Directed by Mike Vejar. PTEN, April 22, 1996.

"Lines of Communication." *Babylon 5*. Written by J. Michael Straczynski. Directed by John Flinn III. PTEN, April 28, 1997.

"The Long Dark." *Babylon 5*. Written by Scott Frost. Directed by Mario DiLeo. PTEN, November 30, 1994.

Marx, Karl. *Grundrisse: Foundations of the Critique of Political Economy*. Translated by Martin Nicolaus. New York: Vintage, 1973.

McCarron, Kevin. "Religion, Philosophy and the End of History." In James and Mendlesohn, 131–44.

Merchant, Paul. *The Epic*. London: Methuen, 1971.

"Mind War." *Babylon 5*. Written by J. Michael Straczynski. Directed by Bruce Seth Green. PTEN, March 2, 1994.

Mueller, Martin. "Oral Poetry, the 'Iliad' and the Modern Reader." In Draper, 171–83.

"The Paragon of Animals." *Babylon 5*. Written by J. Michael Straczynski. Directed by Mike Vejar. TNT, February 4, 1998.

"The Parliament of Dreams." *Babylon 5*. Written by J. Michael Straczynski. Directed by Jim Johnston. PTEN, February 23, 1994.

"Phoenix Rising." *Babylon 5*. Written by J. Michael Straczynski. Directed by David Eagle. TNT, April 1, 1998.

"Rising Star." *Babylon 5*. Written by J. Michael Straczynski. Directed by Tony Dow. PTEN, October 20, 1997.

Sawyer, Andy. "The Shadows out of Time: Lovecraftian Echoes in *Babylon 5*." In James and Mendlesohn, 61–70.

Schofield, Anne M., and Nickianne Moody. "Reconsidering Gender and Heroism." In James and Mendlesohn, 50–59.

"Secrets of the Soul." *Babylon 5*. Written by J. Michael Straczynski. Directed by Tony Dow. TNT, March 4, 1998.

Sharkey, Betsy. "A Man with a 5-Year Plan." *Mediaweek*, October 21, 1996, 20, 24, 28.

"Signs and Portents." *Babylon 5*. Written by J. Michael Straczynski. Directed by Janet Greek. PTEN, May 18, 1994.

Straczynski, J. M. "The Profession of Science Fiction, 48: Approaching Babylon." *Foundation* 64 (Summer 1995): 5–19.

"A Tragedy of Telepaths." *Babylon 5*. Written by J. Michael Straczynski. Directed by Tony Dow. TNT, March 25, 1998.

"A View from the Gallery." *Babylon 5*. Written by J. Michael Straczynski. Directed by Janet Greek. TNT, February 11, 1998.

"The War Prayer." *Babylon 5*. Written by D. C. Fontana. Directed by Richard Compton. PTEN, March 9, 1994.

"War without End." *Babylon 5*. Written by J. Michael Straczynski. Directed by Mike Vejar. PTEN, May 13, 1996, and May 20, 1996.

"Whatever Happened to Mr. Garibaldi?" *Babylon 5*. Written by J. Michael Straczynski. Directed by Kevin Dobson. PTEN, November 11, 1996.

"The Wheel of Fire." *Babylon 5*. Written by J. Michael Straczynski. Directed by Janet Greek. TNT, November 4, 1998.

Winnifrith, Tom. "Postscript." In Winnifrith, Murray, and Gransden, 109–18.

Winnifrith, Tom, Penelope Murray, and K. W. Gransden, eds. *Aspects of the Epic*. New York: St. Martin's, 1983.

"Z'ha'dum." *Babylon 5*. Written by J. Michael Straczynski. Directed by Adam Nimoy. PTEN, October 28, 1996.

STARGATE SG-1 AND THE QUEST FOR THE PERFECT SCIENCE FICTION PREMISE

Stan Beeler

The annals of science fiction television (SFTV) are littered with the hulks of series that, for one reason or another, never made it past a few short seasons of broadcast time. Some, if they appeal to the right kind of audience, live on as cult fiction, their plots never developing any further except in the active imaginations of fans whose textual poachings stretch the boundaries of both decorum and copyright law.[1] Others sink beneath the surface of our cultural consciousness, eliciting no interest except among academics or TV executives who desperately try to determine why they failed. Television is a harsh environment for nurturing new ideas, one where critically acclaimed series from respected creative talent—like Joss Whedon's *Firefly* (2002)—can quickly disappear if they do not live up to market expectations. A series that manages to live past its incubation period, develops an audience that follows it across networks, and generates a spin-off is a rare beast indeed. Notable for its longevity, *Stargate SG-1* endured for ten seasons (1997–2007), and its spin-off, *Stargate Atlantis*, has been on the air since 2004.[2] While many factors contribute to any series' run, in the case of *Stargate SG-1* I would suggest that it is a fortunate match of the series' underlying structures and premise with the dictates of contemporary television's dominant narrative paradigms.

In *The Limits of Interpretation*, Umberto Eco suggests that television narrative is especially representative of a contemporary aesthetic in which "iteration and repetition seem to dominate the whole world of artistic creation" (84). He believes that "every work aesthetically 'well done' . . . must achieve a dialectic between order and novelty, in other words, between scheme and novelty. . . . This dialectic must be perceived by the consumer, who must grasp not only the contents of the message, but also the way in which the message transmits those contents" (91). These criteria reflect a shift away from romantic aesthetics, which emphasized innovation above all, and a return to standards that prize familiar structures such as we find in the music and art of the baroque. Consider, for example, the structure of a fugue, which is based upon variations of a simple theme. Television, like many other contemporary artistic products, also prizes variations on familiar themes.[3] *Stargate SG-1* seems particularly well suited to such narrative imperatives, as it is designed around a plausible pseudoscientific concept—a science fiction premise—that encourages the audience to predict the events that will occur while also giving the illusion that each episode is completely new and in some respects unpredictable.

Certainly, the premise of *Stargate SG-1* is not new; it derives from Roland Emmerich's 1994 film *Stargate* and is brilliant in its simplicity. A circular, gatelike device, discovered in Egypt in the early twentieth century, is powered up by contemporary scientists working for the U.S. Air Force. At the other end of the gate, on a planet circling a distant star, a military and scientific team emerges and discovers a human population enslaved by snakelike parasites (Goa'uld) who possess the bodies of their human slaves. Inherent in this description are a number of concepts that drive the continued popularity of the series: travel to the stars,[4] military science fiction, an unequivocally evil enemy, strongly differentiated characters, and a linking of alien races with familiar human mythology. All of these are major contributing factors in the series' long-term success and are consistent with the predictable/novel nature of television's contemporary aesthetic that Eco describes. Consistent pseudoscience allows the viewer to become comfortable with the parameters of the Stargate world; military drama underpins the structure of the episodes through an archetypal struggle between good and evil; a familiar mythology allows the audience to anticipate the introduction of characters, locations, and plot structures; and the strong differentiation of the characters provides a comfortable template for much of the dialogue and action.

Space Travel

To further its aesthetic balance of familiarity and novelty, *Stargate SG-1* emphasizes the common science fiction activity of space travel but adds significant variations. The Stargate device recalls the effect of the transporter of *Star Trek* (1966–1969), but unlike *Star Trek*'s device, the Stargate provides nearly instantaneous transmission of people and objects across vast distances, thus eliminating the need for a spaceship. This change produces a fundamental difference in the plot structures and even set design of the series. Because the SG-1 team can commute rapidly to distant planets while maintaining contact with the military-political hierarchy and research facilities of Stargate Command, plots that revolve around the disjunction between politics on Earth and the realities of fighting an interstellar war on the other end of the Stargate become common.[5] The structure of a normal television narrative fits extremely well with the premise of the Stargate as a means of immediate transportation between radically different locations. Michael Z. Newman indicates that most television fiction writers "organize their stories into rather short segments, often less than two minutes in length. Viewers might call these scenes, but writers call them 'beats' and they are television's most basic storytelling unit. . . . [The networks] believe that the audience's attention is unlikely to be sustained for much longer than that" (17). These beats are the components of the multiple plot elements that make up an hour-long television episode. The Stargate device thus not only explains the multiple intertwined plotlines set in different locations but also gives reason to the quick shifts on beat from one plot unit to the next while avoiding the use of cramped sets to suggest the relatively small area of a spaceship. The ringlike Stargate itself requires limited computer-related special effects; there is the initial "kawoosh"[6] of water blasting out of a pool-like enclosure that has been turned on its side—usually depicted with stock footage—then a cut to a graphic of a rapid journey through a CGI tunnel, and the travel is done.

Of course, a number of other, more visually demanding means of transportation are used in the series, and *Stargate SG-1* has also developed a host of signature special effects that far exceed the basic Stargate device spectacle. For example, much short-distance transportation is accomplished by means of a series of heavy rings—aptly named the Ring Transporter—that are often buried in sand or earth. The rings flash upward to form a tubelike enclosure over the people or objects to be transported and then drop back into the ground, revealing an empty space. Unexpected activation of Ring Transporters provides for abrupt and surprising changes of location and attendant plot transitions. Furthermore, the Ring Transporters have proven useful devices for advancing a dramatic plot, since the normal structure of an hour-long television episode requires a small narrative climax in the beat before each of the four or so commercial breaks. Transporting an unsuspecting character away from a safe or dangerous location arouses audience interest about events subsequent to a commercial break. After the commercial, that minor climax is quickly resolved, and when the narrative continues, the scene shifts to the new location and movement toward the central plot climax resumes. While the audience is provided with easily understood devices that have a predictable effect on the outcome of the plot, the unexpected introduction of a new location and situation adds the aesthetic experience of novelty to the situation's comfortable repetition.

Characterization as Premise

Stargate SG-1 is not only a conventional space exploration narrative; it also revolves around the dynamic tension between the military and humanist components of the mission. The four members of the initial SG-1 team are Samantha Carter (Amanda Tapping), Jack O'Neill (Richard Dean Anderson), Daniel Jackson (Michael Shanks), and Teal'c (Christopher Judge). Carter and O'Neill are both members of the U.S. Air Force, but they represent widely different aspects of the military. Carter is a physicist and, although cognizant of military discipline, has a strong interest in pure science; that is, she is not primarily interested in military applications of scientific discoveries. In contrast, O'Neill, the SG-1 team leader, is a special ops veteran and considers the battle against aliens to be a primary goal of space travel. He travels to the stars to find new allies and weapons. Jackson is an anthropologist and linguist who is quite uncomfortable with the military bias of the team's mission. This constant tension is exacerbated by his tendency toward mysticism, which culminates in his temporary ascension to another plane of existence in the fifth-season episode "Meridian." Teal'c is a Jaffar (hereditary slave and human incubator to the Goa'uld). Although a warrior by trade, unlike the members of the Earth military he has a strong ethical conception of battle that is highly reminiscent of the courtly behavior of medieval knights.

The unlikely combination of these four radically different character types in a single team of explorers is extremely effective in furthering the series' larger narrative trajectory. For not only does the narrative develop through encounters with varied forms of alien life; it also

Standing before a Stargate portal are *Stargate SG-1*'s Teal'c (Christopher Judge), Samantha Carter (Amanda Tapping), Jack O'Neill (Richard Dean Anderson), and Daniel Jackson (Michael Shanks).

depends upon the tensions between the members of SG-1. This double capacity means that *Stargate SG-1* can transcend the limited depth of characterization common to military science fiction—which can devolve into a simple "good guys versus aliens" story—through its ongoing dialogue among the four distinct viewpoints represented by the characters. Moreover, as the characters develop, we see subtle variations in their natures that further enhance the plot possibilities. This technique of character development is a key to balancing the familiar and the innovative, for after ten years we feel that we know the characters personally, and any development of character must follow logical progressions that coincide with our understanding of human nature.[7] Yet the different backgrounds and goals of the SG-1 team allow for significant innovation, as they react differently to the common dilemmas presented each week.

Mythology

Another key contributing factor to *Stargate SG-1*'s longevity is its use of mythological themes and characters. As indicated above, television narrative strives to maintain its audience through a judicious use of familiar patterns that, when employed successfully, hide their nature through a bravura display of the new—characters, places, and situations. As students of the genre have often noted, science fiction depends heavily upon the creation of a coherent and internally consistent parallel universe; thus, no matter how outlandish the fictional deviations from the "real world," these deviations must logically fit together. This structural coherence is instrumental in providing *Stargate SG-1* with a narrative pattern that delivers all variations in a package that is immediately accessible to an audience already familiar with the underlying assumptions of its universe. The *Stargate* film used Egyptian mythology as a primary component of its basic premise, and it integrated facts and preconceptions about ancient Egypt available in popular culture with the science fiction elements of star travel and alien beings. When the creators of *Stargate SG-1* took over this hybrid mythology, they elaborated upon it, changing the technology of the Stargate to permit travel to a number of other places and times rather than just the ancient Egyptian world of Abydos. As a result, the SG-1 team visits many worlds based on other historical mythologies. And since the Stargate is presented as the basic technology through which the known universe has been populated, it also explains how those cultures came to be on those other planets. As such, it provides a mythological superstructure that explains the existence of all of the other mythologies in the overarching *Stargate* narrative. That the Goa'uld use the Stargate to pretend to be gods also aids in the development of a consistent alternate reality. When a culture that SG-1 contacts identifies its gods, the priests associated with these gods usually prove to be the antagonists for that episode; in this way the audience does not have to puzzle out the moral structure of any new culture the SG-1 team contacts, regardless of its seeming strangeness.

This pattern of mythological underpinning also informs the physical properties of the planets that provide the backdrop for *Stargate SG-1* episodes. A running gag used in the series is to point out the physical similarity of all the worlds that SG-1 visits. That is, the inhabited universe is apparently made up of planets that look remarkably like the heavily forested coast of British Columbia where much of the series is shot. Arid, desertlike Abydos is a notable exception, and this may have a lot to do with the fact that the series inherited Abydos from the film, which was not shot in Canada; rather, it recalls the film's shooting locations in California and Arizona. The basic premise that all planets that have a gate were seeded with human life lifted from various places on Earth at various times also neatly explains why we encounter so few of the "bug-eyed monsters" common in film in the first few seasons, and why the cultures encountered tend to be similar to cultures described in our own history books. (What it does not explain is why all inhabitants speak contemporary North American English.[8]) The Stargate is simply a remarkably flexible device, allowing the writers to foreground character studies and plotlines of the SG-1 team against a rich backdrop of cultures that are readily available for research. It also helps to speed up the exposition of the setting, as the audience is already reasonably familiar with the cultures that are presented. The writers simply drop a few familiar mythological names or have Daniel Jackson identify the historical precedent, and the basic parameters of an alien world are readily understood by the audience.

In addition to establishing external coherence, *Stargate SG-1* obeys one of the primary rules of good science fiction in maintaining a consistent internal mythology as it develops its story lines. Whenever a new planet or race is discovered, the series tries to integrate the new material into the backstory of previous episodes. This means that although the plotlines of individual episodes are often new, self-standing, and accessible to an audience that has not watched the whole series, the mythology that underpins the characters and stories stretches back across the course of the show, lending its varied adventures a compelling internal coherence. Egyptian mythology has proven to be an especially evocative choice for the overarching thematic of the series' first few seasons. The ornate decorations and massive architecture of ancient Egypt add a beautiful and cohesive visual design scheme to the sets and props, even extending to the interior of the unusual Goa'uld spacecraft, whose interiors are lit by torches. The resulting contrast between high technology and low, for example, or between the SG-1 team and troops of loincloth-clad, spear-carrying combatants is quite effective.[9]

But *Stargate SG-1*'s mythologically consistent world is not limited to the unifying scheme of ancient Egypt; it also extends to the numerous other alien races that have been invented to provide allies and enemies for the campaigners from Earth. As each race is added to the pantheon, the writers integrate it into the backstory of the *Stargate* universe and also provide a plausible integration into the mythology of the "real" Earth that exists outside the *Stargate* universe. This care in the creation of mythologically based alien races provides the series with an almost seamless fantasy structure, and although this technique has previously been used by a few SFTV series, the underlying premise of the Stargate effectively explains the existence of historical Earth cultures on distant planets.[10] In fact, each of the cultures involved in *Stargate SG-1*'s mythology helps to develop a reassuring, familiar structure that provides a background for the variations introduced in weekly episodes. Like the basso continuo in a piece of baroque music, the major races of the series that are discussed in the following section give *Stargate SG-1* a structure that allows for significant innovation in incidental characters and events.

Goa'uld

The Goa'uld are the first and most prominent alien race encountered by Stargate Command, and also one of the few nonhuman species to appear in the early seasons of the series. Some SFTV works on the principle of adding a new alien race almost every week, so that the newness counterbalances the familiar patterns of exploration and character development. In contrast, *Stargate SG-1* is judicious in introducing its alien races. The Goa'uld serve as a familiar configuration of the enemy for most of the series' ten seasons, whereas the innovative elements that take the show beyond a simple pattern of dull repetition are most often nonaggressive races of humans who have been transported to remote planets.

The idea of a snakelike creature that invades the human body brings a wealth of Freudian implications that enhance character motivation and allegorical plot dimensions. The mechanism of possession by an alien can also help to explain the character reversals that are common in serial television plots. Jason Mittell has described one variant of this technique as "narrative spectacle": "when the plot makes unforeseen sharp twists that cause the entire scenario to 'reboot,' changing the professional and interpersonal dynamics of almost every character" (36). As an example, we might note that, throughout the course of the series, most of the primary actors have played different versions of their characters (a ploy commonly used in fantasy series that feature vampires, demonic possession, and alternate universe doubles[11]). The idea that these creatures are masquerading as gods is also a moral trigger for North American culture, which, because of its monotheist background, might find offensive the notion of a host of gods who manipulate their devotees into war. The Goa'uld are also a postcolonial theorist's ideal enemy, since they not only transport and enslave the natives but also physically possess their bodies.[12]

Jaffa

The narrative consistency of *Stargate SG-1* depends heavily upon elaborate paired structures, so the series also devotes considerable effort to creating a victim race to contrast with the Goa'uld. Since the Goa'uld live by literally colonizing the bodies of human beings, the Jaffa become symbolic representatives of the problem of colonialism. They are so coopted by their Goa'uld masters that they serve as human incubators for the larval form of the Goa'uld, and the System Lords fight proxy wars using the Jaffa. It is interesting that the series creators have chosen to primarily—but not exclusively—cast African Americans in the Jaffa roles, for the symbolic connections of the Jaffa with slavery are obvious and serve to strengthen the liberation politics that run throughout the *Stargate* franchise. Although the series creators might instead have had the pseudo-Egyptian Goa'uld select Jewish slaves to achieve historical accuracy and create a consistent biblical context, they never relinquish an opportunity to combine concepts from different times and places in a cultural bricolage. In this case, using people of African descent as enslaved people mixes well with the Goa'uld as alien slave masters to resonate with American history. The Jaffa thus become an almost necessary accoutrement to the moral representation of the Goa'uld. They allow the introduction of master-slave narratives familiar to the audience and enable the heroic SG-1 team to perform the expected actions of liberation.

Ori and the Ancients

The underlying moral structure of *Stargate SG-1* is as important to the predictable nature of the episodes as is the consistent science fiction premise. Positive moral forces tend to have balancing negative forces, thus allowing the audience to identify the pattern and enjoy the novelty introduced into its iterations. We see an example of this technique when the race known as the Ancients is introduced. The Ancients are human-like beings who are said to have developed the system of Stargates and all of the technology that goes with it, including the city of Atlantis that is the focus of the *Stargate SG-1* spin-off series. The technology that is scattered around the universe, we learn, was left behind when the Ancients evolved enough to transcend their corporeal matter and ascend to a nonphysical plane of existence. The visual effects involved in this transcendence are fascinating, for as the Ancients become spiritually enlightened, they drift away from their bodies in tentacled spheres of light. The Ancients are another example of the series' use of hybrid mythology, sharing elements of Zen Buddhism, the ancient Greek legend of Atlantis, and a selection of Arthurian tales, including the story of Merlin and the search for the Holy Grail. As a narrative device, this particular mythological mixture allows the series to evoke a surprising variety of literary and religious traditions about contact between humans and spiritual beings and, more generally, to introduce spiritual elements into the plotlines of the series' otherwise "hard science fiction."

The series' ninth season introduces another sort of ascended being, the Ori, who add a Manichaean balance to the *Stargate* universe. Whereas the Ancients are a relatively positive expression of transcendence, the Ori are the evil side of that spirituality. They have discovered that they gain power by being worshipped by beings still on the physical plane. That they pretend to be gods and force people to submit to their quasireligious pronouncements is enough to brand them as evil in the series' context. In fact, some might see the Ori as a shadow form of the Goa'uld. The significant difference is that the Ori promise transcendence to their followers but never provide it, while the Goa'uld depend upon the stick far more than the carrot when dealing with minions. With the introduction of the Ori, the *Stargate* plotline develops a balance of angels and demons, and it reaps the benefits of conflicting spiritual agents. The Ancients do not become involved in the struggle and thereby allow the SG-1 team members to maintain their role as heroic defenders, while the Ori eagerly involve themselves in the physical world, providing truly powerful opponents for the heroes. This moral balance between the Ancients and the Ori clearly echoes that of the Goa'uld and Tok'ra and thus further develops the symmetrical structures at work throughout the series. This symmetry is as important to the familiar feeling of the series as the regular use of well-known mythological figures, for whenever a positive or negative element is introduced, the audience instinctively knows that there will soon be a paired variant, much like the inversion or retrograde of a theme in a fugue.

Metatextual Humor

Most of our discussion of *Stargate SG-1* so far has emphasized the impressive level of narrative coherence that marks the series. There is, however, an aspect of this show that, at first glance, appears to disrupt the familiar structure of its alternate reality. In his discussion of serial narrative, Eco notes how difficult it is "to distinguish between the repetition of the media and the repetition of the so-called major arts" (84). *Stargate SG-1*, although obviously aimed at a popular audience, frequently employs postmodern elements that mark what some call high art, thereby adding another dimension to its predictable/novel mix. In fact, the series often undercuts its narrative coherence with metatextual references to the process of writing and filming an SFTV series. While it might seem counterproductive for a show that relies heavily upon the coherence of its fictional world also to question its elaborately constructed alternate reality, at least three episodes are entirely devoted to plotlines foregrounding the narrative's fictionality. The one hundredth episode of the series, "Wormhole X-Treme," for example, tells of a ne'er-do-well alien, Martin Lloyd (Willie Garson), who has lost significant portions of his memory and has blended into Earth society, taking a job as a writer for the television series *Wormhole X-Treme*. This series follows the primary plotline of *Stargate SG-1*, and characters and writers from the real series appear in parodic representations of themselves. While in other series a narrative turn of this sort might constitute "jumping the shark,"[13] *Stargate SG-1* manages to allow its audience a peek behind the wizard's curtain while maintaining a level of narrative seriousness. This sort of self-parody has been an integral component of the series' makeup since its early years, as well as an accepted part of the postmodern aesthetic that undergirds so much of contemporary science fiction.[14]

In season eight, *Stargate SG-1* takes this reflexive dimension a step further, devoting an entire episode to the disjunction between commonly perceived notions of reality and the science fiction alternate reality developed in the series. In "Citizen Joe," a barber from Indiana, Joe Spencer (Dan Castellaneta[15]), acquires an innocuous-looking stone that is actually an alien device that allows him to share memories with Jack O'Neill, leader of the SG-1 team. Joe, who does not realize the source of his "false" memories, uses them to write science fiction stories. His subsequent failed attempts to publish the stories provide ample opportunity for metanarrative discussions and critiques of various episodes of *Stargate SG-1*. Furthermore, "Citizen Joe" incorporates a metanarrative tour de force when it references "Wormhole X-Treme." The two hundredth episode of the series, simply titled "200," also returns to the basic premise of "Wormhole X-Treme," although in this version the metaseries has been cancelled, and the actors and writers are speculating on the changes this event will bring to their careers. The formal announcement of *Stargate SG-1*'s cancellation at almost the same time this episode was broadcast effectively transformed it into a farewell episode, despite that it appeared well before the season's end.

This discussion of the underlying plot structures of *Stargate SG-1* should make it clear that the series not only incorporates a solid science fiction premise but also has successfully tailored its science fiction formula to accommodate the requirements of the repetitive aesthetic of contemporary television. Perhaps more important, it has deployed that aesthetic to help accomplish one of the important tasks of SFTV: helping cater to the basic human need to mythologize our environment. *Stargate SG-1* does not attempt to create a universe ex nihilo but integrates traditional mythology with contemporary scientific fact, speculation, and conjecture. The series' creators draw upon the audience's underlying cultural knowledge while treading a fine line between a rejection of spirituality and an ingenuous, new age mysticism. The series' basic premise thus allows its audience access to the wealth of human mystic traditions without requiring us to give up our contemporary desire to comprehend the world within a scientific framework. Figures that would have been perceived as gods and demons in the fiction of other eras have thus been transformed through its underlying scientific mythologization. Although the Goa'uld and Ori are no less powerful than their clearly defined mythic predecessors, the source of their power is consistent with contemporary conceptions of the structure of reality.

The series' science, if outlandish at times, manages to be internally consistent and interesting to a broad audience; its incorporation of mythological elements allows for an array of visually impressive sets and costumes; and its concept of near instantaneous travel through the Stargate provides for the rapid switching between multiple plotlines so important to the structure of contemporary television narrative. Yet the series always frames these novel effects within a comfortable pattern of themes and structures, of familiar tropes and histories, thereby producing the delicate balance Eco describes that can help explain why audiences tuned in week after week for ten years. This is, perhaps, the key to *Stargate SG-1*'s success in the highly competitive environment of contemporary television drama. Familiarity encourages habitual watching, and plot innovation, closely integrated into the medium's structural parameters, provides the leaven that makes each new episode interesting. The contemporary audience does not seek something completely new every evening. If this were so, then serial drama would not have gained the popularity it currently enjoys. Nevertheless, like a piece of baroque music, *Stargate SG-1* consistently manages to manipulate the familiar elements of mythology, science, and character templates in new and fascinating configurations.

Moreover, this balancing of familiarity and innovation extends to the series' surprising ability to integrate elements of a postmodern aesthetic into a familiar narrative formula that some still pejoratively term "genre fiction." Under the guise of self-deprecating humor, *Stargate SG-1* uses the techniques of contemporary high art to foreground the narrative and technical imperatives of SFTV. When a plot element is an obvious cliché, television writers will often "hang a lantern on it." That is, they will have a character directly refer to the hackneyed plot element, indicating awareness of the predictable outcome. This series has taken the technique into the realm of postmodern aesthetics through the use of self-reflexive episodes that "hang a lantern" on the series' whole narrative structure. The result is a genre production that employs many of the comfortable conventions without offending the artistic sensibilities of a relatively sophisticated audience. For these reasons—and others—*Stargate SG-1* survived for a decade in a highly competitive media environment, and its successful spin-off, *Stargate Atlantis*, suggests that this franchise will in various forms continue for many years more.

Notes

The "Mythology" section of this chapter was suggested by an interview that I gave for a documentary with the working title "Beyond the Mythology of *Stargate SG-1*," produced for broadcast in April 2007. The documentary will be included on the direct-to-DVD movies that are planned for the series. The interview was conducted by the documentary's coproducer, Kerry Hittinger, in December 2006.

1. For a detailed discussion of this phenomenon, see Henry Jenkins's *Textual Poachers*.

2. *Stargate SG-1* was initially broadcast on the cable network Showtime in 1997 and then moved to the Sci-Fi Channel in 2002. The franchise is owned by MGM, and there is speculation that it will be continued in the form of another film or spin-off.

3. For a study of connections between the musical similarities of the aesthetics of repetition and another contemporary television series, see my article "There Is Nothing New in the Underworld: Narrative Recurrence and Visual Leitmotivs in *Charmed*."

4. The fascination of science fiction has been built upon the founding concept of space travel to such an extent that the term "space opera" has, for many nonfans, come to be synonymous with science fiction.

5. An example of this motif is the episode "Politics," whose plot deals with the struggle by the U.S. Air Force to maintain control of the Stargate, despite efforts by a senator to cut its government funding.

6. Kawoosh! Productions VII is one of the companies involved in production of *Stargate SG1*.

7. In *Seeing through the Eighties*, Jane Feuer argues that characters do not really develop in serial television; their positions just shift in relation to one another (128).

8. In contrast, the *Star Trek* franchise and *The Hitchhiker's Guide to the Galaxy* (2005) constantly reiterate their science fiction solution to the language problem.

9. Of course, the link between ancient Egyptian culture and alien contact is not an invention of the series or the film. Erich von Däniken published a number of books in the 1960s and 1970s based on the ancient astronaut theory. However, *Stargate SG-1* effectively explores the aesthetic potential of this notion.

10. For example, *Star Trek* in its first series occasionally based its fantasy worlds on existing human mythology, but there was rarely any attempt to integrate the mythology into the series' underlying premise.

11. A good example of this technique is the character Angel in the series *Buffy the Vampire Slayer* (1997–2003) and its eponymous spin-off *Angel* (1999–2004). Angel is a vampire with a soul that makes him behave in an altruistic manner, but under certain circumstances the soul is removed and the actor (David Boreanez) has a chance to exercise his full range of acting ability as a villain.

12. The Goa'uld are not the only alien species that masquerade as gods in the *Stargate* franchise. For example, in "Spirits," shape-shifting aliens pose as the protective spirits of a people derived from Salish American Indians.

13. A television series "jumps the shark" when it has reached the end of logical narrative variations. The term refers to an episode of *Happy Days* (1974–1984) in which a character performs the unnecessary feat (jumping a shark) while water skiing.

14. For a more detailed analysis of the self-referential humor of *Stargate SG-1*, see my article "'It's a Zed PM.'"

15. Castellaneta voices Homer Simpson on *The Simpsons*. The series is reported to be one of Richard Dean Anderson's favorites, and subtle references to *The Simpsons* abound in *Stargate SG-1*.

Works Cited

Beeler, Stan. "'It's a Zed PM': *Stargate SG-1*, *Stargate Atlantis* and Canadian Production of American Television." In *Reading Stargate SG-1*, edited by Stan Beeler and Lisa Dickson, 154–66. London: Tauris, 2006.

———. "There Is Nothing New in the Underworld: Narrative Recurrence and Visual Leitmotivs in *Charmed*." In *Investigating* Charmed: *The Magic Power of TV*, edited by Stan Beeler and Karin Beeler, 129–42. London: Tauris, 2007.

Däniken, Erich von. *Chariots of the Gods.* New York: Putnam, 1968.

Eco, Umberto. *The Limits of Interpretation.* Bloomington: Indiana University Press, 1990.

Feuer, Jane. *Seeing through the Eighties: Television and Reaganism.* Durham, NC: Duke University Press, 1995.

Jenkins, Henry. *Textual Poachers: Television Fans and Participatory Culture.* New York: Routledge, 1992.

Mittell, Jason. "Narrative Complexity in Contemporary American Television." *Velvet Light Trap* 58 (2006): 29–40.

Newman, Michael Z. "From Beats to Arcs: Toward a Poetic of Television Narrative." *Velvet Light Trap* 58 (2006): 16–28.

THE ISLAND'S GREATEST MYSTERY

Is *Lost* Science Fiction?

David Lavery

> What we get from science fiction . . . is not different from the thing that makes mainstream stories rewarding, but only expressed differently. *We live on a minute island of known things.* Our undiminished wonder at the mystery which surrounds us is what makes us human. In science fiction we can approach that mystery, not in small, everyday symbols, but in bigger ones of space and time.
>
> —Damon Knight,
> *In Search of Wonder* (my italics)

> The lure of the genre lies at least partly in its capacity to open up imaginative possibilities.
>
> —Geoff King and Tanya Krzywinska,
> *Science Fiction Cinema*

At the beginning of the third season of ABC's hit television series *Lost*, a group of individuals gather in a living room (at the outset the viewer has no idea where) for a meeting of what turns out to be a book club. The host of the gathering, Juliet, whose preparations for the party have included steeling herself before a mirror to the tune of Petula Clark's "Downtown" and carelessly burning some homemade muffins, immediately faces a mutiny. One outspoken member of the group, Adam, has harsh words for her choice of books, *Carrie*, Stephen King's novel about a high school girl whose powers of telekinesis wreak havoc after her humiliation at the senior prom.[1] He dismisses it as "not even literature," as "popcorn," as "by-the-numbers religious hokum-pokum," as . . . "*science fiction*." Claiming to be "absolutely thrilled" that Adam hates her "all-time favorite book," she responds with indignation to his observation that her choice no doubt led to Ben's absence from the meeting.

She sarcastically notes that she was under the impression that "free will actually still existed on the . . ."

Juliet's rant and the book club discussion are, however, interrupted by an apparent earthquake. As the clubbers flee, a man crawls out from under her house (where he had earlier been fixing the plumbing), and veteran *Lost* watchers, now seeing his face for the first time, recognize him as Ethan Rom, the pretend castaway who abducted Claire's baby in season one. We immediately make out as well that a man who emerges out of a nearby house to investigate the disturbance, soon after identified as the book club absentee "Ben," is in reality Henry Gale, who, as we learned in the final episode of season two, may well be the leader (or at least *a* leader) of the mysterious "others."

Now, viewers—and the castaways—have been led to believe that the others live a primitive life on the island, but Juliet, Ben, and Ethan, if they are, in fact, others, seem here to dwell in a pleasant little village of perfectly manicured small cottages. As Ben and the other others look up at the source of a loud noise overhead, *Lost*aholics gasp at the realization that again, as in the opening scene of the previous season, we have been deceived, this time about time as well as place,[2] for the events transpiring before our eyes are from the narrative past. Above, a plane, Oceanic 815, breaks into three pieces and plummets to Earth, and Ben quickly dispatches two trusted but now (in *Lost*'s present tense) dead underlings: Goodwin (killed by Ana Lucia in season two's "The Other 48 Days") and Ethan (shot by Charlie in season one's "Homecoming"), to rush to the scenes of the crash and mix in with the survivors. As the camera pulls away in telephoto jumps—establishing shots that end rather than introduce the sequence—we see that the others' well-manicured settlement is nestled in what appears to be a crater on an island. Another island is visible in the distance. And in the sky overhead, the jet trails of the doomed Oceanic flight are still visible.

That a Stephen King novel would emerge as the latest text on this island, following in the wake of the many books read by Sawyer (*Watership Down, A Wrinkle in Time, Lancelot, Bad Twin*), the volumes in the hatch (*The Turn of the Screw, The Third Policeman, An Occurrence at Owl Creek Bridge*), and Desmond's saved-for-his-deathbed *Our Mutual Friend*, should not surprise us. The best-selling author has championed the series since its inception (King, "*Lost*'s Soul"), and *Carrie*'s cameo is in one sense a shout-out to a friend of the show.[3]

That Adam dismisses *Carrie* as "science fiction," however, does come as a surprise. Few critics of the genre would label the book science fiction. Horror, yes, but horror science fiction. Adam's dismissive charge is, of course, in keeping with at least one usage of a designation about which almost no one seems to agree. When George W. Bush responded to a reporter's suggestion, during the 2000 Republican primary season, that he had avoided military duty during the Vietnam War due to his father's influence, he called the charge "science fiction," meaning that it was not just false but really, really false. We readily recognize that, whatever Adam or "W" meant by the label, it was clearly not intended as praise. But like the inclusion of a King novel as part of *Lost*'s complex narrative, Adam's use of the term resonates on another level: as textual recognition of goings-on outside the series itself.

For had not *Lost* won a Hugo Award in its first season from the World Science Fiction Society? Had it not inspired, in the always quick-to-copy world of network TV, science fiction wannabes: *Surface* on NBC, *Threshold* on CBS, *Invasion* also on ABC (all now off the air). Yet, more than two seasons in (I am writing during the third season), *Lost*'s science fiction–ness remains highly problematic. Certainly, one could argue that *Lost* is not science fiction at all. In this essay I want to test some key aspects of *Lost* against several touchstone definitions of "science fiction" to determine whether or not the series is justifiably science fiction gold.

At the outset, I should stipulate that we have reason to believe network executives have pointedly sought to steer *Lost*'s narrative away from such a genre affiliation (Porter and Lavery, 1st ed. 18–21), evidently fearing that, as was the case with *Twin Peaks* in the early 1990s, too much weirdness would drive away viewers from a prized cash cow. Yet, whatever the intentions of ABC in regard to *Lost*'s science fiction identity, it remains abundantly clear that the series' avid, energized fandom (not to mention the World Science Fiction Society) very much wants to read it as science fiction, with or without the help of its creators.

As *Unlocking the Meaning of* Lost details, fan theorizing about the island's mysteries has often been informed by science (Porter and Lavery, 1st ed. 157–82). For every conspiracy theory of a religious or philosophical nature (e.g., the oft suggested and just as often denied notion that all the characters are in some kind of purgatory), there are a dozen more that suggest that the island is overrun by nanotechnology (another theory repeatedly dismissed by executive producers Damon Lindelof and Carlton Cuse), that Oceanic 815 went through a wormhole into an alternate reality, or that a working knowledge of string theory is absolutely essential to understanding the mysterious island.

That *Lost*'s science fiction–ness is problematic comes with the territory, for more than a century into its history (or is it centuries? millennia?), the very definition of the genre itself still remains a matter of dispute.

Definition One

In *How to Write Science Fiction and Fantasy*, Orson Scott Card states simply, "What SF writers write is SF" (11). Similarly, Damon Knight offers, "Science Fiction is what I mean when I point to it" (quoted in Gunn 71). For both Card and Knight, each a practitioner of the genre as well as a critic, the answer to the question of science fiction's nature is essentially tautological: science fiction is what science fiction authors do; science fiction is the form we recognize as such. Needless to say, neither definition, though representative of one camp in the debate over science fiction's nature, is especially illuminating; neither is likely to enable us to pick science fiction definitively out of a police lineup or differentiate it precisely from other pretenders; and neither is advantageous in testing *Lost*'s science fiction–ness.

Some of *Lost*'s writers have, it is true, authored science fiction in other lives: J. J. Abrams, who cowrote and directed the pilot and then, characteristically, went on to other projects, did introduce clear science fiction elements into *Alias* (2001–2006)—the Rambaldi mythology, for example—and Cuse helped to create and write the quite science fiction western *The Adventures of Brisco County, Jr.* (1993–1994). But does it therefore follow, as Card's perverse gloss would suggest, that *Lost* must therefore be science fiction as well?[4] Thousands (if not more), including a major professional organization, have pointed to *Lost* as science fiction, but thinking does not make it so.

Definition Two

In *The Visual Encyclopedia of Science Fiction*, George Turner explains that Theodore Sturgeon, one of the grand literary masters of science fiction, considered "science fiction" a "term [that] can be applied only to a story wherein removal of its scientific content would invalidate the narrative" (257). John Campbell, best known as the author of the story "Who Goes There?" which inspired two versions of *The Thing* (1951, 1982), concurs: "To be science fiction, not fantasy, an honest effort at prophetic extrapolation of the known must be made. Ghosts can enter science fiction, if they're logically explained, but not if they are simply the ghosts of fantasy. Prophetic extrapolation can derive from a number of different sources, and apply in a number of fields. Sociology, psychology, and para-psychology are, today, not true sciences; therefore, instead of forecasting future results of application of sociological science of today, we must forecast the development of a science of sociology. From there the story can take off" (quoted in Gunn 74). For both writers, science fiction is decidedly not fantasy. Failure to cast science in some central role in the narrative makes it, ipso facto, not science fiction. For Campbell, the seemingly supernatural, not to mention extrapolations from the social—or soft—sciences, can put in appearances in science fiction without inviting disqualification only if they are prehardened— that is, stamped with the episteme of the scientific worldview.

Lost, of course, has not excluded science from the island. The already mentioned inclination of fans to speculate about secret scientific endeavors follows naturally from the presence of the still mysterious Dharma Initiative and its many research projects: "meteorology, psychology, parapsychology, zoology, electromagnetism, and utopian social [experiments]" ("Orientation").

And the island has its ghosts. In "White Rabbit," for example, Jack's father leads him on a journey into the jungle during which he nearly falls to his death and then discovers a new source of water for the castaways. Yemi, Mr. Eko's brother, lures him to his brutal death at the made-from-smoke fist of the monster in "The Cost of Living." Though Christian Shephard's body is onboard Oceanic 815 (Jack finds the missing casket in the Adam and Eve cave), the appearance of his specter is certainly not made "logical" as Campbell means the word. Yemi's body

Several of the castaways of *Lost* set out to explore the jungle of their mysterious island.

is likewise on the island (via the heroin-smuggling plane that, incredibly, crashed there on its flight from Nigeria), but does his "incarnation" in Eko's dreams and, later, outside the Pearl hatch, seemingly as the monster's lethal enticement, meet Campbell's litmus test?

Lindelof and Cuse suggested in "The Official *Lost* Audio Podcast"

(November 6, 2006) that in the much talked about first encounter between Eko and the monster (in "The 23rd Psalm"), he was being "read" by the smoke being: it was mapping his psyche in their face-to-face—hence the holographic representations of his past, including his relationship with his brother, clearly visible in the smoke. An impalpable entity able to read minds and later create a seemingly corporeal manifestation based on its mystical interrogation—is this "logical" in Campbell's sense?

Definition Three

In a difficult, compelling, and ultimately debate-redefining 1979 book, *Metamorphosis of Science Fiction*, Darko Suvin insists the controversy over the nature of science fiction, defined as "the literature of cognitive estrangement" (4), can be solved only by asking epistemological questions. Famously, Suvin identifies the presence of a "novum" as a key science fiction signature. A novum, a "new thing," an element of material culture, an idea, an action or event, when it announces itself in a science fiction tale, simultaneously declares, because of its radical originality, its temporal impossibility in this particular universe, the narrative to be science fiction.

When the first aired episode of Joss Whedon's *Firefly*, "The Train Job," opens in a saloon, a newcomer to the series is not likely to read the scene as science fiction. The setting, in fact, invites the viewer to begin processing the narrative as a western. When the characters begin to use a smattering of Chinese words as part of their colorful language, we are, of course, less certain of the genre locus. When, in an ensuing bar fight, Captain Mal Reynolds is thrown through a window and the evidently holographic pane reforms behind him, we suspect we are not in Kansas anymore. And when, their backs against a cliff, Mal and company are saved from certain doom by a hovering spaceship, the verdict is in: we are watching science fiction. The Chinese words, the holographic window, the spaceship—each is a novum in Suvin's terms; the presence of each estranges us, undermines our expectations, requires us to adapt or expand our imaginative framework and, finally, to begin reading the narrative as science fiction.

A novum may be something radically new. In *The Matrix* we would seem to be watching police chasing a criminal across city rooftops (something we might have seen in, say, Hitchcock's *Vertigo*) until Trinity (and the Agents in hot pursuit) makes a beyond-belief leap from one building to the next. The response of a trailing beat cop—"That's impossible!"—identifies the act as a novum in Suvin's terms. But a novum may also be, in the right context, quite mundane.

In Clifford Simak's short story "Over the River and through the Woods," two young children mysteriously appear on a midwestern American farm in the middle of the nineteenth century, claiming to be the offspring of distant relatives who have sent them away for safekeeping in the rural setting. Gradually the truth is disclosed: the children are from the future, sent back by the farm family's descendents in a time machine from an Earth threatened by alien invasion. The discovery that the children are not who they claim to be (or from where they claim to be from) begins with the farmers' bafflement (a.k.a. estrangement) at a never before seen strip of interlocking metal "teeth" on one of the children's pants. In mid-nineteenth-century America, even a zipper can be a novum.[5]

Now, *Lost* is full of moments of estrangement. Mysterious incidents and events and enigmatic plot and character developments abound. An enigmatic set of numbers (4, 8, 15, 16, 23, 42) recurs, not just on and in the hatch (where, when loaded into a computer every 108 minutes—the sum of these numbers—they disperse a buildup of electromagnetic energy that, if not released, will result in an explosion capable of bringing down a jumbo jet flying overhead), but also in the world at large (on the dashboard reading of a rental car, spelled out by cheerleaders' uniforms in the Sydney airport, chanted by a mental patient). The monster, seemingly made up of a cloud of black smoke, terrorizes the island, killing the pilot of the Oceanic 815 flight and, later, Eko himself. At least two individuals, John Locke, who before the crash had been a paraplegic, and Rose, who was dying from cancer, are miraculously healed by the island. In a burgeoning number of "*Lost* crosses," the survivors of the crash have been anything but strangers. Prior to their common fate on the island, their backstories reveal, many of their paths had already crossed: Hurley and Locke endured the same horrible manager, and Locke worked in a box factory Hurley owned. Libby and Hurley were both patients in a mental hospital, and Libby gave Desmond the sailboat in which he crashed on the island. Kelvin, the man Desmond replaced as the hatch's button pusher (and killed), trained Sayid as a torturer in Iraq. Jack and Desmond met while running the steps in a stadium in Los Angeles. A polar bear seen earlier on a comic book read by Walt (and Hurley) seemingly takes material form on the island. Walt, AWOL for almost all of season two, appears to possess extraordinary though not yet defined powers, including, perhaps, astral projection and telekinesis.

Thus it is not my contention that *Lost* is not full of mysteries, but the presence of mysteries does not, in and of itself, make a television series science fiction.[6] Certainly no one would have claimed that the enigmatic *Twin Peaks*, which featured a supernatural, psychopathic serial killer named BOB, was science fiction. Science fiction, according to Suvin, is characterized by "the presence and interaction of estrangement *and* cognition" (my italics), and the cognition, the explanation, must make scientific sense—must be readable as "not impossible within the cognitive (cosmological and anthropological) norms of the author's epoch" (7–8). *Lost* has given us estrangement enough for ten television series, but believable cognition? Not so much—not yet.

We learned in "Live Together, Die Alone," the final episode of season two, that the much speculated upon mystery of Oceanic 815's crash was caused by one of the island's electromagnetic anomalies (even learned the exact time and date of the crash). But that doesn't make it science fiction, because electromagnetism is a scientific reality.

Even if the island has, in fact, made the lame walk and cured a fatal cancer (although we do not know for certain yet that the island deserves the credit), we cannot for all that brand such developments as science fiction. For in the paradigm of the modern epoch, such miraculous healing must be considered unscientific, probably impossible—a fiction, but not science fiction.

Clearly, we still have much to learn about *Lost*'s monster, but suffice it to say that we cannot at this point conclude that it is a science fiction monster. Unlike the aliens of all those *Alien* and *Predator* movies, classic examples of the genre's fascination with exozoology, or even the "monster from the Id" of *Forbidden Planet* (1956), a beast given form out of the unconscious of Dr. Morbeus and given credence by the theorizing of Sigmund Freud, *Lost*'s monster has yet to be given any real underpinning. It may well turn out to be a science fiction monster, or it all just might go up in smoke.

David Lavery

Definition Four and the End of *Lost*

Early in 2007, a wide variety of print, online, and broadcast media reported that show runners Cuse and Lindelof had begun talks with ABC to establish a definite end point for *Lost*. The negotiations were newsworthy precisely because they were unparalleled, an attempt to prearrange an armistice in the "war between art and commerce" certain to shadow the remainder of the series' run.[7]

As *Unlocking the Meaning of* Lost notes, the advantages of such an agreement are clear enough:

> To know precisely when *Lost*'s creators would need to resolve the show's myriad mysteries, to ascertain in advance when its many character arcs would need to hit their targets, to predetermine when best to pull the plug . . . would be in everyone's best interest. The creators, the network, the fans—all would benefit. To set limits to one of contemporary television's most amazing creations would make it more likely to be remembered as such. The clearly defined terminus of the Harry Potter books (there will be seven and only seven) was cited as a role model. *The X-Files'* extension beyond its natural life was evoked as a cautionary tale. (Porter and Lavery, 2nd ed. 13)

But the end of *Lost*, predetermined or not, will certainly have another effect of great relevance to our present consideration.

The polymathic science fiction writer and critic Samuel R. Delany defines science fiction as "a new way of reading, a new way of making texts make sense—collectively producing a new set of codes." Science fiction writers invented the genre, he claims, "by writing new kinds of sentences and embedding them in contexts in which those sentences were readable" (79). Scholar of the genre Brian Attebery provides a gloss: "What distinguishes science fiction from other kinds of fiction is a peculiar compromise between scientific truth and untruth. Samuel Delany has analyzed this compromise in terms of the SF text's subjunctivity. . . . What he means by this term is the degree to which every statement in the fiction describes a hypothetical condition: something that is not happening, has not happened, could not have happened in the past (unlike realistic fiction), but might happen, given the proper changes in society and scientific knowledge. Another word for subjunctivity might be 'ifness,' the condition of being contingent" (Attebery

29–30). Here, in the last of our definitions, we find a similar but more concise rendering of Suvin's more obscure take on the genre. Drawing on the insights of reader-response literary criticism, Delany proposes that we understand science fiction as a way of knowing a text—as what happens when we read in a certain way.

As we negotiate a text, whether a literary, filmic, or televisual one,[8] reader-response criticism has shown us, we make our way with imperfect knowledge, reading both forward (anticipating with partial understanding what is to come) and backward (reconsidering what we once believed in light of new information). The "consistently changing fictional world" we encounter is "one that appears to us as whole and complete at any given moment during the reading act" (Allen 79), but it is not—until, that is, the end. And at that end we must reread, if not literally—turning back to page one, or watching again the entire movie or television series—then at least in our imaginations, as we rethink what it all meant, whether our once tentative hypotheses, conjectures, and assumptions still hold up.

Delany and Attebery, like Suvin before them, seek to remind us that "reading" science fiction likewise requires a "wandering viewpoint" (Wolfgang Iser, quoted in Allen 79), but one in which one of the conundrums is whether or not what we read is really science fiction. If we think it is, we will read it differently. We will read subjunctively; we will read—and view—with "ifness."

Is *Lost*, then, science fiction? At the risk, very much in the tradition of *Lost* itself, of frustrating or angering my audience, I can only conclude that, at this point in the series' development, we do not know. A series with an obsessed fandom that has become a worldwide cultural phenomenon based largely on the endless speculation its multiple mysteries have generated around the water cooler, in the mass media, and (most of all) on the Internet, *Lost* is now precariously perched on the horns of a dilemma it created. Judging by the drop in ratings that is now worrying everyone involved with the show, viewers may well be growing weary with *Lost*'s indefinitely delayed gratification. When will we know the answers to the still proliferating questions the series has raised? When will we know the true purposes of the others? What exactly is the monster? Can the island really heal its inhabitants? The perils of "serial creativity" (Dolan; Porter and Lavery, 1st ed. 17–21), the very conditions of televisual narrative, necessitate that such mysteries be prolonged to fuel the needs of a long-term story arc, so we could well need to wait until the entire *Lost* skein plays out.

We may not know, then, whether *Lost* is science fiction until the final closing credits, until the final Bad Robot whizzes across the screen and comes face-to-face with the camera and with us, until we have left the island for good, until, as Damon Knight offers, "our undiminished wonder at the mystery" of life itself is over.

A Postscript

Season three of *Lost* was divided into two parts: the so-called miniseries, the first six episodes of the season, concerning Jack, Kate, and Sawyer's captivity by the others—after the conclusion of which the above was written—and the seventeen episodes that followed. Many of those contain nothing even remotely connected to science fiction: "Stranger in a Strange Land," yet another Jack backstory; "Enter 77," which takes us into Sayid's past and introduces us to the supposed "last surviving member of the Dharma Initiative"; "Per Avion," with its revelation that Jack and Claire share a father; the wacky, let's-write-out-characters-nobody-cares-about-in-a-very-self-referential-way "Exposé"; the give-Charlie-one-more-backstory-before-we-kill-him "Greatest Hits." All of these are serviceable enough episodes but do not further this investigation. Two Juliet backstories, "Not in Portland" and "Left Behind," and the Sun and Jin vehicle "D.O.C." all involve science of the ob-gyn variety and introduce the burning question, certain to be important in season four, of why babies conceived on the island and their mothers are all doomed. However, as I hope I have made clear above, science does not equal science fiction.

Season three did, of course, compound the already long list of unsolved *Lost* mysteries. Did the others really have the power to answer Juliet's wish in "Not in Portland" to have her husband run over by a bus? Was the meteor that obliterated Hurley's Mr. Cluck's restaurant (not to mention a certain eponymous newscaster) in "Trisha Tanaka Is Dead" really brought on by the numbers' curse? How did Locke's despicable father end up on the island, as we find in "The Man from Tallahassee" and "The Brig"? Did he really materialize, as Ben explains, from a "capacious magical box," capable of bringing forth anything imaginable? Why has Richard Alpert not aged a day since Ben met him in the jungle as a boy? Perhaps most important, who or what is Jacob? Is he a corporeal being? Why can Ben see him but Locke cannot, though he does hear his plea for help in "The Man behind the Curtain"?

The most important development in these episodes is the revelation, hinted at in the *Lost* miniseries and confirmed in "Flashes before Your Eyes," that Desmond survived the implosion of the hatch at the end of season two with an altered consciousness. In one of *Lost*'s most fascinating episodes, Desmond apparently journeys back in time, relives his past, and breaks up with Penny after meeting a mysterious woman, Mrs. Hawking, who informs him it is destiny to end up on the island, push the button, turn the failsafe key, and save the lives of every single person on the planet. In subsequent episodes Desmond remains able to catch glimpses of the future, including Charlie's death in the season finale (in "Catch-22," Desmond's intervention temporarily prevents it). Judging by the number of critics, bloggers, and Web sites characterizing Desmond as a time traveler, "Flashes" might well have been the long anticipated science fiction smoking gun. And yet whether Desmond actually does go back in time is by no means certain.

Each of these enigmas could find a home in a science fiction narrative, but my earlier position stands: it is by no means clear, yet, if we can label *Lost* as such. What is now certain is that *Lost* will end. Lindelof and Cuse have negotiated a deal with ABC for three more seasons of sixteen episodes each, many of which, if season three's finale "Through the Looking Glass" is any indication, will be filled with flash-forwards instead of the backstories to which we have become accustomed. In May 2010, when we come to the end of *Lost*, we will know whether it was science fiction.

Notes

1. Although the author is mentioned, the cover of the book is never clearly shown on screen. Astute fans (*Lost* has perhaps the most active and inquisitive fan base in the history of television) immediately identified the book (an obscure, out of print edition) and posted their discovery online. *Lost* show runners Damon Lindelof and Carlton Cuse soon after confirmed the title of Juliet's book of choice.

2. Season two began by following Desmond's early morning routine in the hatch (Mama Cass on the phonograph, exercise, breakfast, daily injection) prior

to Jack, Hurley, Kate, and Locke's explosive entry. Until the end of the sequence, which repeats the final shot of season one, we have no idea what we are watching or where we are.

3. King's love of *Lost* may be the result of his having found it King-like, for the show's creators repeatedly cite King's *The Stand* as one of their key influences (see Porter and Lavery, 1st ed. 130–38).

4. Card has edited a book on *Lost*, in which, tellingly, he has little to say about the series as science fiction. See below.

5. Although Elias Howe patented something very like a zipper in 1851, the closure as we know it was not invented until 1917 and was not in common use until the 1930s.

6. Nor is it entirely certain that all the enigmas are unfathomable. As Orson Scott Card notes in his introduction to *Getting Lost*, the show frequently hedges its bets: "Some of [*Lost*'s mysteries] point to science fiction—the laboratory where Claire and her baby were obviously about to be the victims of a mad-scientist plot, the serum that the previous tender of the hatch was injecting himself with, the mechanical explanations that keep turning up for otherwise fantastical events. (Ah, there are polar bears in the training film! Ah, the monster is a *machine!*)" (13).

7. I owe the phrase "war between art and commerce" to series star Matthew Fox (Jack), who predicted it during an interview with Jon Stewart on *The Daily Show* during season two.

8. See Allen's superb conflation of these three types of reading.

Works Cited

Allen, Robert C. "Reader-Oriented Criticism and Television." In *Channels of Discourse: Television and Contemporary Culture*, edited by Robert C. Allen, 74–112. Chapel Hill: University of North Carolina Press, 1987.

Attebery, Brian. *Teacher's Guide to Accompany* The Norton Book of Science Fiction. New York: Norton, 1993.

"The Brig." *Lost*. Written by Damon Lindelof and Carlton Cuse. Directed by Eric Laneuville. ABC, May 2, 2007.

Card, Orson Scott, ed. *Getting Lost: Survival, Baggage and Starting Over in J. J. Abrams' Lost*. Dallas: BenBella Books, 2006.

———. *How to Write Science Fiction and Fantasy*. Cincinnati, OH: Writer's Digest Books, 1990.

———. Introduction to Card, *Getting Lost*, 1–21.

"Catch-22." *Lost*. Written by Jeff Pinkner and Brian K. Vaughan. Directed by Stephen Williams. ABC, April 18, 2007.

"The Cost of Living." *Lost*. Written by Monica Owusu-Breen and Alison Schapker. Directed by Jack Bender. ABC, November 1, 2006.

Delany, Samuel R. Interview by Larry McCaffery. In *Across the Wounded*

Galaxies: Interviews with Contemporary American Science Fiction Writers, edited by Larry McCaffery, 71–104. Urbana: University of Illinois Press, 1990.

"D.O.C." *Lost*. Written by Edward Kitsis and Adam Horowitz. Directed by Frederick E. O. Toye. ABC, April 25, 2007.

Dolan, Marc. "The Peaks and Valleys of Serial Creativity: What Happened to/ on *Twin Peaks*." In *Full of Secrets: Critical Approaches to* Twin Peaks, edited by David Lavery, 30–50. Detroit, MI: Wayne State University Press, 1995.

"Enter 77." *Lost*. Written by Damon Lindelof and Carlton Cuse. Directed by Stephen Williams. ABC, March 7, 2007.

"Exposé." *Lost*. Written by Edward Kitsis and Adam Horowitz. Directed by Stephen Williams. ABC, March 28, 2007.

"Flashes before Your Eyes." *Lost*. Written by Damon Lindelof and Drew Goddard. Directed by Jack Bender. ABC, February 14, 2007.

"Greatest Hits." *Lost*. Written by Edward Kitsis and Adam Horowitz. Directed by Stephen Williams. ABC, May 16, 2007.

Gunn, James. "The Readers of Hard Science Fiction." In *Hard Science Fiction*, edited by George Slusser and Eric S. Rabkin, 70–81. Carbondale: Southern Illinois University Press, 1986.

"Homecoming." *Lost*. Written by Damon Lindelof. Directed by Kevin Hooks. ABC, February 9, 2005.

King, Geoff, and Tanya Krzywinska. *Science Fiction Cinema: From Outerspace to Cyberspace*. London: Wallflower, 2000.

King, Stephen. "*Lost*'s Soul." *Entertainment Weekly*, September 9, 2005, 150.

Knight, Damon. *In Search of Wonder: Essays on Modern Science Fiction*. Chicago: Advent, 1967.

"Left Behind." *Lost*. Written by Damon Lindelof and Elizabeth Sarnoff. Directed by Karen Gaviola. ABC, March 4, 2007.

Le Guin, Ursula K., and Brian Attebery, eds. *The Norton Book of Science Fiction*. New York: Norton, 1993.

"Live Together, Die Alone." *Lost*. Written by Damon Lindelof and Carlton Cuse. Directed by Jack Bender. ABC, May 24, 2006.

"The Man behind the Curtain." *Lost*. Written by Elizabeth Sarnoff and Drew Goddard. Directed by Bobby Roth. ABC, May 9, 2007.

"The Man from Tallahassee." *Lost*. Written by Drew Goddard and Jeff Pinkner. Directed by Jack Bender. ABC, March 21, 2007.

"Not in Portland." *Lost*. Written by Carlton Cuse and Jeff Pinkner. Directed by Stephen Williams. ABC, February 7, 2007.

"Orientation." *Lost*. Written by Javier Grillo-Marxuach and Craig Wright. Directed by Jack Bender. ABC, October 5, 2005.

"The Other 48 Days." *Lost*. Written by Damon Lindelof and Carlton Cuse. Directed by Eric Laneuville. ABC, November 16, 2005.

"Per Avion." *Lost*. Written by Chuck Kim and Jordan Rosenberg. Directed by Paul Edwards. ABC, March 14, 2007.

Porter, Lynnette, and David Lavery. *Unlocking the Meaning of* Lost: *An Unauthorized Guide*. 1st ed. Naperville, IL: Sourcebooks, 2006.

———. *Unlocking the Meaning of* Lost: *An Unauthorized Guide*. 2nd ed. Naperville, IL: Sourcebooks, 2007.

Simak, Clifford. "Over the River and through the Woods." In Le Guin and Attebery, 125–32.

"Stranger in a Strange Land." *Lost*. Written by Christina M. Kim and Elizabeth Sarnoff. Directed by Paris Barclay. ABC, February 21, 2007.

Suvin, Darko. *Metamorphoses of Science Fiction: On the Poetics and History of a Literary Genre*. New Haven, CT: Yale University Press, 1979.

"Through the Looking Glass." *Lost*. Written by Damon Lindelof and Carlton Cuse. Directed by Jack Bender. ABC, March 23, 2007.

"The Train Job." *Firefly*. Written by Joss Whedon and Tim Minear. Directed by Joss Whedon. Fox, September 20, 2002.

"Trisha Tanaka Is Dead." *Lost*. Written by Edward Kitsis and Adam Horowitz. Directed by Eric Laneuville. ABC, February 28, 2007.

Turner, George. "Science Fiction as Literature." In *The Visual Encyclopedia of Science Fiction*, edited by Brian Ash, 257–62. New York: Harmony Books, 1977.

"The 23rd Psalm." *Lost*. Written by Damon Lindelof and Carlton Cuse. Directed by Matt Earl Beesley. ABC, January 11, 2006.

"White Rabbit." *Lost*. Written by Christian Taylor. Directed by Kevin Hooks. ABC, October 20, 2004.

PART V

THE LANDING ZONE

Where Does
Science Fiction Television
Go from Here?

TV TIME LORDS

Fan Cultures, Narrative Complexity, and the Future of Science Fiction Television

Charles Tryon

In a DirecTV commercial that aired in winter 2006–2007, William Shatner and Leonard Nimoy, reprising their roles as Captain James T. Kirk and Mr. Spock, promote the service's picture clarity. A similar commercial, featuring Christopher Lloyd's Dr. Emmett Brown from the *Back to the Future* trilogy, seems to equate DirecTV with a time machine much like the films' famous DeLorean, with Doc Brown touting the service's high-definition capacity and channel selection. The commercials evoke the spirit of these science fiction texts to suggest the birth of a new era of television, one defined by freedom and consumer choice. These nostalgic links to some of science fiction's more famous franchises are quite telling, as DirecTV, like other purveyors of a new televisual world, seeks to position itself in relation to the medium's—and its audience's—future, as well as its futuristic texts. The spirit of exploration embodied in the *Star Trek*–themed commercial in particular reimagines television's "vast wasteland" as an open realm available for exploration and enjoyment.

I mention these advertisements in part because they link science fiction film and television, but also because they reinforce the rhetoric of freedom and consumer choice that has become crucial to our sense of television's future, as television programming increasingly becomes available in contexts and formats other than a traditional broadcast model. In addition to seemingly unlimited channel selection, media content can now be accessed across a variety of platforms, allowing audiences to encounter television shows in multiple viewing contexts and television producers to create new kinds of content to attract audiences.

Of course, with television shows increasingly available on DVD, online, and via short "phonisodes" on mobile phones, it has become difficult to determine what constitutes television, much less how audiences are encountering it. As a result, discussions of television based on models of live broadcasting and limited channel selection often seem imprecise, provoking new questions about both specific series and the larger television experience. The technological changes in TV exhibition and distribution have profoundly altered the relationship between the entertainment industry and its audience. Yet one can begin to assess the impact of these new technologies, as William Boddy argues, by considering "the ways in which their prospect unsettles prevailing textual forms, business models, and audience assumptions" (3). Science fiction television (SFTV), I would suggest, offers a key lead in this direction, already tracing some of the ways in which our digital media are altering textual forms, producing changes in business models, and creating new audience-text relationships. Because science fiction fan cultures have enthusiastically embraced these innovations, SFTV has played a significant role in redefining the television experience. These new televisual modes, which immerse the viewer or user into the world of the show, make it easier to imagine TV as an object to be mixed, altered, or otherwise manipulated, thereby creating a situation in which SFTV fans become active participants in rather than passive viewers of the medium.

New Models of Television

I start from the notion that our experiences of media technologies are shaped by a combination of technological, institutional, and cultural forces, often producing unpredictable audience uses. New delivery systems, such as digital video recorders (DVRs), streaming video, and portable television, have already significantly altered the definition of television and the reception practices that go along with it, while making it possible for fans and other amateurs to produce and distribute their own shows, often based on the expansive universes of popular SFTV series. In addition, because audiences equipped with DVRs no longer rely on the program schedules associated with broadcast television, approaches based on earlier concepts like "liveness" and "flow" become less central to the form, as producers try to attract an increasingly fragmented audience.[1] Furthermore, audiences can now engage in repeat viewings of shows, using DVDs or DVRs to watch more attentively, leading producers to create increasingly sophisticated narrative worlds that sustain and reward intensive fan involvement on a variety of levels, a process particularly appropriate to the complex narrative worlds associated with SFTV series ranging from *Star Trek* to *The X-Files* to more recent shows such as *Heroes* and *Battlestar Galactica*.

While new media technologies are producing new forms of fan interaction in terms of both new rhythms of audience attention and fan productions, they are also building easily recognizable demographics. Thus Sara Gwenllian-Jones and Roberta Pearson note that "channels such as the Sci-Fi Channel constitute and target 'cult' audiences by defining their programming content in terms of genre. Such strategies allow them to establish their own brand identity and attract audiences that constitute a relatively identifiable, specific, and consistent demographic that can be further targeted by advertisers" (7). Such synergies include the Sci-Fi Channel's marketing of high-tech entertainment technologies to fans who check its Technology Blog. This blog often positions viewers as on the cutting edge because of their purchase of high-end entertainment technologies and draws them into what Jeffrey Sconce has called "*Wired* magazine's marketing discourse" (192). These synergies can also feed other forms of consumerism. Josh Stenger notes how *Buffy the Vampire Slayer*'s "fiercely loyal and highly participatory fan base" provided 20th Century-Fox with an enthusiastic market for *Buffy* memorabilia auctioned on eBay soon after the show was cancelled (28). The resulting frenzy, which featured fans and collectors aggressively bidding on everything from Sarah Michelle Gellar's blue jeans to obscure props, underscored the degree to which fans sought to incorporate aspects of *Buffy* into their lives, although the competitive, anything-goes bidding alienated many fans who were priced out of the auctions.

Accompanying the notion of watching television on one's own schedule is a corollary desire to watch television wherever one wants. Like the temporal flexibility offered by DVRs, portable entertainment technologies such as video iPods seemingly offer entertainment at any moment and in any location. These technologies are promoted around desires for freedom, consumer choice, and convenience, invoking what Lisa Parks has called the "distinct culture organized around middle-class fantasies of transport, personal freedom, and citizenship" (137). Such fantasies of mobility and freedom are evident in the marketing of Apple's iPods, as well as the new cell phone technologies that promise streaming live television. Of course, the small screens, usually no more than three or four inches diagonally, make watching anything more than a short segment tedious at best. Thus content made specifically for portable screens tends to be short, with an emphasis on informative segments that can be watched in a state of distraction.

This understanding of the new desire for a portable entertainment shows up in the *Doctor Who* "Tardisodes," short promotional clips delivered to mobile phones, directed at members of *Doctor Who*'s "tweenage" demographic. The Tardisodes efficiently play to the parameters of the new medium, making use of the rhetoric of news bulletins to promote the show, while to some extent mocking that same rhetoric. For example, in "Tardisode B," which serves as a preview for the second season's "Doomsday" episode, a BBC-style news broadcaster warns viewers of the attack of the Cybermen, although astute viewers will also recognize the voice of the Daleks heard off-screen during the message. The historical reference to Orson Welles's *War of the Worlds* broadcast is unmistakable here, with "Tardisode B" cleverly negotiating the parameters of the miniature screen, much like Welles's *War of the Worlds* broadcast sought to navigate the limits of the medium of radio in its time. While this strategy cannot be separated from the attempt to promote the upcoming *Doctor Who* episode, it also seems explicitly linked to the nature of the phonisode as an emerging genre.

However, this model of choice and access does not always produce a positive or pleasurable result. A primary characteristic of what has been termed the "post-television" era is the seemingly unlimited choices made possible by digital media and relentlessly promoted by the entertainment industry. While we can produce more programming than ever before, allowing for the cultivation of niche audiences, the new technologies and their promotion have also produced feelings of being overwhelmed by the options and by the impossibility of watching everything. As a result, there have been various expressions of frustration against the new televisual environment. John Kiesewetter describes "TiVo trauma," the stress that many television viewers face in finding time to watch the programs they have saved before they are automatically deleted because the TiVo's memory is full. Kiesewetter emphasizes the sheer volume of entertainment now available because of our capacity to record shows. In short, these disparate TV watching practices and the anxieties they produce raise a number of questions not only about configurations of public and private space but also about configurations of attention as new forms of television bring with them new rhythms of TV watching.

Narrative Complexity and Transmedia Storytelling

New media technologies have also fundamentally changed television narrative, and they have profound implications for the kinds of programming and for the ways in which audiences are understood. Because of new viewing technologies and viewing practices like streaming video, portable entertainment, DVD collections, and DVRs, programmers have developed increasingly sophisticated narratives to retain audience attention. Jason Mittell argues that "television's narrative complexity is predicated on specific facets of storytelling that seem uniquely suited to the series structure that sets television apart from film" (29). This narrative complexity is augmented by new technologies that make it possible to view television outside its normal broadcast schedule. As a result, the current moment is characterized by narrative experimentation, as programmers, aware that television itself is undergoing great change, find themselves free to challenge narrative conventions.

These changes are often attributed to changes in audience, with Steven Johnson arguing in *Everything Bad Is Good for You* that audiences have become increasingly sophisticated and now seek shows that provide them with more of a cognitive workout. Noting the multithreaded narratives and multiple character relationships of popular shows like *24*, *The Sopranos*, and *ER*, Johnson argues that such complex programming invites a level of cognitive engagement that older shows—he cites examples ranging from *Starsky and Hutch* to *The Dukes of Hazzard*—do not, and in support he points to the detailed, often deeply personal analyses of television series appearing in online discussion forums. But instead of simply claiming that audiences are becoming "more sophisticated," we might ask why they seem increasingly attracted to highly serialized narratives and more complicated story lines. Although serial narratives have existed since television's earliest days, most evidently in the oft maligned genre of the soap opera, seriality has been, over the last decade, reinvented as a sign of realism, thereby linking such complex narratives as *Battlestar Galactica, Babylon 5, Lost, Heroes*, and *Jericho* with "quality" programming. In fact, shows that fail to observe the dictates of serial plotting (or that do so poorly) are often faulted for what Marcus Alexander Hart refers to as "the *Voyager* Reset," in which everything within the show world returns to the status quo at the end of the episode. While it is important to emphasize that complex programming does not necessarily mean better television, a desire for complexity may suggest new modes of audience engagement with television quite unlike the image of the passive couch potato of previous decades.

This trend toward narrative complexity continues a much longer trajectory in television evolution that has been particularly tied to SFTV. Jan Johnson-Smith's discussion of the form underscores the degree to which the genre's narratives have become increasingly complex since the 1980s. Quoting John Thornton Caldwell's influential *Televisuality*, she notes the development of a television practice that "plays with the limits of what can be done 'within the constraints and confines of the limited television frame'" (49), emphasizing the influence of *Hill Street Blues* on a variety of genres. In fact, *Battlestar Galactica* producer Ronald Moore cited *Hill Street Blues* as a key influence on the storytelling structure of his series while acknowledging the challenge he faced in keeping the series from becoming inaccessible to casual viewers. Later, Chris Carter's *X-Files* series furthered this push for narrative complexity. Negotiating between the larger conspiracy narrative and "monster-of-the-week" episodes, *The X-Files* often struggled to keep both casual and obsessive fans satisfied with the show. And such struggles continue to inform more recent efforts, especially as shows deploy a range of media to construct their show worlds.

Unlike a two-hour film, or even a trilogy of films, a television series opens up possibilities for multiple narrative modes. *Babylon 5*, for example, challenged televisual norms in that it was conceived as a long-term but predetermined epic story. Television's new narrative complexity is also defined by its interplay between serial and episodic formats with little obligation for narrative closure at the end of every episode. Thus a series like *Battlestar Galactica* may juggle multiple narrative threads—the romance between Starbuck and Apollo, Boomer's discovery that she is a Cylon, the political conflict between Roslin and Zarek—over the course of several episodes, while the larger mission of battling the Cylons and finding Earth persists throughout the series. In SFTV today the goal is typically for the new serial narrative to avoid the melodramatic and character-driven elements associated with the soap opera. However, those boundaries can become blurred, as Katee Sackhoff's comments on her character Starbuck illustrate: she faults the show for becoming a space opera analogous to "*90210* in space" (quoted in Cullen). But while these boundaries may be difficult to maintain, the emphasis on serial narratives may also produce more consistent viewing practices.

These new narrative modes also cannot be separated from what Henry Jenkins has called "transmedia storytelling," the use of multiple media to create an increasingly elaborate world (*Convergence Culture* 9). While transmedia storytelling is typically motivated by economic concerns, it also provides audiences with new pathways into the world of the show, with series such as *Lost, Heroes, Battlestar Galactica*, and *Jericho* managing to incorporate Webisodes, graphic novels, alternate reality games, and other narrative forms to keep audiences engaged. Thus fans can enter NBC's *Heroes* through the show when it is broadcast, through the graphic novel series that appears online, or through an alternate reality game at a mock Web site for Primatech Paper, the mysterious company featured on the show. In *Jericho*'s online series, *Countdown*, the messages Robert Hawkins receives from "Delta One" often speculate on how populations might react in the case of a nuclear attack, often using interviews with researchers in trauma studies or political science. Other episodes feature news reports of the North Korean nuclear test in October 2006 and footage of Secretary of State Condoleezza Rice announcing the United States' response to the tests. These Webisodes expertly mix documentary and fictional footage in positioning *Jericho* as a commentary on contemporary U.S. politics, a focus that manifests itself in several of the first-season episodes.

At the same time, individual show Web sites often incorporate advertising into the world of the show. In the *Countdown* Webisodes, which typically run for about three or four minutes, Hawkins is invariably seen logging into his "ruggedized" laptop, which conspicuously displays the AT&T logo, illustrating in part that these Webisodes can serve as alternative sites for product placement, in this case seamlessly inserted into the diegetic world of the show. While such product placement is not unusual on broadcast television, it does illustrate one potential avenue for making online content more profitable, if also producing an uneasy relationship to the narrative world of the show. However, even with these explicit—and often transparent—attempts at marketing to SFTV audiences, the online content of shows such as *Jericho* and *Heroes* emphasizes audience engagement and participation while expanding the world of the show beyond the parameters of the weekly hour-long series.

Fan Practices

These changes in our experience of televisual time are also measured in fan practices, as these new technologies invoke new rhythms of fan attention. In his discussion of TV fandom, Matt Hills characterizes these changes in reception in terms of economic shifts, arguing that "fans have themselves become more responsive to the scheduling patterns of these serials, exhibiting what could be termed a form of '*just-in-time fandom*'" (178). Hills compares the flood of posts that appear on discussion boards immediately after a cult TV episode airs, or even during the show's commercial breaks, to post-Fordist production processes characterized by "specific and highly temporal rhythms" (179). Although these audience rhythms persist, the development of streaming video has introduced some flexibility, with casual fans capable of watching and commenting on individual episodes hours or days after they appear. Many of their comments constitute what Hills calls "narratives of anticipation and speculation" (180), that is, fan discussions about potential directions a series or narrative arc might take. While we might be cautious in describing such new media texts in purely affirmative terms, they do suggest a number of alternatives allowing audiences, particularly those of SFTV, to engage with the stories and with each other in new ways, often accelerating the development of fan cultures and making audiences more aware of their status as producers as well as consumers of media.

These fan cultures must be understood in terms of the longer history of SFTV fandom. In *Textual Poachers*, Jenkins reminds us that "the history of media fandom is at least in part the history of a series of organized efforts to influence programming decisions" (28), as in the notable example of *Star Trek*. In the late 1960s, its fans, or "Trekkies," organized to pressure NBC into keeping *Star Trek* on the air despite low ratings, and more recently fans similarly fought to keep Joss Whedon's *Firefly* on television. Although their efforts were not rewarded, Columbia did commission Whedon to make a film based on the series. And as these examples suggest, fans are increasingly involved in the entertainment industry's operations and understand how to pressure the networks. In fact, the new models of fandom are helping to generate a new public sphere surrounding television. The Web, for example, has been used to organize social gatherings based on shared enthusiasm for specific television shows, such as the "frak parties" associated with the TV series *Battlestar Galactica* and built on the house party model popularized during Howard Dean's 2004 presidential campaign (Doctorow). These parties have been incorporated into the promotion of *Battlestar Galactica* as a show that warrants collective viewing, with executive producer and writer Ron Moore personally calling several of the larger parties.

Another common practice is the creation of fan videos that edit, annotate, and sometimes rewrite show episodes. Fan videos have been distributed via fan culture networks and at science fiction conventions for decades, but the new digital technologies have made them easier to produce and distribute. YouTube, for example, allows users to share videos, which can move through the Web rapidly and gain audiences of thousands, or even millions, within just a few days. Fans of *Battlestar Galactica* have adopted this practice, producing slash videos playing out the sexual tension between male characters such as Apollo and Anders, who are competing for the affections of Starbuck, and between female characters such as President Laura Roslin and Starbuck. In such cases, the videos typically demonstrate a solid understanding of how these TV shows use cinematography and editing to encode sexual desire.[2] And these fan videos are only one example of such productions, as fans frequently participate in discussion boards, maintain unofficial series Weblogs to review and discuss specific episodes, and design wikis that explain plot details and provide biographical information for key characters.[3]

In addition to creating videos and Web sites, fans continue to produce homemade episodes of shows based in the worlds of their favorite science fiction franchises, and these productions too now gain a wider audience than ever before. With the availability of relatively inexpensive digital cameras and distribution channels such as YouTube, SFTV fans have seized upon the do-it-yourself media production model, not only creating and posting slash videos but also producing entirely new content based on long-term science fiction franchises such as *Star Trek* and *Doctor Who*. Like the fan videos that draw on existing episodes, these "original" programs raise interesting questions about copyright and "ownership" of the characters and worlds depicted in a series. A notable example is the fan-produced *Star Trek* series *Starship Farragut*. Using homemade effects and makeup and filming primarily in a Virginia state park, the creators have put together a series that expands on the already massive *Star Trek* universe, producing what series director Paul Sieber describes as an "online community theater" (quoted in Hakim). Because the makers of *Starship Farragut* do not profit financially from the series, Paramount, which owns the rights to *Star Trek*, has allowed it to proceed. Again, we might recall that such fan productions have a long history. As Jenkins points out in *Fans, Bloggers, and Gamers*, British fans of the original *Doctor Who* series often produced home movie episodes using Super 8 and other domestic technologies in the very same quarries where the actual series was filmed (144). Of course, that fan videos appear online raises new questions about their relationship to the network-produced series, especially since actors from the original *Star Trek* series, including Walter Koenig and George Takei, have appeared in one of the more popular *Star Trek* fan series, *Starship Exeter*, further blurring the boundary between fan and "official" productions.

Generally, though, show producers have embraced such opportunities for interaction, seeing the blogs and discussion boards as a chance to sustain (or build) an active, enthusiastic audience. Jan Johnson-Smith observes that J. M. Straczynski, creator of *Babylon 5*, "was available to discuss the work with fans on the internet, named ships and transient personnel after those same fans and posted countless messages with his responses to alternately inane and in-depth questions on internet message boards" (65).[4] In addition to reaching out to the fan-created frak parties, *Battlestar Galactica*'s Moore has emulated Straczynski's strategy of cultivating the fan relationship. His podcasts and DVD commentary tracks, ranging from observations about how specific scenes were produced to explicitly interpretive observations about specific episodes, have actively shaped interpretations of the text while continuing to cultivate a larger, more enthusiastic fan community. For example, during his discussion of the "Colonial Day" episode, Moore indicates the degree to which he reads *Battlestar Galactica* as a commentary on the present, noting that he wanted to construct an episode based around President Laura Roslin's political management style. Of course, these podcasts also bring a new temporal experience of television. Thus, *Slate* television reviewer Adam Rogers notes, "Die-hards painstakingly synchronize their iPods and TiVos every week." In addition to the regular podcasts and commentary tracks, Moore has provided audiences with podcast recordings of *Battlestar* writers' meetings featuring Moore and show writers Bradley Thompson and David Weddle. Significantly, Rogers's comments about the *Battlestar* podcasts attempt to distance the show from its SFTV predecessors. Identifying the *Star Trek* franchise as the bad object against which *Battlestar Galactica* is defined, Rogers emphasizes that the *Battlestar* podcasts are "about more than geeky plot points," suggesting an implicit connection between new models of television and valuations of quality.

Other attempts to incorporate fan communities into SFTV include cable experiments with interactive television. The cable channel G4 has produced the interactive *Star Trek* series *Star Trek 2.0* and *Star Trek: The Next Generation 2.0*, which seek to lure the fans of the shows to watch the channel through real-time online chats designed to respond to elements of specific episodes and which, in G4's first experiments, generated millions of lines of chat.[5] The Sci-Fi Channel has conducted similar experiments during *Battlestar Galactica* reruns. During the episode, the chat text appears as a crawl at the bottom of the television screen, much like the news tickers seen on cable news shows. However, the resulting chats often seem highly structured, with specific questions guiding the conversation about the series rather than commenting on or interpreting the episode. Often the questions have a "promotional" tone, as fans are asked to name what plot point they are most anticipating, to guess which human might be a Cylon, or even to identify which characters are the most attractive. Taken in this direction, the interactive episodes can become not sites of unlimited public engagement but instead ones of limited response range, structured around a restricted sense of fandom. While G4's interactive experiment with *Star Trek 2.0* has been touted as "revolutionary,"[6] some would see it as essentially a ratings stunt for a relatively obscure cable channel, taking familiar programming and repackaging it for the purposes of channeling attention and cultivating a live audience. Still, the explicit appeal to fantasies of community embodied in the real-time chats clearly gestures toward a level of interactivity that normal television does not offer.

In a 2003 speech at a Royal Television Society dinner, Ashley Highfield described the current state of television as having reached a "tipping point" in that future TV would necessarily be much different from the broadcast model that dominated in the twentieth century: "Future TV may be unrecognizable from today, defined not just by linear TV channels, packaged and scheduled by television executives, but instead will resemble more of a kaleidoscope, thousands of streams of content, some indistinguishable as actual channels." Highfield's comments anticipate many of the utopian aspects of the emerging convergence culture wherein consumers become active participants in the circulation of media content.[7] Such predictions about television's future often sound like science fiction narratives, invoking new worlds of public and private space, new modes of engagement and interactivity, even new levels of human response. Certainly, Highfield anticipates a new sort of viewer, toggling back and forth between not only different programs but also different media. We can glimpse this futuristic vision of TV spectatorship already operating in anecdotal accounts of TiVo households, as viewers increasingly find themselves liberated from the broadcast schedule, even if that liberation comes at the price of an excess of choices. In addition, streaming video, video sharing, and other interactive Web features change not only when and where we watch television but how we watch it, allowing viewers to become more actively engaged in the production of the worlds of their favorite characters and series. As the examples of the fan cultures surrounding such series as *Star Trek*, *Battlestar Galactica*, and *Heroes* suggest, SFTV audiences are already actively involved in this rather science fictional process of reimagining our relationship with television and, along with it, reimagining ourselves.

Notes

1. For Raymond Williams's most explicit mapping of the concept of flow, see *Television* 78–118. For more recent attempts to reconsider this concept for a postnetwork era, see Uricchio's "Television's Next Generation" and Spigel's introduction to *Television after TV*.

2. All of the videos described here are available via YouTube (http://www.youtube.com).

3. See, for example, the Battlestar Wiki (http://www.battlestarwiki.org/) or the Primatech Paper blog (http://www.primatechpaper.org/), a parody of NBC's "official" Primatech Paper Web site, which serves in part as a portal for the alternate reality game, *Heroes 360*, affiliated with the series.

4. In *Fans, Bloggers, and Gamers*, Jenkins also discusses the fan culture that Straczynski cultivated for *Babylon 5*. Significantly, Jenkins notes that Straczynski was warned by the show's lawyers that his participation in the *Babylon 5* fan culture could open him up to plagiarism lawsuits (146).

5. In his *TrekWeb* review, Steve Krutzler refers to the chat as a "stream-of-consciousness narrative from real viewers that is different every time."

6. G4 president Neal Tiles suggests that watching *Star Trek 2.0* is "akin to peering into the future because this is how every demo is going to be consuming media in the future" (quoted in Nordyke).

7. For Jenkins's definition of this concept, see *Convergence Culture* 3–4.

Works Cited

Boddy, William. *New Media and Popular Imagination: Launching Radio, Television, and Digital Media in the United States*. Oxford: Oxford University Press, 2004.

Caldwell, John Thornton. *Televisuality: Style, Crisis, and Authority in American Television*. New Brunswick, NJ: Rutgers University Press, 1995.

Cullen, Ian M. "Sackhoff Admits to Hating the Viper Scenes." *SciFi Pulse*. January 30, 2007. http://scifipulse.net/battlestarnews/Sackhoff_Vipers.html.

Doctorow, Cory. "Online Activists Launch *Battlestar Galactica* Party-Planner." *Boing Boing*. September 20, 2006. http://www.boingboing.net/2006/09/20/online-activists-lau.html.

Gwenllian-Jones, Sara, and Roberta E. Pearson. *Cult Television*. Minneapolis: University of Minnesota Press, 2004.

Hakim, Danny. "'Star Trek' Fans, Deprived of a Show, Recreate the Franchise on Digital Video." *New York Times*, June 18, 2006. http://www.nytimes.com/.

Hart, Marcus Alexander. "My Gods! Is *Battlestar* Going All *Voyager* on Us?" *Geek Monthly*, February 2007, 26.

Highfield, Ashley. "TV's Tipping Point: Why the Digital Revolution Is Only Just

Beginning." *BBC*. October 6, 2003. http://www.bbc.co.uk/pressoffice/speeches/stories/highfield_rts.shtml.

Hills, Matt. *Fan Cultures*. London: Routledge, 2002.

Jenkins, Henry. *Convergence Culture: Where Old and New Media Collide*. New York: New York University Press, 2006.

———. *Fans, Bloggers, and Gamers: Exploring Participatory Culture*. New York: New York University Press, 2006.

———. *Textual Poachers: Television Fans and Participatory Cultures*. London: Routledge, 1992.

Johnson, Steven. *Everything Bad Is Good for You: How Today's Popular Culture Is Making Us Smarter*. New York: Riverhead, 2005.

Johnson-Smith, Jan. *American Science Fiction TV: Star Trek, Stargate and Beyond*. New York: Tauris, 2005.

Kiesewetter, John. "Call It TiVo Trauma." *Cincinnati (OH) Enquirer*, December 17, 2006. http://news.enquirer.com/.

Krutzler, Steve. "G4 Following *Star Trek 2.0* with *The Next Generation 2.0*." *TrekWeb*. December 4, 2006. http://trekweb.com/articles/2006/12/04/G4-Following-Star-Trek-20-With.shtml.

Mittell, Jason. "Narrative Complexity in Contemporary American Television." *Velvet Light Trap* 58 (2006): 29–40.

Nordyke, Kimberly. "G4 Tries to Keep Men's Attention." *Hollywood Reporter*, December 13, 2006. http://www.hollywoodreporter.com/.

Parks, Lisa. "Flexible Microcasting: Gender, Generation, and Television-Internet Convergence." In Spigel and Olsson, 133–56.

Rogers, Adam. "Captain's Log: Want to Understand *Battlestar Galactica*? Eavesdrop on Its Writers." *Slate*, November 29, 2006. http://www.slate.com/id/2154625/?nav=tap3.

Sconce, Jeffrey. "Tulip Theory." In *New Media: Theories and Practices of Digitextuality*, edited by Anna Everett and John T. Caldwell, 179–93. New York: Routledge, 2003.

Spigel, Lynn. Introduction to Spigel and Olsson, 1–34.

Spigel, Lynn, and Jan Olsson, eds. *Television after TV: Essays on a Medium in Transition*. Durham, NC: Duke University Press, 2004.

Stenger, Josh. "The Clothes Make the Fan: Fashion and Online Fandom when *Buffy the Vampire Slayer* Goes to eBay." *Cinema Journal* 45, no. 4 (2006): 26–44.

Uricchio, William. "Television's Next Generation: Technology/Interface Culture/Flow." In Spigel and Olsson, 163–82.

Williams, Raymond. *Television: Technology and Cultural Form*. New York: Schocken, 1974.

FURTHER READING

Anderson, Christopher. *Hollywood TV: The Studio System in the Fifties*. Austin: University of Texas Press, 1994.

Barnouw, Erik. *Tube of Plenty: The Evolution of American Television*. New York: Oxford University Press, 1975.

Barrett, Michele, and Duncan Barrett. Star Trek: *The Human Factor*. London: Polity Press, 2001.

Beeler, Stan, and Lisa Dickson. *Reading* Stargate SG-1. London: Tauris, 2006.

Bernardi, Daniel Leonard. Star Trek *and History: Race-ing toward a White Future*. New Brunswick, NJ: Rutgers University Press, 1998.

———. "*Star Trek* in the 1960s: Liberal-Humanism and the Production of Race." *Science-Fiction Studies* 24 (1997): 209–25.

Bignell, Jonathan, and Stephen Lacey, eds. *Popular Television Drama: Critical Perspectives*. Manchester: Manchester University Press, 2005.

Boddy, William. *New Media and Popular Imagination: Launching Radio, Television, and Digital Media in the United States*. Oxford: Oxford University Press, 2004.

Booker, M. Keith. *Science Fiction Television: A History*. Westport, CT: Praeger, 2004.

Bould, Mark. "Film and Television." In James and Mendlesohn, 79–95.

Boyer, Paul. *By the Bomb's Early Light: American Thought and Culture at the Dawn of the Atomic Age*. Chapel Hill: University of North Carolina Press, 1994.

Braun, Beth. "*The X-Files* and *Buffy the Vampire Slayer*: The Ambiguity of Evil in Supernatural Representations." *Journal of Popular Film and Television* 28, no. 2 (2000): 88–94.

Britton, Piers D., and Simon J. Barker. *Reading between Designs: Visual Imagery and the Generation of Meaning in* The Avengers, The Prisoner, *and* Doctor Who. Austin: University of Texas Press, 2003.

Brooks, Tim, and Earle Marsh. *The Complete Directory to Prime Time Network and Cable TV Shows, 1946–Present*. 8th ed. New York: Ballantine, 2003.

Burns, Christy L. "Erasure: Alienation, Paranoia, and the Loss of Memory in *The X-Files*." *Camera Obscura* 15 (2000): 195–224.

Buxton, David. *From* The Avengers *to* Miami Vice: *Form and Ideology in Television Series*. Manchester: Manchester University Press, 1990.

Chapman, James. *Saints and Avengers: British Adventure Series of the 1960s*. London: Tauris, 2002.

Clareson, Thomas D. *Many Futures, Many Worlds: Theme and Form in Science Fiction*. Kent, OH: Kent State University Press, 1977.

Cook, John R., and Peter Wright, eds. *British Science Fiction Television: A Hitchhiker's Guide*. London: Tauris.

Dery, Mark. *Escape Velocity: Cyberculture at the End of the Century*. New York: Grove, 1996.

Eco, Umberto. *Travels in Hyperreality*. Translated by William Weaver. New York: Harcourt Brace, 1986.

Ellington, Jane Elizabeth, and Joseph W. Critelli. "Analysis of a Modern Myth: The *Star Trek* Series." *Extrapolation* 24 (1983): 241–50.

Ellis, John. *Seeing Things: Television in the Age of Uncertainty*. London: Tauris, 2000.

Erickson, Hal. *Syndicated Television: The First Forty Years, 1947–1987*. Jefferson, NC: McFarland, 1989.

Erisman, Fred. "*Stagecoach* in Space: The Legacy of *Firefly*." *Extrapolation* 47 (2006): 249–58.

Garcia, Frank. "*Crusade*: The Doomed Sequel Series to *Babylon 5* Premieres on TNT." *Cinefantastique* 31, no. 7 (1999): 56–58.

Geraghty, Lincoln. "Homosocial Desire on the Final Frontier: Kinship, the American Romance, and *Deep Space Nine*'s 'Erotic Triangles.'" *Journal of Popular Culture* 36 (2003): 441–65.

Gitlin, Todd. *Inside Prime Time*. Rev. ed. London: Routledge, 1994.

Gregg, P. B. "England Looks to the Future: The Cultural Forum Model and *Doctor Who*." *Journal of Popular Culture* 37 (2004): 648–61.

Hardy, Sarah, and Rebecca Kukla. "A Paramount Narrative: Exploring Space on the Starship *Enterprise*." *Journal of Aesthetics and Art Criticism* 57 (1999): 177–92.

Helford, Elyce Rae, ed. *Fantasy Girls: Gender in the New Universe of Science Fiction and Fantasy Television*. London: Rowman and Littlefield, 2000.

Heller, Lee E. "The Persistence of Difference: Postfeminism, Popular Discourse, and Heterosexuality in *Star Trek*." *Science-Fiction Studies* 24 (1997): 226–44.

Hurd, Denise Alessandra. "The Monster Inside: 19th Century Racial Constructs in the 24th Century Mythos of *Star Trek*." *Journal of Popular Culture* 31 (1997): 23–36.

Iaccino, J. F. "*Babylon 5*'s Blueprint for the Archetypal Heroes." *Journal of Popular Culture* 34 (2001): 109–20.

Jackson, Rosemary. *Fantasy: The Literature of Subversion*. London: Methuen, 1981.

James, Edward. *Science Fiction in the 20th Century*. New York: Oxford University Press, 1994.

James, Edward, and Farah Mendlesohn. *The Cambridge Companion to Science Fiction*. Cambridge: Cambridge University Press, 2003.

Jameson, Fredric. "Towards a New Awareness of Genre." *Science-Fiction Studies* 9 (1982): 322–24.

Johnson, Catherine. *Telefantasy*. London: BFI, 2005.

Johnson, William, ed. *Focus on the Science Fiction Film*. Englewood Cliffs, NJ: Prentice-Hall, 1972.

Johnson-Smith, Jan. *American Science Fiction TV*: Star Trek, Stargate *and* Beyond. Middletown, CT: Wesleyan University Press, 2005.

Kapell, Matthew. "'Speakers for the Dead': *Star Trek*, the Holocaust, and the Representation of Atrocity." *Extrapolation* 41 (2000): 104–14.

Kellner, Douglas. "*The X-Files* and the Aesthetics and Politics of Postmodern Pop." *Journal of Aesthetics and Art Criticism* 57 (1999): 161–76.

Kuhlman, Martha. "The Uncanny Clone: *The X-Files*, Popular Culture, and Cloning." *Studies in Popular Culture* 26, no. 3 (2004): 75–88.

Kuhn, Annette, ed. *Alien Zone: Cultural Theory and Contemporary Science Fiction Cinema*. London: Verso, 1990.

———, ed. *Alien Zone II: The Spaces of Science Fiction Cinema*. London: Verso, 1999.

Lancaster, Kurt. "Web of Babylon." In Redmond, 308–12.

Lavery, David, Angela Hague, and Marla Cartwright, eds. *Deny All Knowledge: Reading* The X-Files. Syracuse, NY: Syracuse University Press, 1996.

Lucanio, Patrick, and Gary Coville. *American Science Fiction Television Series of the 1950s: Episode Guides and Casts and Credits for Twenty Shows*. Jefferson, NC: McFarland, 1998.

———. *Smokin' Rockets: The Romance of Technology in American Film, Radio and Television, 1945–1962*. Jefferson, NC: McFarland, 2002.

Lyotard, Jean-François. *The Postmodern Condition: A Report on Knowledge*. Translated by Geoff Bennington and Brian Massumi. Minneapolis: University of Minnesota Press, 1984.

Marling, Karal Ann. *As Seen on TV: The Visual Culture of Everyday Life in the 1950s*. Cambridge, MA: Harvard University Press, 1994.

McNeil, Alex. *Total Television: The Comprehensive Guide to Programming from 1948 to the Present*. 8th ed. New York: Penguin Books, 2003.

Miller, Mark Crispin. *Boxed In: The Culture of TV*. Evanston, IL: Northwestern University Press, 1988.

Morton, Alan. *The Complete Directory to Science Fiction, Fantasy, and Horror Television Series: A Comprehensive Guide to the First 50 Years, 1946 to 1996.* Peoria, IL: Other Worlds Books, 1997.

Murray, Janet. *Hamlet on the Holodeck: The Future of Narrative in Cyberspace.* Cambridge, MA: MIT Press, 1997.

Napier, Susan J. *Anime from* Akira *to* Howl's Moving Castle: *Experiencing Contemporary Japanese Animation.* Rev. ed. London: Palgrave, 2005.

Nelson, Robin. *TV Drama in Transition: Forms, Values, and Cultural Change.* Basingstoke: Macmillan, 1997.

Newman, Kim. *Doctor Who.* London: BFI, 2005.

Osgerby, Bill. "'Stand-By for Action!' Gerry Anderson, Supermarionation and the 'White Heat' of Sixties Modernity." In *Unruly Pleasures: The Cult Film and Its Critics,* edited by Xavier Mendik and Graeme Harper, 121–35. London: FAB, 2000.

Osgerby, Bill, and Anna Gough-Yates, eds. *Action TV: Tough Guys, Smooth Operators and Foxy Chicks.* London: Routledge, 2001.

Peary, Danny, ed. *Omni's Screen Flights/Screen Fantasies.* Garden City, NY: Doubleday, 1984.

Porter, Lynette, and David Lavery. *Unlocking the Meaning of* Lost: *An Unauthorized Guide.* Naperville, IL: Sourcebooks, 2006.

Redmond, Sean, ed. *Liquid Metal: The Science Fiction Film Reader.* London: Wallflower Press, 2004.

Roberts, Robin. "Performing Science Fiction: Television, Theater, and Gender in *Star Trek: The Experience.*" *Extrapolation* 42 (2001): 340–56.

———. "Rape, Romance, and Consent in *Star Trek: The Next Generation.*" *Extrapolation* 40 (1999): 21–35.

Robinson, Murray. "Planet Parenthood." *Collier's,* January 5, 1952, 31, 63–64.

Rovin, Jeff. *The Great Television Series.* Cranbury, NJ: Barnes, 1977.

Sander, Gordon F. *Serling: The Rise and Fall of Television's Last Angry Man.* New York: Plume, 1994.

Scheibach, Michael. *Atomic Narratives and American Youth: Coming of Age with the Atom, 1945–1955.* Jefferson, NC: McFarland, 2003.

Silbergleid, Robin. "'The Truth We Both Know': Readerly Desire and Heteronarrative in *The X-Files.*" *Studies in Popular Culture* 25, no. 3 (2003): 49–62.

Sobchack, Vivian. "Images of Wonder: The Look of Science Fiction." In Redmond, 4–10.

Sontag, Susan. "The Imagination of Disaster." In *Against Interpretation,* 212–28. New York: Dell, 1966.

Stark, Steven D. "*The Twilight Zone*: Science Fiction as Realism." In *Glued to the Set: The 60 Television Shows and Events That Made Us Who We Are Today*, 85–89. New York: Free Press, 1997.

Stewart, Garrett. "The 'Videology' of Science Fiction." In *Shadows of the Magic Lamp: Fantasy and Science Fiction in Film*, edited by George E. Slusser and Eric S. Rabkin, 159–207. Carbondale: Southern Illinois University Press, 1985.

Storm, Jo. *Approaching the Possible: The World of* Stargate SG-1. Toronto, ON: ECW Press, 2005.

Suvin, Darko. *Metamorphoses of Science Fiction: On the Poetics and Discourse of a Literary Genre*. New Haven, CT: Yale University Press, 1979.

Telotte, J. P. "Disney in Science Fiction Land." *Journal of Popular Film and Television* 33, no. 1 (2005): 12–21.

———. *Replications: A Robotic History of the Science Fiction Film*. Urbana: University of Illinois Press, 1995.

———. *The Science Fiction Film*. Cambridge: Cambridge University Press, 2001.

Todorov, Tzvetan. *The Fantastic: A Structural Approach to a Literary Genre*. Translated by Richard Howard. Ithaca, NY: Cornell University Press, 1975.

Tulloch, John. *Television Drama: Agency, Audience, and Myth*. London: Routledge, 1990.

Tulloch, John, and Manuel Alvarado. Doctor Who: *The Unfolding Text*. London: Macmillan, 1983.

Tulloch, John, and Henry Jenkins. *Science Fiction Audiences: Watching* Doctor Who *and* Star Trek. London: Routledge, 1995.

Virilio, Paul. *The Art of the Motor*. Translated by Julie Rose. Minneapolis: University of Minnesota Press, 1995.

———. *The Lost Dimension*. Translated by Daniel Moshenberg. New York: Semiotext(e), 1991.

Wakefield, Sarah R. "'Your Sister in St. Scully': An Electronic Community of Female Fans of *The X-Files*." *Journal of Popular Film and Television* 29, no. 3 (2001): 130–37.

Wardle, Paul. "*Total Recall*: Showtime's New Sci-fi Series Does Justice to Philip K. Dick." *Cinefantastique* 31, no. 3 (1999): 40–41.

Weinstein, D. "*Captain Video*: Television's First Fantastic Voyage." *Journal of Popular Film and Television* 30, no. 3 (2002): 148–57.

Westfahl, Gary. *The Mechanics of Wonder: The Creation of the Idea of Science Fiction*. Liverpool: Liverpool University Press, 1999.

Whitfield, Stephen E., and Gene Roddenberry. *The Making of* Star Trek. New York: Ballantine Books, 1968.

Wildermuth, Mark. "The Edge of Chaos: Structural Conspiracy and Epistemology in *The X-Files.*" *Journal of Popular Film and Television* 26, no. 4 (1999): 146–57.

Wolfe, Peter. *In the Zone: The Twilight World of Rod Serling.* Bowling Green, OH: Bowling Green State University Popular Press, 1996.

Woodman, Brian J. "Escaping Genre's Village: Fluidity and Genre Mixing in Television's *The Prisoner.*" *Journal of Popular Culture* 38 (2005): 939–56.

Woolery, George W. *Children's Television: The First Thirty-Five Years, 1946–1981.* Vol. 2, *Live, Film and Tape Series.* Metuchen, NJ: Scarecrow, 1989.

Worland, Rick. "Sign-Posts Up Ahead: *The Twilight Zone, The Outer Limits,* and TV Political Fantasy, 1959–1965." *Science-Fiction Studies* 23 (1996): 103–22.

SELECTED VIDEOGRAPHY

In keeping with the focus of this volume, what follows is a select listing of American and British science fiction television series. It does not include miniseries, television movies, or series that lasted less than half of a typical season, nor does it include those series, such as a number of anthology programs of the 1950s, that only sporadically included science fiction or fantasy episodes. Each listing provides the series' primary title (that by which it is best known), dates of original run, the production company and, if not syndicated, the network or cable channel on which it appeared, a brief note of focus or type, the producer and/or creator of the series, and its primary cast. In compiling this list, I have relied on a variety of sources, including Lucanio and Coville's *American Science Fiction Television Series of the 1950s*, Booker's *Science Fiction Television*, Brooks and Marsh's *The Complete Directory to Prime Time Network and Cable TV Shows*, Fulton's *The Encyclopedia of TV Science Fiction*, and *The Internet Movie Database* (http://www.imdb.com).

Adam Adamant Lives! (1966–1967). BBC. Time travel adventure. Producer: Verity Lambert. Cast: Gerald Harper, Juliet Harmer, Jack May, Peter Ducrow.

Adventures of Superman (1953–1957). National Periodicals Inc./ABC. Superhero. Producers: Bernard Luber, Robert Maxwell, Whitney Ellsworth. Cast: George Reeves, Phyllis Coates, Noel Neill, Jack Larson, John Hamilton.

ALF (1986–1990). Alien Productions Inc./NBC. Comic alien on Earth. Producer and creator: Paul Fusco. Cast: Max Wright, Anne Schedeen, Andrea Elson, Benji Gregory, Paul Fusco (voice of ALF).

Andromeda (2000–2005). Fireworks Entertainment/Tribune Entertainment/MBR Productions/Sci-Fi Channel. Space adventure. Creator: Gene Roddenberry. Cast: Kevin Sorbo, Lisa Ryder, Brandy Ledford, Lexa Doig, Steve Bacic.

Animorphs (1998–1999). Angel/Brown Productions/Nickelodeon. Alien invasion, superheroes. Executive producers: Deborah Forte, Bill Siegler. Cast: Boris Cabrera, Shawn Ashmore, Brooke Nevin.

Babylon 5 (1994–1998). Babylonian Productions/Warner Bros. Television. Space travel adventure. Creator: J. Michael Straczynski. Producers: Robert Latham Brown, John Copeland. Cast: Michael O'Hare, Bruce Boxleitner, Claudia Christian, Jerry Doyle, Tracy Scoggins.

Battlestar Galactica (1978–1980). Glen A. Larson Productions/ABC. Space travel adventure. Creator and writer: Glen A. Larson. Producer: John Dykstra. Cast: Richard Hatch, Dirk Benedict, Lorne Greene, Herb Jefferson Jr., Maren Jensen.

Battlestar Galactica (2004–present). R&D TV/USA Cable Entertainment/ Sci-Fi Channel. Space adventure. Creator: Glen A. Larson. Producers: Paul M. Leonard, Trisha Brunner. Cast: Edward James Olmos, Mary McDonnell, Katee Sackhoff, Jamie Bamber, James Callis, Tricia Helfer.

Beyond Reality (1991–1993). USA Network. Investigations of unexplained parapsychological phenomena. Executive producers: Jon Slan, Ron Ziskin. Cast: Shari Belafonte, Carl Marotte, Nicole deBoer.

The Bionic Woman (1976–1978). Harve Bennett Productions/Universal TV/ ABC. Superhero. Creator and supervising producer: Kenneth Johnson. Special effects: Greg C. Johnson. Cast: Lindsay Wagner, Richard Anderson, Martin E. Brooks, Lee Majors.

Blake's 7 (1978–1981). BBC. Space travel adventure. Creator and writer: Terry Nation. Cast: Michael Keating, Paul Darrow, Peter Tuddenham, Jan Chappell, Jacqueline Pearce, Gareth Thomas.

Buck Rogers (1950–1951). ABC. Futuristic adventure. Producers: Joseph Cates, Babette Henry. Cast: Kem Dibbs, Robert Pastene, Harry Sothern, Lou Prentis.

Buck Rogers in the 25th Century (1979–1981). John Mantley Productions/ Glen A. Larson Productions/Universal TV/NBC. Futuristic adventure. Creators: Glen A. Larson, Leslie Stevens. Producers: Richard Caffey et al. Cast: Gil Gerard, Erin Gray, Pamela Hensley, Tim O'Connor, Mel Blanc.

Bugs (1995–1998). Carnival Films/BBC. Futuristic adventure. Creators and producers: Brian Eastman, Stuart Doughty. Cast: Craig McLachlan, Jaye Griffiths, Jesse Birdsall, Jan Harvey, Paula Hunt.

Captain Midnight (a.k.a. *Jet Jackson, the Flying Commando*; 1954–1956). Screen Gems Television/CBS. Scientific action-adventure. Producer: George Bilson. Director: D. Ross Lederman. Cast: Richard Webb, Sid Melton, Olan Soule.

Captain Video and His Video Rangers (1949–1955). DuMont. Scientific action-adventure. Producers: James Caddigan, Frank Telford, Olga Druce. Cast: Richard Coogan, Al Hodge, Don Hastings, Hal Conklin, Stephen Elliott, Ben Lackland.

Chocky (1984–1986). Thames Television/Independent Television. Children's alien encounters. Creators and writers: John Wyndham, Anthony Read. Cast: Andrew Ellams, James Hazeldine, Carol Drinkwater, Zoe Hart.

Cleopatra 2525 (2000–2001). Renaissance Pictures. Postapocalyptic conflict. Executive producers: Sam Raimi, Eric Gruendemann, R. J. Stewart, Robert G. Tapert. Cast: Jennifer Sky, Gina Torres, Victoria Pratt, Patrick Kake.

Commando Cody: Sky Marshal of the Universe (1955). Republic Pictures/NBC. Superhero-scientist adventure. Producer: Franklin Adreon. Writers: Ronald Davidson, Barry Shipman. Cast: Judd Holdren, Aline Towne, Richard Crane, John Crawford, Gregory Gay.

Counterstrike (1969). BBC. Alien invasion. Creator: Tony Williamson. Producer: Patrick Alexander. Cast: Jon Finch, Sarah Brackett, Katie Fitzroy.

Crusade (1999). Babylonian Productions/TNT. Space adventure. Continuation of *Babylon 5*. Creator, writer, and executive producer: J. Michael Straczynski. Cast: Gary Cole, Peter Woodward, Carrie Dobro, Daniel Dae Kim.

Dark Angel (2000–2002). 20th Century-Fox Television. Genetically enhanced superheroes. Creators and writers: James Cameron, Charles H. Eglee. Executive producers: James Cameron, Charles H. Eglee, and Rene Echevarria. Cast: Jessica Alba, Michael Weatherly, Valarie Rae Miller, Richard Gunn.

Dark Skies (1996–1997). Bryce Zabel Productions/Columbia Pictures Television/NBC. Alien conspiracy. Producers: Bruce Kernan, Brad Markowitz. Creator: Bryce Zabel. Cast: Eric Close, Megan Ward, J. T. Walsh, Tim Kelleher.

Deadly Games (1995–1996). Paramount Television/UPN. Virtual reality adventure. Executive producers: Paul Bernbaum, Leonard Nimoy. Cast: Christopher Lloyd, James Calvert, Cynthia Gibb, Stephen T. Kay.

Doctor Who (1963–1989, 1996, 2005–present). BBC/BBC Wales/Canadian Broadcasting Corp. Interdimensional and time travel adventure. Creators: Sydney Newman, Donald Wilson, C. E. Webber. Cast: William Hartnell, Patrick Troughton, Jon Pertwee, Tom Baker, Peter Davison, Colin Baker, Sylvester McCoy, Paul McGann, Christopher Eccleston, David Tennant (Doctors).

Doomwatch (1970–1972). BBC. Investigation of scientific dangers. Creators: Gerry Davis, Kit Pedler. Producer: Terence Dudley. Cast: John Paul, Simon Oates, Vivien Sherrard, Elizabeth Weaver.

Earth: Final Conflict (1997–2002). Roddenberry/Kirschner Productions/NBC. Alien invasion. Creator: Gene Roddenberry. Cast: Kevin Kilner, Lisa Howard, David Hemblen, Majel Barrett, Von Flores.

Earth 2 (1994–1995). Amblin Entertainment/Universal TV/NBC. Space adventure. Creators, writers, and executive producers: Michael Duggan,

Carol Flint, Mark Levin, Billy Ray. Cast: Debrah Farentino, Joey Zimmerman, Clancy Brown, Jessica Steen, Antonio Sabato Jr.

Eureka (2006–present). Universal TV/Sci-Fi Channel. Secret government experiments. Writers and executive producers: Andrew Cosby, Jaime Paglia. Cast: Colin Ferguson, Salli Richardson-Whitfield, Debrah Farentino, Joe Morton, Matt Frewer.

Farscape (1999–2003). Jim Henson Productions/Sci-Fi Channel. Space travel adventure. Creator and writer: Rockne S. O'Bannon. Cast: Ben Browder, Jonathan Hardy, Claudia Black, Anthony Simcoe, Gigi Edgley, Virginia Hey, Wayne Pygram.

Firefly (2002). 20th Century-Fox Television/Sci-Fi Channel. Space travel adventure. Creator, writer, and executive producer: Joss Whedon. Cast: Nathan Fillion, Gina Torres, Alan Tudyk, Morena Baccarin, Adam Baldwin, Jewel Staite, Sean Maher, Summer Glau, Ron Glass.

First Wave (1998–2001). Sugar Entertainment/Vidatron Entertainment/Sci-Fi Channel. Alien invasion. Creator and writer: Chris Brancato. Cast: Sebastian Spence, Rob LaBelle, Roger R. Cross, Traci Lords, Robert Duncan.

Flash Gordon (1954–1955). Inter-Continental Television Films/King Features. Space adventure. Producers: Wenzel Luedecke, Edward Gruskin. Directors: Wallace Worsley Jr., Gunther von Fritsch. Cast: Steve Holland, Irene Champlin, Joe Nash, Henry Beckman.

The Girl from Tomorrow (1991–1993). Nine Network/Film Australia. Time travel adventure. Executive producer: Ron Saunders. Cast: Katherine Cullen, Melissa Marshall, James Findlay, Helen O'Connor.

The Guardians (1971). London Weekend Television/Independent Television. Futuristic dystopian adventure. Creators: Rex Firkin, Vincent Tilsley. Producer: Andrew Brown. Cast: John Collin, Gwyneth Powell, Cyril Luckham, Edward Petherbridge.

H. G. Wells' Invisible Man (1958–1959). Official Films/ITP/Independent Television. Fantastic invention. Creator: Larry White. Producer: Ralph Smart. Cast: Tim Turner, Lisa Daniely, Deborah Watling.

Halfway across the Galaxy and Turn Left (1994). Crawfords Australia Productions. Comic space travel adventure. Executive producer: Terry Ohlsson. Cast: Lauren Hewett, Jeffrey Walker, Silvia Seidel, Bruce Myles, Jan Friedl.

Hard Time on Planet Earth (1989). Demos-Bard/Shanachie Productions/CBS. Alien superhero on Earth. Writer and producer: Michael Piller. Cast: Martin Kove, Danny Mann, Charles Fleischer, Marita Geraghty.

Heroes (2006–present). NBC Universal Television/NBC. Common people with unusual powers. Creator and writer: Tim Kring. Cast: James Kyson Lee, Hayden Panettiere, Masi Oka, Sendhil Ramamurthy, Ali Larter.

The Hitch-Hiker's Guide to the Galaxy (1981). BBC. Comic space adventure. Creator and writer: Douglas Adams. Producer: Alan J. W. Bell. Cast: Simon Jones, David Dixon, Peter Jones, Mark Wing-Davey, Sandra Dickinson.

Homeboys in Outer Space (1996–1997). Sweet Lorraine Productions/Touchstone Television/UPN. Comic space travel. Executive producer: Ehrich Van Lowe. Cast: Flex Alexander, Darryl M. Bell, Paulette Braxton, Kevin Michael Richardson.

Honey, I Shrunk the Kids (1997–2000). Buena Vista Television/Disney Channel. Fantastic machine. Creators and writers: Ed Ferrara, Kevin Murphy. Cast: Peter Scolari, Barbara Alyn Woods, Hillary Tuck, Thomas Dekker, George Buza.

Hyperdrive (2006–present). BBC. Comic space adventure. Creators, writers, and producers: Kevin Cecil, Andy Riley. Cast: Nick Frost, Kevin Eldon, Miranda Hart, Dan Antopolski, Petra Massey.

The Incredible Hulk (1978–1982). Marvel Productions/Universal TV/CBS. Superhero adventure. Creator and executive producer: Kenneth Johnson. Consultant: Stan Lee. Cast: Bill Bixby, Lou Ferrigno, Jack Colvin.

The Invaders (1967–1968). Quinn Martin Productions/ABC. Alien invasion. Creator and writer: Larry Cohen. Executive producer: Quinn Martin. Cast: Roy Thinnes, Hank Simms, William Woodson, Kent Smith.

Invasion (2005–2006). Warner Bros. Television/Shaun Cassidy Productions/ABC. Alien invasion. Creator and writer: Shaun Cassidy. Cast: William Fichtner, Eddie Cibrian, Kari Matchett, Lisa Sheridan, Tyler Labine.

The Invisible Man (1975–1976). Silverton Productions/Universal TV/NBC. Fantastic invention. Producers: Harve Bennett, Steven Bochco. Cast: David McCallum, Jackie Cooper, Melinda Fee, Henry Darrow.

The Invisible Man (2000–2002). Stu Segall Productions/USA/Sci-Fi Channel. Writers and producers: Jonathan Glassner, David Levinson, Craig Silverstein. Cast: Vincent Ventresca, Paul Ben-Victor, Shannon Kenny, Eddie Jones, Michael McCafferty.

Jake 2.0 (2003–2004). Viacom/David Greenwalt Productions/UPN. Computer-enhanced man. Creator: Silvio Horta. Executive producers: David Greenwalt, Silvio Horta, Robert Lieberman, Gina Matthews, Grant Scharbo. Cast: Christopher Gorham, Judith Scott, Philip Anthony-Rodriguez, Miranda Frigon.

Jeremiah (2002–2004). Platinum Studios/Jeremiah Productions/Lionsgate Television/Showtime. Postapocalyptic adventure. Creator, writer, and producer: J. Michael Straczynski. Cast: Luke Perry, Malcolm-Jamal Warner, Sean Astin, Ingrid Kavelaars.

Jericho (2006–present). Junction Entertainment/CBS Paramount Network Television. Postapocalyptic mystery. Executive producers: Jon Turteltaub, Carol Barbee, Stephen Chbosky. Cast: Skeet Ulrich, Ashley Scott, Sprague Grayden, Kenneth Mitchell, Darby Stanchfield.

Journey of Allen Strange (1997–2000). Lunch Entertainment/Nickelodeon. Comic alien on Earth. Creator, writer, and executive producer: Tommy Lynch. Cast: Arjay Smith, Erin Dean, Shane Sweet, Jack Tate.

Journey to the Unknown (1968). 20th Century-Fox Television/Hammer Films/ABC. Anthology series. Executive producers: Joan Harrison, Norman Lloyd. Cast: Robert Reed, Milo O'Shea, David Hedison, Jane Asher.

Jupiter Moon (1990). Primetime/Andromeda/BSB. Space adventure. Creator: William Smethurst. Cast: Andy Rashleigh, Caroline Evans, Phil Willmott, Nicola Wright.

Land of the Giants (1968–1970). 20th Century-Fox Television/Irwin Allen Productions/ABC. Space travel. Creator and producer: Irwin Allen. Cast: Stefan Arngrim, Kurt Kaszner, Deanna Lund, Gary Conway, Don Marshall, Kevin Hagen.

Lexx (1997–2002). Salter Street Films/Chum Television/Showtime/Sci-Fi Channel. Space adventure. Executive producers: Paul Donovan, Wolfram Tichy. Cast: Brian Downey, Michael McManus, Patricia Zentilli, Jeffrey Hirschfield, Xenia Seeberg.

Logan's Run (1977–1978). MGM Television/CBS. Dystopian world. Writers: Harlan Ellison, William F. Nolan, Shimon Wincelberg. Executive producers: Ivan Goff, Ben Roberts. Cast: Gregory Harrison, Heather Menzies, Donald Moffat, Randy Powell.

Lois & Clark: The New Adventures of Superman (1993–1997). December 3rd Productions/Roundelay/Warner Bros. Television/ABC. Superhero. Creators: Joe Shuster, Jerry Siegel. Cast: Dean Cain, Teri Hatcher, Lane Smith, Justin Whalin.

Lost (2004–present). Touchstone Television/Bad Robot/ABC. Mysterious adventure. Creators: Jeffrey Lieber, J. J. Abrams, Damon Lindelof. Writer and executive producer: J. J. Abrams. Cast: Dominic Monaghan, Evangeline Lilly, Matthew Fox, Jorge Garcia, Naveen Andrews, Josh Holloway.

Lost in Space (1965–1968). 20th Century-Fox Television/Irwin Allen Productions/CBS. Space travel adventure. Creator, writer, and producer: Irwin Allen. Cast: Guy Williams, June Lockhart, Jonathan Harris, Mark Goddard, Billy Mumy, Angela Cartwright, Marta Kristen.

Luna (1983–1984). Central Television/Independent Television. Futuristic sitcom. Creator and producer: Mickey Dolenz. Cast: Patsy Kensit, Joanna Wyatt, Aaron Brown, Frank Duncan.

The Man and the Challenge (1959–1960). Ziv Television Programs/NBC. Scientific adventure. Creator and producer: Ivan Tors. Cast: George Nader, Lynn Allen, Raymond Bailey.

The Man from Atlantis (1977–1978). Solow Productions/NBC. Superhero and undersea researcher. Creators: Herbert F. Solow, Mayo Simon. Producers: Herbert F. Solow, Robert H. Justman, Herman Miller. Cast: Patrick Duffy, Belinda Montgomery, Victor Buono.

Mann & Machine (1992). Universal TV/Wolf Films/NBC. Future cop with robot partner. Creators and producers: Robert De Laurentiis, Dick Wolf. Cast: David Andrews, Yancy Butler, S. Epatha Merkerson, Christine Belford.

M.A.N.T.I.S. (1994–1995). Universal TV/Renaissance Pictures/Fox. Scientist and superhero. Creator and executive producer: Bryce Zabel. Cast: Carl Lumbly, Gary Graham, Roger Rees, Galyn Gorg.

Max Headroom (1987–1988). Lorimar Productions/Chrysalis/Lakeside/ABC. Futuristic society. Producers: Phillip DeGuere, Peter Wagg, Brian Frankish. Cast: Matt Frewer, Amanda Pays, William Morgan, Chris Young.

Men into Space (1959–1960). Ziv Television Programs/United Artists/CBS. Space exploration. Producer: Lewis J. Rachmil. Space concepts: Chesley Bonestell. Cast: William Lundigan, Angie Dickinson, Joyce Taylor, Charles Herbert, Tyler McVey.

Mike & Angelo (1989–1991, 1993–2000). Thames Television/Tetra Films/Carlton Television. Comic alien on Earth. Creators and writers: Lee Pressman, Grant Cathro. Cast: Matt Wright, Michael Benz, Shelley Thompson, Tyler Butterworth, Tim Whitnall.

Mission Genesis (a.k.a. *Deepwater Black*; 1997). Empire Entertainment/Yorkshire Television/Sci-Fi Channel. Postapocalyptic space adventure. Executive producers: Wilf Copeland, Alex Nassar. Cast: Nicole de Boer, Jason Cadieux, Julie Khaner, Craig Kirkwood.

Mork and Mindy (1978–1982). Paramount Television/Henderson Productions/ABC. Comic alien on Earth. Creators: Garry Marshall, Joe Glauberg, Dale McRaven. Cast: Robin Williams, Pam Dawber, Robert Donner.

Mutant X (2001–2004). Marvel Studios/Tribune Entertainment/Fireworks Entertainment/Sky One. Genetic experimentation. Creator and writer: Avi Arad. Cast: Forbes March, Victoria Pratt, Victor Webster, John Shea, Lauren Lee Smith.

My Favorite Martian (1963–1966). Jack Chertok Television Productions/ CBS. Comic alien on Earth. Creator: John L. Greene. Producer: Jack Chertok. Cast: Ray Walston, Bill Bixby, Pamela Britton, Alan Hewitt.

My Living Doll (1964–1965). Jack Chertok Television Productions/CBS. Robot assimilation. Creators and writers: Bill Kelsay, Al Martin. Executive producer: Jack Chertok. Cast: Bob Cummings, Julie Newmar, Jack Mullaney, Doris Dowling.

Night Gallery (a.k.a. *Rod Serling's Night Gallery*; 1970–1973). Universal TV/NBC. Anthology series. Creator and writer: Rod Serling. Producer: Jack Laird. Cast: Rod Serling (host), Burgess Meredith, Dana Andrews, Vincent Price (guest stars).

Now and Again (1999–2000). CBS Productions/Paramount Network Television Productions/Picturemaker Productions/CBS. Government project for genetic engineering. Creator and writer: Glenn Gordon Caron. Cast: Eric Close, Dennis Haysbert, Gerrit Graham, Kim Chan, Heather Matarazzo.

Operation Neptune (1953). NBC. Scientist-hero, undersea adventure. Creator and writer: Gen Genovese. Cast: Tod Griffin, Richard Holland, Harold Conklin, Rusty Lane.

Otherworld (1985). MCATV/Independent Television. Parallel dimension adventure. Creators and producers: Roderick Taylor, Philip DeGuere. Cast: Sam Groom, Gretchen Corbett, Tony O'Dell, Jonna Lee.

The Outer Limits (1963–1965). Villa Di Stefano/Daystar Productions/ MGM/UA/ABC. Anthology series. Creator and producer: Leslie Stevens. Writers: Leslie Stevens, Joseph Stefano, Harlan Ellison, et al. Cast: Vic Perrin (control voice).

The Outer Limits (1995–2002). Alliance Atlantis Communications/Trilogy Entertainment Group/Showtime/Sci-Fi Channel. Anthology series. Writers: Sam Egan, Brad Wright, Naren Shankar, et al. Cast: Kevin Conway (control voice).

Out of the Unknown (1965–1967, 1969, 1971). BBC/BBC2. Anthology series. Creator and producer: Irene Shubik. Cast: David Hemmings, Milo O'Shea, Rachel Roberts (guest stars).

Out of This World (1962). ABC/Independent Television. Anthology series. Creator: Irene Shubik. Producer: Leonard White. Cast: Boris Karloff (narrator).

Out There (1951–1952). CBS. Anthology series based on well-known science fiction stories. Writer: Arthur Heinemann. Executive producer: Donald Davis. Cast: Robert Webber, Casey Allen, Nancy Franklin.

Painkiller Jane (2007–present). Insight Films/IDT/Kickstart Productions/

Sci-Fi Channel. Mutant superhero adventure. Creator: Gil Grant. Executive producer: Gil Grant. Cast: Kristanna Loken, Rob Stewart, Noah Danby, Sean Owen Roberts, Alaina Huffman.

Phil of the Future (2004–2006). Brookwell-McNamara/Kid Brother Productions/Disney Channel. Comic time travel. Creators and writers: Tim Maile, Douglas Tuber. Cast: Ricky Ullman, Alyson Michalka, Amy Bruckner, Craig Anton.

The Phoenix (1981). Mark Carliner Productions/ABC. Alien fugitive on Earth. Executive producer: Mark Carliner. Writers: Anthony Lawrence and Nancy Lawrence. Cast: Judson Earney Scott, Shelley Smith, E. G. Marshall.

Phoenix 5 (1970). Artransa Park Production/Australian Broadcasting Commission/Independent Television. Space adventure. Writer: John Warwick. Producers: Peter Summerton, John Walters. Cast: Mike Dorsey, Damien Parker, Patsy Trench, Owen Weincott.

Planet of the Apes (1974). 20th Century-Fox Television/CBS. Postapocalyptic culture conflict. Executive producer: Herbert Hirshman. Cast: Ron Stein, Eldon Burke, Roddy McDowall, Ron Harper.

The Powers of Matthew Star (1982–1983). Paramount Television/NBC. Teenage alien on Earth. Creator: Harve Bennett. Executive producer: Bruce Lansbury. Cast: Peter Barton, Louis Gossett Jr., Michael Fairman, Gary Imhoff.

The Pretender (1996–2000). 20th Century-Fox Television/MTM Entertainment/Mitchell/Van Sickle Productions/NBC. Human with powers of simulation and emulation. Writers and executive producers: Craig W. Van Sickle, Steven Long Mitchell. Cast: Michael T. Weiss, Andrea Parker, Patrick Bauchau, Jon Gries.

Prey (1998). Edelson Productions/Lars Thorwald Inc./WB/ABC. Mutant menace. Creator and writer: William Schmidt. Cast: Debra Messing, Adam Storke, Larry Drake, Frankie Faison.

The Prisoner (1967–1968). Everyman Films/Associated Television. Dystopian prison escape drama. Creator, writer, and executive producer: Patrick McGoohan. Cast: Patrick McGoohan, Angelo Muscat, Peter Swanwick, Leo McKern.

Project UFO (1978–1979). Mark VII/Worldvision/NBC. Dramatizations of UFO investigations. Creator and writer: Jack Webb. Executive producers: Jack Webb, Gene Levitt. Cast: Caskey Swaim, William Jordan, Edward Winter, Aldine King.

Quantum Leap (1989–1993). Belisarius Productions/Universal TV/NBC. Time travel. Creator, writer, and executive producer: Donald P. Bellisario. Cast: Scott Bakula, Dean Stockwell, Dennis Wolfberg, Deborah Pratt.

Quark (1978). Columbia Pictures Television/NBC. Comic space opera. Creator, writer, and producer: Buck Henry. Cast: Richard Benjamin, Tim Thomerson, Richard Kelton, Bobby Porter.

Ray Bradbury Theater (1985–1992). Alberta Filmworks/Atlantis Films/Ellipse Programme/Granada Television/Showtime/HBO/USA. Anthology series. Creator and writer: Ray Bradbury. Executive producer: Larry Wilcox. Cast: Ray Bradbury (host), Peter O'Toole, Drew Barrymore, Jeff Goldblum, William Shatner (guest stars).

Red Dwarf (1988–1989, 1991–1993, 1997, 1999). BBC/Grant Naylor Productions/Paul Jackson Productions/BBC2. Comic space adventure. Creators and writers: Rob Grant, Doug Naylor. Cast: Craig Charles, Danny John-Jules, Chris Barrie, Robert Llewellyn.

Robocop: The Series (1994–1995). Robocop Productions/Rysher Entertainment/Skyvision Entertainment. Robot crime fighter. Executive producers: Stephen Downing, Kevin Gillis, Brian K. Ross. Cast: Richard Eden, Yvette Nipar, Andrea Roth, Blu Mankuma.

Rocky Jones, Space Ranger (1954). Roland Reed Productions/Space Ranger Enterprises. Space adventure. Producer: Roland Reed. Director: Hollingsworth Morse. Cast: Richard Crane, Scotty Beckett, Sally Mansfield, Maurice Cass, Robert Lyden.

Rod Brown of the Rocket Rangers (1953–1954). CBS. Space adventure. Writers: Jack Weinstock, Willie Gilbert. Producer: William Dozier. Cast: Cliff Robertson, Jack Weston, Bruce Hall, John Boruff.

Roswell (1999–2002). 20th Century-Fox Television/Regency Television/WB/UPN. Alien teenagers adventure. Creator: Jason Katims. Executive producers: Jason Katims and Jonathan Frakes. Cast: Jason Behr, Katherine Heigl, Brendan Fehr, Shiri Appleby.

Salvage 1 (1979). Bennett/Katleman Productions/Columbia Pictures Television/ABC. Comic space adventure. Creator: Mike Lloyd Ross. Executive producers: Harve Bennett, Harris Katleman. Cast: Andy Griffith, Trish Stewart, Joe Higgins, Richard Jaeckel.

Sapphire & Steel (1979–1982). Associated Television/Independent Television. Time travel adventure. Creator and writer: P. J. Hammond. Executive producer: David Reid. Cast: Joanna Lumley, David McCallum, David Collings.

Science Fiction Theatre (1955–1957). Ziv Television Programs. Semidocumentary anthology series. Writer and producer: Ivan Tors. Cast: Truman Bradley (host).

SeaQuest DSV (1993–1995). Amblin Entertainment/Universal/NBC. Fantastic machine. Creator: Rockne S. O'Bannon. Producers: Steven Spielberg, David Burke, Patrick Hasburgh, Rockne S. O'Bannon. Cast: Roy Scheider, Don Franklin, Jonathan Brandis.

The Secret Adventures of Jules Verne (2000). Filmline International/Talisman Crest/Sci-Fi Channel. Nineteenth-century scientific adventure. Creator and writer: Gavin Scott. Producer: Neil Zeiger. Cast: Chris Demetral, Michel Courtemanche, Francesca Hunt, Michael Praed.

Seven Days (1998–2001). Paramount Network Television Productions/ UPN. Time travel through alien technology. Writer and producer: Christopher Crowe. Cast: Jonathan LaPaglia, Don Franklin, Norman Lloyd, Justina Vail.

The Six Million Dollar Man (1974–1978). Harve Bennett Productions/Universal Television/ABC. Bionic superhero. Executive producer: Harve Bennett. Cast: Lee Majors, Richard Anderson, Farrah Fawcett, Lindsay Wagner.

Sliders (1995–2000). Fox/Sci-Fi Channel. Space warp, interdimensional travel. Creators: Tracy Torme, Robert Weiss. Cast: Jerry O'Connell, John Rhys-Davies, Sabrina Lloyd, Cleavant Derricks, Kari Wuhrer, Tembi Locke.

Smallville (2001–2006). Tollin/Robbins Productions/WB. Superhero. Creators and writers: Alfred Gough, Miles Millar. Executive producers: Steven S. DeKnight, Ken Horton, Alex Taub, Michael W. Watkins. Cast: Tom Welling, Michael Rosenbaum, Allison Mack, Kristin Kreuk.

Space: Above and Beyond (1995–1996). 20th Century-Fox Television/Hard Eight Pictures/Fox. Space travel adventure. Creators and writers: Glen Morgan, James Wong. Cast: Morgan Weisser, Kristen Cloke, Rodney Rowland, Lanei Chapman.

Space: 1999 (1975–1977). Group 3 Ltd./ITC/Radiotelevisione Italiana. Space adventure. Creators and producers: Gerry Anderson, Sylvia Anderson. Cast: Martin Landau, Barbara Bain, Nick Tate, Zienia Merton.

Space Patrol (1950–1955). Tower Productions/Mike Moser Enterprises/ ABC. Crime fighters in space. Producers: Mike Moser, Dick Darley. Director: Dick Darley. Cast: Glenn Denning, Bela Kovacs, Ed Kemmer, Virginia Hewitt, Lyn Osborn, Ken Mayer.

Space Precinct (1994–1995). Grove Television/Mentorn/Sky One. Detective in space. Creator, writer, and producer: Gerry Anderson. Cast: Rob Youngblood, Ted Shackelford, Simone Bendix, Nancy Paul.

Space Rangers (1993). Ranger Productions/RHI/Trilogy Entertainment/ CBS. Space opera. Creator, writer, and producer: Pen Densham. Cast: Linda Hunt, Jeff Kaake, Jack McGee, Marjorie Monaghan.

Star Maidens (1976). Portman Productions/Independent Television. Comic space adventure. Producer: James Gatward. Cast: Judy Geeson, Dawn Addams, Pierre Brice, Gareth Thomas.

Star Trek (1966–1969). Desilu/Paramount Television/NBC. Space travel adventure. Creator and producer: Gene Roddenberry. Cast: William Shatner, Leonard Nimoy, DeForest Kelley, Nichelle Nichols, James Doohan, George Takei, Walter Koenig.

Star Trek: Deep Space Nine (1993–1999). Paramount Television. Space station adventure. Creator: Gene Roddenberry. Writers: Gene Roddenberry, Rick Berman, Ira Steven Behr. Executive producers: Rick Berman, Ira Steven Behr. Cast: Avery Brooks, Rene Auberjonois, Cirroc Lofton, Alexander Siddig, Colm Meaney, Armin Shimerman.

Star Trek: Enterprise (originally *Enterprise*; 2001–2005). Braga Productions/Paramount Television/Rick Berman Productions/UPN. Space travel adventure. Creator: Gene Roddenberry. Writers and executive producers: Rick Berman, Brannon Braga. Cast: Scott Bakula, Jolene Blalock, John Billingsley, Dominic Keating.

Star Trek: The Next Generation (1987–1994). Paramount Television/CBS. Space travel adventure. Creator and executive producer: Gene Roddenberry. Cast: Patrick Stewart, Jonathan Frakes, LeVar Burton, Brent Spiner, Marina Sirtis, Michael Dorn.

Star Trek: Voyager (1995–2001). Paramount Television/UPN. Space travel adventure. Creator: Gene Roddenberry. Executive producers: Rick Berman, Brannon Braga, Kenneth Biller, et al. Cast: Kate Mulgrew, Robert Beltran, Robert Duncan McNeill, Jeri Ryan, Ethan Phillips.

Stargate Atlantis (2004–present). Sony/MGM Television/Sci-Fi Channel. Time travel, space warp. Creators, writers, and executive producers: Brad Wright, Robert C. Cooper. Cast: Torri Higginson, Joe Flanigan, David Hewlett, Rachel Luttrell.

Stargate SG-1 (1997–2007). Sony/MGM/Showtime/Sci-Fi Channel. Time travel, space warp. Creators, writers, and producers: Jonathan Glassner, Brad Wright. Cast: Richard Dean Anderson, Michael Shanks, Amanda Tapping, Christopher Judge, Ben Browder.

Starhunter (2000–2001). Chum Television/Danforth Studios/Greystone International. Space bounty hunters. Executive producers: Silvio Astarita, Stefan Jonas, Elaine Scott. Cast: Michael Pare, Tanya Allen, Claudette Roche, Murray Melvin.

The Starlost (1973). Glen Warren Productions/20th Century-Fox Television. Ecologically oriented space adventure. Creator: Harlan Ellison. Cast: Keir Dullea, Gay Rowan, Robin Ward, William Osler.

Starman (1986–1987). Columbia Pictures Television/Henerson/Hirsch Productions/ABC. Alien on Earth. Creators and writers: Mike Gray, John Mason. Cast: Robert Hays, Christopher Daniel Barnes, Michael Cavanaugh, Erin Gray.

Superboy (later *The Adventures of Superboy*; 1988–1992). Alexander Salkind/Cantharaus/Lowry Productions/Viacom. Superhero. Writer and executive producer: Ilya Salkind. Cast: Gerard Christopher, Stacy Haiduk, John Haymes Newton, Jim Calvert, Scott Wells, Sherman Howard.

Super Force (1990–1992). Paramount Television/MCA/Universal. Futuristic crime fighters. Creator and writer: Larry Brody. Producer: Michael Attanasio. Cast: Ken Olandt, Larry B. Scott, Patrick Macnee.

Survivors (1975–1977). BBC. Postapocalyptic adventure. Creator: Terry Nation. Producer: Terence Dudley. Cast: Carolyn Seymour, Lucy Fleming, Stephen Dudley, Ian McCulloch.

Tales of Tomorrow (1951–1953). George F. Foley Productions/ABC. Anthology series based on classic and contemporary science fiction stories. Producers: George F. Foley, Mort Abrahams, Richard Gordon. Cast: Jean Alexander, Martin Brandt, Lon McCallister, Walter Abel.

Tekwar (1995–1996). Atlantis Films/Universal/USA Network. Futuristic private eye adventure. Creators and executive producers: William Shatner, Peter Sussman. Cast: Greg Evigan, William Shatner, Eugene Clark, Torri Higginson.

3rd Rock from the Sun (1996–2001). Carsey-Werner Company/YBYL Productions/NBC. Comic aliens on Earth. Creators and writers: Bonnie Turner, Terry Turner. Cast: John Lithgow, Kristen Johnston, French Stewart, Jane Curtin.

Threshold (2005–2006). Paramount Television/Heyday Productions/Braga Productions/CBS/Sky One. Alien invasion fought by government task force. Creator: Bragi F. Schut. Executive producers: Brannon Braga, David S. Goyer, David Heyman, Anne McGrail. Cast: Carla Gugino, Charles S. Dutton, Brent Spiner, Robert Patrick Benedict.

Timeslip (1971). Associated Television/Independent Television. Time travel adventure. Producer: John Cooper. Cast: Cheryl Burfield, Spencer Banks, Derek Benfield, Iris Russell, Denis Quilley.

Time Trax (1993–1994). Gary Nardino Productions/Lorimar Television/Warner Bros. Television. Time traveling crime fighter. Creators and writers: Harve Bennett, Jeffrey M. Hayes, Grant Rosenberg. Cast: Dale Midkiff, Elizabeth Alexander, Peter Donat.

Time Tunnel (1966–1967). Irwin Allen Productions/20th Century-Fox Television/ABC. Time travel. Creator, writer, and producer: Irwin Allen. Cast: James Darren, Robert Colbert, Lee Meriwether, Whit Bissell.

Tom Corbett, Space Cadet (1950–1955). Rockhill Productions/CBS/ABC/ NBC/DuMont. Space adventure. Based on the novel by Robert Heinlein. Producers: Allen Ducovny, Albert Aley. Cast: Frankie Thomas, Jan Merlin, Al Markim, Jack Grimes.

The Tomorrow People (1992–1995). Central Independent Television/Thames Television/Tetra Films/Independent Television. Futuristic superheroes. Creator: Roger Price. Producers: Grant Cathro, Alan Horrox, Lee Pressman, Roger Price. Cast: Kristen Ariza, Jeff Harding, Gabrielle Hamilton, Christian Tessier.

Total Recall 2070 (1999–2000). Showtime. Futuristic society. Writer and executive producer: Art Monterastelli. Cast: Michael Easton, Karl Pruner, Michael Rawlins, Cynthia Preston.

Tracker (2001–2002). Chum Television/Lionsgate Television/Tandem Communications. Alien police officer on Earth. Creator and executive producer: Gil Grant. Cast: Adrian Paul, Amy Price-Francis, Geraint Wyn Davies.

Tremors (2003). Stampede/Chum Television/Sci-Fi Channel. Fantastic creatures. Creators and writers: Brent Maddock, Nancy Roberts, S. S. Wilson. Cast: Victor Browne, Gladys Jimenez, Marcia Strassman, Lela Lee.

The Tripods (1984–1985). Fremantle International/7 Network/BBC. Alien invasion. Producer: Richard Bates. Cast: John Shackley, Ceri Seel, Jim Baker, Robin Hayter.

The Twilight Zone (1959–1964). Cayuga Productions/CBS. Anthology series. Creator, writer, and executive producer: Rod Serling. Producers: Buck Houghton, William Froug, Bert Granet, Herbert Hirschman. Cast: Rod Serling (narrator).

The Twilight Zone (1985–1989). Atlantis Films/London Film Productions/ Persistence of Vision/MGM/CBS. Anthology series. Executive producers: David P. Berman, Michael MacMillan, Mark Shelmerdine, Philip DeGuere. Cast: Charles Aidman, Robin Ward (narrators).

The Twilight Zone (2002–2003). Joshmax Productions/New Line/Spirit Dance Entertainment/Trilogy Entertainment/UPN. Anthology series. Writer and executive producer: Ira Steven Behr. Cast: Forest Whitaker (narrator), Michalla Petersen.

UFO (1970–1971). Century 21 Television/ITC. Alien invasion defense force. Creators and writers: Gerry Anderson, Sylvia Anderson. Executive producer: Gerry Anderson. Cast: Ed Bishop, George Sewell, Michael Billington, Gabrielle Drake.

V (1984–1985). Warner Bros. Television/NBC. Alien invasion. Creator:

Kenneth Johnson. Writer and supervising producer: Garner Simmons. Cast: Marc Singer, Faye Grant, Jane Badler, Jennifer Cooke, Jeff Yagher.

Viper (1994, 1996–1999). NBC. Futuristic crime fighters, fantastic machine. Executive producers: Danny Bilson, Paul De Meo. Cast: Dorian Harewood, Carrie Fleming, Gavin Buhr.

The Visitor (1997–1998). 20th Century-Fox Television/Centropolis Television. Aliens on Earth. Executive producers: Dean Devlin, Roland Emmerich, John Masius. Cast: Adam Baldwin, Granville Ames, Richard Cox.

Voyagers (1982–1983). James D. Parriott Productions/Universal Television/NBC. Time travel. Writer and executive producer: James D. Parriott. Cast: Jon-Erik Hexum, Meeno Peluce.

Voyage to the Bottom of the Sea (1964–1968). Irwin Allen Productions/20th Century-Fox Television/ABC. Fantastic machine. Creator, writer, and producer: Irwin Allen. Cast: Richard Basehart, David Hedison, Del Monroe, Henry Kulky.

VR.5 (1995). Samoset Productions/Chum Television/Fox. Virtual reality adventure. Creators: Thania St. John, Michael Ketleman, Geoffrey Hemwall, Jeannine Renshaw, Adam Cherry. Cast: Lori Singer, Michael Easton, Will Patton, David McCallum.

War of the Worlds (1988–1990). Hometown Films/Paramount Television. Alien invasion. Executive producer: Greg Strangis. Cast: Jared Martin, Lynda Mason Green, Philip Akin, Richard Chaves.

Welcome to Paradox (1998). Chelser/Perlmutter Productions/Sci-Fi Channel. Anthology series based on science fiction literature. Creators and executive producers: Lewis Chesler, Jeremy Lipp. Cast: Michael Philip (host).

The X-Files (1993–2002). 20th Century-Fox Television/Ten Thirteen Productions/Fox. Investigations of paranormal and alien phenomena. Creator, writer, and producer: Chris Carter. Cast: David Duchovny, Gillian Anderson, Mitch Pileggi, Robert Patrick.

CONTRIBUTORS

Stan Beeler is chair of English at the University of Northern British Columbia. His areas of interest include film and television studies, popular culture, and comparative literature. His publications include *Reading Stargate SG-1* (Tauris, 2006), *Investigating* Charmed: *The Magic Power of TV* (Tauris, 2007), and *Dance, Drugs, and Escape: The Club Scene in Literature, Film, and Television* (McFarland, 2007).

M. Keith Booker is the James E. and Ellen Wadley Roper Professor of English at the University of Arkansas. He has authored or edited more than thirty books on literature, film, and television, including *Monsters, Mushroom Clouds, and the Cold War: American Science Fiction and the Roots of Postmodernism, 1946–1964* (Greenwood, 2001), *Strange TV: Innovative Television Series from* The Twilight Zone *to* The X-Files (Greenwood, 2002), *Science Fiction Television: A History* (Praeger, 2004), *Alternate Americas: Science Fiction Film and American Culture* (Praeger, 2006), and *Postmodern Hollywood: What's New in Film and Why It Makes Us Feel So Strange* (Praeger, 2007).

Mark Bould is a senior lecturer in film studies at the University of the West of England. Coeditor of the journal *Science Fiction Film and Television* and associate editor of *Science Fiction Studies, Historical Materialism,* and the *Journal of Horror Studies,* he has authored *Film Noir: From* Berlin *to* Sin City (Wallflower, 2005) and *The Cinema of John Sayles* (Wallflower, 2007) and coedited *Parietal Games: Critical Writings by and on M. John Harrison* (Science Fiction Foundation, 2005). He is currently coediting *Neo-Noir, The Routledge Companion to Science Fiction,* and *Fifty Key Figures in Science Fiction.* Other projects include *The Routledge Concise History of Science Fiction* and *The Routledge Science Fiction Film Guidebook.*

Wheeler Winston Dixon is the James Ryan Professor of Film Studies at the University of Nebraska–Lincoln. With Gwendolyn Audrey Foster, he is coeditor in chief of the *Quarterly Review of Film and Video.* His newest books include *Film Talk: Directors at Work* (Rutgers University Press, 2007), *Visions of Paradise: Images of Eden in the Cinema* (Rutgers University Press, 2006), and *Lost in the Fifties: Recovering Phantom Hollywood* (Southern Illinois University Press, 2005). He has edited *American Cinema* *of the 1940s: Themes and Variations* (Rutgers University Press, 2006) and *Film and Television after 9/11* (Southern Illinois University Press, 2004). Forthcoming in 2008 is *A Short History of Film*, coauthored with Gwendolyn Audrey Foster. A highly regarded filmmaker as well, he has been honored by the Museum of Modern Art in New York with a retrospective of his films, which are now part of the museum's permanent collection.

Gerald Duchovnay, professor of English and film at Texas A&M University–Commerce, has published numerous articles on literature, film, and media. His books include *Humphrey Bogart: A Bio-Bibliography* (Greenwood, 1999) and *Film Voices: Interviews from* Post Script (State University of New York Press, 2004), and he is the founding and general editor of *Post Script: Essays in Film and the Humanities.*

Susan A. George is a lecturer at the University of California, Davis, and holds a PhD in cultural studies and feminist theory. Focusing on gender construction in science fiction film and television, her work has appeared in the *Journal of Popular Film and Television, Post Script, Science Fiction Research Association Review, Reconstruction,* the *Journal of the Fantastic in the Arts,* and in various anthologies, including *Space and Beyond: The Frontier Theme in Science Fiction* (Greenwood, 2000), *Fantastic Odysseys: Selected Essays from the Twenty-second International Conference on the Fantastic in the Arts* (Praeger, 2003), and *Why We Fought: America's Wars in Film and History* (University Press of Kentucky, 2008).

Rodney Hill, assistant professor at Georgia Gwinnet College, holds a PhD in film from the University of Kansas. Coauthor of *The Encyclopedia of Stanley Kubrick* (Facts on File, 2002), he has also published essays in *Film Quarterly, Cinema Journal, Post Script, Literature/Film Quarterly,* and elsewhere.

Lacy Hodges is a PhD candidate at the University of Florida. Her dissertation offers a feminist examination of genre and postmodernism in various popular science fiction television series.

Samantha Holloway is a freelance writer, editor, and independent scholar whose work focuses on science fiction and fantasy, specifically in the area of visual media. Her first novel, *The Two-Thirds Queen*, is in the editing stage, and she is currently working on a scholarly book on the fantastic death wish.

David Lavery holds a chair in film and television at Brunel University in London. He is the author of numerous essays and reviews and author, coauthor, editor, or coeditor of fifteen books, including Seinfeld, *Master of Its Domain: Revisiting Television's Greatest Sitcom* (Continuum, 2006), *Unlocking the Meaning of* Lost: *An Unauthorized Guide* (Sourcebooks, 2006), *Reading* Deadwood: *A Western to Swear By* (Tauris, 2006), *Reading* The Sopranos: *Hit TV from HBO* (Tauris, 2006), *Dear Angela: Remembering* My So-Called Life (Lexington Books, 2007), *Saving the World: A Guide to* Heroes (EWC, 2007), Lost's *Buried Treasures* (Sourcebooks, 2007), *The Essential Cult Television Reader* (University Press of Kentucky, forthcoming), and *Joss Whedon: A Creative Portrait* (Tauris/St. Martin's, 2008). Lavery also coedits the e-journal *Slayage: The Online International Journal of Buffy Studies*, edits *Intensities: The Journal of Cult Media*, and is a founding editor of the new journal *Critical Studies in Television: Scholarly Studies of Small Screen Fictions*.

Christine Mains is a PhD candidate at the University of Calgary, completing a dissertation on the figure of the genius in popular culture. She has published articles on fantasists Patricia McKillip and Charles de Lint and on the television series *Stargate SG-1* and *Stargate Atlantis*.

Dennis Redmond holds a PhD in comparative literature from the University of Oregon and researches multinational media and cultural studies. He is the author of *The World Is Watching* (Southern Illinois University Press, 2003), a study of late-twentieth-century video culture. He is completing a second PhD in communication at the University of Illinois while editing *Uplink*, a Webzine on contemporary video game culture.

J. P. Telotte is professor of film and media in the School of Literature, Communication, and Culture at the Georgia Institute of Technology, where he teaches courses in film history, film genres, and film and television. Author of more than one hundred articles on film, television, and literature and coeditor of the journal *Post Script*, he has also published numerous books, the most recent of which are *Science Fiction Film* (Cambridge University Press, 2001; Spanish translation, 2002), *Disney TV* (Wayne State University Press, 2004), and *The Mouse Machine: Disney and Technology* (University of Illinois Press, 2008).

Charles Tryon is assistant professor of film and media studies at Fayetteville State University in North Carolina. He has published articles on *Dark*

City and *Sans Soleil* and is currently completing a book on film and new media audiences.

Sherryl Vint, assistant professor in the Department of English at Brock University in Ontario, is the author of *Bodies of Tomorrow: Technology, Subjectivity, Science Fiction* (University of Toronto Press, 2007) and coeditor of the journal *Science Fiction Film and Television.* She is currently coediting *The Routledge Companion to Science Fiction, Beyond the Reality Studio: Cyberpunk in the New Millennium, Remaking Worlds: Critical Essays on China Miéville,* and *Fifty Key Figures in Science Fiction*; cowriting *The Routledge Concise History of Science Fiction*; and writing *Animal Alterity: The Question of the Animal in Science Fiction.*

Lisa Yaszek is associate professor in the School of Literature, Communication, and Culture at the Georgia Institute of Technology, where she curates the Bud Foote Science Fiction Collection. Her research interests include science fiction, gender studies, and contemporary literature. She is the author of *The Self Wired: Technology and Subjectivity in Contemporary Narrative* (Routledge, 2002) and *Galactic Suburbia: Gender, Technology, and the Creation of Women's Science Fiction* (Ohio State University Press, 2008). Yaszek's essays on science, society, and science fiction have appeared in such journals as *Extrapolation, NWSA Journal,* and *Rethinking History.*

INDEX